Understanding the American South

Americans in the twenty-first century find themselves searching for new understandings of their history. They seek explanations for chronic political polarization, acute pandemic polarization, social media addiction, heightened concern over global warming and armed global conflict, widening cultural and economic gaps between city and countryside, persistent racial tensions, gender divides, tensions over abortion rights and the public school curriculum, and a forty-year pattern of increasing economic inequality in the United States. Americans are looking for a past that can help them understand the divided and fractious present, a past that enlightens and inspires. In this collection of original essays, Lacy K. Ford uses the past to inform the present, as he provides a deeper, more nuanced understanding of American history and the American South's complicated relationship with it.

Lacy K. Ford is a scholar-in-residence at the Institute for Southern Studies, University of South Carolina, where he served as Dean of the College of Arts and Sciences from 2016 to 2020. The author of two prize-winning books, he has also been interviewed by the *New York Times*, *CBS Evening News*, CNN, and NPR's *All Things Considered*.

CAMBRIDGE STUDIES ON THE AMERICAN SOUTH

Series Editors:

Mark M. Smith, *University of South Carolina, Columbia*

Peter Coclanis, *University of North Carolina at Chapel Hill*

Editor Emeritus:

David Moltke-Hansen

Interdisciplinary in its scope and intent, this series builds upon and extends Cambridge University Press's longstanding commitment to studies on the American South. The series offers the best new work on the South's distinctive institutional, social, economic, and cultural history and also features works in a national, comparative, and transnational perspective.

Titles in the Series

Lacy K. Ford, *Understanding the American South: Slavery, Race, Identity, and the American Century*

David Stefan Doddington, *Old Age and American Slavery*

John C. Rodrigue, *Freedom's Crescent: The Civil War and the Destruction of Slavery in the Lower Mississippi Valley*

Elijah Gaddis, *Gruesome Looking Objects: A New History of Lynching and Everyday Things*

Damian Alan Pargas, *Freedom Seekers: Fugitive Slaves in North America, 1800–1860*

Sebastian N. Page, *Black Resettlement and the American Civil War*

Hayden R. Smith, *Carolina's Golden Fields: Inland Rice Cultivation in the South Carolina Lowcountry, 1670–1860*

Wilson Jeremiah Moses, *Thomas Jefferson: A Modern Prometheus*

Joan E. Cashin, *War Stuff: The Struggle for Human and Environmental Resources in the American Civil War*

David Stefan Doddington, *Contesting Slave Masculinity in the American South*

Lawrence T. McDonnell, *Performing Disunion: The Coming of the Civil War in Charleston, South Carolina*

Enrico Dal Lago, *Civil War and Agrarian Unrest: The Confederate South and Southern Italy*

Daniel J. Vivian, *A New Plantation World: Sporting Estates in the South Carolina Low Country, 1900–1940*

Eugene D. Genovese, ed. Douglas Ambrose, *The Sweetness of Life: Southern Planters at Home*

Donald G. Mathews, *At the Altar of Lynching: Burning Sam Hose in the American South*

Keri Leigh Merritt, *Masterless Men: Poor Whites and Slavery in the Antebellum South*

Katherine Rye Jewell, *Dollars for Dixie: Business and the Transformation of Conservatism in the Twentieth Century*

Sarah Gardner, *Reviewing the South: The Literary Marketplace and the Southern Renaissance, 1920–1941*

William Thomas Okie, *The Georgia Peach: Culture, Agriculture, and Environment in the American South*

Karlos K. Hill, *Beyond the Rope: The Impact of Lynching on Black Culture and Memory*

William A. Link and James J. Broomall, eds., *Rethinking American Emancipation: Legacies of Slavery and the Quest for Black Freedom*

James Van Horn Melton, *Religion, Community, and Slavery on the Colonial Southern Frontier*

Damian Alan Pargas, *Slavery and Forced Migration in the Antebellum South*

Craig Friend and Lorri Glover, eds., *Death and the American South*

Barton A. Myers, *Rebels against the Confederacy: North Carolina's Unionists*

Louis A. Ferleger and John D. Metz, *Cultivating Success in the South: Farm Households in Postbellum Georgia*

Luke E. Harlow, *Religion, Race, and the Making of Confederate Kentucky, 1830–1880*

Susanna Michele Lee, *Claiming the Union: Citizenship in the Post–Civil War South*

Kathleen M. Hilliard, *Masters, Slaves, and Exchange: Power's Purchase in the Old South*

Ari Helo, *Thomas Jefferson's Ethics and the Politics of Human Progress: The Morality of a Slaveholder*

Scott P. Marler, *The Merchants' Capital: New Orleans and the Political Economy of the Nineteenth-Century South*

Ras Michael Brown, *African-Atlantic Cultures and the South Carolina Lowcountry*

Johanna Nicol Shields, *Freedom in a Slave Society: Stories from the Antebellum South*

Brian Steele, *Thomas Jefferson and American Nationhood*

Christopher Michael Curtis, *Jefferson's Freeholders and the Politics of Ownership in the Old Dominion*

Jonathan Daniel Wells, *Women Writers and Journalists in the Nineteenth-Century South*

Peter McCandless, *Slavery, Disease, and Suffering in the Southern Lowcountry*

Robert E. Bonner, *Mastering America: Southern Slaveholders and the Crisis of American Nationhood*

Understanding the American South

Slavery, Race, Identity, and the American Century

LACY K. FORD
University of South Carolina

CAMBRIDGE
UNIVERSITY PRESS

Shaftesbury Road, Cambridge CB2 8EA, United Kingdom

One Liberty Plaza, 20th Floor, New York, NY 10006, USA

477 Williamstown Road, Port Melbourne, VIC 3207, Australia

314–321, 3rd Floor, Plot 3, Splendor Forum, Jasola District Centre,
New Delhi – 110025, India

103 Penang Road, #05–06/07, Visioncrest Commercial, Singapore 238467

Cambridge University Press is part of Cambridge University Press & Assessment,
a department of the University of Cambridge.

We share the University's mission to contribute to society through the pursuit of
education, learning and research at the highest international levels of excellence.

www.cambridge.org
Information on this title: www.cambridge.org/9781009522021

DOI: 10.1017/9781009522038

© Lacy K. Ford 2024

This publication is in copyright. Subject to statutory exception and to the provisions
of relevant collective licensing agreements, no reproduction of any part may take
place without the written permission of Cambridge University Press & Assessment.

When citing this work, please include a reference to the DOI 10.1017/9781009522038

First published 2024

A catalogue record for this publication is available from the British Library

Library of Congress Cataloging-in-Publication Data
NAMES: Ford, Lacy K., author.
TITLE: Understanding the American South : slavery, race, identity, and the
American century / Lacy K. Ford, University of South Carolina.
Other titles: Slavery, race, identity, and the American century
DESCRIPTION: Cambridge, United Kingdom ; New York, NY : Cambridge
University Press, 2024. | Series: Cambridge studies on the American
South | Includes bibliographical references and index.
IDENTIFIERS: LCCN 2024011923 | ISBN 9781009522021 (hardback) |
ISBN 9781009522014 (paperback) | ISBN 9781009522038 (ebook)
SUBJECTS: LCSH: Southern States – History. | Southern States – Social
conditions. | Southern States – Race relations – History. | Political
culture – Southern States – History. | Slavery – Southern States – History. |
National characteristics, American.
CLASSIFICATION: LCC F209 .F67 2024 | DDC 975–dc23/eng/20240327
LC record available at https://lccn.loc.gov/2024011923

ISBN 978-1-009-52202-1 Hardback
ISBN 978-1-009-52201-4 Paperback

Cambridge University Press & Assessment has no responsibility for the persistence
or accuracy of URLs for external or third-party internet websites referred to in this
publication and does not guarantee that any content on such websites is, or will
remain, accurate or appropriate.

This book is dedicated to my family, Janet, Travis, Cheryl, Michelle, and Emma, Sonya, Will, Calvin and Bert, as well as my many supportive friends, for their affection, support, and encouragement

Contents

Introduction   *page* 1

PART I UNDERSTANDING THE AMERICAN SOUTH AND THE CIVIL WAR IN A NEW CENTURY

1   A Twenty-First Century Meaning for the American
Civil War: A Post-Cold War Reflection   13

PART II UNDERSTANDING THE SOUTH AND THE AMERICAN IDENTITY

2   The Liberal Tradition: Southern Exceptionalism,
the Civil War, and the Future of American Liberalism   39

3   The "Genius of American Politics": The South, Ideology,
and American Identity   66

4   The "People of Plenty": Abundance and the American
South in the Age of Inequality   89

PART III UNDERSTANDING SLAVERY, RACE, AND INEQUALITY IN THE AMERICAN SOUTH

5   The Problem of Slavery Reconsidered: The South, the
Nation, and a Reflection on "The Travail of Slavery"   115

6   The Legacy of W. E. B. DuBois: Slavery and Race in
Southern and American History   139

7   An American Elegy: The American South during
the Ages of Capital and Inequality   169

8   Transforming Southern History: The Role of
Women Historians   192

x   *Contents*

9 The Fraying Fabric of Community: The Unraveling of
   Southern White Working-Class Culture   225

           PART IV UNDERSTANDING HISTORY AND IRONY

10 The Irony of Southern History and the Problem of Innocence
    in American Life   255

Bibliography   269
Index   287

Introduction

As readers find themselves approaching the middle of the third decade of the twenty-first century, many Americans are searching for new understandings of their history, ones that can explain chronic political polarization, acute pandemic polarization, rampant social media addiction, heightened concern over global warming and armed global conflict, widening cultural and economic gaps between city and countryside, persistent racial tensions, growing gender divides, deep cultural tensions over public school curriculums, abortion rights, and what we term affirmative action. Moreover, and perhaps most significantly, a forty-year pattern of increasing economic inequality in the United States grows steadily more visible. Americans are looking for a past, not a past rendered usable for partisan advantages and brief news bites but one that can help them understand the divided and fractious present, a past that informs and inspires. Americans seek to make sense of the state of the nation as it stands now, not thirty, fifty, or seventy-five years ago. But they are searching for new and more complex understandings of the nation's history to better comprehend its present.

As an American and southern historian who has spent a lifetime studying the politics, economy, and social fabric of the American South and its relationship with the rest of the nation, I have long asked the enduring question: Can we, as Americans and as southerners, learn from our history? And, if so, how? After decades of reflection, my answer now is essentially the same one that nudged me toward a career as a historian several decades ago. That answer was and is that any effort to understand our nation's or region's present and future challenges inevitably leads both citizen and scholar alike into an examination of our

Understanding the American South

history, including an examination of the American South's often critical role in making that history. After all, is it not better to learn from our history, however complicated, burdensome, and even painful, than to forget, ignore, or try to erase that history? The past should never be our only guide, but it is a valuable, and arguably indispensable, one, and one we ignore at our individual and collective peril.

I have also learned over the course of my career that as we seek to learn from the past, we must approach the endeavor with a deep sense of humility. And with that humility in mind, I have undertaken to offer my understanding of how the American South shaped the nation and its future through this book of essays, recognizing that at times the South offers a counterpoint to the prevailing national story, and quite often offered anger, bitterness, meanness, and tragedy rather than uplift and wisdom. Even a brief look at the writings of William Faulkner revealed more meanness, sadness, and tragedy than inspiration or even comic relief while offering the assurance that the human spirit will endure and, ultimately, even prevail. We can at least do our share and trust Providence for the rest.

This book of original essays does not pretend to cover every important facet of the history of the American South and its full impact on the American nation, rather it reflects my desire to draw on my areas of expertise, which lean toward political and economic history as well as slavery to help bring a deeper understanding of American history, and of the American South's complicated relationship with it, to bear on our twenty-first-century world and its many challenges. These essays attempt an innovative approach to seeking new understandings and using them to shape our interpretations of the present. The essays use the past to inform the present, but they also acknowledge that the pressures of the present require us to ask new and different questions about the past. These questions not only emerge from current trends but also from probing unexamined corners of the past and seeking new connections with it. We also must recognize that, however well-meaning our endeavors, at some future point we will all look as foolish to future generations as past generations sometimes look to us. Differently put, this book of essays seeks to both use the present to interrogate the past and to use the past to interrogate the present, and to do so more openly and directly than traditional historical scholarship typically allows or encourages.

Most of the essays in the volume start by considering and reevaluating a landmark work authored by a well-known scholar or writer dealing with a pivotal question about the nature of the American South, its

Introduction

3

history, and its impact on the nation. Each of the essays not only explicates the major arguments of historical scholarship but also explores how these interpretations have fared over time. Most importantly, these essays look for insights emanating from both the original work and its subsequent critiques and elaborations, so that we might enhance our current efforts to understand and meet the challenges facing twenty-first-century America. In brief, the book's aim is to promote a dynamic and nuanced understanding of our past to illuminate our future and guide us as we negotiate a path forward.

To fulfill its purpose, the book travels down four related avenues of inquiry. The first avenue explores a hardy but often revealing perennial – the meaning of the American Civil War – from the standpoints of the nineteenth, twentieth, and most importantly the twenty-first centuries. To do so, the book's lead essay evaluates historian David Potter's 1968 assertion that, from an international perspective, the defeat of the American South's bid for independent nationhood and the emancipation of enslaved Blacks in the American Civil War resulted in an unprecedented marriage (or at least a civil union in twenty-first-century terms) of liberalism and nationalism, a union unique in the formation of nineteenth-century nation-states. This fortuitous marriage not only gave liberalism a strength it might otherwise have lacked but also lent nationalism a democratic legitimacy, and even a morality, that it may not otherwise have deserved. The essay also provides a close examination of how, during the late twentieth and early twenty-first centuries, the end of the Cold War and the emergence of multiple decentralizing technologies (including cell phones and social media) and other polarizing forces raise serious questions about whether a more than 150-year-old marriage can survive the alluring centrifugal temptations and frustrations of the new century.

The book's second line of inquiry examines several scholarly manifestations and cautions advanced following *Time* and *Life* publisher Henry Luce's 1941 prediction of a coming "American Century," an epic golden age characterized by the spread of democracy and prosperity around the globe under American auspices. The extended post-World War II economic boom and the advent the Cold War facilitated something approaching a triumphal American Century, at least in the eyes of some influential scholars who seized on the new national mood of triumphalism to produce an influential literature arguing the case for American exceptionalism and grappling with the place of the once-defeated South in the presumably triumphant American nation. Emerging from the

4 Understanding the American South

confidence and optimism of the immediate postwar years, a series of sweeping historical interpretations appeared, each designed to precisely define the unique character of the American nation and explain its "triumph" as the leader of the "free world," while also trying to explain, or explain away, the place and history of the American South in this phase of triumphalism.

Three of the nation's leading scholars (Louis Hartz, Daniel Boorstin, and David Potter) crafted broadly interpretative books trying to define the American national character while also cautioning the nation against embracing Luce's uber-optimistic proclamation of an American Century too eagerly or too literally, at least in terms of foreign policy. Each essay in Part II explores one of these three efforts to define the cohesive essence of the nation and the role the American South played (whether supporting or contradictory). These essays also examine how later scholars have refined and challenged the original arguments, casting new light on the original interpretations. The subject of Part II's first essay, Louis Hartz's triumphalist manifesto for an enduring American liberal tradition, *The Liberal Tradition in America*, certainly did not underestimate the role of ideology in American history, but it badly misinterpreted the origins and content of the nation's prevailing ideologies. Hartz's underlying argument that all American ideologies emerged from a liberal core (rejecting monarchy, aristocracy, and state religion) contained a kernel of truth. But the battle-scarred terrain of American politics reveals that its political ideologies have been far more complex and nuanced than Hartz comprehended when he wrote during the 1950s. Hartz's fundamental misunderstanding of the ideology of the founders led him into a thicket of problems in defining the fluid liberalism that flourished in American life. But ironically, his insistence on explicating American liberalism produced in Hartz's work an original understanding of American conservatism, whether of southern slaveholders trying to fashion the Tory conservatism of a landed gentry or twentieth-century businessmen trying to find a conservative ideology that was consistent with the constant churn, uncertainty, and creative destruction that define capitalism. Hartz's more enduring legacy may be his insight into the flaws of southern and American conservatism rather than his understanding of liberalism.

Part II's second essay, "The 'Genius of American Politics': The South, Ideology, and American Identity," examines historian Daniel Boorstin's contention that historically Americans' special genius grew from their taking a practical, nonideological approach to politics and government. In Boorstin's view, such a pragmatic approach, one unfettered by ideology,

Introduction

allowed Americans to react to changing circumstances on the ground with confidence and alacrity. The practical problem-solving of the moment realized within a stable historical and constitutional context constituted Boorstin's "genius" of American politics. Boorstin boldly argued that the American Civil War was a nonideological conflict. Instead, in his mind, the conflict emerged directly from a practical sectional disagreement over the need to adopt appropriate measures for managing the problem of slavery in the United States and its expansion into new territories. Over the seven decades since Boorstin published *Genius*, scholarship has revealed that Boorstin failed to grasp the intensely ideological nature of American politics in the Age of Civil War and the conflicting ideologies that drove both North and South to war while Boorstin constructed a fictitious consensus that could hardly explain the human cost of the war. Given the horrific conflict, the sweeping nature of emancipation, and the promise, later abandoned, of full citizenship to African Americans, how can we now, as a nation, have confidence that the elusive political "genius" of American politics can survive the current era of polarization and disillusionment?

The concluding essay in Part II turns again to David Potter and focuses on his compelling argument that American exceptionalism emerged neither from a practical, nonideological political genius, nor a prevailing faith in an inherited ideology, but rather on the influence of widespread and enduring economic abundance on the American character. Potter's *People of Plenty* argued that the broad availability of abundance, or simply the broadly available opportunity to amass at least a sufficiency and perhaps an abundance, became the nation's single most defining characteristic. Potter's argument proved especially convincing during the broadly shared prosperity of the post-World War II years. Yet Potter's explanation never quite accounted for the enduring postbellum poverty of the American South that lingered long enough for President Franklin Roosevelt to label the South the "nation's no. 1 economic problem" in 1938. Moreover, as the nation's economic growth slowed significantly and inequality worsened since 1980, there are now new reasons to question whether Potter's argument can remain influential, especially if the problem of growing and apparent hardening of economic inequality and the related class anger persists or worsens.

For its third avenue of exploration, the volume turns to a direct reexamination of the American South and its peculiar yet formative relationship with the rest of the American nation. Part III, comprising five essays, opens by focusing on historian Charles Sellers' argument that by the mid-nineteenth century, many white southerners, influenced by the spirit of American democracy and the values of evangelical Christianity, could never fully embrace the proslavery argument and maintained only a half-hearted commitment to the region's peculiar institution out of a mix of economic necessity and racial fear. Sellers argued that most white southerners experienced moral unease if not full-fledged guilt over how to justify living in a slaveholding society. In Sellers' view, this "travail of slavery" burdened white southerners throughout the late antebellum period and even beyond emancipation.

For at least a decade or so after the publication of Sellers' essay in 1960, subsequent scholarship supported and embellished Sellers' argument that white southerners experienced varying measures of guilt over slavery. But during the 1970s, an impressive array of new scholarly studies not only revealed that most white southerners eagerly defended slavery as either a necessary or a benign institution but, more importantly, that they accepted the racial justification for slavery and retained a deep commitment to white supremacy, white privilege, and Black subordination for at least a century after the end of slavery and the defeat of the Confederacy. One lingering legacy of slavery remains the dynamic of white domination and Black subordination that informs some white southern attitudes down to the present day. The manifestation of that legacy reveals much more rekindled anger than lingering guilt.

The second essay is Part III addresses the critical historical contributions of the Black scholar W. E. B. Du Bois, one of the most important, and most radical, American intellectuals of the twentieth century, and his influence on historical scholarship down to the present day. His *Souls of Black Folk* (1903) and *Black Reconstruction* (1935) created a field in Black history with particular emphasis on its intersection with the history of the American South. DuBois' *Souls of Black Folk* (1903) lyrically introduced the idea of the "two-ness" of the Black experience in the United States, and lent DuBois prestige he used as a co-founder of the National Association for the Advancement of Colored People (NAACP). Later in his life, DuBois' *Black Reconstruction* (1935) stood as a bold interpretive challenge to much of the existing historical literature. DuBois emphasized the democratic achievements of Black politicians and their allies during Reconstruction, achievements which were later eroded and dismantled by white supremacist politicians of the post-Reconstruction era. Decades later, as the direct action phase of the postwar civil rights movement gained momentum, a new generation of scholars turned to DuBois' work on Reconstruction as an example of how Black agency in

Introduction

history could be recognized and serve as the impulse for new understandings of slavery as well as Reconstruction. DuBois' work inspired impressive later work on slave resistance, slave communities, slave religion, the slave family, and slave political awareness, as well as a reinterpretation of the Reconstruction era as one of expanding democracy and the era's end as the dawn a truly tragic era in southern and American history. The essay also examines the rich historiography spawned from DuBois pioneering work and its progress down to the present day, including the revived emphasis on caste privilege and economic inequity. Moreover, this essay explores the role of DuBois' work as the basis for the creation of an anti-triumphalist interpretive thrust to American history, a thrust which persists down to the present day.

For nearly three-quarters of a century after the Civil War, the American South seemed the exception to American exceptionalism. As the late British historian Eric Hobsbawm put it, after the end of Reconstruction, the South remained "agrarian, poor, backward, and resentful; whites resenting the never-forgotten defeat and Blacks the disfranchisement and ruthless subordination imposed by whites when reconstruction ended." Confederate defeat and the emancipation of slaves (who constituted not only the majority of the South's agricultural labor force but also its largest single capital investment), left the American South faced with the challenge of embarking upon the "Age of Capital" while largely bereft of the era's key resource: capital. Using Hobsbawm's *Age of Capital* as a starting point, the third essay in Part III focuses on how the southern capital shortage turned much of the rural South into a "vast pawn shop" with financing for planting crops coming from a mortgage on a crop not yet produced. Moreover, as beggars for capital and wanting in skilled labor, the American South became the ragged stepchild of the industrializing American economy, an economic backwater forming a sort of "colonial economy" largely controlled by outside capital. Unable to control their economic destiny, white southerners defined success as reestablishing white supremacy in the region through disfranchisement and the creation of Jim Crow laws that clearly relegated the region's emancipated Black population to second-class citizenship. Even in the twenty-first century, active economic legacies of the capital-starved South haunt the region's economic landscape in the form of underdeveloped human capital and dependence on outside investment.

While most of the essays in this volume are organized around or in response to a particular interpretation shaping the discourse of American and southern history, the striking reality about the role of women in

American and southern history remained that for many years the absence of scholarship about women, and the even more pronounced absence of women historians in the profession, left large gaps in the nation's history and its history profession. Women seeking to find their way into the profession and to gain a voice in important historical discussions found many obstacles looming in their path. In particular, the journey of women into the world of professional historians involved overcoming many stereotypes and prejudices. A few women emerged as professional historians who made major contributions into new areas of scholarship during the early post-World War II era, but the ratio of women to men only began to increase in the late 1970s and early 1980s. Recent Nobel Prize winner in economics Claudia Goldin, whose expertise included the participation of women in the workforce, found that the "quiet revolution" of women entering the history profession that ran from 1950 to 1970 exploded as women rushed into the profession in full force during the 1970s, largely in search of job satisfaction. But more importantly than the enhanced ratio of women entering the profession, the influx of talented women opened new fields of study (women, family, social history topics, etc.) and their role shaped the profession dramatically as the extent of male dominance that had prevailed for many decades diminished. Chapter 8 examines the influence of talented women who opened and shaped new areas of study largely, or at least partially, little noticed or explored by men, while also offering new perspectives on longstanding questions of scholarly inquiry. Through their scholarship, women historians both opened new fields and enriched contributions of already established areas of scholarship. This essay reveals how valuable contributions made by women scholars have been in both opening new lines of inquiry as well as deepening the previously male-dominated dialogue on existing topics.

The fifth and concluding essay in Part III explores the rapid and dramatic "coming apart" of white working-class communities across the American South as the New Age of Inequality (post-1980) settled in, bringing stagnation and decline to rural areas, small towns, and even medium-sized cities. As the economic doldrums took hold across swaths of the American South and its diaspora during the decades since 1980, social dysfunction emerged with a vengeance in white working-class communities, a phenomenon that captured national attention through J. D. Vance's depiction in his best-selling *Hillbilly Elegy* (2016). While some southern urban areas boomed and diversified into attractive "brain hubs," other cities, small towns, and rural areas became mired

Introduction

in economic stagnation and decline. And even some older, chiefly industrial cites also suffered and declined as the economy deindustrialized. The many challenges the faltering economy presented white southern workers and their communities stimulated a visceral response from disaffected workers, a response manifest in angry efforts to reclaim white privilege and the aggressive championing of "traditional" values, and ultimately an unprecedented level of death and despair among white working-class southerners during the opioid epidemic. The complex story of disruptive economic forces, lingering racial resentments, and fierce atavistic loyalties led white southern workers to choose clinging to cultural values over building alliances that might redress their economic grievances.

The book's final essay returns to the larger but crucial point of what we can expect to learn from history, and how the study of history can enrich our understanding of our present, including our predicaments as well as our gifts. The late dean of southern historians, C. Vann Woodward, once asserted that the poor, defeated, and pessimistic South could serve as a counterpoint to the overweening confidence and optimism expressed by rest of the American nation. But Woodward later conceded that rather than offer a counterpoint to the national myths of virtue and prosperity, white southerners, at least, emerged as avid champions of American power and eager boosters for American capitalism, despite the region's history of poverty, defeat, and racial antagonism.

This essay, drawing not only on Woodward but also on the insights of Reinhold Niebuhr, Garry Wills, and Abraham Lincoln, among others, suggests that the irony of history should explode our innocence, chasten our arrogance, scold our self-righteousness, and alert us to the folly of ignoring inconvenient history. In sum, history, at its best, should give us a keen awareness of the irony embedded in the human experience, and, as it does, it should temper our pride even when showing mercy and our zeal even when seeking justice, while strengthening our recognition of the need to walk with humility in all our endeavors.

PART I

UNDERSTANDING THE AMERICAN SOUTH AND THE CIVIL WAR IN A NEW CENTURY

I

A Twenty-First Century Meaning
for the American Civil War

A Post-Cold War Reflection

A half century ago, historian David Potter, a titan even in a generation
of American historians which included C. Vann Woodward, Richard
Hofstadter, Daniel Boorstin, John Hope Franklin, Kenneth Stampp,
and others, offered an original interpretation of the meaning of the
American Civil War for the "modern" world of the mid-twentieth century.[1] In a brief essay published in 1968, Potter argued that despite all
of the political calculation and miscalculation that led to disunion and
civil war, the immense carnage produced by the war, and the failure of
the Reconstruction era to nurture or sustain a national commitment to
racial equality or even basic civil rights, the American Civil War had
succeeded not only in saving the American nation and ending the enor-
mity of slavery within its borders but also in preserving the viability of a
representative democracy (with all its flaws). In doing so, Potter claimed,
the American Civil War united liberalism and nationalism in a marriage
unique in the history of nineteenth-century nationalist movements. Over
the next 100 years, Potter maintained, this fateful union of liberalism
and nationalism gave liberalism a power that it might otherwise have
lacked and lent nationalism a popular legitimacy and moral sanction
that it would not necessarily have enjoyed. As a result, in Potter's view,
America's liberal nationalism served both the nation and the world well.[2]

Since Potter's essay appeared over fifty years ago, it has awakened the
imaginations of scholars of his own and later generations. Historians
have grappled with the full meaning of a war that cost the nation over
700,000 lives (from a total population of roughly 35 million) and yet also
saved the Union and freed nearly four million slaves.[3] By taking a comparative perspective, by internationalizing the scope of the inquiry, Potter

provided an analysis that reached beyond the question of how the Civil War should be understood in the American master historical narrative to address an even larger question: What legacy did the American Civil War leave for the future world as a whole?

In recent years, however, Potter's arguments have received less and less scholarly attention and prompted less and less reflection. Perhaps the lapse in attention owes to the extent to which Potter's argument has grown axiomatic in the minds of many experts. Or perhaps the lapse grows from an increasing sense that Potter's conclusions no longer seem relevant. The excesses of American nationalism and the growing illiberalism of American policies have raised fresh questions about the value of the marriage of nationalism and liberalism. Nevertheless, at the distance of a half century from its publication, Potter's analysis, and the continuing relevance of his interpretation for scholars and citizens of the twenty-first century, invites reexamination. In particular, the quarter of a century since the end of the Cold War has produced dramatic changes that have reshaped American habits and values in ways that have garnered too little attention. The experience of those years has also raised fundamental questions about the current and future health of the American marriage of nationalism and liberalism. But before examining the impact of the end of the Cold War on this long, if not always happy, marriage, we must first understand how Potter explained that relationship.

The emergence of nationalism as a major ideological and cultural force dominated the nineteenth century, especially in Europe. According to Potter, nationalism, in its modern form, "scarcely existed before the French revolution," but "by the end of nineteenth century, Britain, France, Germany, Italy and Japan had become the prototypes for modern nationality." Yet, after promising beginnings in Britain and France in the late eighteenth and early nineteenth century, nationalism foundered for a half century after the French defeat at Waterloo. The Union triumph in the American Civil War gave it renewed vigor. Moreover, nationalism had been not so much stalled as suppressed throughout Europe during the first half of the nineteenth century, with even Britain leading one of the major efforts to subdue unwanted examples (Irish nationalism). Unification efforts in Germany and Italy had sputtered and Louis Napoleon had declared himself emperor of France in 1852. When the Union victory restored the American nation-state in 1865, it gave nationalism a much-needed boost. The triumph of the Union not only preserved the American nation, Potter concluded, but also "forged a bond between

A Twenty-First Century Meaning for the Civil War

nationalism and liberalism at a time when it appeared that the two might draw apart and move in opposite directions."[4]

In analyzing the nationalist movements of the nineteenth century, Potter noted that the chief obstacles to the formation of "modern" nation-states in Europe were supranational entities such as the Habsburg, Hohenzollern, and Ottoman empires and the vast influence, including political influence, of the Roman Catholic Church. In the case of emerging European nationalist movements (in Germany, France, and Italy), these large superstructures, boasting significant military and political power, not to mention the power inherent in centuries of tradition, had to be displaced by revolutions from below – revolutions in which people had to find a common identity across local, ethnic, and linguistic barriers and then hammer out degrees of independence from larger empires and the church.[5]

By contrast, Potter maintained, the primary obstacles to nationalism and the formation of a powerful nation-state within the American Union came from conflicting and overlapping local and regional loyalties. These provincial loyalties were expressed in the numerous state's rights arguments expressed throughout the antebellum era, arguments that emanated from northern states on numerous occasions but even more consistently from southern states, where slaveholders often sought to use state sovereignty to protect slavery from presumed threats of federal intervention. Further, within individual slaveholding states, slaveholders frequently advocated the retention of political power at the local level (the county or parish), to protect the interests of slaveholders in Black belt areas from white-majority counties eager to tax slave property. Even at the local level, slaveholders zealously championed their rights as masters to govern their plantations and slaves as they saw fit with minimum interference from those living outside the Big House or beyond the plantation boundaries. To be sure, southern localism rested, as Potter noted, on support for a social order headed by an elite consisting of large landholders that often, though not always, expressed some suspicion of democracy, much as supranational obstacles to nationalism in Europe and Japan defended traditional hierarchies and related notions of social order.[6] But the fact remains that the American opposition to nationalism generally emanated from champions of localism and decentralization, while in other parts of the world imperial and other centralized powers stood in the way of emerging nation-states. Hence, the nature of the challenges facing emergent nationalism looked radically different in Europe than in the United States.

16   *Understanding the American South*

From its inception, the United States was a federal republic based on the novel concept of divided sovereignty. After detailed study of classical and modern efforts at creating lasting republics undertaken in preparation for the Convention of 1787, founder James Madison settled on the creative concept of divided sovereignty as a solution to the history of failure of popular republics.[7] The resulting United States Constitution called for popular but divided sovereignty. Sovereignty resided in the people, but that popular sovereignty was divided between the people of the states and the people of the nation. After a series of revisions of state constitutions in the 1780s and 1790s, the power of individual states was often shared with local governing units known variously as counties, parishes, districts, or townships. The primary challenge facing incipient American nationalism was to limit state and local authority to its sphere and build a shared sense of national loyalty.[8] Moreover, making a nation from the American states was as much a matter of cultivating emotional attachments as a matter of constitutional or political structure.[9] Thus nation-building in the United States had to occur from both above and below. In sum, the American nationalist project faced greater challenges from existing local and provincial loyalties than from transnational entities such as empires or Catholicism.

In Potter's account, the liberalism that married America's emerging nationalism during and after the Civil War was not an elaborate creed of political and economic ideas, such as Adam Smith's anti-mercantilist economic liberalism, or the political liberalism associated with John Locke, which emphasized property rights and representative government, though American liberalism enveloped elements of both. Rather it was the practical liberalism of a democratic republic, of Abraham Lincoln's "government of the people, by the people, and for the people" that could not be allowed to perish even under a crisis of disunion and a brutal civil war. It was an American experiment in a republican government based on a written constitution, popular yet divided sovereignty, and a well-defined system of checks and balances embedded within its government, and, after 1865, a liberalism infused by "a new birth of freedom" emanating from the emancipation of the nation's nearly four million slaves.[10]

Ironically, given the rhetoric of the twentieth and twenty-first centuries, American-style liberalism of the Civil War era only incidentally fostered notions of a free market economy. In fact, a free market ideology never emerged as a political force until well after the Civil War. Yet market revolution upon market revolution swept across the United States at various paces in different places throughout the antebellum era.

A Twenty-First Century Meaning for the Civil War

These sequential and overlapping market revolutions were spurred by land acquisition, western expansion, canals, railroads, shipping and navigation technology, a better postal service, and even, perhaps especially, a lucrative domestic slave trade that flourished long after Congress banned the international slave trade in 1808.[11] Faith in the idea of a thriving, expanding economy with a significant market orientation certainly became embedded in the minds of many antebellum American producers and consumers, as well as its capitalists, and, as much recent literature insists with remarkable surprise, even among the slaveholding planters across the American South who were as involved in global markets as any economic actors on earth. Yet national faith in the ideas or ideals of a free market economy emerged much more slowly than the market economy itself, gaining significant traction only well after the Civil War, and arguably not until concerted efforts by pro-business groups to promote free market ideas launched well into the twentieth century.[12] During the pre-Civil War years, considerable anti-corporation sentiment coexisted with support for active government promotion of economic development (chiefly through internal improvement projects and banking practices), with the former often garnering greater public support than the latter. By the time of the Civil War, market-oriented economic activity, along with laws protecting private property and limiting corporate liability, had become the reality of daily economic life in most of the United States, but the "free market" had not yet emerged as a treasured American ideal.[13]

For much of the twentieth century, the American marriage of liberalism and nationalism appeared to be a bulwark for freedom and democracy in a threatening world. During the first half of the century Americans saw the dark side of nationalism in the Kaiser's Germany and especially in the later reactionary and murderous regimes of Nazis and Fascists. Americans stared into the abyss of the extremes produced when nationalism unleavened by liberalism falls into the wrong hands. At the same time, Americans also saw fresh fruits of the union of nationalism and liberalism in their own country. The turn-of-the-century Progressive movement, which originated as an array of local reform movements that gradually forced their way into the national arena, generated an appetite for clean politics and national legislation to address some major social questions (sanitation and education foremost among them) that, on balance, appeared to strengthen the bonds between liberalism and nationalism in the American setting. During the 1930s, Franklin Roosevelt's New Deal, offered as a response to the worst depression in the nation's history, initiated the construction of both a national regulatory structure

18 *Understanding the American South*

and a social safety net that protected many ordinary Americans from the occasional depredations of the market economy and gave business a measure of protection as well.[14]

Moreover, by the time Potter crafted his essay in the late 1960s, the strengths of the American marriage of nationalism and liberalism seemed obvious. It was clear that American power had secured the defeat of Nazis and Fascists in Europe and the Japanese imperialists in the Pacific, and that victory appeared to ensure that liberal nationalism rather than conservative or chauvinistic nationalism would prevail, or at least could prevail, against powerful opponents with great malignancy of intent. In addition, the Allied victory in World War II provided the ideological high ground for Americans in their Cold War of ideas and ideology with the Soviets and the Chinese communists, who despite their commitment to communism derived a great deal of their support from the long-deferred fulfillment of the ambitions of Russian and Chinese nationalism. Specifically, the American marriage of nationalism and liberalism gave the United States, as the leader of the "West" (the NATO coalition), the moral and ideological high ground when judged against the brutality and repression of the Stalinist and post-Stalinist regimes in the Soviet Union, not to mention the China of Chairman Mao and the brutal purge of the Cultural Revolution. The so-called vital center, the loose post-World War II coalition of liberals, moderates, and even some conservatives who came together on certain basic tenets of American anti-communist principles, rallied American democracy against a common and menacing enemy with appeals to liberal, democratic nationalism.[15]

At its best, such common national purpose served the nation well, sustaining popular support for both capitalist creativity and an expanding social safety net, and for the emergence of what a wary President Eisenhower called the "military-industrial complex," as well as a fledgling environmental movement. It had encouraged public investment in schools and research universities and supported a far-ranging system of community and technical colleges to enhance workforce preparedness and workplace skills in a sweeping effort to create an ever better-educated citizenry and ensure that the United States remained a leader in research and knowledge in an increasingly competitive world economy.[16]

In fact, the expanding support for American higher education during the Cold War era shaped both economic opportunity and the American university system as we know it. First, the GI Bill offered broad and affordable access to college to American veterans for the first time, and the baby boom following the GIs' return home combined with later federal

A Twenty-First Century Meaning for the Civil War

scholarship and loan programs to sustain demand for higher education and the rapid expansion of American universities, especially in the 1960s. Second, federally funded research agencies provided indirect funding for university-sponsored research through grants to faculty. In 1950, the postwar United States established the National Science Foundation, at least in part, to "secure the national defense" and funded its initial year of operations with $3.5 million. When American anxiety spiked after the Soviet launch of Sputnik in 1957, National Science Foundation funding escalated to $40 million in 1958, and that same year the government created NASA to spearhead the space program and further expand federal funding of the nonhealth sciences. Funding for the preexisting National Institutes of Health, which stood at just under $5 million at the end of World War II, exploded to over $1 billion by 1970 (and to $16 billion by 2000) in the postwar era. Even the humanities and social sciences were affected. In a move closely related to Cold War tensions, the 1958 Education Act provided federal funding for university-based area studies centers for Africa, Asia, Latin American, and other areas where the United States perceived itself as confronting communism.[17]

Over the long term, this dramatic expansion of federal support for research, and particularly university research, spurred initially by the Cold War and its drive for technological and scientific supremacy, established the federal government as the primary funder of basic research in the nation and created and sustained the modern research university as a critical component in the struggle for world economic competitiveness (if not dominance). Such policies appeared to be crafted by and for the expanding middle class and the baby boomers of the post-World War II era. These efforts represented a determination to preserve the American economic and knowledge infrastructure as the envy of the world.

Yet the sense of common purpose and the solid anti-communist front the United States projected in the early years of the Cold War also revealed the weaknesses of the American marriage of liberalism and nationalism. Despite the rising tide of post-World War II prosperity throughout the United States, questions of social and racial justice were often pushed to the background in favor of either the Cold War arms race or the race to capitalist expansion. It also appeared that the United States could be tempted toward adventurism in those parts of the world where capitalism and free markets were not gaining favor in the avowed competition with communist ideology. The penchant of Cold War America to prop up anti-democratic and illiberal regimes internationally and oppose internal reform movements in the so-called Third World damaged the

20   *Understanding the American South*

nation's reputation in the developing world. Such American shortsightedness gave momentum to considerable and justifiable suspicion around the world that the United States sought to become (or had become) an imperial power.[18]

American imperialism would rely on the power of the nation's amassed capital, as well as its military might, to forge an economic empire, not to mention a sense of national cultural hauteur that failed to take into consideration either American excesses or the deep virtues represented by other cultures. At home, McCarthyism, the suppression of internal dissent, and the overall "domestic security" crisis of the 1950s suggested that the United States would struggle to both control Cold War anxieties and live up to its ideals at home as well as abroad. The pressure for conformity, the squashing of dissent, and the emergence of "the company man" as the ideal citizen and head of the middle-class American household gave post-World War II America an illiberal and conformist patina.[19]

Yet beneath the conformist urge, and ironically stimulated by it, lay vibrant subcultures of protest and dissent. During the 1950s and 1960s, the direct action phase of the civil rights movement produced fresh successes which ultimately toppled Jim Crow and ended formal African American disfranchisement in the American South with the passage of the Civil Rights Act of 1964 and the Voting Rights Act of 1965. These formal successes stood as tributes to the courageous grassroots activism of African American communities throughout the South, where dozens, hundreds, and even thousands of communities and churches supplied the disciplined ground troops of nonviolent protest needed to win the battles of politics and perception on behalf of the civil rights movement.[20] By the 1960s, reaction to pressure for conformity amid persistent injustice stimulated yet another anti-establishment social movement, one driven by a very nonconformist segment of the nation's youth population. Through youth protests, mostly on college campuses, many young Americans sought greater freedom of expression in a variety of areas. Through this movement, whether directed at social injustices, personal freedoms (and even indulgences), or ultimately against the deepening American involvement in Vietnam, the fear of state power emerged as a matter of generational concern in the United States.[21]

By the middle of the 1960s, these protest movements became intertwined to different degrees with the escalating domestic debate over the war in Vietnam. An increasingly active antiwar movement gained substantial popularity among the young (draft-age) population on college

A Twenty-First Century Meaning for the Civil War   21

campuses and within the larger intelligentsia. This movement eventually received the endorsement of the nation's best-known civil rights leader, the Rev. Dr. Martin Luther King, Jr., much to the consternation of President Lyndon Johnson and his administration, which had successfully maneuvered major civil rights legislation through Congress.[22]

This antiwar protest movement highlighted the ways in which the military and economic adventurism undertaken by the United States under the cover of the Cold War tarnished the image of the world's most powerful democracy in the eyes of many Americans. Together, these protest movements, acting both independently and in combination, focused much attention on the adventurism and exploitation that the American nation, for all its professed good intentions, practiced. These movements also brought irreconcilable tension to the nation's "vital center" coalition and generated deep divisions within American society, dividing the nation to the point that many Americans feared that the nation was coming apart. It was at almost precisely at this moment in 1968 that Potter published his essay on nationalism and liberalism.

But, while deep domestic divisions persisted until the war in Vietnam ended in 1975, the fears of the nation coming apart eventually proved overblown, and few could have imagined that roughly twenty years following the publication of Potter's essay the Cold War itself would be on the verge of extinction and that the great international experiment in socialism would collapse due to its failure to provide either meaningful freedom or a decent material standard of living for most people living within its scope. Moreover, the Soviets' penchant for foreign interventionism and adventurism around the world matched that of previous imperial powers and squandered Soviet blood and treasure in Afghanistan and elsewhere. Soviet economic scarcity produced internal protests, with incidents in Boris Yeltsin's Moscow the most prominent among them. Mikhail Gorbachev's efforts to "reform" the Soviet regime through glasnost and perestroika not only proved inadequate but arguably accelerated the disintegration of the Soviet Union rather than forestalling it.[23]

The precise endpoint of the Cold War remains a matter of some debate. But many Americans' remembrance of the end of the Cold War is framed by President Ronald Reagan standing at the Brandenburg Gate in Berlin and demanding, "Mr. Gorbachev, tear down this wall," followed by later scenes of East Berliners crossing the formerly forbidden zone to visit West Berliners under relaxed restrictions, and soon stopping to chip souvenirs off the slowly eroding wall. But no matter exactly when the Cold War ended, its conclusion marked a quiet turning point in the history of the modern American nation. From its entry into World War I through this "fall" of the Berlin Wall, the American nation, with its blend of nationalism and liberalism, however flawed, defining its character, stood formidably against extremism in various forms. By the early 1990s, it had added outlasting brutal and authoritarian communist regimes in the Cold War to its resume of defeating Fascists across the globe in world war. Moreover, during the 1960s, the nation had at least partially redeemed the long-deferred promises of the Reconstruction era for equal citizenship and greater opportunity for African Americans, and to an extent all people regardless of race or gender.[24]

The end of the Cold War produced more than its share of celebratory triumphalism in the United States, much of it undeserved. Such triumphalism emerged with special vigor from various points on the political right eager to capture the credit for victory for their revered political icon, Ronald Reagan, and to bootstrap support for their own neoconservative international agenda. That agenda emerged from a commitment to the worldwide domination of free market capitalism, constitutional democracy, and enlightened secularism. Some observers even confused the end of the Cold War, meaningful though it was, with the end of history. Indeed, American triumphalism received perhaps its most emphatic expression in Francis Fukuyama's article (and later book), "The End of History," published in 1989. Fukuyama's work posited a near universal triumph of American values, political democracy, capitalist economics, and secular culture – all American style – around the world. The scattered remaining redoubts of localism, authoritarianism, or socialism would slowly but surely crumble when challenged by the allure of those irresistible American exports: prosperity and democracy.[25]

A skeptical conservative, Samuel Huntington, warned his bullish younger colleagues that such self-confident American universalism and exceptionalism (an older secular faith that became embattled in the aftermath of Vietnam and Watergate) would appear as imperialism to others around the world. Moreover, the champions of the "End of History" somehow ignored the rise of religious fundamentalism worldwide between 1970 and 2000 in reaction to modernity in all its many guises.[26] This fundamentalist movement reasserted itself with vengeance in the Islamic world after the ill-conceived twenty-first-century American war with Iraq, which proceeded despite the lack of proof that Iraqi dictator Saddam Hussein had either a role in the 9/11 attacks on the World Trade Center or a program close to producing nuclear weapons.

A Twenty-First Century Meaning for the Civil War 23

The end of the Cold War did not prove to be the "End of History." Not even the flourishing hyperbole of conservative triumphalism could obscure the fact that after the Cold War's end the old American union of nationalism and liberalism has grown frayed and maybe even strained. With the common ideological and military opponent seemingly vanquished, the purpose of the liberal nationalist fusion seemed less clear and compelling, and certainly less focused. The chief causes of the fraying ties between liberalism and nationalism appear to lie in the strong decentralizing currents unleashed when Americans no longer had to nurture unity and promote strength to face down a common enemy of global reach and roughly commensurate military power. In the weakening of centralizing forces, the end of the Cold War has been abetted by other trends that have served to strengthen decentralizing forces just as the Cold War's demise weakened centralizing ones. Among the most powerful of these decentralizing forces stand the personalization of technology, increasing economic inequality, and the growing dysfunction of intentionally polarized politics. Together, the strength of such decentralizing forces, operating in the absence of the Cold War's centralizing counterweight, has placed enormous strain on the American marriage of nationalism and liberalism.

The trend toward increased personalization of technology in recent decades is unmistakable, and the decentralizing tendencies emanating from this technological revolution came in at least two phases.[27] During the first phase, major changes in the computer and television industries expanded access to information and entertainment and eroded the centralizing influence of national oligopolies. Computing evolved from big mainframes produced by mega-firms such as IBM ("Big Blue") to personal computers, which both put computing power in the homes and offices of many Americans and allowed the emergence of newcomers such as Apple and Dell to become mega-firms, outstripping IBM in wealth, with the entire process facilitated by the emergence of a dominant software mega-provider, Microsoft. These changes distributed significant computing and communicating capacity much more broadly across the nation, democratizing information in the process and expanding communication opportunities through email. Also, in this first phase, cable television broke the grip of major networks on the viewing public and brought diversity in news and entertainment options to millions with cable access. News and entertainment channels proliferated and television viewing became a much more segmented market. Over time, viewers could even choose a cable news channel whose "slant" on the world comported well with their own.[28]

The second phase of the decentralizing movement in technology came with the rise of personal devices such as cell phones, the Palm, and the Blackberry, and emerged with a vengeance with the smartphones (especially Apple iPhones) of the twenty-first century. These smartphones placed a powerful computer, which provided access to vast knowledge as well as a sense of connection, in the hand of the user 24/7, and spawned as offspring new forms of communication discussed later in this chapter. These inventions and improvements tended to enhance personal autonomy while at the same time making people feel better connected, if only virtually, to the larger world. These inventions have decentralized knowledge and communication while simultaneously enhancing a sense of being in touch and of being on top of things, thus fulfilling the needs of both inner- and outer-directed personalities.[29]

The rise of the personal computer and related connectivity during this first phase of the technology revolution were not the only forces driving decentralization and an eroding a sense of common purpose during the last quarter of the twentieth century. The growing inequality of wealth and income in the United States since the 1970s also enhanced the sense of decentralization. Real (inflation-adjusted) wages in the United States have not increased appreciably since 1979. The incomes of average families have not increased since 2000. Between 2000 and 2011 worker output increased by 2.5 percent, but worker incomes increased by only 1 percent during the same period. At the same time, the share of total income earned by the nation's top 1 percent has increased from 11 percent in 1994 to 23 percent in 2012.[30] Taking a longer view, from 1979 through 2007, the after-tax income of households in the top 1 percent of households grew by 275 percent, compared to 65 percent for the next 19 percent of households, to just under 40 percent for the next 60 percent, and only 18 percent for the bottom fifth of households. The income of the 1 percent of highest-income households nearly tripled between 1979 and 2007, while the share received by low- and middle-income households declined.[31]

A look at the distribution of wealth is even more troubling. While the top 10 percent of American households control roughly a quarter of all income, they control just over three-quarters of all wealth, with the richest 5 percent controlling over 50 percent of the wealth. By contrast, the bottom 40 percent controls virtually no wealth and the next 40 percent only 12 percent. Such a wealth distribution may or may not mean the presence of a permanent moneyed aristocracy of unprecedented power in the United States, but it certainly suggests the emergence of an

A Twenty-First Century Meaning for the Civil War 25

economic order French economist Thomas Picketty labeled "patrimonial capitalism," a system centered on the power of inherited wealth, which gradually squeezes the life from the American dream of ongoing upward social mobility.[32]

It has also been easy to notice how the phenomenon of economic globalization at least appears to have enhanced inequalities in wealth and income.[33] On balance, globalization seems to have benefited better-educated, more technologically sophisticated Americans – the creative classes, high-level technology "geeks," and financial wizards – significantly. But at the same time, blue-collar Americans, with lower levels of education and fewer job skills, have faced lower or stagnant wages, the outright loss of jobs, and/or a shift to the lower-paying service sector with the decline of the proportion of manufacturing jobs in the American economy. Such polarization of gains and loss by class has divided Americans even further, produced ongoing political contretemps, and added a new dimension to centrifugal pull.[34]

Increasing inequalities in the distribution of wealth and income in the United States have also heightened disturbing class divisions in other tangible ways. A society which a half century ago sought security primarily against external threats through large nuclear arsenals and the theory of "mutually assured destruction" now seeks safety from nearby dangers, often based on both real and exaggerated concerns about random street crime, through the perquisites of wealth: gated communities, penthouse suites, private schools, and exclusive clubs of various sorts. Opportunity, especially in the form of a college education, is not so much a public good as a privilege available in proportion to how much people can afford to pay for it.[35] Political campaigns, given their dependence on fundraising for expensive yet critical media buys, have become more influenced than ever by Big Money, whose funding efforts and advertising (through Political Action Committees) now enjoy Supreme Court sanction as rights of free speech.

Taken together, the technological revolutions and growing economic inequalities have generated powerful decentralizing forces that tend to diminish the national sense of common purpose and enhance the pressures working to disrupt Potter's uniquely American marriage of nationalism and liberalism. Yet perhaps the most striking development appearing after the end of the Cold War has been the emergence of long-term political and governmental division and dysfunction which surfaced in the absence of Cold War imperatives. It was hardly a coincidence that just as the Soviet Union, the nation's chief Cold War antagonist,

26 *Understanding the American South*

disintegrated into its constituent parts, the American nation that had outlasted it spun into increasingly sharp political divides over questions related to political centralization. As the galvanizing centripetal pull of the Cold War, with its insistence on thwarting the designs of a powerful and threatening external adversary, rapidly diminished, the United States itself experienced its own, more modest, version of coming apart.[36] Differently put, once former Soviet Premier Nikita Khrushchev's vow to "bury" the United States became harmless hyperbole rather than genuine menace, the lack of a unifying outside threat, such as Soviet communism, allowed disintegration of the "vital center." That center had advocated, to varying degrees, on behalf of a balanced economy, a commitment to both the public good and private initiative, an adequate social safety net, and a sense of common national purpose. The weakening of this once "vital center" itself proved a major factor in the growing strength of decentralizing tendencies in the United States.

The gradual weakening of the political center in the United States is a complicated story, and a full examination lies well beyond the scope of this chapter, but a partial examination can illustrate the larger point about the loss of a centralizing pull. Ironically, a key to the diminished power of the center lay in the success of the democratic reform impulse of the 1960s that informed the court decision applying the "one person, one vote" principle to the drawing of Congressional and state legislative election districts. African Americans, Hispanics, and other minorities understandably pushed hard for increased representation drawn from their ranks in legislative bodies, and Democrats responded to the desire of significant portions of their base and the new demands of federal law by encouraging the drawing of majority minority districts to insure minority representation. At the same time, Republicans seized the advantage they derived from the herding of Democratic voters into overwhelmingly Democratic districts to increase Republican competitiveness in districts which had lost Democratic votes. As Republicans won more and more districts and eventually gained control of more state legislatures, they created as many safe GOP seats as possible through redistricting. The safer these Republican seats became, the more conservative the Republican candidates who could win them.

As safe seats became the rule, incumbents in both parties became far more concerned about primary challenges than about opposition in the general elections. This growing logic of safe seats, examined in mere outline form here, created more minority (and generally more liberal) representation from safe Democratic districts, more conservative winners from safe Republican districts, and fewer competitive districts in which representation was truly decided in the general election rather than in the primary. The electoral pressures meant that popularity among the party faithful meant more than the ability to appeal to swing voters. As a result, the power of the political center at the ballot box diminished. The Democratic party grew more liberal and the Republican party more conservative, leaving centrists with fewer appealing choices.

At the presidential level, the losses suffered by avowed liberals Walter Mondale and Michael Dukakis in the 1984 and 1988 elections chastened Democrats back toward the center. Bill Clinton's success with the "New Democrat" label in the 1992 and 1996 convinced the party that centrist strategies could work in presidential elections. While Clinton led chastened Democrats back to the center after Reagan-era defeats, to date there is little evidence that Barack Obama's solid presidential victories in 2008 and 2012 nudged Republicans back toward the center. Instead, the GOP responded to defeat with increasingly sharp and divisive attacks on Obama and his supporters that polarized the electorate even more dramatically. In fact, the nation's once muscular vital center is now threatened primarily by the continued, and even erratic, rightward drift of a Republican party still seeking a repeat of the success of the Reagan years. If the modern conservative political movement in the United States surfaced with Barry Goldwater's disastrous 1964 presidential defeat, it crested with Ronald Reagan's popular presidency in the 1980s. Yet in most recent election cycles, the GOP has attempted to recapture such success by lurching even further to the right.[37]

At the national level, the boundaries of the right wing's popularity have been successfully delineated and exploited by skillful Democratic politicians, such as Bill Clinton and Barack Obama, who appealed to common ground and understood the importance of wooing the center. But, frankly, the calculus of political success for both Clinton and Obama was narrow and required either considerable help from either third-party candidates (Ross Perot) or an aggressive mobilization of their party's base. Increasingly, the traditional pro-business wing of the Republican party struggled to retain its usual prominence within the GOP. In 2012, when the pro-business faction of the party produced a presidential nominee (Mitt Romney) who was deeply one of its own, and who also wore even a thin veneer of conservative populism uncomfortably, that nominee failed to arouse enough passion among Republican loyalists to match George W. Bush's majority of 2004, despite one exceedingly poor debate performance by the usually articulate Democratic incumbent (Obama).[38]

Even the stunning 2016 success of rhetorical flame-thrower and unbridled political and personal attacker Donald Trump in routing a covey of small-government conservative ideologues in the Republican presidential primaries, not to mention his shocking November victory in the electoral college, have arguably only moved the party further from the mainstream in its views. Trump's general election upset appears driven by narrow popular vote wins in key industrial states in which blue-collar white voters swung to Trump in unexpected numbers. But this victory did little to close the gap between the self-styled outsider candidate become president and the national mainstream, given that the losing candidate, Democrat Hillary Clinton, won the popular vote comfortably (by 2 percent and nearly four million votes) despite her strongly negative popularity ratings.

But, while hard-right conservative success at the national level has been intermittent at best since Reagan left office in 1989, the story in the states has been quite different. Nowhere has the hard-right influence grown more apparent than in Republican primaries held in safely "red" states and districts. The hard right's growing dominance there has given it enhanced influence across the larger political landscape. For example, in 2018, Republicans controlled governorships and held legislative majorities in over thirty states, giving them not only power in those states but also added leverage nationally (in the United States Senate and the Electoral College). It was an underappreciated fact that in the disputed presidential election of 2000, George W. Bush's victory hinged on carrying ten more states than Al Gore and winning the twenty electoral votes (two per state) granted to each state by the US Constitution in addition to the electoral votes allocated to each state based on its representation in Congress. Without those electoral votes, Gore would have defeated Bush regardless of the outcome in Florida. In 2016, Trump's winning effort consisted of carrying many more states than Hillary Clinton while winning many fewer popular votes than the Democratic nominee.

Since at least 1994, but especially during the final six years of the Obama presidency, gridlock has often prevailed in national politics. In the legislative branch simple majorities will no longer do. A three-fifths majority is needed to push most bills through the US Senate. In the US House, the majority caucus and its leadership control which bills even make it to the floor (a tactic employed by both parties). Continuing resolutions substitute for actual budgets and debt ceiling issues periodically threaten to shut down the government. In the executive branch, legislative achievements have given way to governing by executive order. Such inert government, disdained and routinely dismissed as intolerable during

A Twenty-First Century Meaning for the Civil War   29

a Cold War era characterized by urgency and the need for strength, now regularly prevails. Such political dysfunction and inaction clearly fueled the Trump candidacy in 2016, as the Republican insurgent vowed to ignore both ideological purity and political correctness in his professed determination to get things done. In fact, Trump's ego and narcissistic desire for the spotlight triggered even more dysfunction and reckless confrontation.

The reign of the politics of stalemate and the empowerment of champions of decentralization need not inevitably mean the weakening of liberal nationalism, but in the late twentieth- and early twenty-first-century United States, resurgent localism has been laced with significant measures of chauvinism and atavism. The polarized politics of the post-Cold War era has given new vigor and license to the expression of such ideas. But even beyond partisan politics, there can be little doubt that national confidence in the public sector, a shared understanding of common purpose, and a sense of mutual obligation to fellow citizens have all eroded with the end of the Cold War. Localism and even libertarianism threaten the 100-year-old marriage of nationalism and liberalism that David Potter so artfully explained. Our politics are not calling us back toward the center. And if not our politics, what is?

Perhaps surprisingly, but perhaps not, religion hardly exerts much cohesive pull in America today. As recent scholarship confirmed, American Christianity has long been marked by intense denominational competition with frequent schisms creating even more competition among churches for members. Differentiation of message rather than a message of common purpose drives church growth.[39] Moreover, repeated polls suggest that the twenty-first-century United States is a less overtly religious, less churchgoing society than ever in its history. Yet despite shrinking overall numbers, the range of religious affiliations with meaningful numbers of followers is larger than ever before. Within the dominant religious tradition, Christianity, there are more denominations and sects than ever but less unity and sharper internal divisions than during the middle of the twentieth century when mainline Protestantism, informed and instructed by public theologians such as Reinhold Niebuhr, served as something approaching a civil religion.[40] In the early twenty-first century, no matter how much social good through service emanates from churches, synagogues, mosques, shrines, temples, and other centers of worship and belief – and without question life in America would be much more callous without them – religious divisions often do as much to accelerate polarization as to promote common purpose.

30 *Understanding the American South*

Nor has American popular culture offered much help. A familiar tool of nationalism, and one often abused, a shared "national" popular culture can often and perhaps ultimately supersede the scores of folk cultures enveloped by most nation-states. During most of the Cold War years, an increasingly strong American popular culture was defined by three television networks, a handful of powerful movie studios, and a music industry dominated by a few recording labels. Moreover, television networks and movie producers had something of a preoccupation with the Cold War. For example, the immensely popular, iconic James Bond films of the 1960s and beyond emerged from the public fascination with the Cold War mindset of espionage and intrigue. The three major commercial television networks not only offered thorough coverage of the Cold War but also delivered pretty much the same news to American households every night. Anchors such as Edward R. Murrow, whose *See It Now* program unmasked Senator Joseph McCarthy's red-baiting campaign against the military, and Walter Cronkite, whose coverage of civil rights and the war in Vietnam informed riveted viewers, emerged as among the most trusted people in the nation. Such trust produced an era in which people were entitled to their own opinions but not to their own facts, at least not in public discourse. Later in the evening, the major networks delivered common entertainment at regular times to national audiences, creating shared viewing experiences across much of the nation.[41] Professional sports of the era created a new national pastime, as football, NFL-style, replaced baseball, MLB-style, as the nation's most popular sport. Often deemed shallow and distracting by the intelligentsia of the age, the vigor of a widely shared national popular culture nonetheless emerged as a key source of common identity in an increasingly diverse nation.

But as the second phase of the ongoing technological and communication revolution of the late twentieth and early twenty-first centuries emerged in full force, mobile personal devices and social media eventually undermined the common popular culture cultivated by Big Media and Big Entertainment to a significant degree. The personalization of entertainment, communication, and information have at the very least decentralized American popular culture if not shattered it into dozens of pieces sorted by niche markets, generational patterns, peer pressures, and, of course, income. Entertainment and information are now delivered on very personalized time schedules as "on demand" or "on your time" technologies rise to dominance. Television programming is available on laptop and tablet computers as well as ubiquitous smartphones and watched whenever and wherever by streaming viewers. The so-called millennial generation that serves as the driving edge of these trends has

A Twenty-First Century Meaning for the Civil War   31

even earned the label of "cord-cutters" for their aversion to any signal delivered by cable or to an immobile device. Moreover, programming is now generated by a broad variety of entities, including cable networks and video-streaming enterprises. HBO, Netflix, AMC, Amazon, and others have in recent years produced hit series such as *The Wire, Mad Men, The Parent, House of Cards*, and *The Magnificent Mrs. Maisel*. News, and even more opinion, gushes forth 24/7 from a variety of sources, including websites and online tabloid equivalents. Vinyl albums and CDs are a thing of the past, as music, first purchased one song at a time for a while from Apple's iTunes, is now obtained from streaming services such as Pandora or Spotify through "apps."

Interpersonal communications have been revolutionized by new technology and innovative entrepreneurship. A new category of media – social media – emerged as entrepreneurs such as Mark Zuckerberg fathomed the popular appeal of giving individuals the ability to communicate with groups of friends using the internet. Facebook, with its systems of friends, posts, and likes, connected and reconnected people across distances great and small into multitudinous communities (as many in number as there are users of Facebook), where members share pictures and posts as frequently as they choose with those who have "friended" them. Businesses and other organizations now maintain Facebook pages to reach customers. Land phone lines gave way to cell phones (some estimates suggest that fewer than 40 percent of American households now maintain land lines), and the postal service and phone calls yielded to emails. Email has now been partially replaced by text messaging, and among younger Americans, by another social media tool, X (nee Twitter), and its imitators. With its own lingo of hashtags, handles, and "emojis" (symbols connoting emotions), Twitter allows brief and pithy communication through short "tweets" of 280 characters or less. Initially, the character limit per tweet was 140 characters. People follow celebrities, athletes, and even politicians as well as networks of friends or people with similar interests, as subject lines "trend" when they become popular. Connections through social media such as Facebook and Twitter have promoted the creation of virtual communities fostering a sense of connection and belonging, but they do so in a highly decentralized fashion that is entirely voluntary, carries little obligation, and remains, at the end of day, "virtual."[42]

The technology, communication, personal device, and social media marketplaces are full of competitors and personal choice in consumption prevails, but any sense of shared community beyond the choice of entertainment and information dissolves. The once shared experience of the family TV room, stultifying and conformist as it may have been for many, is replaced by scattered viewers and readers on commuter trains, at bus stops, on walks and jogs, across tables from each other at restaurants, and, well, just about anywhere reachable by a signal. As liberating and diversity-encouraging as these trends may be, they are nonetheless powerful centrifugal forces pulling society away from a common center. They are scattering rather centering influences, highlighting the absence of a strong magnet-like pull emanating from the national core like that of the Cold War era.

In the face of such powerful decentralizing tendencies, a fervent rhetorical patriotism flourishes, especially in terms of support for the nation's all-volunteer armed services. Yet doubters wonder if such ardent patriotism disguises the decline of actual commitment to nation with loud and vehement expressions of arch-loyalty. At times, even the current rhetoric of patriotism is divisive, often chauvinistic in tone, and exclusive rather than inclusive in its scope. Make no mistake, the actual sacrifices for freedom made by those in uniform under the Stars and Stripes, though genuinely appreciated by most Americans, are often disproportionately borne by those Americans – women, African Americans, and Hispanic Americans – long excluded from full privileges of citizenship.

Given all of this, what, if anything, is left to hold the center against the tumult? Can any of the traditional mechanisms or ideals stand against the tide? Constitutional checks and balances? Genuine love of nation? Faith in shared prosperity? The ongoing affinity of newcomers to their chosen and adopted nation? Confidence in a rickety political system that is more than 200 years old to sort matters over the long term, if not in the short? Good, old-fashioned American common sense? Perhaps none of the above independently but all or some mixed together?

The answer, in this historian's view, remains in the end more a matter of faith than a subject of proof. But the long narrative of American history, which is far from a foolproof guide yet still indisputably the best guide we have, suggests that there may well be something in that Lincolnian blend of nationalism and liberalism, especially when economic opportunity, real and imagined, is folded in, that still exerts a powerful unifying pull that might effectively countervail the protean forces dividing us and tugging us apart. Above the din of inflammatory rhetoric and the dysfunction of daily politics in Washington and elsewhere, there is still much in that elusive American character that seems to hear and respond to calls to rally for the common good on occasion, to respond affirmatively when "the promise of American life," as progressive-era journalist Herbert Croly aptly labeled it a hundred years ago, appears at stake.[43]

A Twenty-First Century Meaning for the Civil War

Using the language of that century-old era, Croly's shorthand prescription for protecting that promise called for using "Hamiltonian means" to achieve "Jeffersonian ends." Twenty-first-century political commentators would translate this message as a call to use centralized public power to countervail concentrated private power to enhance freedom and opportunity for all. Such a call represents an updated reassertion of an even older American (Jacksonian-era) rallying cry that the few should never prevail at the expense of the many.[44]

Faith in the "promise of American life" may simply mean believing that, among Americans as whole, decency still exceeds meanness, a commitment to fairness still reigns over fascination with wealth and power, hope in expanding opportunity can override fears of lost security, the nation of immigrants can still welcome more immigrants, becoming better at being global is a better strategy than trying futilely to wall ourselves off from the rest of the world, or simply recognizing that people are unique but overall they are more alike than different. Summoning what Lincoln called "the better angels of our nature," we can "still bind up the nation's wounds" and care for each other while working together to seek justice and lasting peace in our nation and world, as our greatest president challenged us to do amid a grave crisis some 150 years ago.[45]

Reviving the "promise of America life" for the twenty-first century will nonetheless involve some hard work. It will require the recovery of a sense of common purpose – a common purpose for all Americans, including African Americans and Hispanics and Muslims and Asian and gay and transgender people and all others, not just white Americans, who are a shrinking portion of the population. It will involve helping those injured by economic globalization as well as those who are enriched by it. It will involve moving beyond the politics of stalemate. It will involve the rediscovery of the politics of compromise. It will involve an informed citizenry getting their heads out of sound bites, cell phone conversations, and social media and instead paying serious attention to issues and not just to barbed chatter and political dog-and-pony shows. It will involve calling forth the America we often see after crises and tragedies, after floods, hurricanes, and mass killings, the America we glimpsed too briefly after the 9/11 attacks in New York City, in Boston after the marathon bombing, and in South Carolina after the racist slaying of African Americans in Charleston's historic Emmanuel AME church. It will involve citizens embracing as a model the example of the biblical Good Samaritan who stopped to help the suffering stranger, who found him in need and ministered to him, who found the victim lodging and paid for

34   *Understanding the American South*

continuing care. If the nation can do these things, then, a hundred years after Herbert Croly coined the phrase, the enduring appeal of the "promise of American life," and renewed calls for its fulfillment, can surely resonate once again.

Notes

1. David M. Potter, "Civil War," in C. Vann Woodward, ed., *The Comparative Approach to American History* (New York: Oxford University Press, 1968), 135–145. This essay was reprinted that same year as "The Civil War in the History of the Modern World: A Comparative View," in David M. Potter, ed., *The South and Sectional Conflict* (Baton Rouge: Louisiana State University Press, 1968), 287–299. See Denis Brogan, "David M. Potter," in Robin Winks and Marcus Cunliffe, eds., *Pastmasters: Some Essays on American Historians* (New York: Harper Row, 1969), 316–344.
2. Potter, "Civil War," 138–139.
3. On the revised death tolls for the American Civil War, see J. David Hacker, "A Census Based Count of the Civil War Civil War Dead," *Civil War History* 57 (December 2011): 307–348; see also J. David Hacker, "Recounting the Dead," *New York Times*, September 20, 2011; Drew Gilpin Faust, *The Republic of Suffering: Death and the American Civil War* (New York: Alfred A. Knopf, 2008).
4. Potter, "Civil War," 142–144.
5. Potter, "Civil War," 138–140.
6. Potter, "Civil War," 136–139.
7. Drew R. McCoy, *The Last of the Fathers: James Madison and the Republican Legacy* (New York and Cambridge: Cambridge University Press, 1989), 39–84; Jack Rakove, *James Madison and the Creation of the American Republic* (Glenview, IL: Scott, Foresman, 1990), 39–93; Jack Rakove, *Original Meanings: Politics and Ideas in the Making of the Constitution* (New York: Random House, 1996), 35–56.
8. McCoy, *Last of the Fathers*, 39–84; Rakove, *James Madison*, 70–91; Lacy K. Ford, "Inventing the Concurrent Majority: Madison, Calhoun and the Problem of Majoritarianism in American Political Thought," *Journal of Southern History* 60 (February 1994): 19–58.
9. Gordon S. Wood, *Empire for Liberty: A History of the Early Republic* (New York: Oxford University Press, 2009), 5–275; Gordon S. Wood, *The Creation of the American Republic, 1776–1787* (Chapel Hill: University of North Carolina Press, 1969), 471–518.
10. Eric Foner, *Second Founding: How the Civil War and Reconstruction Remade the Constitution* (New York: W. W. Norton & Company, 2019).
11. Charles G. Sellers, *The Market Revolution: Jacksonian America, 1815–1846* (New York: Oxford University Press, 1992), especially 70–171; George Rogers Taylor, *The Transportation Revolution, 1815–1860* (New York: Rinehart, 1951); Carter Goodrich, *Government Promotion of American Canals and Railroads, 1800–1890* (New York: Columbia University Press,

A Twenty-First Century Meaning for the Civil War   35

1965); Richard R. John, *Spreading the News: The U.S. Postal Service from Franklin to Morse* (Cambridge, MA: Harvard University Press, 1995); John Larson, *National Public Works and the Promise of Popular Government in the United States* (Chapel Hill: University of North Carolina Press, 2001); Paul F. Paskoff, *Troubled Waters: Steamboats, Disasters, River Improvements, and American Public Policy, 1821–1860* (Baton Rouge: Louisiana State University Press, 2007).

12. Lawrence B. Glickman, *Free Enterprise: An American History* (New Haven: Yale University Press, 2019).

13. Sellers, *The Market Revolution*, 364–395.

14. David M. Kennedy, *Over Here: The First World War and American Society* (New York: Oxford University Press, 1980); David M. Kennedy, *Freedom from Fear: The American People in Depression and War, 1929–1945* (New York: Oxford University Press, 1999).

15. Arthur M. Schlesinger, Jr., *The Vital Center: Our Purpose and Perils on the Tightrope of American Liberalism* (Boston: Houghton Mifflin, 1949).

16. James T. Paterson, *Grand Expectations: The United States, 1945–1974* (New York: Oxford University Press, 1996), 407–446; Stephen Ambrose, *Eisenhower: Soldier and President* (New York: Simon and Schuster, 1990), 497–548.

17. Enrico Moretti, *The New Geography of Jobs* (Boston: Houghton Mifflin, 2012), 217–221.

18. John Lewis Gaddis, *The United States and the End of the Cold War: Implications, Reconsiderations, and Provocations* (New York: Oxford University Press, 1992); Odd Arne Westad, *The Cold War: A World History* (New York: Basic Books, 2017).

19. David Oshinsky, *A Conspiracy So Immense: The World of Joe McCarthy* (New York: The Free Press, 1983); Larry Tye, *Demagogue: The Life and Long Shadow of Joe McCarthy* (Boston: Houghton Mifflin, 2020).

20. For a stimulating brief history, see Thomas Holt, *The Movement: The African American Struggle for Civil Rights* (New York: Oxford University Press, 2021).

21. Holly V. Scott, *Younger than That Now: The Politics of Age in the 1960s* (Amherst: University of Massachusetts Press, 2016).

22. Fredrik Logevall, *Embers of War: The Fall of an Empire and the Making of America's Vietnam* (New York: Random House, 2012); Taylor Branch, *At Canaan's Edge: America in the King Years, 1965–1968* (New York: Simon and Schuster, 2007).

23. Sean Wilentz, *The Age of Reagan: A History, 1974–2008* (New York: HarperCollins, 2008), 151–175, 243–263.

24. Wilentz, *Age of Reagan*, 284, 295–296.

25. Francis Fukuyama, "The End of History," *The Public Interest* 16 (Summer 1989): 1–5; Francis Fukuyama, *The End of History and the Last Man* (New York: The Free Press, 1992).

26. Samuel Huntington, "Clash of Civilizations," *Foreign Affairs* 72 (Summer 1993): 22–49.

27. Nancy Baum, *Personal Connections in the Digital Age* (Cambridge, MA: Polity Press, 2015).

36   *Understanding the American South*

28. See, for example, Gabriel Sherman, *The Loudest Voice in the Room: How the Brilliant, Bombastic Roger Ailes Built Fox News and Divided a Country* (New York: Random House, 2014).
29. David Reisman with Nathan Glazer and Reuel Denny, *The Lonely Crowd: A Study of the Changing American Character* (New Haven: Yale University Press, 1963).
30. *US News and World Report*, March 27, 2015.
31. Robert J. Gordon, *The Rise and Fall of American Growth: The U.S. Standard of Living since the Civil War* (Princeton: Princeton University Press, 2016), 605–624; Joseph Stiglitz, *People, Power, and Profits: Progressive Capitalism for an Age of Discontent* (New York: W. W. Norton & Company, 2019), 37–46; Paul Krugman, *Arguing with Zombies: Economics, Politics and the Fight for a Better Future* (New York: W. W. Norton & Company, 2020), 259–293.
32. Thomas Piketty, *Capital in the Twenty-First Century* (Cambridge, MA: Harvard University Press, 2014), 336–376.
33. Stiglitz, *People, Power, and Profits*, 79–100; Angus Deaton, *The Great Escape: Health, Wealth, and the Origins of Inequality* (Princeton: Princeton University Press, 2013), 218–263.
34. Moretti, *The New Geography of Jobs*, 178–214.
35. Abhijit V. Banerjee and Esther Duflo, *Good Economics for Hard Times* (New York: Public Affairs, 2019), especially 10–97; Deaton, *The Great Escape*, 267–266.
36. William O'Neill, *Coming Apart: An Informal History of the 1960s* (Chicago; Quadrangle Books, 1971).
37. Wilentz, *Age of Reagan*, 432–458; Thomas B. Edsall, *Building Red America: The New Conservative Coalition and the Drive for Permanent Power* (New York: Basic Books, 2006), especially 50–105.
38. Wilentz, *Age of Reagan*, 450–458.
39. Jon Butler, *Awash in A Sea of Faith: Christianizing the American People* (Cambridge, MA: Harvard University Press, 1990).
40. Robert M. Bellah, "Civil Religion in America," *Daedalus* 6 (Winter 1967): 1–21.
41. A. M. Sperber, *Murrow: His Life and Times* (New York: Fordham University Press, 1999); Douglas Brinkley, *Cronkite* (New York: HarperCollins, 2012).
42. Zoetanya Sujon, *The Social Media Age* (Los Angeles: Sage, 2021).
43. Herbert Croly, *The Promise of American Life* (New York: Macmillan, 1909).
44. Charles Forcey, *The Crossroads of Liberalism: Croly, Weyl, Lippman and the Progressive Era, 1900–1925* (New York: Oxford University Press, 1961); David Noble, *The Paradox of Progressive Thought* (Minneapolis: University of Minnesota Press, 1958).
45. Eric Foner, *The Fiery Trial: Abraham Lincoln and American Slavery* (New York: W. W. Norton & Company, 2010).

PART II

UNDERSTANDING THE SOUTH AND THE AMERICAN IDENTITY

2

The Liberal Tradition

Southern Exceptionalism, the Civil War, and the Future of American Liberalism

In *The Liberal Tradition in America*, published in 1955, Harvard political scientist Louis Hartz joined the chorus of voices trying to explain the apparent success of the American republic, the success that publisher Henry Luce boldly proclaimed to be the "American Century" in 1941. Shortly after World War II ended, Arthur Schlesinger Jr.'s *The Vital Center* (1948) tempered Luce's triumphalism with a strong caution that the American political center must hold if the United States stood to prevail in the global struggle with the Soviet Union for power and influence. Schlesinger had observed Soviet power emerge as the Red Army played a crucial role in defeating the Nazis followed later by the Soviet entrance into the world of atomic powers. The key to success in the struggle with the Soviets, in Schlesinger's view, lay in hewing to the New Deal path of pragmatic centrism in domestic affairs, avoiding either an excessive drift to the right to combat communist ideology or the temptation to move further left as the success of the social safety net created by the New Deal revealed that the measured economic redistribution could improve overall economic outcomes.[1]

Other theories explaining American "greatness," marked by the nation's recent ascent to the role of political and economic "leader of the free world," paraded forth readily in the postwar era. Daniel Boorstin's *The Genius of American Politics* found the key to the republic's unique success in its practical conservatism, its tendency to avoid the impulsive embrace of new political theories but also its willingness to make whatever modest changes were necessary to preserve and strengthen the republic. Historian David Potter offered a boldly materialist explanation for American success. Americans enjoyed the privilege of being a "People

40 *Understanding the American South*

of Plenty." They were blessed first by abundant land, and later by ingenious mechanics, inventers, engineers, entrepreneurs, and investors who together and independently organized enterprises that took advantage of the nation's many natural resources as well as the continually expanding influx of labor from overseas to build an economy which delivered on the promise of broadly shared upward mobility for many Americans.[2]

A few years later, C. Vann Woodward presented an interpretation of American uniqueness that depended less on national character and more on geographic and technological considerations. Woodward argued that from 1815 until World War I, America enjoyed a century of "free security," primarily due to the breadth of three oceans and the state of military (and particularly naval) technology throughout the nineteenth century. During this "Age of Free Security," the United States enjoyed protection from European threats and entanglements simply because of its comparative geographic isolation and the state of military and transportation technology. As a result, Woodward emphasized, the nineteenth-century United States spent very little on defense, supported only a small military, which focused mainly on pushing back the Native American population on the nation's southern and western frontiers, and devoted the bulk of its resources and energy toward economic and territorial expansion. Even during the bloody American Civil War, which occupied millions of men, the United States enjoyed a geographic buffer from interference by international powers. Some fifty years later, free security weakened during World War I as German submarines proved capable of creating havoc for American efforts to ship supplies to Britain and France. The Japanese surprise attack on Pearl Harbor that drew the United States fully into World War II revealed that long-range bombing attacks could be launched from islands in the Pacific, and, of course, all security evaporated when the Soviet Union developed atomic weapons in the early 1950s. Security immediately became very expensive rather than free, and even all that spending failed to guarantee security except through the deterrent of nuclear retaliation.[3]

Hartz's emphasis on the formative power of liberalism on the American character fell more in the camp occupied by Boorstin and Potter in emphasizing a national character rather than historical accidents in creating American exceptionalism. Yet Hartz fell on the opposite end of the spectrum from Boorstin and Potter in finding the origins of American exceptionalism in an ideology rather than in experiences and circumstances (Boorstin) or in opportunity (Potter). For Hartz, the uniqueness of America lay in its specific and generally monolithic ideological tradition,

The Liberal Tradition

liberalism, from which he believed the nation emerged and continued to embrace. Moreover, Hartz insisted that the liberal ideological tradition had stood the test of time, with only a few mutations.

In Hartz's view, the American nation was born liberal, at least once it won its independence from the British Crown. It had no aristocracy or nobility to overthrow. It had no established church to defy or shove aside, no historic feudal society to remake, and after George III, it had no king who could claim sovereignty over them. The people were sovereign, even though many disputes would arise during the nation's first century over exactly "which people" were sovereign (usually this consisted of debate between the "national people" and the "the people of individual states"). The liberal ideas which Hartz saw as defining the vision of the American founders consisted of liberalism defined by John Locke and his latter-day disciples. Locke's liberalism rested on the foundation of property rights, the rule of law, and some level of popular participation or representation in government. Locke believed that there must be allegiance to the state for that state to govern effectively, but that there also had to be some restraint or check on the power of the state, a function best provided by a set of fundamental laws enjoying the consent of the governed.[4]

Hartz argued that Lockean liberalism faced formidable challenges in Britain from all the forces associated with an *ancien régime*: royalty, aristocracy, an established church, plus an old and rigid class structure. But on American (or New World) ground, Hartz contended, all the conservative institutions and influences which challenged liberalism in Britain were absent, leaving liberalism free to stand not only as the ideal but the reality of American politics. Moreover, Hartz asserted, the modest social upheaval which accompanied the Revolution further cleared the way for the triumph of liberalism in America.[5]

While the absence of both a debilitating feudal past and a limiting conservative influence from church or aristocracy were critical to the emergence of a liberal democracy in America, Hartz was not entirely convinced that the absence of conservative counterweights to the prevailing liberalism was a good thing. Hartz saw American liberalism as vulnerable to a division into two of its key components: democracy and capitalism. When Hartz used the term capitalism (at least in these battles with democracy) he was referring to a constellation of ideas that Americans today would describe as pro-business conservatism, including active governmental support for expanding business opportunities. Hartz's capitalists were those who sought to align politics and government behind the drive for economic development and wealth accumulation. Democracy was essentially

42 *Understanding the American South*

structured governance by popular will. Despite the energy democracy brought to American liberalism, and the needed restraint on the power of capitalism it provided, Hartz worried that liberal energy and egalitarianism too often lacked wisdom. But, whatever his own reservations, in Hartz's mind there was no doubt that liberalism was the ideology of the American Revolution and America's later history as a nation.[6]

Since the publication of *The Liberal Tradition in America* in 1955, Hartz's historical analyses of various periods of American history have been challenged. But no part of Hartz's argument in the *Liberal Tradition* has received as much fulsome, and devastating, criticism as his emphasis on Lockean liberalism as the founding ideology of the United States. By the 1970s, American historians understood the ideological origins of the American republic very differently than Hartz had during the 1950s. Within the first two decades following the publication of Hartz book, historians of the American Revolution developed a very different ideological interpretation of the Revolution and the subsequent writing of the Constitution in 1787, one that firmly displaced Hartz's emphasis on Lockean liberalism as the basis of the founders' ideology. Led by Harvard historian Bernard Bailyn, Brown University professor Gordon Wood (a former doctoral student of Bailyn), and soon followed by a large and impressive cadre of Revolutionary-era and early republic historians, scholars offered a thoughtful and well-documented challenge to the prevailing notion that Lockean liberalism provided the ideological framework of the American Revolution and the subsequent writing of the Constitution.[7]

To be sure, both middle and late eighteenth-century American political leaders knew Locke's ideas, especially his views on the strong relationship between property and liberty, the importance of representation, and the rule of law. But the larger context of what property meant politically to the founders and the ideological world they inhabited had evolved radically since Locke developed his theory in the seventeenth century. The new post-Hartz wave of scholarship proved beyond doubt that the dominant ideological influence on the American founders were the ideas of the British opposition during the rule of King George I and his Prime Minister Robert Walpole. The critiques offered by opponents of Walpole and the king retained some key Lockean principles but jettisoned others as they advanced a very different set of ideas for defending balanced government from corruption through patronage and spoils.[8]

The essence of the British opposition's critique of the so-called Whig coalition built by Walpole and George I centered on the idea that the

The Liberal Tradition

balanced government prescribed by Britain's unwritten constitution and the Whig settlement of 1688 had been corrupted by Walpole's ability to build a strong political faction within Parliament loyal to the king. The Whig settlement had presumed that British sovereignty lay with the "King-in-Parliament" and that British liberty and rights were protected by the "balanced government" provided through the representation of royalty (king), aristocracy (lords), and commoners (property owners, merchants, etc.) in the unitary sovereign body (Parliament). But Walpole built a coalition through the deliberate and skillful use of the vast patronage at the king's disposal that created a powerful "Court" faction in the other two houses of Parliament, a faction pliable to the king's (or Walpole's) wishes. Walpole's skillful use of royal patronage produced very popular and effective policies during most of his time as "prime minister" and retained considerable popularity afterwards.[9]

But Walpolean practices and the creation of a "Court" faction drew criticism from opposition pamphleteers known as "radical Whig" and "Country" thinkers, who saw Walpole's use of patronage as a form of corruption and a tool for enhancing royal power. Patronage, Walpole's critics maintained, compromised the independence of members of Parliament by rendering them financially dependent on and obligated to the Crown and its ministers. The opposition's ideology held that independence gave members of Parliament the ability to make political judgments free of corrupting influence. Such independence, Walpole's critics insisted, sustained the prevailing system of balanced government in Great Britain.

While the opposition's critique never gained more than limited traction in Britain, their ideas fell on fertile ground among the American colonists once they began looking for reasons behind what they perceived as George III's increasingly harsh or even punitive policies toward the colonies during and after the Seven Years (or French and Indian) War. Over time, the ideas of the British opposition evolved into a new ideology the founders used to justify their bid for American independence. Later termed "republicanism," this ideology served as the foundation for the Revolution and the state and federal constitutions written during the 1780s, and these republican ideas continued to shape the ideological dimensions of Americans politics to some extent for decades to come.[10]

The key points of the ideology involved independence, representation, balanced government, and checks on power. For American leaders, these points served as the prescription for preserving liberty and self-government. The question of who should be allowed to participate

44   *Understanding the American South*

in the creation and management of government remained critical, and most American colonists embraced the views of the radical Whig and Country pamphlets that only "independent" men, men above the dependence and corruption growing from the temptation of spoils, should be considered citizens. In American eyes, ownership of productive property lay at the heart of such independence. But contrary to Hartz's assertion, it was hardly a Lockean understanding of the importance of property that made it central to the American governing project. In Locke's view, property endowed its holders with a stake in society, a vested interest in the government. From the tradition of the British opposition, however, Country and radical Whig thinkers held that property allowed those who possessed it to resist manipulation through spoils or patronage (the corrupting temptation in Walpole's Britain). At least in theory, such independence allowed citizens (and politicians) to rise above the temptations of either self-interest or spoils and act on behalf of the common good.[11]

Even before independence was won, Americans had to decide, both at the national and state level, exactly what form of governance they would create. Lacking the balance of social class (Crown, aristocrat, and commoner) that undergirded the British idea of balanced government, Americans had to find alternative mechanisms to achieve balance within their governing framework. At the state level, new constitutions were adopted, and despite their variety, most embraced the concept of checks and balances in government and the need to use balancing influences to prevent threats to liberty. At the national level, the Articles of Confederation lent a strong tilt toward state sovereignty, in part because each colony had generally engaged the Crown separately rather than as a group before the Revolution. But the thirteen colonies also needed unity – a nation – to conduct the revolution. By 1787, the struggle of running a national government under the Articles led to the calling of the Philadelphia Convention, which went well beyond its charge to revise the Articles and undertook, in closed session, an effort to write a new constitution for the new nation.[12]

James Madison, who emerged as the primary architect of the US Constitution, spent months prior to the 1787 convention reading and studying not only political theory but also the history of republics and why they failed as he prepared proposals that would, as a rule, drive the debate at the Philadelphia convention in 1787. As historian Jack Rakove explained, Madison came to the Convention armed with "a comprehensive theory of government that consciously challenged many axioms of eighteenth-century political science," including even some of the axioms

The Liberal Tradition 45

held dear by the Country and radical Whig thinkers who inspired the leaders of the Revolution. Madison believed that his pre-convention studies had revealed the faults "not only of the Confederation but also of the republican constitutions of the states." It was at the Convention and during the subsequent ratification debates that Madison helped place a fresh American stamp on new, improved republican ideas.[13]

In May 1787, Madison headed to Philadelphia convinced that the chief threat facing the new nation lay in the "vicious" legislation passed by state legislatures too often preoccupied with the narrow self-interests of their individual states or even simply their legislative majorities. Madison decided the nation need a much stronger national government to check the power of irresponsible state governments. The Virginian's studies and his knowledge of state legislative activity under the Articles led him to abandon the notion that individuals (and especially politicians) could ever achieve the "disinterestedness" prescribed by prevailing "Country" or inherited republican theory and that only the structural checking and balancing of such self-interest could achieve the goal of protecting either individual rights or national interests from abuse at the hands of runaway state majorities.[14]

One of Madison's major theoretical innovations emerged from his belief that by "extending the sphere" of the republic, thus expanding the number of interests included, a national government could better stymie majorities by making them less likely to form if representation spread across a much broader territory. With this assertion, Madison distanced himself from the long-prevailing theory that republics must be small and homogenous, asserting instead that larger, more diverse republics provided the diversity of interests needed to check and balance one another and prevent potentially tyrannical local majorities from doing widespread harm. Madison also recognized that, lacking the distinctions of class and status that provided some checks and balances within Britain's sovereign "King-in-Parliament," sovereignty itself must be divided in the new United States. A national government must be strong enough to check the power of sovereign states, which Madison saw as the great danger threatening the new nation. Hence Madison wanted to divide sovereignty between the states and the federal government and to use the large size of the republic to check the power of local factions that might cohere in an individual state. Drafted during a period of reaction to prior abuses of royal governors, the state constitutions of the Confederation period placed too much power, Madison believed, in the state legislatures with inadequate checks and balances on those elected bodies.[15]

46 *Understanding the American South*

For Madison, the fear of rampaging local majorities stemmed from the Confederation-period actions in favor of debt relief and the issuance of paper money, which he saw as inimical to property interests and a threat to the nation's financial stability, a critical matter for the new government. Also, Madison, a slaveholder who lived in the state with by far the largest number of slaves, worried that local majorities might even threaten, at some future point, the property rights enjoyed by slaveholders through high levels of taxation or a desire to restrict the sale or movement of slaves. Such concerns lay behind Madison's desire for a national veto on state laws. In fact, Madison worried so much about the exercise of self-serving populism in the individual states that he arrived in Philadelphia determined to seek a national veto over all state laws. Madison presented his proposed veto to the Convention as a means of protecting the financial integrity of the new nation. But his effort failed quickly, much to Sage of Montpelier's chagrin. After the defeat of his proposed national veto, Madison scrambled to find other ways to limit damaging state legislation.[16]

The Convention's work, driven by Madison's proposals presented under the sponsorship of the Virginia delegation, looked for a system of checks and balances, for popular sovereignty, or the rule of the people, or at least the eligible voters, and intentional constraints on the power of the majority. Madison's ingenuity produced ways of placing checks and balances into the new Constitution while giving it enough authority and vigor to govern the nation, and particularly its finances, economy, and defense, effectively, while allowing sufficient protections against majoritarian tyranny, which Madison believed to be the most likely form of tyranny in a republic.[17]

Even though the new constitution called for a republic with a separation of powers, mechanisms for checks and balances, and both population and states represented, Madison left the Convention doubting that the new document would prevent disruptions coming from the whims of runaway local majorities. Enough of his preferred provisions failed to survive the Convention's numerous compromises and revisions to make the Virginian question whether the new Constitution was strong enough to protect national as opposed to parochial interests. He expressed fear that the new document "would neither effectually answer its national object nor prevent the local mischiefs." But Madison muted his pessimism and moved on to defend the proposed Constitution in the public press during the ratification process of 1788.[18]

Most of the formulations of Madison's political theory that Americans remain aware of today came from his efforts to influence the ratification

The Liberal Tradition

debates, particularly in the crucial state of New York where substantial opposition to ratification flourished, through his contributions to what we now know as *The Federalist Papers*. In his contributions as "Publius," Madison laid out both his concerns and his theoretical innovations. He reiterated the importance of "extending the sphere" of the republic rather than trying to limit a republic to a small and homogenous area. No area could be homogenous enough or its people disinterested enough to make small republics work, Madison contended. But by enlarging republics so that more interests are embraced within the republic's boundaries, these interests will naturally check and balance each other, and that it would be unlikely that such numerous interests spread over a broad space could cohere long enough to become a threat to a large republic. Moreover, Madison emphasized that the new American republic would be a "compound republic," including thirteen state governments as well as the national government. In a compound republic, the national and state governments could check and balance each other. Madison's strategy here arose from his desire to create a national government strong enough to restrain the excesses of state governments. He envisioned the need for a national government strong enough to check "mischief" and "iniquity" emanating from state governments due to popular excesses and the power of local majorities. He also believed that such popular excesses were much more likely to emerge unchecked within small, rather than large and populous, states, which in themselves enveloped multiple interests.[19]

The myth of the American nation being founded on Lockean liberalism has now long since been exploded, and a rich variety of ideological perspectives introduced over subsequent decades reshaped the founding ideas considerably. The remaining question is whether Hartz's argument for a defining American liberalism still holds any merit for explaining the character of the American nation across two centuries. Throughout the antebellum era and even through the Civil War, the ideological terrain in the American nation rested on ideas received from the republican consensus of the founding era, but those ideas modified significantly as new circumstances emerged. As the nation entered the Jacksonian era, new doses of popular democracy and organized partisanship, both generally distrusted and even feared by Madison, invaded the inherited republican mix. Popular democracy called for a broadening of the suffrage – usually to all or almost all white men (and taking great care to exclude Blacks and women). As the energy of white man's democracy strengthened, it diluted the republican preference for property requirements for voting in

48   *Understanding the American South*

favor of accepting militia services or taxes paid or simply being a white male as an appropriate qualification for suffrage rights. State constitutional requirements tilted more and more toward favoring population as a basis for representation in state legislatures and toward an elected judiciary, elected local governments, and popularly elected governors. Above the surge in democracy for white men, the ideological jousting between Democrats and Whigs at the national level lay chiefly in differences over the appropriate role of government in facilitating economic and moral improvement. The popularization of politics and even the debates over the nation's political and moral economy during the era of the Second American Party System remained well within the larger framework of the founders' republicanism, just a more democratic, and less elitist, republicanism.[20]

Arguably the second most problematic, and certainly the most provocative, of Hartz's interpretations of American history emerged in his treatment of the antebellum South's rearguard attempt to establish a formidable conservative tradition in a predominantly liberal (or, more accurately, republican) world. If Daniel Boorstin had failed to perceive the highly ideological nature of sectional conflict and Civil War, Hartz was quick to recognize the deep ideological dimensions of disunion and war. Again, Hartz mischaracterized the prevailing collection of ideas in the American North as liberalism, but he recognized that a least some thinkers in the Old South had attempted to launch what he labeled a "Reactionary Enlightenment," a conservative ideology not simply to preserve slavery but to offer a compelling intellectual justification for doing so. In essence, Hartz argued, some southern thinkers tried to invent an aristocratic or seigneurial culture in the Old South, termed by Hartz "the Feudal Dream of the South," that represented a break with the prevailing "liberalism" of the rest of the nation.[21]

To support his point, Hartz explored South Carolina's John C. Calhoun's determined political effort to preserve slavery as it had been secured at the founding. This effort fell, in Hartz's view, into the Reactionary Enlightenment category, even though Calhoun, hardly a feudal dreamer, used the Constitution and other well-known tenets of the founders' republicanism as his guide in defending the South's slaveholding society. Seeking to preserve and protect an existing institution, slavery, Calhoun invented new mechanisms (the concurrent majority and sectional veto) designed to buttress the existing constitutional protections defending the rights of the nation's slaveholding minority. But in Calhoun's mind these new mechanisms stood as new formulations

The Liberal Tradition

of existing republican doctrines not as part of an effort to invent a quasi-feudal slaveholding South, but they did recast the founders' ideology in a more conservative manner.[22]

Hartz contended that a handful of other southern thinkers, with Virginia intellectual George Fitzhugh arguably foremost among them, went much further than Calhoun in mounting a reactionary critique of American liberalism. Their efforts were intellectual, or at least ideological, but hardly a serious political movement. Calhoun was in the fight to win, to achieve a single longstanding goal: the protection of the South's ability to own and trade enslaved property, the region's main source of wealth and income. Calhoun sought to find enough conservatism in the Constitution to justify the concept of minority veto. Nearing death from "consumption" (tuberculosis) in 1850, Calhoun proposed constitutional amendments urging major concessions to the South to stave off secession and save the Union. At the time the amendments were offered, most southern politicians in either political party (Democrat or Whig) thought slavery could still be defended by traditional partisan political maneuvering and judicial interpretation, leaving Calhoun, and his ideas, with only scattered support even from the rest of the deep South.[23]

Those late antebellum southern thinkers who pondered a truly reactionary, quasi-feudal society for the slaveholding South had far less influence that Calhoun, and thus hardly made a ripple on the political waters of the 1850s. Yet Hartz's fascination with the idea of a neo-feudal social order for the South and the emergence of a true conservative tradition remains worthy of attention. Hartz recognized that the purpose of these southern reactionary thinkers was not so much an effort to chart a bold new course for the South (perhaps Calhoun could do such things in Congress but they held no such illusions about their influence). Instead, they mounted a scathing critique of the emerging free labor capitalism in the North. These southern critics of "free labor" scored more than a few polemical points even if they had little influence on the politics of slavery. In their critique of "free societies," these reactionary southern thinkers aggressively called attention to the potential errors of northern ways. These "southern Tories" did not seriously look back for a feudal past as a model for southern society, but they certainly envisioned a future of tension between labor and capital perhaps ending in the triumph of socialism. They worried, given the European patterns of the 1840s, that inevitable conflict between capital and labor could end in socialist majorities. These southern thinkers were, after all, defenders of private property, including property in other human beings or "property in man." These most conservative southern

50 *Understanding the American South*

thinkers mounted an aggressive critique of free labor capitalism, even going to the provocative if absurd length of comparing "chattel slavery" in the South favorably with "wage slavery" in Britain and the antebellum North. Such critiques of free society tweaked northern insecurities but did little more. And in the South as a whole, any political reorientation away from the white man's democracy was a slight drift of wealthy conservatives toward a posture of Tory paternalism joined at the hip with Tory-sponsored capitalism. The irony of the flirtation of the late antebellum South's intellectual fringe with a critique of capitalism lies in the fact that the death of the Confederacy and the end of slavery facilitated American capitalism's move into its Gilded Age without a counterpoint from the South, but rather a faint plaintiff cry seeking a larger share of the capitalist system's benefits for their defeated region.[24]

The American ideological innovation of the mid-nineteenth century came not from the fringes of the slaveholding South but from the mainstream North, where the ideas encapsulated in the popular slogan "free soil, free labor and free men" became the rallying cry of the new Republican party that rose from nonexistence in 1852 to a large partisan plurality and electoral college majority in 1860 without the support of a single slaveholding state.[25] Free labor Republicans still emphasized the need for independent citizens with productive capacity. The majority of citizens in free states, Abraham Lincoln maintained in his 1859 speech at the Wisconsin State Fair, were "neither hirers nor hired." Instead, they were "men, with their families" who "work for themselves, on their farms, in their houses, and at their shops, taking the whole product to themselves, and asking no favors of capital on the one hand, nor hirelings and slaves on the other." Independent men who had enjoyed upward mobility and owned property became ideal republican citizens. Lincoln then added an affirmative case for upward mobility under free labor: the idea that laborers need not remain laborers but could work hard and procure productive property. As Lincoln explained, a hireling

labors for a while, saves a surplus with which to buy tools or land for himself; then labors on his own account for another while, and at length hires another new beginner to help him, this is ... free labor – the just, generous, and prosperous system which opens the way for all – and gives energy, progress and improvement of condition to all.

As evidence of the possibility of upward mobility under the free labor system, Lincoln appealed to his audience's own experience, noting that "many independent men" attending his speech, "doubtless a few years ago were hired laborers."[26]

The Liberal Tradition

51

While Lincoln's primary concern in the pre-Civil War years was to champion free labor in contradistinction to the South's slave labor system, he also understood that the relationship between labor and capital was increasingly a matter of concern to independent citizens. Lincoln held that, despite claims neither capital and labor were superior to the other, labor and capital everywhere existed in a relationship with each other in which neither was independent of the other. And even after Lincoln's assassination, the main thrust of the Republican party's approach to Reconstruction consisted of a strong desire to expand suffrage and render the freed people independent enough to enjoy the franchise and a measure of economic opportunity under a free labor system. The Republican approach worked reasonably well for the freedpeople until Reconstruction was abandoned and southern whites moved as quickly as they could to reestablish control of the state and local government in the region.[27]

During the Gilded Age, however, the ideological drift of the nation moved it away from the republicanism of the founders as policy discourse picked up and expanded Lincoln's musing on the relationship of capital and labor. By the late 1870s, it became impossible to overlook the powerful and growing role of capital in the both the world and the American economy. The first industrial revolution had generated enough new capital, when added to the substantial financial and commercial capital already in existence, that the relationship of capital and labor became too important to ignore and too inclined to reshape the national political economy. Hartz's styling of these postwar developments as the creation of a "new Whiggery" for America understates the transformation. Jacksonian-era Whigs could be characterized as pro-development and protective of capital, but they chiefly looked to positive government, specifically subsidies for infrastructural improvements and protective tariffs, rather than agreement from government to wield whatever power it had at its disposal in favor of capital.[28]

The new political economy of Gilded Age America emerged as an economy of capitalists (including manufacturers), workers (mostly industrial and railroad), and independent producers (chiefly farmers). The last of these launched several movements, such as the Grange, the Farmers' Alliance, and the Populist party, aimed at reversing the trend of diminishing capital's political influence, but none of these movements succeeded for more than a brief time. The political reorientation toward capital produced a great increase in national wealth but also much greater inequality in wealth, an inequality that also materialized in political influence as well as income distribution. With wealth enjoying political influence, capitalists generally garnered the needed support from government to suppress both regulation and the new labor movement. Capital was power, and capital used that power to its advantage.[29]

Hartz saw Gilded Age America as the time of the new Whiggery in the United States, with Republicans morphing into a party of capitalism modeled on the remnant of the antebellum American Whig party while also accepting portions of Lincoln's free labor republicanism of the 1850s and embracing the myth of Horatio Alger. Gilded Age Democrats (chiefly southern) were scarcely different ideologically, just more determined to protect white supremacy and more "strict constructionist," but almost equally pro-business. To Hartz, postbellum American Whiggery lacked even the veneer of Tory paternalism that the British system offered. The rough-and-tumble capitalism of the Gilded Age, however, left America open to the emergence of the early twentieth-century Progressive movement and even, to a limited extent, a hearing for a socialist critique.[30]

To be sure, Gilded Age industrialization and the widening of economic inequality gave rise to more class conflict than previously existed, as industrial and mining workers formed unions of varied levels of radicalism and even farmers organized in cooperatives and supported Populist politicians at times during the era. But the chief "reform" of the era was progressivism, starting first, as we now know, at the local level and ultimately working its way up into state and national politics (complicating but never really disrupting the nation's two-party system).[31]

Yet American progressivism proved a class movement of a very different kind. Convincing scholarship has revealed that progressivism was a middle-class movement designed to bring order and improvement to an increasingly helter-skelter capitalist society sporting too many rough edges. The movement, led by middle-class reformers drawing heavily on organization and efficiency concepts developed by business, aimed at infusing order, rationality, and efficiency throughout the entire society, uplifting the working class and curbing the excesses of upper-class power. Progressives sought reform through a system of social control mechanisms whose effectiveness had been proven in private and public sector bureaucracies and through legislation regulating the behavior of business, enhancing safety standards in industry, and providing education for previously unreached classes of American children. Doubtless a key element in the Progressives' education plan was the desire teach children, especially immigrant children, precisely how to become better Americans, and even to make the next generation less likely to succumb

The Liberal Tradition

to any form of international radicalism. That such an educational movement was not entirely successful is hardly a surprise, but the extent to which it nudged Americans toward a middle-class norm was surprising.[32]

Progressivism was a class revolt in the sense that it championed middle-class rationality against upper-class excess, middle-class modesty versus upper-class ostentation, and middle-class checks on upper-class power. Progressives also sought to inculcate the working class with middle-class values to the extent possible. Above all, Progressives championed, as historian Robert Wiebe declared, a "search for order." It was a search for order that looked both up and down the social hierarchy. The working and lower classes often chafed under the middle-class search for order and rationality, and that resistance to "reform" aided the wealthy in their effort to limit progressive influence. The middle-class nature of the movement resulted in curbing some abuses of power by the titans of industry and finance and the launching of uplift initiatives aimed at improving the lives and character of the working classes, whether or not the working class desired the improvements encouraged. The Progressive movement stopped well short of supporting a full pro-labor agenda as proffered by labor unions and usually proceeded with caution on labor management issues. Moreover, in the South, progressivism proved an entirely "for whites only movement" if for no other reason than that the survival of reform depended on appearing to promote, sustain, or strengthen Jim Crow.[33]

In Hartz's view, as in that of many others, it took the New Deal to really bring liberal reform to American politics. It did so under the cover of economic necessity of the worst depression in the nation's history. President Franklin D. Roosevelt, more practical than ideological, inserted the public sector where it had never been before, regulating the private sector as never before, and weaved the first social safety net worthy of the name in American history. He did all this to bring relief and recovery from the Great Depression. That the more radical left was weak in America likely helped the New Deal more than hindered it, making conservative (Republican) rhetoric about a drift toward collectivism look far-fetched.[34]

Elected president four times, FDR reshaped American liberalism, likely even more than Hartz believed. "New Deal pragmatism," as Hartz called it, reflected Roosevelt's personality and proved to be an intriguing blend of boldness and caution, innovation and reluctance, a transformation propelled by the desire to preserve an existing system by modifying rather than jettisoning it. To be sure, the New Deal took actions

54 *Understanding the American South*

considered radical in the face of a half century or more of pro-business conservativism in American life. The Roosevelt administration passed direct relief measures of unprecedented financial proportion, and FDR attempted to directly regulate business and agriculture through National Recovery Act and the Agricultural Adjustment Act. He also stepped in to save the nation's financial system, or what was left of it. Roosevelt built a social safety net through Social Security, expanded unemployment insurance, and implemented direct government hiring programs to provide Americans with jobs. He even passed legislation (highlighted by the National Labor Relations Act of 1935) which encouraged labor organization and enhanced the bargaining power of unions.[35]

All of this could have been considered radical by American standards, and it was, in fact, radical in some ways, but it often passed as simply doing what needed to be done to bring the nation out of the Depression and provide some measure of relief to the unprecedented suffering and want the Depression had caused. Roosevelt persuaded the government to spend money to stimulate the economy, even though he personally remained unconvinced of the Keynesian argument that government spending was the answer to depressions arising chiefly from inadequate demand. If nothing else, however, Roosevelt's pragmatism, his willingness to experiment (though not necessarily systematically) to find what worked, kept socialism largely at bay in the nation during the 1930s, the moment in American history which should have proved most fertile for its growth. While socialism in the United States gained a modicum of support in this era, it remained little more than a thorn in the New Deal's side – and perhaps even an interesting counterweight to keep moderates on FDR's side – rather than a true threat to the New Deal.[36]

Over time, once unprecedented government spending supporting European allies at war finally pulled the United States out of the Great Depression, FDR recast American liberalism with his "Four Freedoms" peroration in his third inaugural address, delivered on January 6, 1941, nearly eleven months before the Japanese attack on Pearl Harbor. Roosevelt reasserted two basic human freedoms, the freedom of speech and freedom of religion (or freedom to worship), freedoms seemingly well protected by the Constitution and Bill of Rights. But Roosevelt went further, asserting two new basic human rights, and committing, to the extent he could, American protection for them: freedom from want and freedom from fear. These two basic human rights emerged from the caldron of the Great Depression and the rise of Fascism in Europe and Asia, and from the conditions of the era which had left too many Americans

The Liberal Tradition

and too many people around the world in need of life's basics. Freedom from want stood as a commitment to meeting the basic survival needs of all the world's people. FDR also sought an even more elusive freedom, a universal "freedom from fear," that great ravager of the human spirit, both during World War II, the subsequent Cold War, and even today. Foremost in Roosevelt's mind at the time loomed the fear of Nazi and Fascist brutality toward those "not like them." In asserting these basic human rights, FDR went beyond law and constitution to assert American democracy's support for four basic human rights, the foundation, he believed, of a civilized world.[37]

The mobilization for war ultimately did much in the short term to address "freedom from want," at least for Americans. The promised "Arsenal of Democracy" turned out armaments and supplies at record levels and ultimately turned the tide of the war in Europe and the Pacific. Freedom from fear proved more difficult. Before World War II was over, Americans had unveiled the most destructive weapon the world had ever seen – the atomic bomb – and only a few years later the Soviet Union, an ally morphed into an archenemy, revealed the possession of a similar weapon. In the new world of nuclear weapons, freedom from fear hinged on the effectiveness of a doctrine provocatively termed "Mutually Assured Destruction," hardly a name designed to calm fears.[38]

Nevertheless, the Four Freedoms stood as a foundation for American liberalism and American pragmatism going forward, allowing enough government intervention in the economy not only to produce a healthy national economy but also a comfortable social safety net. Stimulating and maintaining a strong economy became the essence of pragmatism and liberalism in America. New Deal pragmatism and tinkering and its undeniable success left American socialism stranded, and reduced, at least for a time, the influence of conservative business interests, which Hartz persisted in calling American Whiggery. Collectivists lacked the resources to stage a comeback. The advocates of the free market had an abundance of resources and ultimately orchestrated a successful return to power and influence with the popularity of Ronald Reagan in the 1980s. Like Banquo's ghost, they would not down.[39]

Hartz concluded his volume by arguing that the chief threat to the future of American liberalism no longer lay in the domestic realm but for the first time in American history in the arena of foreign policy. Both communism and anti-communist hysteria presented grave threats to American liberalism, and especially to the pragmatic liberalism that stood as Roosevelt's legacy. Hartz worried, with considerable justification, that

56   *Understanding the American South*

America's spread-eagled triumphalism and self-righteous tone in the ideological Cold War would drive many poor nations across the world into the embrace of communism. Hartz's familiar pessimism shaped his conclusion, leaving even measured optimism about the future of the American national character to scholarly competitors such as Daniel Boorstin and David Potter.[40]

To the extent that Hartz's emphasis on American liberalism flourished in the decades following its publication, its success as a lingering influence had less to do with the accuracy of his history, which other experts in various fields quickly modified or replaced, nor his writing, which could be dense and academic at times, or with Hartz's penchant for pretentiously displaying his knowledge of European political theory, than with the broad popular appeal of a living American liberal tradition. The idea that a continuous strain of liberalism, standing generically for property rights, democracy, constitutional protections for the individual, and the rule of law that ran through all eras of American history, regardless of their intellectual origins, resonated with many Americans. As they looked for continuity and virtue in their history as well as in the nation's present, liberalism, like opportunity and practicality, and seemed both logical and flattering as national character traits.[41]

Yet the bulk of more than a half century of post-Hartz scholarship on American politics and political ideology has challenged the notion of a hegemonic liberal tradition. Instead, intense ideological conflict, albeit generally avoiding the radical extremes (socialism and some more polite version of fascism), has often pervaded American politics. Though the boundaries of ideological debate were often drawn narrowly by the nation's political history, rival political ideologies have generated much heated debate and even required vast human sacrifice on at least one occasion (the American Civil War). So, before conceding too much ground to Hartz's liberal tradition, we need to take an even closer look at the ideological conflicts that have provided the central theme of the American political tradition.

Closer to the mark than Hartz's emphasis on dominant liberalism would be a tradition or history emphasizing both a liberal and a conservative tradition running in dialectical tension throughout American history but also evolving as that history unfolds. Sometimes one gained the upper hand and sometimes the other gained it, but the grip was always tenuous and contested. And the definitions of liberalism and conservatism used were never textbook and morphed readily over time. The American contest between liberalism and conservatism must be understood as one side

The Liberal Tradition

advocating a move toward a more democratic or egalitarian (even if for white men only), and later a more inclusive, system embracing those previously denied access, and their opponents preferring to defend the status quo, protect property rights and wealth accumulation, and maintain the role of elites in decision making. In the Revolutionary and Constitution era, the idea of a republic served as the more liberal idea, with conservatives protecting aristocratic or elitist features in the framework of government, chiefly by protecting property and wealth from majoritarian assault. In the Jackson era, a struggle emerged between an egalitarian republicanism which advocated voting rights for almost all white men, apportioning legislatures largely according to population, and the popular election of judges and local officials (so these officials would be more responsive to the people). The more conservative or elitist republicans (operating under the label of Whigs) wanted to protect property and other forms of capital, limit the power of popular majorities, prevent the use of government for majority plunder, and steer government support toward internal improvements and other actions designed to advance commerce and encourage collective moral improvement.[42]

As the movement to stop the expansion of slavery into western territories gained strength, a new party, the Republican party, coalesced behind the call for a nation committed to "free soil, free labor, and free men." That party emerged as the liberal or progressive side, one opposed by Democrats and a battered remnant of southern Whigs who, in some form or fashion, sought to protect the rights of slaveholders and the concurrent influence of slaveholding states within the Union. By 1860, the Republicans enjoyed a large national plurality in the popular vote and elected a president with an overwhelming electoral majority which included all nonslaveholding states.[43]

The American Civil War cost over 700,000 lives but became part of the process of emancipation of nearly four million slaves. The end of slavery and the triumph of free labor left the Republicans with a core of largely traditional Whig economic ideas (stable currency, protective tariffs, policies favorable to business) with its remaining liberal agenda item focused on securing freedom and establishing basic civil rights for the freed Blacks in southern states. But even the party's resolve in that key area waned rapidly in the face of an economic recession during the 1870s. Their Democratic rivals could hardly be called anything but conservative, still favoring states' rights and an economic agenda little different from the Republicans, except perhaps on tariff issues. For the next half century or so, American politics settled into a largely pro-business

58 *Understanding the American South*

ideology that did little to challenge or soften any negative impact of a large-scale industrialization and the rise of big business. Intermittent challenges emerged to the pro-business orthodoxy, which was associated more strongly with the Republicans than the Democrats, but these challenges came not from existing parties but from third-party insurgencies such as the Populists or the Progressives or from labor unions such as the Knights of Labor, the American Federation of Labor, and the more radical International Workers of the World.[44]

The liberal, progressive, or popular impulse in the nation during these years fragmented and found itself advanced piecemeal by various groups unable to find a comfortable home in either party or form a coalition of all progressive discontents. The Populists presented challenges from farmers across the nation, seeking cheaper credit and price supports. The Progressives sought reforms in education, curbs on the raw power of big business, and a drive to expand both expertise and efficiency in government and to secure enough governmental power to provide some check on both big business and labor. The challenges of coalition-building proved insurmountable. The specific needs of farmers and labor were fundamentally different. Labor saw little need to subsidize farmers when the result would be workers paying higher prices for food. Wage and hour legislation demanded by labor had little relevance or appeal to farmers. Progressives expressed sympathy for the underdog, but their programmatic support generally focused on uplift programs and education for workers and rural people as the best answer to farmer and worker problems.[45]

While the national political debate during and after World War I focused primarily on the choice between Wilsonian internationalism and a domestic-oriented isolationist argument, with the latter generally prevailing, Gilded Age pro-business supremacy reigned on the domestic front throughout the 1920s as many of the major consumer products of the modern age, including automobiles, radios, movies, and refrigeration gained popularity during the decade.

But the liberal versus conservative tug of war reappeared with a vengeance during the Great Depression once President Franklin Roosevelt's New Deal introduced an unprecedented level of government intervention in the American economy, an economy that for all its past achievements had collapsed under its own weight after the Stock Market Crash of 1929. Republican Herbert Hoover's flailing foray into activism proved radically insufficient, leading to Roosevelt's landslide victory in 1932. Roosevelt's determination to actively experiment until he found working solutions to the problems of relief and recovery and the reform of a system that had collapsed so completely produced his administration's advocacy for workers and farmers as well as government intervention to stimulate demand and regulate supply.[46]

Such New Deal activism once again generated a political and ideological struggle between New Dealer liberalism and conservative business and finance interests, who argued that such government tinkering would only make matters worse. This tension between New Deal activism (liberalism) and staunch business opposition (conservatism) revived the bipolar competition of American political ideologies. But the desperation of the Depression years and the credit Roosevelt won for at least trying to do something about it established Democratic hegemony, though that agenda depended at least in part on support of more conservative Democrats from the solid white South. The ultimate success of the New Deal, or more pointedly the massive government spending needed to fund the mobilization for World War II, made the argument very one-sided well into the 1950s and beyond. Moreover, economic prosperity fed the triumphal spirit of postwar America. As he wrote *Liberal Tradition*, Hartz could see only the faint outlines of a resolute and exceedingly well-funded pro-business counterattack, one painting the virtues of the free market in glowing terms and urging the government to stay out of the economy and allow the market to self-regulate. What seemed at the time a fantastic pro-business, free market fairy tale eventually emerged as a formidable force in American politics driving the conservative resurgence of the 1980s and beyond. Liberalism's inevitable failures and its tendency to overreach played a role in conservatism's rejuvenation. But that rejuvenation occurred only after a unique economic boom lasting a quarter century finally ran out of gas in the mid-1970s in the face of the decade's Oil Crisis (triggered by the Organization of the Petroleum Exporting Countries embargo) and the increasingly detrimental impact of globalization on the nation's manufacturing employment.[47]

Since the end of the postwar (1948–1973) economic boom, the liberal spirit in America has often found itself on the defensive and struggling to regain its popular appeal. No small part of that difficulty emerged from exceedingly well-financed conservative efforts to mobilize support for conservative causes and candidates – from courthouse to statehouse to Congress and White House. Yet Ronald Reagan remains the only conservative president in the past forty years to leave office enjoying popularity. As such, he remained the touchstone for conservative candidates even in 2020. In the more than three decades since Reagan's second term ended

60 *Understanding the American South*

in 1989, Democrats and Republicans have each held the presidency for sixteen years. But Democrats Clinton and Obama both left the oval office with higher approval ratings than Republicans George Bush, George W. Bush, and Donald Trump.[48]

Still, when Hartz published *Liberal Tradition* in the mid-1950s, liberalism appeared triumphant despite the Eisenhower presidency. It had seemingly won most major arguments and become the dominant national ideology, and even mainstream Republicans of the 1950s seemed committed to a social safety net and federal regulation of the economy (at least up to a point). To be sure, the American liberalism of the 1950s stood as a pragmatic, self-made, hybrid liberalism rather than a doctrinaire liberalism espoused by Locke or any other liberal theorist, and it was certainly not socialism as extreme right-wing critics such as the John Birch Society claimed. The American liberal tradition had carried the day when it produced results. But its triumph had not been uncontested and its critics never fully vanquished. Its foes were never monarchy, nor aristocracy, nor church, but elites: moneyed elites with mercantile, commercial, industrial, and financial interests.

At least since the beginning of the Jacksonian era, American political debate emerged from the complex interplay between ideology and interests. Popular ideologies emerged when ideas seemed to fit or explain facts or existing circumstances. Once ideologies emerged, skilled political practitioners used them to explain (or explain away) whatever circumstances appeared anomalous or required elaboration. On occasion, circumstances presented themselves that the prevailing ideologies could not explain or absorb. New ideologies then morphed from the old or were born from the new circumstances (even if ideologies rarely bear no resemblance to their ideological parentage). In the United States, ideologies were carefully crafted to make coherent cases for broadly liberal interests and broadly conservative interests (given the understanding of those terms at any given time), and those ideologies brought a semblance of clarity to political discourse throughout the nation. Ideologies emerging from interests became very powerful forces when it came to shaping the public understanding of new circumstances, polarizing the electorate, and mobilizing popular support. Moreover, ideologies sometimes became so powerful that they altered public perceptions of reality.

Looking back to the founding, we must recognize the brilliance but also the transience of Madison's remarkable insights and achievements at the Grand Convention of 1787, where the Virginian sought a large republic which encompassed a multitude of interests. So many interests, Madison

The Liberal Tradition

hoped, that they could not cohere long enough to forge an oppressive, enduring majority. Yet we must also concede that Calhoun's challenge to the Madisonian formulation carried much weight. By the 1830s and 1840s, the transportation and communication revolutions and the rise of national political parties had rendered even a multiplicity of interests an insufficient check on the formation of durable majorities. And we must also acknowledge that however accurate his critique, Calhoun's idea of government by concurrent majority loomed as a remedy far worse than the disease.[49]

In fact, the American political system has fundamentally relied on partisan competition itself to balance power and interests in the republic. While unsound as a theoretical model for checking power, the party competition model for balancing interests and restraining their excesses has worked tolerably well throughout most of the American past. When in opposition, each party tries to chip away, or blast away, at the other party's popularity, so that the opposition might gain the majority. And the challengers are always poised to take advantage of a major political misfortune on the incumbent party's watch. Still, experts readily concede that despite the seeming "success" of party competition as a mechanism for checking power and achieving balance, it remains an inefficient and undependable remedy. Moreover, if Madison's constitutional innovations had limited durability, the wisdom of his judgment that "parchment barriers," pieces of paper, even constitutions, are not adequate checks on power remain remarkably appropriate as the nation heads well into the 2020s. We still often look to the Constitution and the rule of law to check power, hoping against hope that they can sustain the republic against tyranny and anarchy, but also relying on the good sense and energy of the American people to make it so.

Notes

1. Alan Brinkley, *The Publisher: Henry Luce and His American Century* (New York: Alfred A. Knopf, 2010), 263–276; Arthur Schlesinger, Jr., *The Vital Center* (New York: Alfred A. Knopf, 1949), 243–246.
2. Daniel Boorstin, *The Genius of American Politics* (Chicago: University of Chicago Press, 1953); David Potter, *People of Plenty: Economic Abundance and the American Character* (Chicago: University of Chicago Press, 1954).
3. C. Vann Woodward, "The Age of Reinterpretation," *American Historical Review* 66, no. 1 (1960): 1–19.
4. Louis Hartz, *The Liberal Tradition in America* (New York: Harcourt, 1955), especially 3–32.

62 *Understanding the American South*

5. Hartz, *The Liberal Tradition*, 35–66.
6. Hartz, *The Liberal Tradition*, 203–227.
7. Bernard Bailyn, *Ideological Origins of the American Revolution* (Cambridge, MA: Harvard University Press, 1967), 55–143; Gordon Wood, *The Creation of the American Republic, 1776–1787* (Chapel Hill: University of North Carolina Press, 1969), 3–90; Robert E. Shalhope, "Toward a Republican Synthesis," *William and Mary Quarterly* 29, no. 1 (1972): 49–80; Drew R. McCoy, *The Elusive Republic: Political Economy in Jeffersonian America* (Chapel Hill: University of North Carolina Press, 1980), 13–75.
8. Bailyn, *Ideological Origins*, 27–28, 242–243; J. R. Pole, *Political Representation in England and the Origins of the American Republic* (New York: St. Martin's Press, 1966).
9. Bailyn, *Ideological Origins*, 47–50.
10. Robert M. Weir, "'The Harmony We Were Famous For': An Interpretation of Pre-Revolutionary South Carolina," *William and Mary Quarterly* 36 (1969): 473–501.
11. Bailyn, *Ideological Origins*, 33–54.
12. Jack Rakove, *James Madison and the Creation of the American Republic* (Glenview, IL: Little Brown, 1990), 30–52; McCoy, *The Elusive Republic*, 120–135; Wood, *Creation of the American Republic*.
13. Rakove, *James Madison*, 30–43; McCoy, *The Elusive Republic*, 120–135.
14. Rakove, *James Madison*, 53–69.
15. Rakove, *James Madison*, 44–52.
16. Rakove, *James Madison*, 44–69.
17. Rakove, *James Madison*, 53–79.
18. Rakove, *James Madison*, 66–69; "From James Madison to Thomas Jefferson, 6 September 1787," in Robert A. Rutland, Charles F. Hobson, William M. E. Rachal, and Frederika J. Teute, eds., *The Papers of James Madison*, Vol. 10, *27 May 1787–3 March 1788* (Chicago: The University of Chicago Press, 1977), 163–165.
19. Rakove, *James Madison*, 70–79.
20. Sean Wilentz, *The Rise of American Democracy: From Jefferson to Lincoln* (New York: W. W. Norton & Company, 2006); Daniel Walker Howe, *What God Hath Wrought: The Transformation of America, 1815–1848* (New York: Oxford University Press, 2007); Charles G. Sellers, *The Market Revolution: Jacksonian America, 1815–1846* (New York: Oxford University Press, 1992).
21. Hartz, *The Liberal Tradition*, 144–177.
22. Hartz, *The Liberal Tradition*, 158–167; Lacy Ford, "Inventing the Concurrent Majority: Madison, Calhoun and the Problem of Majoritarianism in American Political Thought," *Journal of Southern History* 60 (1994): 19–58.
23. Ford, "Inventing the Concurrent Majority," 19–58; Eugene Genovese, *The World the Slaveholders Made: Two Essays in Interpretation* (New York: Pantheon, 1969), 118–246; and Eugene Genovese, *The Slaveholders' Dilemma: Freedom and Progress in Southern Conservative Thought, 1820–1860* (Columbia, SC: University of South Carolina Press, 1992).

The Liberal Tradition   63

24. Elizabeth Fox-Genovese and Eugene D. Genovese, *The Mind of the Master Class: History and Faith in the Southern Slaveholders' Worldview* (New York: Cambridge University Press, 2005); Elizabeth Fox-Genovese and Eugene D. Genovese, *Slavery in White and Black: Class and Race in the Southern Slaveholders' New World Order* (New York: Cambridge University Press, 2008).

25. Eric Foner, *Free Soil, Free Labor, and Free Men: The Ideology of the Republican Party before the Civil War* (New York: Oxford University Press, 1970).

26. Abraham Lincoln, "Speech on Kansas-Nebraska Act, 1854, at the Wisconsin State Fair," in Richard N. Current, ed., *The Political Thought of Abraham Lincoln* (Indianapolis: The Bobbs-Merrill Company, 1967), 72–76.

27. Eric Foner, *The Fiery Trial: Abraham Lincoln and American Slavery* (New York: W. W. Norton & Company, 2010); Eric Foner, *Reconstruction: America's Unfinished Revolution, 1863–1877*, updated edition (New York: Harper Perennial Modern Classics, 2014).

28. Hartz, *The Liberal Tradition*, 89–113; Michael Holt, *The Rise and Fall of the American Whig Party: Jacksonian Politics and the Onset of the Civil War* (New York: Oxford University Press, 1999), 1–458.

29. Steven Hahn, *A Nation without Borders: The United States and Its World in the Age of Civil Wars, 1830–1910* (New York: Penguin Books, 2016), 449–500.

30. Hartz, *The Liberal Tradition*, 203–227.

31. Hahn, *A Nation without Borders*, 363–447; Robert Wiebe, *The Search for Order, 1877–1920* (New York: Hill and Wang, 1967), 44–224.

32. William A. Link, *The Paradox of Southern Progressivism, 1880–1930* (Chapel Hill: University of North Carolina Press, 1992); Dewey W. Grantham, *Southern Progressivism: The Reconciliation of Progress and Tradition* (Knoxville: University of Tennessee Press, 1983).

33. Wiebe, *The Search for Order*, 111–195; Hahn, *A Nation without Borders*, 448–518.

34. David M. Kennedy, *Freedom from Fear: The American People in Depression and War, 1929–1945* (New York: Oxford University Press, 1999) 121–248; William E. Leuchtenberg, *Franklin D. Roosevelt and the New Deal, 1932–1940* (New York: Harper and Row, 1963), 1–196; Paul K. Conkin, *The New Deal*, 3rd ed. (New York: Wiley-Blackwell, 1991). For more on the radical left, communism, and socialism during the 1930s, see Harvey Klehr, *The Heyday of American Communism: The Depression Decade* (New York: Basic Books, 1984); Robin D. G. Kelley, *Hammer and Hoe: Alabama Communists during the Great Depression*, 25th anniversary edition (Chapel Hill: University of North Carolina Press, 2015); Lashawn Harris, "Running with the Reds: African American Women and the Communist Party during the Great Depression," *Journal of African American History* 94, no. 1 (2009): 21–43; Michael Kazin, "The Agony and Romance of the American Left," *American Historical Review* 100, no. 5 (1995): 1488–1512; and Jack Ross, *The Socialist Party of America: A Complete History* (Lincoln: University of Nebraska Press, 2015).

35. Leuchtenberg, *Franklin D. Roosevelt and the New Deal*, 41–62, 143–196.
36. Zachary D. Carter, *The Price of Peace: Money, Democracy, and the Life of John Maynard Keynes* (New York: Random House, 2020), 296–325.
37. Kennedy, *Freedom from Fear*, 465–666; Carter, *The Price of Peace*, 310–316.
38. For more on Mutually Assured Destruction, see Robert P. Jameson, "Armageddon's Shortening Fuse: How Advances in Nuclear Weapons Technology Pushed Strategists to Mutually Assured Destruction, 1945–1962," *Air Power History* 60, no. 1 (2013): 40–53; Henry D. Sokolski, ed., *Getting MAD: Nuclear Mutual Assured Destruction, Its Origins and Practice* (Carlisle, PA: US Army War College Press, 2004), https://press.armywarcollege.edu/monographs/32; and Edward Kaplan, *To Kill Nations: American Strategy in the Air-Atomic Age and the Rise of Mutually Assured Destruction* (Ithaca, NY: Cornell University Press, 2015).
39. Hartz, *The Liberal Tradition*, 203–227; Sean Wilentz, *The Age of Reagan: A History, 1974–2008* (New York: Harper Perennial, 2009), 288–322.
40. David Oshinsky, *A Conspiracy So Immense: The World of Joe McCarthy* (New York: Free Press, 1983). For more on the Second Red Scare and anti-communist hysteria in the 1950s, see chapter 7, "Red Scares Abroad and at Home," in James T. Patterson, ed., *Grand Expectations: The United States, 1945–1974* (New York: Oxford University Press, 1996), 165–205; Landron R. Y. Storrs, *The Second Red Scare and the Unmaking of the New Deal Left* (Princeton: Princeton University Press, 2013); Landon R. Y. Storrs, "Red Scare Politics and the Suppression of Popular Front Feminism: The Loyalty Investigation of Mary Dublin Keyserling," *The Journal of American History* 90, no. 2 (2003): 491–524; Ellen Schrecker, "McCarthyism: Political Repression and the Fear of Communism," *Social Research* 71, no. 4 (2004): 1041–1086; and James H. Smith, "Red-Baiting Senator Harley Kilgore in the Election of 1952: The Limits of McCarthyism during the Second Red Scare," *West Virginia History* 1, no. 1 (2007): 55–74.
41. Hartz, *The Liberal Tradition*, 284–309.
42. Michael Holt, *The Rise and Fall of the American Whig Party: Jacksonian Politics and the Onset of the Civil War* (New York: Oxford University Press, 1999); Harry L. Watson, *Liberty and Power: The Politics of Jacksonian America* (New York: Hill and Wang, 1990).
43. Eric Foner, *Free Soil, Free Labor, and Free Men: The Ideology of the Republican Party before the Civil War* (New York: Oxford University Press, 1970).
44. Hahn, *A Nation without Borders*, 401–447.
45. Hahn, *A Nation without Borders*, 439–482.
46. Leuchtenberg, *Franklin D. Roosevelt and the New Deal, 1932–1940*, 18–62.
47. Wilentz, *Age of Reagan*, 35–39, 95–98.
48. Gerhard Peters, "Final Presidential Job Approval Ratings," in John T. Woolley and Gerhard Peters, eds., *The American Presidency Project* (Santa Barbara: University of California, 1999–2021), www.presidency.ucsb.edu/statistics/data/final-presidential-job-approval-ratings. The data were

The South, Ideology, and American Identity
67

Constitution) needed little adjusting, they seldom grew enamored with other political theories, whether new or old. Boorstin called this proposition "givenness," a "belief that values in America are in some way or other automatically defined: given by certain facts of geography or history peculiar to us." Initially, these values came as a "gift from the past," from the founders and other early settlers who gave us all the theory we need. Yet "givenness," as Boorstin presents it, also holds that values are "a gift from the present," that our institutions are somehow defined by and perpetuate our values and our "way of life." Americans think and feel that their "living experience" reveals and fulfills the nation's underlying governing theory. Finally, Boorstin maintains, "givenness" posits a continuity or homogeneity in our nation's history. The American national experience has been largely one of continuity, he argues, with the nation's past flowing seamlessly into its present and its future.[3]

In his brief volume, the historian Boorstin skimmed through the American past to find evidence for his claims. He argued that the American Revolution was remarkable for its nonideological character, and the founders for their lack of interest in political theory. The American revolutionaries, were, in Boorstin's view, simply seeking to conserve a way of life that had already developed in the colonies. Boorstin maintained that neither political theory nor ideology much influenced the founders; instead, their focus remained on the realities of life on the ground in the thirteen colonies. Boorstin acknowledged *The Federalist Papers* as a notable exception to his contention that the founders rarely appealed to political theory, but he dismissed the founding essays as post hoc justifications for a constitution whose drafting had been driven by practical necessity.[4] Within three decades of Boorstin's claim that the American founding stood as a nonideological event, a convincing new wave of historical scholarship argued that during the late colonial and revolutionary eras, the nation's founders were extremely well versed in the political ideologies and theories of the day, and the American political environment highly charged with ideological concerns. Moreover, leading American historians of the Revolution and Constitution argued that the founders grappled within an ideology known to scholars as the "republican synthesis," which dominated both the public and private political discourse both leading up to the Revolution and at the later Constitutional Convention in 1787.[5]

Still, despite Boorstin's dramatic underestimation of the importance of ideology to the American Revolution, the greatest challenge to his interpretation of American history was and remains the American Civil War.

68   *Understanding the American South*

Americans fought a deadly and destructive Civil War over an intensely ideological issue: the definition of freedom, and the extent to which that freedom should extend to all people. The Civil War, a conflict rightly known in official records as "The War of the Rebellion," was nothing less than a conflict over the scope of human freedom in our inherited constitutional republic. One side ultimately fought to extend as well as preserve freedom, the other fought to limit freedom by defending and expanding slavery across territory and generations, in the interest of protecting slaveholder wealth and preserving racial privilege for all whites. This sectional conflict, and the resulting civil war, stands as the one great American political problem that defied compromise or constitutional resolution and was resolved only at the cannon's mouth – at the price of over 700,000 American lives (Union and Confederate). The Civil War still stands today as a serious challenge to Boorstin's argument in favor of a unique American political genius.[6]

Boorstin's analysis of the Civil War anticipated the approach used by Sargent Joe Friday (Jack Webb) on the popular 1960s police show "Dragnet," in which Friday repeatedly insisted on "just the facts." Boorstin's analysis stuck very closely to presumed facts with little attention to the power of ideas or emotions in creating the conflict. Boorstin maintained that the Civil War emerged from two distinct sources: evolving sectional differences and different views of the federalism that lay at the heart of the American Constitution. He insisted that it was not a conflict driven by competing ideologies. Sectionalism, Boorstin argued, emerged because different societies had grown up in different sections of the country (North and South) and that each society had a sociology (but not an ideology) of its own. Southern society was rooted in slavery, and all that slavery entailed, while northern society rested on a foundation of family farms and free labor. These realities constituted what Boorstin called the "givenness" of American society, that is a recognition of things as they are and a general desire to preserve them. In that sense, white northerners and white southerners were each conservative people who came to armed conflict to preserve their own version of American society against threats emanating from the other.[7]

Boorstin argued that both sections made the case for their cause from sociology (which Boorstin understood as facts about a given society) rather than ideology. The debate behind the war was simply over which existing society was the better one. In Boorstin's view, this presented an empirical question rather than a conceptual or ideological one. He saw the characteristics and behavior of societies as their sociology and

The South, Ideology, and American Identity   69

assumed they existed without necessarily exerting much influence on the
ideas emanating from or the self-conceptions and social constructions
emerging within the society. Writing before the idea of a relationship
between base and superstructure became fashionable in the discipline of
sociology, Boorstin assumed that the base exerted only nominal influence on the superstructure and vice versa. Thus Boorstin saw the "sociology" of the two sections as "stand ins" for ideology. Neither "North nor
South was pursuing a new vision of society," Boorstin insisted, since each
side presented their respective arguments on "an empirical rather than a
metaphysical playing field." Both sides, Boorstin believed, wanted simply
to argue the "facts" about their society, transforming every "statistical
detail" into a "clue" to their section's "way of life." For Boorstin, this
tendency bore witness to the American sense of "givenness" in both sections because it revealed the "assumption that life as it was in America –
whether in North or in the South – gave the outlines of life as it ought
to be."[8]

Boorstin conceded that the concept of a sociology for society helped
white southerners evade the larger moral question of slavery – a question
central to the northern critique of southern life. But Boorstin was quick
to note that northern opposition to slavery, or at least to its expansion,
was "based less on love for the Negro than on concern for the white
working man, less on a feel for the present sufferings of the slave than on
a fear for the future plight of white men if everywhere in the Union he
should have to compete with the Negro."[9]

Boorstin also contended that American federalism also defined and
limited the terms of political debate between North and South. Just as
the American Revolution had been defined by a well-established British
colonial framework, the sectional conflict leading to the American Civil
War emerged within an established constitutional framework. The
Constitution-burning abolitionists loomed as the major exception to the
rule, since many, though far from all, secessionists made the controversial claim that their movement offered a constitutional remedy.[10]

Each side in the conflict, Boorstin claimed, insisted that they were
defending the principles of the Declaration and the Constitution rather
than breaking free from or redefining those principles. Each section
claimed to be "defending the authentic original doctrine, to be defending the Constitution." Their conflict grew out of the southern concern
that the northern states wanted too much power to rest in federal hands
while the southern slaveholding states preferred keeping the balance
of power in the individual states in order to protect slavery. Boorstin

Understanding the American South

conceded that these constitutional arguments largely served each side's sectional interest. The slaveholding South feared that the northern desire to contain slavery within its existing boundaries would eventually tilt power in the American constitutional system so far toward the northern or federal side that the existence of slavery itself might be in jeopardy. The free labor northern states feared that unless slavery was restricted to those areas where it already existed, then the expansion of slave labor would limit the opportunity of free farmers and free workers to profit from their own initiative, whether to retain, or to rise into, the status of propertied freeholder.[11]

Hence southerners developed a fondness for a state's rights and the strict construction of the United States Constitution, as they feared that a growing majority of nonslaveholding states would eventually overwhelm the South within the Union and force emancipation. On this point, Boorstin turns to John C. Calhoun to speak for the South. While alive, Calhoun often yearned to speak for the South, yet during much of his career, he seldom persuaded other leading southern politicians to assign him that role, especially after the failure of nullification to gain broad support in 1832–1833.[12] Boorstin devoted much of his discussion on southern views of the Constitution to Calhoun's idea that the power of a concurrent majority could be used to limit the power of a numerical majority. Calhoun saw the Constitution as a living document which attempted to share power between its two primary organizing elements: the people of the nation and the people of the individual states which compose the nation. The South Carolinian saw the Constitution as an attempt to balance the two by giving each the power of the concurrent majority through the nation's federal structure. Over time, in Calhoun's estimation, the transportation and communication revolution in the antebellum era and the concomitant rise of national political parties promoted the growth of what the South Carolinian denounced as a "consolidated national government," a government which could become a means used by one section to dominate the other. Calhoun thought such a power contradicted the will of the founders and required remedy. Using arguments that echoed those of the founders about the dangers of uncontrolled majorities, Calhoun insisted that minority rights could be protected through the concept of the concurrent majority, a concept which gave a unified minority the right to veto majority-approved legislation. Such a constitutional structure, Calhoun argued, would encourage moderation and compromise in the spirit of goodwill and yet leave the government strong enough to function effectively. After Calhoun's death in 1850, but before the rise of the

The South, Ideology, and American Identity 71

Republican party in 1854, the fear of an oppressive northern majority pushed more and more southerners toward open advocacy of secession as a remedy for the protection of slavery.[13]

Boorstin interpreted sectional conflict as profoundly conservative in nature, as growing out of a dispute between two existing social systems, both rooted in the same political and constitutional context. As a result, there existed no larger dispute with the Constitution itself but sharp differences over key points of interpretation. In Boorstin's view, this was an argument between competing constitutional orthodoxies. He viewed it not as a matter of competing political ideologies but as a dispute between socially different sections operating within an agreed upon constitutional framework, but with each professing different interpretations of the Constitution. According to Boorstin, both sections styled themselves as preservers of an old order, as defenders of established doctrine, and as the true descendants of the founding fathers. Yet they held different views of the old order, the established doctrine, and the true intent of the founders. Neither side repudiated or even disputed the American Constitution; each side believed themselves to stand for the true values of the founders and both sides believed they were even better custodians of the founding wisdom than the other.[14]

Boorstin noted the irony that a radical remedy such as secession had been presented using "such a conservative vocabulary" and added the phenomena to his list of reasons that the South saw secession as an effort to preserve rather than recreate its form of government. Yet Boorstin concluded his treatment of the Civil War by pointing out that the South's response to a humbling defeat which ended slavery, the interest and institution the war was fought to preserve, emerged not as one of continued guerilla resistance but instead as continued political argument defending the constitutionality of their failed efforts.[15] As evidence, Boorstin examined former Confederate Vice-President Alexander Stephens' lengthy constitutional defense of secession written shortly after the end of the war. Boorstin pondered why such a crushing defeat of great practical and emotional impact prompted a constitutional argument in reply. To Boorstin, Stephens' approach revealed the depth of the South's underlying commitment to constitutional government and even its loyalty to the US Constitution. The enduring constitutionalism of the American South revealed, in Boorstin's view, that its dispute with the United States was sociological and constitutional in nature and not a matter of ideology.[16]

In Boorstin's eyes, there was nothing radical about the American Civil War despite its transformative impact on both the South and the nation. In Boorstin's view, the southern sociology proved vulnerable to the northern sociology. A bloody war was fought between two conservative societies, each holding and fighting for a set of political and constitutional values that differed very little on many points but disagreed so fundamentally about one question – the question of the territorial expansion of slavery – a difference that could not be compromised but settled only by force of arms.

Moreover, Boorstin did not see his argument for competing sociologies as a denial that slavery lay at the heart of the conflict. The competing sociologies were slavery and slaveholding on the one side and a free labor society on the other, but he does not see that either of these societies produced or adhered to a political ideology that was unacceptable to the other. But the different sections' sociologies, slave labor versus free labor, spawned very specific self-interests that eventually came into conflict. Ultimately, it required much human sacrifice to resolve this conflict. But, for Boorstin, the magnitude of the sacrifice did not suggest that the war involved a conflict of ideologies rather than interests. Interpreted in this manner, the American Civil War reaffirmed rather than challenged the continuity of American political thought. And for Boorstin, the war not only saved the Union but also reinforced a commitment to the common destiny of the nation.

Boorstin's argument that the American Civil War did not constitute a failure, or a collapse, of the much-touted "genius" of American politics stood as strained, if not disingenuous, given the savage warfare, death toll and human suffering the conflict produced, and when the stakes of the outcome are considered. As prominent historian Drew Gilpin Faust described in detail, the nation became a "Republic of Suffering," and the military conflict officially known as the "War of the Rebellion." Such nomenclature hardly makes a case for continuity, consensus, or political genius in American history.[17]

Long before the publication of *Genius*, other interpretations of the American Civil War had appeared that presented challenges to Boorstin's argument. That literature is vast, but perhaps most prominent among those earlier works loomed Charles and Mary Beard's controversial but well-known economic interpretation of the conflict. The Beards judged the Civil War a "Second American Revolution" in which the agrarian interest, as embodied by the American South, rose to defend itself against growing commercial and industrial interests centered in the American North. By nudging slavery into the background and arguing that war represented the conflict of an agrarian society with an increasingly

The South, Ideology, and American Identity 73

commercial and industrial society, the Beards cast the conflict not merely as one of competing sectional interests but as an ideological battle between Jeffersonian agrarian values trying to prevent the triumph of Hamiltonian capitalist values. As Midwesterners hailing from a region still largely dependent upon agriculture, the Beards' sympathies seemed to run largely with the South, despite the slaveholding nature of the region. The concentration of power that the Beards feared most was the concentrated power of capital, which they saw emerging in the American North rather than in the anti-democratic "slave power" that many had claimed ruled the prewar American South.[18]

The provocative if overdrawn Beardian interpretation of the American Civil War hardly stood as the only historiographical challenge confounding Boorstin's argument during the 1950s. The debate over whether the American Civil War was a repressible or irrepressible conflict was already underway, as was the argument that a Union victory proved necessary to give the American nation the power to sustain itself and protect the world in the face of twentieth-century extremism. Yet Boorstin's work retained a significant measure of influence among scholars until later generations of historians emerged who defined ideology more broadly, who embraced an understanding of the influence that flowed between the socioeconomic base and ideological superstructure in societies and cultures, and who found, in a variety of nuanced forms, that the American Civil War was nothing less than a profound ideological conflict between the slaveholding South and the free labor North.[19]

Much of the new scholarly understanding of sectional conflict that left Boorstin's hypotheses shattered grew out of an explosion of scholarship on the nature of the Second American Party System as well as on the relationship of political ideology to social and economic systems within both North and South, and to the role that highly politicized definitions of independence, manhood and citizenship played in shaping the popular understanding of issues that led to the American Civil War. Moreover, both the transportation and communication revolutions which swept across the republic in the first half of the nineteenth century transformed both American politics and the nation's economy. First canals and later railroads dramatically enhanced transportation and the rise of a national postal system improved communication. These improvements conquered space and diminished the role of a large republic in preventing the formation of powerful majorities in ways which the founders had not anticipated. The mobilization of political parties on a national scale became possible. By the time of Andrew Jackson's presidency (1829–1837), the

74 *Understanding the American South*

emergence of a strong, active party system pitted Jackson-led Democrats against an opposition coalition that took the name Whigs in almost every state in the Union.[20]

While both Jacksonian-era national parties were coalitions, there were nonetheless clear patterns of membership. Democrats favored policies that protected independent producers from exploitation at the hands of speculators and large commercial interests. At least in their rhetoric, the Democrats attempted to defend the interests of these independent producers from the machinations of ambitious entrepreneurs, financiers, or capitalists, and to leave matters of moral influence to churches and individual consciences. The Whig party, on the other hand, stood for broad material and moral improvement. Whigs supported the efforts of entrepreneurs and investors to bring expanding material prosperity and enhancing economic development. They also favored the efforts of reformers to usher in major social improvements, including temperance and Sabbatarianism. Democrats sought to use the power of government negatively to protect the producer from exploitation. Whigs sought to use that power positively to assist the entrepreneur and investor in building a broader and deeper material basis for prosperity. Whigs believed that a broadly shared prosperity could better sustain the independence of the citizenry.[21]

The Whig party tended to favor institutions and policies which supported economic development and moral improvement, including a national bank, federal subsidies for internal improvements, and in some instances protective tariffs to encourage infant industries. By contrast, Democrats saw almost any alliance of government with specific economic interests which sought enhanced advantage as a dangerous concentration of power which could erode the position of the independent producer in the American economy. Based on these assumptions, the Democratic party developed an ideology of protecting individuals from the power of economic concentration and government alliances with powerful economic interests. The Whig party developed an ideology which advocated the moral and material improvement of society and favored using the power of government actively to produce such improvement. These differences and these ideologies defined political debate in the United States for nearly two decades.[22]

During the 1850s, however, the politics of that decade eroded public confidence in the existing party system, first in the North but eventually in the South as well. The key issue that the Second American Party System proved unable to handle was the issue of the expansion of slavery into additional western territories. Following the acquisition of California and

The South, Ideology, and American Identity 75

other western territories of the Mexican Cession the issue of the expansion of slavery loomed larger and larger. Increasingly, white northerners, while not generally enamored with the appeals of the abolitionists, came to embrace arguments favoring the containment of slavery to those areas where it already existed. Allowing slavery to expand into newly acquired or newly opened territories would force free farmers, free artisans, and free workers to compete with enslaved Black labor, a competition that they considered demeaning as well as impossible to win. Because both the Democratic and Whig parties were national in nature, these two existing parties found it very difficult to contain this growing northern sentiment against any expansion of slavery. Both parties had important southern wings and leaders of both parties knew that alienating their southern support would leave them vulnerable to defeat and even demolition at the hands of the other party.[23]

The exact causes and timing of the decline and fall of the Second American Party System are matters of a scholarly debate that falls well beyond the scope of this chapter, but by the mid-1850s, a new party emerged in the North, the Republican party, dedicated to the principles of "free soil, free labor and free men." Republicans favored stopping the expansion of slavery as a means of expanding opportunity for free white people in the nation's western territories. Nonetheless, radical white northerners interested in broader antislavery concerns, including abolition, found the Republican party attractive, even if its "free soil, free labor" agenda represented only half a loaf. Restricting the expansion of slavery was a start, and it was a policy more in alignment with the antislavery cause than those offered by either of the existing Jacksonian-era parties, each replete with their substantial southern constituencies. The Republican principles of "free soil, free labor and free men" emerged as a powerful ideology, one which argued convincingly that protecting the "right to rise" of northern whites required the restriction of slavery to existing slaveholding areas. The appeal of the "free labor" ideology also fit readily with a growing northern fear of a potent southern "slave power" determined to impose the will of a proslavery southern minority on an antislavery northern majority, a fear magnified in the 1850s by the repeal of the restrictions on the expansion of slavery imposed by the Missouri Compromise, the minority imposition of the Lecompton Constitution in Kansas, and by the pro-southern Dred Scott decision handed down by the US Supreme Court in 1857.[24]

The growing popularity that the "free labor" ideology enjoyed in the North during the 1850s triggered a predictable reaction in many parts of

76   *Understanding the American South*

the South. White southerners feared that as they became outnumbered not only in terms of popular votes but also in terms of state representation in the United States Senate, their region would become vulnerable to a full-scale assault on slavery. That such an assault did not seem imminent, or even entirely logical to free labor advocates, did not slow the southern embrace of arguments that "northern aggression" must be stopped at its threshold. As the South's ability to build coalitions with Democratic elements in the North to win elections and keep the Republicans out of power eroded, more and more white southerners turned to secession, or at least the threat of secession, as the only viable remedy.[25]

In a very real sense, the sectional conflict that led to the American Civil War involved an ideological contest between the champions of the free labor ideology of the Republican North and an avowedly proslavery southern rights ideology in the South. The southern rights movement argued that slavery was not only an appropriate bulwark for republican citizenship but by far the most appropriate foundation since it defined the dependent working class (enslaved Blacks) out of the body politic.[26]

Boorstin's work largely ignored the late antebellum efforts of the new Republican party and its future leader, Abraham Lincoln of Illinois, to dramatically redefine the meaning of the American Union. As early as 1854, during the Kansas–Nebraska debates, Lincoln observed that "when a white man governs himself that is self-government, but when he governs himself as well as another man, that is more than self-government, that is despotism." If "the negro is a man," Lincoln continued, "then ... there can be no moral right in connection with one man making a slave of another." By identifying masters as despots, Lincoln challenged the very core of arguments that slavery strengthened white independence. Lincoln was no immediate abolitionist, but he challenged the morality of slavery, not simply its influence on the nation's political balance of power.[27] Still, Lincoln stopped short of calling for racial equality. "Let it not be said," Lincoln declared, that "I am contending for the political and social equality between the whites and blacks." Lincoln questioned the moral authority of slave holding, yet while doing so, claimed that he was only trying to stop "the extension of a bad thing," conceding that "where it [slavery] already exists, we must of necessity, manage as best we can." Lincoln called on the nation to "re-adopt the Declaration of Independence" by turning slavery back from its "claims of 'moral right'," back upon its existing legal rights and its arguments of "necessity." Lincoln was clear about his purpose. The expansion of slavery, he insisted, affected the "whole nation" and not just the people hoping

The South, Ideology, and American Identity

to move to the disputed territories. "We want them [territories] for the homes of free white people," Lincoln declared, a goal which, in his view, required the exclusion of slavery.[28]

During the 1850s, Lincoln saw the contradictions within the Constitution concerning the issue of slavery. To be sure, the founding document had done things to restrict and limit slavery. The document appeared to reflect a vision of the national future in which slavery would enjoy diminished importance over time and (somehow) even come to an end. But he also saw that the Constitution, as delegates from the slave-holding states at the Constitutional Convention had worked hard to guarantee, provided slavery with protection and gave slaveholding states disproportionate power in the federal government.[29]

As Lincoln began to see the need to limit the power of slavery within the American Union, he turned not only to the Constitution but also to the Declaration of Independence to gain support from founding documents. In Lincoln's view, the Declaration was far less ambiguous on the issue of slavery. By lifting "life, liberty and the pursuit of happiness" as fundamental American rights and not specifying those as aspirations qualified by race or other social condition, Lincoln linked freedom inextricably with the American experiment in self-government. Simply put, Lincoln saw liberty as a human right which slavery denied.[30]

During the secession crisis and early months of the war, Lincoln initially showed a willingness to accommodate slavery to save the Union. In fact, he emphatically claimed that he would do whatever it took to save the Union, whether it took freeing all the slaves, freeing none of the slaves, or freeing some and not others. Initially, he firmly denied that his administration intended to do anything to interfere with slavery in the states where it already existed. But as the war progressed and the human cost mounted, Lincoln came to recognize that the wartime sacrifice could only be justified by bringing slavery to an end. He used many opportunities to make himself clear on these issues.

Before the war Lincoln had spoken of the "right to rise," understood as an opportunity for upward social mobility, as a key component of American ideology. The "right to rise" required the freedom to move from worker to farmer or artisan or shopkeeper, and the freedom to enjoy the fruits of one's labor.[31] It was this right to rise, the right to be free of bondage, the right to be self-owned individuals, that lay at the heart of Lincoln's beliefs about slavery. Before the war, Lincoln often denied any belief in racial equality, and he made statements that suggested he did not, in fact, believe in the equality of the races. Over time,

78 *Understanding the American South*

however, his experience and observations as commander-in-chief led him to believe that, in some instances at least, African Americans deserved full political rights.[32]

Lincoln began his Gettysburg address with the words "four score and seven years ago," immediately and intentionally linking the founding with the Declaration of Independence rather than the Constitution. Throughout that address he stressed the nobility of sacrifice involved in the war in which the nation was engaged and the need for the nation to derive from it an accomplishment that could justify the depth of sacrifice. Referring to the emancipation of slaves as a "new birth of freedom," President Lincoln suggested that this new birth was the only thing that could conceivably justify the sacrifice of the war.[33]

The thrust of the historical literature that has appeared over the more than half century since Boorstin penned *Genius* strongly suggests that he seriously underestimated the role of ideology in the coming of the Civil War, and thus perhaps in other periods of American history as well. To be sure, self-interest, history, geography, identity, and other circumstances on the ground (matters Boorstin considered "givenness") played strong roles in the formation of the ideologies that led to the American Civil War, but doubtless the war was also in large part an ideological conflict. Interest and identity become especially powerful when matured into and expressed as ideology. Boorstin's concept of "givenness" allows for a world view, but not exactly an ideology, to emerge from history, the facts on the ground, and a willingness to change (but also a desire to change as little as possible). But "givenness" only allows ideological drivers to come into play in decidedly subordinate roles.[34]

Like all works of history, Boorstin's work was a product of its time. As one of several books that appeared after World War II, Boorstin's *Genius* formed part of the corpus of American triumphalism: intellectual and scholarly efforts seeking to explain the qualities that allowed the United States to survive the Great Depression and play a (perhaps the) decisive role in defeating the Nazis and Fascism in the war. Moreover, the abundance of rich historiography on the ideological conflicts that played such an active role in leading the American nation down the road to Civil War were not fully available to Boorstin when he wrote *Genius* in the early 1950s. Yet surely it was a serious moment of scholarly myopia that led to Boorstin's failure to recognize the American Civil War as a radical turning point in the nation's history, one requiring the sacrifice of over 700,000 lives and violently ending the enslavement of some four million Americans. Boorstin should have recognized that such a momentous

The South, Ideology, and American Identity 79

and deadly civil war did not emerge from slight differences in regional sociology or modest disagreements within a fundamental political consensus. At least for a time, Boorstin's vaunted "givenness" found itself ruptured to its very core and the American consensus shattered by a war for southern independence that took more American lives than any other war. The American Civil War exploded the case for a perennial national, and largely nonideological, consensus. Historians can argue that a too quickly abandoned Reconstruction process restored a broad consensus (albeit one founded on white supremacy) in fewer than two decades. But the radical disruption of continuity by secession, Civil War, and emancipation defies Boorstin's claims for continuity, slow and gradual change, and the tractability of all conflicts.

Yet the context of Boorstin's myopia remains easy to understand. His work fell clearly into the body of literature of arguing for American exceptionalism while standing in an uneasy if not dissenting relationship with other triumphalist arguments. Boorstin's emphasis on "givenness" and a slowly adaptable way of life fell toward the conservative end of efforts to explain American exceptionalism. Yet while writing *Genius* from an identifiably conservative point of view, Boorstin presented his main arguments as if taking a nonideological position. The practical-minded Boorstin saw both the American nation and its people as temperamentally conservative. They did not, in his view, tend to follow ideologies or ideologically driven leaders, instead preferring to chart a cautious course based on experience, keeping things as they are as much as possible and amending them just enough when circumstances suggested that such alterations were needed. This temperamental conservatism represented the practical genius that Boorstin contended had served the American nation well over the decades.[35]

Boorstin celebrated the American way of life created by "givenness" and yearned for its longevity. Yet he underestimated the extent to which the turning of a blind eye to how much and how rapidly the nation's economic system, revolving as it did around private market-driven decisions, introduced powerful drivers of change for which "givenness" could hardly keep pace. Capitalism, through its drive for large profits in international trade and its voracious appetite for new markets, created the slave economies of the New World. In fact, arguably modern capitalism has its origins in the seventeenth, eighteenth, and nineteenth centuries as world trade and a strong market orientation created slave economies in the New World, where valuable commodities such as sugar, tobacco, rice, cotton, and coffee brought high prices in the world market in an era

80   *Understanding the American South*

when labor that was not coerced proved hard to mobilize for production. These economies produced valuable commodities which international markets valued highly and generated great fortunes for slave masters. And during its peak periods, the international slave trade itself yielded some of the greatest fortunes the world had ever seen to slave traders.[36]

Eventually, and with considerable irony, capitalism eventually sought the weakening, and perhaps the ultimate demise, of slavery. By the time of the America Civil War and its aftermath, the needs of capitalism in its American context had shifted. Those needs included continued territorial expansion and the creation of an industrial working class that was skilled, mobile, and motivated by wages. The rise of a free American working class did not require the end of slavery, but it did necessitate that slavery be limited or constrained geographically. The defenders of the enslaved Black labor system were simply not willing to accept such restrictions, in large part because their own involvement and investment in world capitalism bred quite different interests and understandings of how the system worked.[37]

The appeal of the "free labor" ideology and the concomitant fear of the "slave power" (which could wield excessive influence within the American democracy) in the American North fueled the rise of the Republican party. Republican opposition to the expansion of slavery led to radical southern resistance and ultimately secession across the lower South. Northern whites sought to defend and enhance an emerging economic system based on "free soil, free labor, and free men." This project required wresting control of the levers of economic power away from those holding them who used an increasingly anachronistic system of enslaved labor. If this argument sounds Marxist in tone and language, it need not. It is simply a clear way of expressing that continuity and conservatism in American life, particularly if continuity and conservatism are defined as defending and preserving a society as it exists, as they were for Boorstin, are often at odds with the dynamic market economy that many Americans embraced. The market juxtaposed on a desire to preserve existing societies may produce a peculiar kind of conservative politics, but not the type of conservativism that Boorstin saw as growing organically from "givenness."[38]

Ultimately Boorstin's brand of conservatism runs up against a problem that almost every strain of American conservatism must eventually confront: Capitalism is not a profoundly conservative economic system. Defenders can present capitalism in conservative terms and label it a conservative economic and social system in the sense that it works to limit or

The South, Ideology, and American Identity

control the role of government in the economy. But when examined from a larger perspective, capitalism is anything but a conservative system. Capitalism is a promoter of ongoing, often rapid, and sometimes radical change, change by the moment, the minute, the hour, the week, the quarter, the year, and the business cycle. Capitalism's pace of change, in search of efficiency and profit, is far more rapid than most people in any society find comfortable, regardless of whether they are liberal or conservative in their political leanings. Capitalism is, in Joseph Schumpeter's famous phrase, "creative destruction." It is relentlessly destructive of the status quo. Hence it is profoundly destructive of Boorstin's "givenness." It is driven not by values or social preferences but by profit and gain and productivity and many other good or harmless or bad things, but it is not driven by keeping things as they are or by conservatism, if conservatism is defined by the idea of keeping things as they are until change is necessary. Indeed, a society devoted to keeping things as they are serves as a poor host for capitalism. Capitalism requires a societal maelstrom of churn, evolution, creative destruction, and regeneration. To be sure, the pace of change that capitalism promotes appears more rapid today than it did in the era of sectional conflict, but even at the time capital was a powerful driver of social as well as economic change.[39]

Moreover, Boorstin's own faith in "givenness" faced potent challenges during the first half of the twentieth century, with the strength of the challenge increasing with each passing decade. The gradual melting of numerous distinct American regional and folk cultures into a single national popular culture largely created by national corporate media, mass communications, and product marketing shook Boorstin's faith that Americans could readily distinguish the authentic from the artificial, the homemade from the mass-produced, the facts on the ground from the fictions being broadcast to persuade or sell to the public. Boorstin's own deep fears of a media-generated faux culture appeared first in his *The Image* (1962), a book reflecting his concern that sophisticated media-created images of American life could so distort history and complicate reality that Americans would not be able to distinguish fact from fiction or image from reality. If our guide is merely an image and not reality, then how can Americans discern what is "given" and what is artificial. The influence of mass commercial culture in creating a distorted reality stood as a major theme of in the third volume of Boorstin's American trilogy, *The Americans: The Democratic Experience*. Throughout a long and entertaining volume, Boorstin expressed concern that the essence of American "givenness" might be first corrupted and ultimately lost.[40]

Boorstin also doubted that American success could be exported or replicated by emerging nation-states in other parts of the world. Indeed, *Genius* was written largely to caution against the ideological imperialism emerging in national counsels during the Cold War. In Boorstin's view, much about the American experience and landscape had produced the unique elixir for "givenness" that guided the success of American democracy. As a result, it was not a product made to sell in international markets – as often happened during the Cold War. Rather, in Boorstin's view, the American experience was a caution against political and ideological imperialism. American democracy was not a readily exportable commodity because it was a product the unique American experience – of "givenness."

In *Genius'* concluding chapter on "Our Cultural Hypochondria," Boorstin explicitly lamented the increased pressure from both national leaders and international events for the United States to define its governing theory and promulgate that theory in a way that might persuade the world of its value. Boorstin blamed intellectuals of all stripes for this temptation to lead American society away from the "givenness" he believed made America great. Boorstin scolded Americans, and especially their leaders, for succumbing to the temptations of theory and philosophy. He appealed to Americans to recognize that historically they had shown "no enthusiasm for plans to make society over" because they had "actually made a new society without a plan."

Boorstin offered an emphatic "no" to the question of whether the United States "could export its political institutions," a question that often arose as the Cold War with Soviet and Chinese communism emerged. "We must refuse to become crusaders for liberalism in order to remain liberals," Boorstin insisted. "We must refuse to become crusaders for conservatism in order to conserve the institutions and the genius which have made American great." Boorstin, as he concluded the book, turned back to Abraham Lincoln as an example of American practicality that more American leaders should emulate. Like Lincoln, Boorstin advised, Americans should "doubt their capacity to make a perfect world."[41]

In retrospect, Boorstin's confidence in the American nation's mysterious sense of "givenness" was not entirely without foundation. There is (or was) an unmistakably practical or pragmatic streak running through American history. The American people have not flocked en masse to ideologues, whether radical or conservative, in times of national crisis, although some demagogues have made considerable progress with the electorate at times. Boorstin sees this wisdom of the people as rooted

The South, Ideology, and American Identity

in their comfort with "givenness," with the existing reality of American society, and their willingness to make modest adjustments when necessary, as the keys to the success and longevity of the American experiment in self-government.

Without question, the American political system has displayed more than its share of genius at times, such as finding Lincoln as a leader at the time the Union was rent asunder or producing Teddy Roosevelt and Woodrow Wilson at a time when big business and big finance approached obtaining unrestrained power in American society, or electing Franklin Delano Roosevelt at the time of a world economic collapse that threatened the very future of both capitalism and democracy. FDR took a pragmatic and experimental approach to patching up the American economic system and weaved a social safety net that prevented free fall. Roosevelt also guided the nation into and through a war that defeated fascism in several guises. A generation later, American politics produced Lyndon Johnson at a moment of national tragedy. Johnson saw and embraced the opportunity to expand civil and voting rights to all Americans and to expand the American social safety net dramatically.

There have also been times in which the genius of American politics seems to have gone to ground, such as during the collapse of the Second Party System or during portions of the Gilded Age. Whether or not the nation is in one of those periods as this chapter is written may depend on one's partisan point of view and who is in power, but certainly the culture of politics has recently become full of insult and invective and seldom characterized by common courtesy and civility much less compromise and bipartisanship. Would Boorstin be comfortable with the "givenness" of American society during this era of cell phone and social media addiction?

Nevertheless, even as Boorstin developed reservations about the growing power of a national popular culture that appeared capable of undermining "givenness," he remained buoyed by his view that Americans had previously stumbled and yet the nation had still overcome its great follies with even greater achievements. Be that as it may, his concern about the highly ideological tenor of the Cold War hinted at the underlying reluctance of Americans to see themselves in real time, reluctance to see faults in themselves, and certainly reluctance to see themselves as an empire, even if mainly an economic one sustained by the presence of its military prowess, or, domestically, as a generally prosperous nation marred by growing inequality yet displaying little regard for the public sector investments that might mitigate against the growth of extreme inequality.

84 *Understanding the American South*

Harkening back to the nation's sectional Civil War, many historians now perceive that both North and South were proceeding (and competing) on imperial journeys long before the war, moving westward and wresting territories from Native Americans, Mexicans, and others in their quest for empire. The rule of a continent that had not been theirs but seemed theirs for the taking proved too appealing to forego. In the end, the difficulty of dividing the spoils of their quest satisfactorily between North and South, or between free labor and slavery, led to bloody internecine conflict. After the war, the slaveholding South's imperial ambitions were shattered and the free labor North's were redirected for a time by new space for settlement and expansion but would reemerge with some vengeance in the late nineteenth and early twentieth centuries as American business amassed capital, searched for markets and suppliers, and eventually sought world economic dominance.

The vaunted Soviet empire that the United States competed against so bitterly during the Cold War ultimately disintegrated, collapsing under its own weight during the 1980s. The United States, both for its own economic reasons and to stand strong against the Soviets, expanded and used its own empire to espouse a desire for democracy and freedom all while reaping large economic benefits from its status. The American empire of the twentieth century remained an economic empire that flourished without a political structure but with an always looming and often intimidating military strength. American business and finance recognized that the federal government could use its power to support the needs of the economic empire if necessary.

After the demise of the Soviet Union left the United States as the world's single superpower, the nation grew seemingly more vulnerable to random attacks from disgruntled opponents around the world (terrorism) and witnessed the emergence of China as an economic superpower as strict communist management of the economy yielded to allow capitalist incentives to build a strong command economy based on an abundance of low-wage labor and a high level of technological proficiency.

Over the last forty years, except for a brief period under the Clinton presidency during the 1990s, a slow-growing United States economy has not been able to generate and distribute enough resources to jump-start another "Great Compression," like the one fashioned during the period from 1940 through 1973, in which not only did economic output and per capital income rise dramatically, but income and wealth also became more evenly distributed. In recent decades, the growing inequality of income and wealth distribution in the US has produced social tension

The South, Ideology, and American Identity 85

and political polarization that Boorstin would have frowned upon. Boorstin worried about the dangers of excessive commercialization of American culture, largely because that culture provided a key reflection of the "givenness" that he saw as bringing a treasured authenticity to American life and serving as the repository of America's political genius. As the inequality in income and wealth increase even as America enjoys only modest economic growth, more and more questions arise about the future of the American economic empire. In an age in which the moral categories presented in the impressive *Star Wars* saga are widely known, good American republicans must know that all empires come to an end.

Notes

1. Alan Brinkley, *The Publisher: Henry Luce and the American Century* (New York: A. A. Knopf, 2010); Arthur M. Schlesinger, Jr., *The Vital Center: The Politics of Freedom* (Boston: Houghton Mifflin, 1949). See also James L. Baughman, *Henry Luce and the Rise of the American News Media* (Baltimore: Johns Hopkins Press, 2001).
2. Daniel Boorstin, *The Genius of American Politics* (Chicago: University of Chicago Press, 1953), 161–189.
3. Boorstin, *Genius of American Politics*, 8–35.
4. Boorstin, *Genius of American Politics*, 66–98.
5. Bernard Bailyn, *Ideological Origins of the American Revolution* (Cambridge, MA: Harvard University Press, 1967); Bernard Bailyn, *The Origins of American Politics* (New York: Random House, 1967); Gordon Wood, *The Creation of the American Republic, 1776–1787* (Chapel Hill: University of North Carolina Press, 1969); Robert E. Shalhope, "Toward a Republican Synthesis," *William and Mary Quarterly* 29 (January 1972): 49–80; Robert E. Shalhope, "Republicanism and Early American Historiography," *William and Mary Quarterly* 39 (April 1982): 334–356; Drew R. McCoy, *The Elusive Republic: Political Economy in Jeffersonian America* (Chapel Hill: University of North Carolina Press, 1980), 48–75 and 136–165.
6. David Potter, *The Impending Crisis: America before the Civil War, 1848–1861*, completed and edited by Donald E. Fehrenbacher (New York: HarperCollins, 1976); James McPherson, *Battle Cry of Freedom: The Civil War Era* (New York: Oxford University Press, 1988); Eric Foner, *Free Soil, Free Labor, and Free Men: The Ideology of the Republican Party before the Civil War* (New York: Oxford University Press, 1970); Sean Wilentz, *The Rise of American Democracy: From Jefferson to Lincoln* (New York: W. W. Norton & Company, 2006).
7. Boorstin, *Genius*, 94–132.
8. Boorstin, *Genius*, 101–106; Immanuel Wallerstein, "The Rise and Future Demise of the World Capitalist System: Concepts for Comparative Analysis," *Comparative Studies in Society & History*, 16 (September 1974): 387–415, and *The Modern World System IV: Centralist Liberalism Triumphant, 1789–1914* (Berkeley: University of California Press, 2011).

86 *Understanding the American South*

9. Boorstin, *Genius*, 111–112.
10. James Brewer Stewart, *Holy Warriors: Abolitionists and American Slavery* (New York: Hill and Wang, 1976); Elizabeth Varon, *Disunion! The Coming of the American Civil War, 1789–1859* (Chapel Hill: University of North Carolina Press, 2008); Charles B. Dew, *Apostles of Disunion: Southern Peace Commissioners and the Coming of Civil War* (Charlottesville: University of Virginia Press, 2001).
11. Boorstin, *Genius*, 99–118; Sean Wilentz, *The Rise of American Democracy*, 668–744.
12. Lacy K. Ford, "Prophet with Posthumous Honor: John C. Calhoun and the Southern Political Tradition," in Charles Eagles, ed., *Is There a Southern Political Tradition?* (Jackson: University Press of Mississippi, 1996), 3–25 and 207–211.
13. Boorstin, *Genius*, 122–124; Ford, "Prophet with Posthumous Honor: John C. Calhoun and the Southern Political Tradition," 3–25; William Freehling, *The Road to Disunion: Secessionists at Bay*, Vol. 1 (New York: Oxford University Press, 1990), 487–565.
14. Boorstin, *Genius*, 129–132.
15. Boorstin, *Genius*, 126–132.
16. Boorstin, *Genius*, 128–129.
17. Drew Gilpin Faust, *The Republic of Suffering: Death and the American Civil War* (New York: Random House, 2008); Steven Hahn, *A Nation without Borders: The United States and Its World in an Age of Civil Wars, 1830–1910* (New York: Penguin Books, 2016), 192–269.
18. Charles and Mary Beard, *The Rise of American Civilization*, 2 vols. (New York: Macmillan, 1927).
19. Eric Foner, "The Causes of the American Civil War: Recent Interpretations and New Directions," *Civil War History* 20 (September 1974): 197–214; Thomas J. Pressley, *Americans Interpret Their Civil War* (Princeton: Princeton University Press, 1954).
20. George Rogers Taylor, *The Transportation Revolution, 1815–1860* (New York: Rinehart, 1951); Charles G. Sellers, *The Market Revolution: Jacksonian America, 1815–1846* (New York: Oxford University Press, 1992); Richard R. John, *Spreading the News: The U.S. Postal Service from Franklin to Morse* (Cambridge, MA: Harvard University Press, 1995); John Larson, *National Public Works and the Promise of Popular Government in the United States* (Chapel Hill: University of North Carolina Press, 2001).
21. Wilentz, *The Rise of American Democracy*, 359–419; William J. Cooper, Jr., *The South and the Politics of Slavery, 1828–1856* (Baton Rouge: Louisiana State University Press, 1978), 23–224.
22. Michael Holt, *The Rise and Fall of the American Whig Party: Jacksonian Politics and the Onset of the Civil War* (New York: Oxford University Press, 1999); Harry L. Watson, *Liberty and Power: The Politics of Jacksonian America* (New York: Hill and Wang, 1990); J. Mills Thornton, *Politics and Power in a Slave Society: Alabama, 1800–1860* (Baton Rouge: Louisiana State University, 1978).

The South, Ideology, and American Identity   87

23. Michael Holt, *The Political Crisis of the 1850s* (New York: Wiley, 1978); Freehling, *The Road to Disunion*, Vol. 1, 511–535.

24. Foner, *Free Soil, Free Labor and Free Men*; William Gienapp, *The Origins of the Republican Party, 1852–1856* (New York: Oxford University Press, 1987).

25. Foner, *Free Soil, Free Labor and Free Men*, 40–72; Wilentz, *The Rise of American Democracy*, 633–706; William Freehling, *The Road to Disunion: Secessionists Triumphant 1854–1861*, Vol. 2 (New York: Oxford University Press, 2007), 48–144.

26. Thornton, *Politics and Power in a Slave Society*, 333–461; Lacy K. Ford, *Origins of Southern Radicalism; The South Carolina Upcountry, 1800–1860* (New York: Oxford University Press, 1988), 338–373. For discussion of the more problematic states of the upper South, see Daniel W. Crofts, *Reluctant Confederates: Upper South Unionists in the Secession Crisis* (Chapel Hill: University of North Carolina Press, 1989).

27. Abraham Lincoln, "Speech on Kansas-Nebraska Act, 1854," in Richard N. Current, ed., *The Political Thought of Abraham Lincoln* (Indianapolis: The Bobbs-Merrill Company, 1967), 72–73.

28. Lincoln, "Speech on Kansas-Nebraska Act, 1854," in Current, ed., *The Political Thought of Abraham Lincoln*, 76.

29. Eric Foner, *The Fiery Trial: Abraham Lincoln and American Slavery* (New York: W. W. Norton & Company, 2010); James Oakes, *The Crooked Path to Abolition: Abraham Lincoln and the Antislavery Constitution* (New York: W. W. Norton & Company, 2021); William W. Freehling, *Becoming Lincoln* (Charlottesville: University of Virginia Press, 2018).

30. Foner, *The Fiery Trial*, 63–131; Oakes, *The Crooked Path to Abolition*, 1–53.

31. Foner, *The Fiery Trial*, 132–205; Oakes, *The Crooked Path to Abolition*, 99–133.

32. Foner, *The Fiery Trial*, 206–322; Oakes, *The Crooked Path to Abolition*, 176–204.

33. Garry Wills, *Lincoln at Gettysburg: The Words That Remade America* (New York: Simon and Schuster, 1992).

34. Boorstin, *Genius*, 103–106.

35. Boorstin, *Genius*, 175–189.

36. Sven Beckert, *Empire of Cotton: A Global History* (New York: Penguin, 2014), 29–135. For more narrowly focused accounts on the reach of slaveholder ambitions, see Walter Johnson, *River of Dark Dreams: Slavery and Empire in the Cotton Kingdom* (Cambridge, MA: Harvard University Press, 2013); and Edward E. Baptist, *The Half Has Never Been Told: Slavery and the Making of American Capitalism* (New York: Basic Books, 2014); for works raising questions regarding Beckert's argument for cotton as the primary driver of the emerging world economy, see Alan L. Olmstead and Paul W. Rhode, "Cotton, Slavery and the New History of Capitalism," *Explorations in Economic History* 67 (2018), 1–17; Peter A. Coclanis, "Slavery, Capitalism and the Promise of Misprision," *Journal of American Studies* 52 (August 2018): 1–9.

88   *Understanding the American South*

37. Steven Hahn, *A Nation without Borders*, 193–230; Eric Hobsbawm, *The Age of Capital, 1848–1875* (London: Widenfield and Nicolson, 1975), 140–142.
38. Boorstin, *Genius*, 8–10. 29–35.
39. Joseph Schumpeter, *Capitalism, Socialism and Democracy* (New York: Harper and Brothers, 1942); Thomas K. McGraw, *Prophet of Innovation: Joseph Schumpeter and Creative Destruction* (Cambridge, MA: Harvard University Press, 2007), especially 247–484.
40. Daniel Boorstin, *The Image: A Guide to Pseudo-Events in America* (New York: Vintage, 1962) and *The Americans: The Democratic Experience* (New York: Random House, 1973).
41. Boorstin, *Genius*, 161–189.

4

The "People of Plenty"

Abundance and the American South in the Age of Inequality

The post-World War II years produced more than their share of probing inquiries into the shaping of the American national character. Few of these studies have enjoyed as much enduring influence as historian David Potter's *People of Plenty: Economic Abundance and the American Character*, published in 1952. Potter's analysis in *People of Plenty* proved appealing to a nation entering the strongest sustained economic boom in its history while also guaranteeing the interpretation durability. To weave his interpretation together, Potter's concise volume considered the impact of abundance (or plenty) from a variety of perspectives: economic, historical, sociological, cultural, psychological, and even spiritual. A historian unafraid to tackle big questions and cross disciplinary boundaries, Potter devoted nearly half the volume to surveying the broad range of social science literature on the nature of character formation and the role abundance might play in shaping attitudes before narrowing his focus to the impact of abundance on the American national character.[1]

To fully assess Potter's interpretation advanced in the *People of Plenty*, it must be examined as a respectful but intentional and long-overdue corrective to Frederick Jackson Turner's well-known and long-influential essay, "The Significance of the Frontier in American History," originally presented at the 1893 meeting of the American Historical Association (AHA).[2] In this pathbreaking essay, Turner argued that the American national character had been defined primarily by the existence of a frontier: a physical frontier of available land. Turner's frontier generated and regenerated an agricultural society populated largely by self-sufficient farmers seeking both security and opportunity. Once firmly established

90 *Understanding the American South*

on a foundation of self-sufficient agriculture and household competence, these farmers expanded their market output for gain.

Turner's frontier was sustained by the abundance of cheap land available in the nation's thinly settled areas. Indeed, the meaning of the frontier for Turner was not so much a borderland region, or even a cutting edge of human settlement, but the availability of cheap land wherever it existed. In Turner's view, available land fostered the specific character traits in Americans: nationalism, democracy, and individualism. This unique blend of traits, Turner argued, defined the American character.[3] Of the three traits, individualism seemed the most logical product of the frontier. Living where institutions were weak and land cheap offered special opportunities but also special challenges. It took determined individuals and families to settle, tame, and rise on the frontier. In Turner's view, independent households made their own way with little help or support from institutions of any kind. The frontier, Turner argued, also fostered democracy.[4] Self-sufficient, landholding farmers generally met the minimal property requirements for voting and their independence arose from their self-sufficiency. Such independence encouraged an egalitarian ethos and rendered the people of the frontier the ideal republican citizens. On or near the frontier, heredity and background counted for little, actions and results mattered far more. Neither fear nor favor determined their political choices.[5]

The idea that the frontier bred individualism and a spirit of democracy among settlers seemed plausible to many historians and citizens for decades, but Turner's insistence that the frontier nurtured nationalist sentiments appeared questionable at first glance and required further explanation. Turner claimed that the "frontier promoted nationalism" because the people on the frontier, where local institutions were weak, relied on the national government to provide order and security in their areas through the organization of territorial governments, the formation and admission of new states, the funding of internal improvements, and providing military defense against foreign intrusion and the potential hostility of Native American nations. Historians writing during the second half of the twentieth century have argued differently, pointing out, for example, that empirical evidence revealed that Whiggish ideas of national development enjoyed less support from self-sufficient farmers on the frontier than did the rival Democratic appeal for the protection of the independent freeholder from emerging concentrations of economic and political power. Turner likely overstated his case, but without question, the protection the national government offered against external

Abundance and the South in the Age of Inequality 91

foes remained the chief guarantor of safety and opportunity in frontier areas.[6] Turner's essay emerged from its time. Turner wrote his essay in the final decade of the nineteenth century, a century in which westward expansion represented opportunity and prosperity in the minds of many American families craving upward mobility. Some of these families came from northern free soil regions; others came from southern slave-based economies as white southerners, both with and without slaves, moved aggressively into prosperous new cotton-growing regions in Alabama, Mississippi, Louisiana, and later Texas. From the upper South and lower North, farm families moved to Ohio, Indiana, Illinois, and eventually Kansas to produce corn and grain in abundance. Further North, hard-pressed New England farmers flowed into Michigan, Wisconsin, Minnesota, and northern Illinois to escape the limited fertility and hilly terrain of their counties of origin in favor of the open plains of new "western" states. Turner wrote at a time in which the geographic frontier had visibly shaped American life in powerful ways.[7]

Abraham Lincoln's Illinois of the 1850s provides a perfect example of a Turnerian frontier. Even though part of a well-established state, rich agricultural land in central and southern Illinois remained thinly settled by farmers scratching out a hard living until railroads arrived in the 1850s, transforming an isolated rural hinterland into a thriving region for commercial agriculture as profitable crops of grain were easily transported by rail to Chicago and emerging urban markets further north and east as well as by boat down the Mississippi River to supply plantations owned by southern slaveholders. The pre-presidential Lincoln's character and his Whiggish worldview was much formed by his participation in bringing improvement and enhanced prosperity to central and southern Illinois during this era.[8]

During the 1890s, however, the United States Bureau of the Census announced, using a technical definition of "frontier" – one based on the number of inhabitants living within a certain number of square miles – that the American frontier had officially closed. This Census Bureau finding had no impact on population mobility or settlement patterns, but the announcement stimulated Turner's thinking, leading to his AHA paper and subsequent essay considering the impact of the frontier's closing on the American character. In view of the Census Bureau's announcement, Turner worried the official closing of the frontier might initiate a gradual erosion of those defining qualities that made America great and simultaneously render it vulnerable to European-style social stratification, deference, and hierarchy. In that sense, Turner's work stood as both a

92 *Understanding the American South*

celebration of the role of the frontier in shaping the American nation but also a lament over the possible consequences of its closing.[9]

Though appearing nearly sixty years later, Potter's work presents a long-forming critique and refutation of Turner's thesis. In fact, recognizing the lingering popularity the frontier thesis still occupied in the public mind, Potter devoted an entire chapter of *People of Plenty* to a critique of Turner's argument. Though aware of the many penetrating critiques historians and others had offered of Turner's thesis in the sixty years since it first appeared, Potter focused on incorporating Turner's insights while subordinating them into his own interpretation emphasizing American abundance. In Potter's view, the frontier had not exerted the primary formative influence on the American national character, as Turner argued, but, in the nineteenth century, it had played a key role in generating the agricultural abundance that did provide that dominant influence.[10]

Potter judged Turner's frontier a vague and ill-defined construct which seemed more a synonym for economic opportunity than a geographic area. To be sure, Potter acknowledged, the frontier, conceived broadly as the availability of land for settlement and the development for agriculture and commerce in new regions, opened doors of opportunity for an ever-growing population to achieve economic competence and upward social mobility. But, Potter argued, Turner's frontier served as the location rather than the source of prosperity. Open land was a place of opportunity, but it was the abundance produced there, rather than the frontier itself, that shaped the character of nineteenth-century Americans.[11]

Potter conceded that the frontier facilitated the creation of economic abundance throughout the nineteenth century, but in twentieth-century America industry and commerce extended abundance long after the agrarian frontier had officially "closed." In the twentieth century, the location of abundance shifted from the nation's productive farms to its towns and cities where industry emerged, factories appeared, and finance and commerce flourished. Geographic mobility played a key role in the shift of American opportunity from rural areas to towns and cities. While not a guarantee of upward mobility, geographic mobility facilitated new economic opportunity. Perhaps most importantly for Potter, geographic mobility allowed Americans to embrace the myth of equality; not equality of circumstances but equal opportunity to seek better circumstances.[12]

Opportunity shifted from the agricultural frontier of the nineteenth century to industry and commerce in the nation's towns and cities during the twentieth century. By the 1920s, a majority of Americans lived in towns and cities rather than rural areas. The republic of Jefferson's

Abundance and the South in the Age of Inequality 93

yeoman farmers became a democracy of shopkeepers, captains of industry, and factory workers as well as farmers. Moreover, Potter thought that abundance, and the ideological claim it had on the American public, emerged not from the existence of economic equality but from the broad availability of a rough-hewn equality of opportunity, a reasonable chance for success, for upward social mobility. The availability of upward mobility did not mean all would rise but that all would have a chance to rise.[13]

By the time Potter wrote his volume, the Turner thesis had been challenged by historical and sociological studies which documented the existence of social stratification in virtually every area of the country during their frontier years. Almost without exception, these studies found class division and social hierarchy in community after community, both in the nineteenth and early twentieth century. And this hierarchy and these classes appeared soon after the communities formed on the frontier. By the late nineteenth century, these divisions generally formed broad social categories best described as moneyed elite, middle class, working class, and poor. But whatever the reality, Potter believed, social class in the United States was presumed malleable. One could rise into the middle class and fall out of it, and rise into it again, all in one lifetime.[14]

In addition to geographic mobility, a second characteristic of American abundance, in Potter's analysis, was its support for the nation's democratic political system. Potter argued, with considerable justification, that American abundance made American democracy both possible and durable. In nations of scarcity, class conflict usually ended with a revolt of the many, often successfully suppressed, against the tyranny of the few. Typically, the few were from an upper class, the military, and the church, but in the twentieth century the few sometimes emerged initially from the peasantry or the proletariat. Abundance made it possible for Americans not to descend into the class warfare common in areas in which scarcity reigned. American abundance allowed the nation's robust democracy to flourish without the emergence of intense and bitter class conflict because it both allowed social mobility and nurtured the larger myth of social mobility to flourish in the United States.[15]

Potter also worried that American plenty had encouraged the nation's commitment to serving as champions of democracy around the world. This national mission, Potter feared, stood as an article of faith to most Americans. This faith concerned Potter, who thought that too many Americans were unaware that many of the circumstances which made democracy work in the United States were lacking in other parts of the

94   *Understanding the American South*

world, or that illiberal and undemocratic forces that remained weak in the United States flourished in other parts of the world. Such undemocratic forces consisted of state-supported churches, powerful monarchies, ruling aristocracies, imperial powers, and restless masses. In nineteenth-century America, critics of slavery had deemed it just such an illiberal and undemocratic institution. But the broad embrace by southern slaveholders of the idea of a "democracy for white men" as a suitable form of government coupled with the racism of many northern whites effectively blunted or contained the critique that slavery was anti-democratic for many decades.[16]

Essentially Potter worried that Americans had conceived of democracy as an "absolute value largely ideological in content and equally valid in any environment." Instead, Potter argued, American democracy stood simply as "as one of the major by-products of abundance." Such a national misunderstanding of democracy's origins, Potter believed, led the American nation to embarrassing misadventures around the world and sustained a certain naiveté about how to address the nation's internal challenges. Americans' arrogance, or perhaps merely shortsightedness, too often rendered them hypocrites in the eyes of the world. What Americans touted as equality meant rough equality of opportunity in an environment where abundance made opportunity available on a widespread basis. Such conditions did not exist in much of the world, and certainly not in all places where Americans tried to export their democratic ideas. What was truly unique about the American experience in self-government, in Potter's view, was not its attachment to democracy but its experience of plenty.[17]

In Potter's view, the importance of abundance in shaping the American national character received even further amplification through the explosion of advertising in the early twentieth century. Nothing repeatedly reminded Americans of the expansive national plenty and their personal access to the advantages of that abundance like advertising, and particularly mass media advertising. Advertising had been around in some form for centuries, and nineteenth-century publications (chiefly handbills and newspapers) were full of advertisements of one sort or the other, but in the twentieth century, first with the rise of modern mass-circulation newspapers and magazines, quickly followed by movies, radio, and ultimately television, changed the nature and scope of advertising dramatically.[18]

Advertising, once dominated by local or regional products, became a tool for developing national brand identity. For example, the rise of

Abundance and the South in the Age of Inequality

major national brands of cigarettes, a large money-maker for most of the twentieth century, would have been improbable without advertising, leaving the industry where it started with a variety of local and regional tobacco products. The same could be said for automobiles and the rapid emergence of three major automakers dominating the American landscape. In Potter's view, advertising did not cause the rise of a consumption (as opposed to production) mentality in the United States, but it greatly accelerated the advance of a consumer culture. This culture hastened the transformation of Americans from a people who drew their identity from what they produced to an identity defined largely by what they consumed.[19]

Advertising served as a major driver of an increasingly consumer-oriented society. Potter compared its influence with that of schools and churches, arguing that while religious and educational institutions cultivated a measure of social control and a common standard of social values, advertising served only to stimulate an emotional desire to acquire and enjoy. Churches, Potter insisted, "sought to inculcate virtue and consideration of others," and schools had "made it their business to stimulate ability and to impart skills." Together, churches and schools "have been very conscientious about their roles as guardians of the social values," Potter contended, and "have conducted themselves with a considerable degree of social responsibility." Potter even credits the free enterprise system with at least "stressing hard work and the sinfulness of unproductive occupations," though the validity of the latter claim may have weakened over time.[20]

But the consumption ethic often proved oblivious to the broader social good or even individual responsibility. Advertising, Potter maintained, had "no motivation to seek to improve the individual or to impart qualities of social usefulness." Advertising, in Potter's view, exercised "immense social influence" over the public but "has no social goals" concerning its influence except that of promoting the sale and consumption of a particular product. In his judgment, advertising lacked any "inherent social purpose." The scope of advertising's influence, compared to that of religion and education, led Potter to voice "concern" about its role in shaping the American character in the middle of the twentieth century. Advertising possessed "vast power to influence values and conduct," Potter contended, but its ultimate purpose was simply "one of stimulating [people] to consume or to desire to consume." More simply put, advertising encouraged people to consume with little concern for the broader social value, if any, of the product consumed.[21]

96   *Understanding the American South*

Potter's judgments revealed his considerable discomfort about the nation's emerging consumer society. He worried out loud about the decline of institutions teaching citizenship and social values and the rise of an institution, backed with extraordinary funding from those who profited from it, dedicated to the "exploitation of material drives." In Potter's mind, Jefferson's producers' republic had been transformed into a consumer's democracy preoccupied with enjoying a cornucopia of goods and services. Yet despite his personal judgment of the transformation, Potter knew that the transformation was facilitated by an economy of abundance rather than an economy of scarcity. Advertising's emergence as a powerful influence reinforced Potter's larger argument: The driving influence of economic abundance (or plenty) in shaping the American national character. An economy of abundance shaped the character of Americans as a "people of plenty."[22]

Ironically, Potter's final chapter, devoted to concluding his case for abundance as the single most formative influence on the American national character, ended his overall argument with a whimper rather than a bang. Potter drew heavily on human psychology and human development theory as part of closing argument for the influence of abundance on the formation of the American family. Potter sought to prove that even practices of child-rearing and human development in the United States were strongly shaped by abundance. His examples, clearly tied to practices and trends in early postwar America, failed to stand the test of time. For example, Potter perceived feeding babies with formulas and bottles rather than through breast milk as a positive scientific advance made possible by national abundance. In more recent decades, health and medical experts have established that, in most instances, breast milk provides the best sustenance for infants and helps them acquire needed immunities.[23]

Potter's book hit closer to its target when he attributed the emergence of the nuclear family in the immediate postwar years to American abundance. The nuclear family and its attendant division of labor emerged chiefly from plenty. In agricultural America, a family division of labor flourished. Virtually everyone in the household worked, with the division of labor falling largely along the lines sentimentally portrayed in the television series *The Waltons*, which enjoyed immense popularity in the 1970s. In that elegiac saga, beginning in the Depression era, the father, John Walton, his eldest son, John-Boy, and eventually younger sons Jason, Ben, and Jim-Bob, ran a sawmill business while also working on a farm. John's wife, Olivia, and their three daughters along with John's

Abundance and the South in the Age of Inequality 97

aging mother performed cooking, housework, and other farm chores. In the new urban industrial economy, families in the industrial workforce often sported two wage-earners, though women almost always held lower-paying jobs and generally retained the primary role in caring for children. The emerging middle-class nuclear family of the 1950s looked more *Leave It to Beaver* than *The Waltons*. *Leave It to Beaver* sported a two-parent nuclear family with two children. The dad, Ward Cleaver, trekked off daily to an unspecified white-collar job (and occasionally working overtime in his study at his comfortable two-story home in a nice neighborhood). June Cleaver, the attractive stay-at-home mom, cooked meals and performed housework, often in nice dresses, usually wearing heels; the happy homemaker as fashion-setter.[24]

However exaggerated these television images were, Potter pointed out that households had grown smaller and their residences larger. Extended families were giving way to nuclear ones as household incomes rose. In 1950, the average household in the United States had 4.6 rooms with 3.1 people living within and 84 percent of all dwellings reported fewer than one person per room. Potter believed this data affirmed his points that child development, family structure, and residential preferences in the nation were powerfully shaped by abundance. Abundance influenced the private and familial as well as the public lives of Americans, and hence exerted a "pervasive influence in the shaping of American character."[25]

Potter advanced a powerful case that for over a century and a half abundance had exercised the predominant influence on the American national character. He effectively argued that the frontier Turner posited as the chief formative influence on the American character had only served as a surrogate for the truly dominant influence: economic abundance and opportunity. The influence of abundance remained formative as the United States shifted from an agricultural to an industrial nation in the late nineteenth and twentieth centuries. Industrialization and the rise of consumer products encouraged Americans to express that fondness for plenty in the marketplace.

Yet Potter failed to note that "plenty" was in decidedly short supply in the postbellum American South. The formerly enslaved Blacks, now emancipated, to a significant degree due to their own efforts during the war, had earlier represented a large proportion of wealth as well as labor in the region. With new labor arrangements uncertain and more and more global competition from other cotton suppliers, per capita income in the American South fell to not much more than half the national average and remained there, at least in the lower South, until the World War II era.

98 *Understanding the American South*

The single great exception to American prosperity remains the Great Depression of the 1930s, which lasted from the stock market collapse in late in 1929 until the acceleration of production for World War II which occurred in 1940 and 1941. As the Depression deepened from 1929 to 1933, public confidence in the economy waned. Misery spread across the nation with levels of unemployment reaching 25 percent and per capita income falling so dramatically that it did not return to 1929 levels for eight years. Radical movements from left and right enjoyed a short-lived resurgence.[26]

Fear stalked the land in 1932 and 1933. When Franklin Roosevelt took over as president in March 1933, he felt compelled to rally Americans by telling them they had "nothing to fear but fear itself."[27] During the early years of Roosevelt's New Deal, relief, recovery, and reform legislation produced modest but clearly insufficient economic gains, but even those modest gains were undermined early in FDR's second term by both the administration and Congressional efforts to reduce spending before such reductions made fiscal sense. Full recovery did not occur until FDR and the nation stumbled its way into the Keynesian remedy of stimulus from deficit spending as the nation poured money into gearing up for a worldwide fight against Nazis and Fascists. As spending rose and the New Deal social safety net moved into place, prospects for upward mobility in America were restored.[28] Even then, however, the Roosevelt administration recognized the underperformance of the American South when compared to national norms and labeled the South the "nation's no. 1 economic problem." Overall, the Great Depression had threatened the American confidence in abundance that Potter later described as the defining trait in the American national character. But the threat had proven short-lived, and the robust long-term recovery more than restored the nation's underlying confidence in abundance.[29]

During the post-World War II era, other sweeping theories explaining the American national character challenged Potter's "people of plenty" for preeminence. Urban historian Arthur Schlesinger argued that the formation of large cities shaped the modern character of the American nation.[30] Scholars from Oscar Handlin to John Higham reminded readers that America was a nation of immigrants, and that immigration shaped the national character in critical ways, including through the concept, however flawed, of America as a "melting pot" nation. C. Vann Woodward, the distinguished southern historian, argued that the "Age of Free Security," the inexpensive safety which the nation enjoyed from 1815 to 1914, allowed Americans to resolve their differences and expand

Abundance and the South in the Age of Inequality 99

territorially while paying little for defense because they enjoyed the protection of oceans and the British navy in an era of limited military, especially naval, technology.[31] Harvard political scientist Louis Hartz argued that the absence of strong conservative bastions of power, such as an established church, a hereditary, titled aristocracy, or a monarchy and royal family allowed for the nation's founding in a liberal constitutional tradition that thrived across generations.[32] Historian Daniel Boorstin argued that something in the nation's practical, anti-ideological DNA gave America a "givenness" that sustained its success.[33] But while there remained many players on the stage, Potter's insistence on understanding Americans as a people of plenty still enjoyed respect and influence, and perhaps preeminence, especially as American prosperity grew to become the envy of the world during the post-World War II economic boom.[34]

Ironically, the periodic recessions and the occasional depression scattered through American history strengthened rather than weakened Potter's argument for abundance as the dominant trait in the American national character. The American response to these periodic hard times has seldom involved widespread doubt about the capacity of Americans to bounce back. Instead, the American response has most often been predicated on a drive to sacrifice in the short term while striving to restore good times. Americans make do with less for a while but usually for only short periods of time, and chiefly for the purpose of returning to prosperity as soon as possible.

World War II produced new anxieties, but wartime spending and production also brought strong signs of coming prosperity. After immediate postwar struggles with the economy's shift to peacetime production, postwar prosperity took hold by 1948 and prevailed with only brief disruptions until the international Oil Crisis of 1973. The latter crisis ushered in a long period of "stagflation," that damning combination of high inflation and high unemployment. Stagflation not only doomed Jimmy Carter's presidency but also lent momentum to the emergence of a new pro-business, limited government political agenda (labeled "movement conservatism") optimistically projected by Ronald Reagan as candidate and president in 1980. This agenda, featuring large tax cuts and large deficit spending (chiefly on defense), combined with the lingering benefits of Carter's unpopular but necessary austerity program to produce the seemingly vigorous economic boom of the mid-1980s.[35]

The overall economic story of American life since 1973, however, has been one of episodic booms and busts. The booms have generally lasted a bit longer than the busts, but since the early 1970s prosperity has proven thin and quite unevenly shared, even by American standards. The top 1 percent of the nation's population has garnered a much a larger share of the income and wealth over the past fifty years while a large majority of Americans shared a shrinking portion of national income and national wealth. As income and wealth gaps widened, social dislocation, resentment, and alienation have deepened among growing portions of the population.[36]

In recent years, a flurry of works by academic economists have focused on the causes and effects of slow economic growth with benefits unevenly shared across the population. This impressive wave of scholarship has confirmed that the century between 1870 and 1970, the era of the second industrial revolution, provided 100 years of unprecedented increases in productivity that generated high rates of growth and raised the American standard of living dramatically while reducing income inequality, despite the negative impact of the Great Depression during the 1930s. The 1870–1970 period, the true American Century in terms of the economy, produced impressive growth and spawned the notable inventions and innovations of the second industrial revolution, which included electricity, the internal combustion engine, the automobile, refrigeration, home appliances, air travel, and many others. These innovations transformed American lifestyles by bringing electricity into homes, making automobile transportation common, rendering groceries, even ones requiring refrigeration, readily available, and generally creating the comforts of modernity for more and more Americans between 1920 and 1970, and especially during the quarter century following World War II.[37]

With the highly significant exception of the Great Depression era, 1929–1941, the years between 1917 and 1948 produced both strong economic growth and increasing income equality. Using national income tax data available since 1917, studies show that between 1917 and 1948 American household incomes grew at an average annual rate of 1.11 percent, with the incomes of the bottom 90 percent of households growing faster (1.43 percent) than those in the top 10 percent (0.58 percent). The lower rate of income growth for the nation's top 10 percent was largely due to the collapse of the great fortunes of the wealthy during the Great Depression.[38]

The vaunted post-World War II economic boom, which lasted roughly from 1948 to 1973, brought unprecedented prosperity to Americans as personal incomes grew more rapidly than ever. The annual growth rate for the postwar boom period was more than twice that of the 1917–1948 period. Moreover, during the postwar era, the incomes for the bottom

Abundance and the South in the Age of Inequality 101

90 percent and the top 10 percent grew at the same rate, an exceedingly robust 2.58 percent annually. No period before or since has matched the remarkable, and evenly shared, growth exhibited during the postwar boom. The broadly shared prosperity of this postwar quarter century made this period resemble the "American Century" Henry Luce had proclaimed in 1941. But it only lasted about thirty years.[39]

The remarkable surge in postwar prosperity triggered a significant qualitative change among American household attitudes that held long-term significance. Americans gradually shifted their primary identity away from that of producers to that of consumers. Several factors contributed to this transformation of identity. The identity of Americans as producers dated back to its pre-Civil War-era self-image as a nation of farmers, artisans, and craftsmen and continued well into the late nineteenth and early twentieth centuries. The producer identity followed Americans from farm and craft work into factories, where they produced steel and cars and engines and a variety of other tangible goods, taking considerable pride in their work ethic and craftsmanship still. Workers were drawn to unions that protected that identity. But during the unprecedented postwar boom, as discretionary income rose at a record pace and the availability of modern conveniences multiplied and television emerged as a powerful advertising medium in virtually every home, household consumption exploded. Average American families prided themselves more on what they purchased, consumed, and owned than on what they produced. While the rapid growth of income which spurred the new consumerist orientation did not prove sustainable, the dominant role of consumerism and consumer identity persisted. Giving sustenance to Potter's theory regarding abundance, and the American standard of living became the nation's social glue. A family's consumption patterns reflected its identity. The producer ethic waned slowly but surely.

Since the postwar boom ended in the early 1970s, overall income growth has slowed dramatically compared to that during the postwar boom. In fact, the annual growth rate of all incomes since 1973 has been a mere 0.58 percent, less than a quarter that of the postwar boom years. This slow growth rate has undermined the comparative economic standing of the United States compared to the rest of the world. The much-bruited American standard of living is no longer the highest in the world, at least in terms of the commonly used metrics, but rather the 13th highest, just ahead of Great Britain, a nation viewed by many Americans as a nostalgic remnant of its former greatness. If levels of inequality are factored in, the United States performance looks even worse, falling to 24th,

102   *Understanding the American South*

well behind Singapore, Japan, and South Korea. Moreover, not only has the growth rate been modest, but gains made during the period of slow growth remain stunningly unevenly shared. The incomes of the nation's top 10 percent doubled from $161,000 in 1972 to $324,000 in 2013. But during those same decades, the incomes of the lower 90 percent rose very slightly from $35,411 in 1972 to $35,653 in 2013 (after peaking at a modest $37,053 in 2000 and then falling back).[40]

Upon closer examination, the growing inequality problem within the American income distribution proves even more troubling than it first appears. Over two-thirds of the income growth in the period was captured by the top 1 percent of households. Calculations developed by Nobel laureate Paul Krugman revealed that even within the flourishing top 10 percent, the benefits of growth were skewed radically to the top 1 percent and not the trailing 9 percent. Between 1977 and 1989 the incomes of the households in 90th to the 95th percentiles increased by 18 percent, and the incomes of those in the 95th through the 99th percentile rose by 24 percent, both substantial increases, but the income of the top 1 percent rose by a whopping 100 percent. Simply put, the income of the top 1 percent doubled in just over a decade. Moreover, of all the income growth American households experienced between 1977 and 1989, 70 percent went to the top 1 percent. Since the 1990s, slow growth and a more unequal distribution of income have only worsened. The share of the nation's income captured by the top 1 percent of earners has increased by 1,200 percent while the share of the lower 90 percent has remained essentially flat since 1970. As the trend continued, corporate CEOs who earned only about twenty times worker pay in 1973 earned over 250 times worker pay by the early 2000s.[41]

American wealth is even more unevenly distributed than income. In the early 1990s the top 1 percent earned 12 percent of the income but controlled 37 percent of the wealth. By 2013, the top 1 percent received 20 percent of income but owned 40 percent of the wealth. Worse still, the share of the top 0.1 percent's wealth has increased by 400 percent. Moreover, race, ethnicity, and gender still matter. In the United States, women's wages are 83 percent of men's, Black men average 73 percent of white men's pay, and Hispanic men's only 69 percent of white men's wage.[42]

Moreover, the trend toward even slower growth and greater inequality appears likely to continue for the next several decades. Why? As economist Robert Gordon noted, growth is now sailing into at least four strong economic headwinds: rising inequality, the declining quality of

Abundance and the South in the Age of Inequality 103

K-12 educational outcomes in the United States compared to the rest of the world, the changing demography of the American workforce due to an aging population and a declining birth rate, and the possible challenge of future national debt service. All the factors serve as possible drags on efforts to achieve higher growth rates.[43]

So, why did the incomes of the bottom 90 percent remain flat or fall since the 1970s? The earnings (chiefly wages and salaries) of the bottom 90 percent have experienced many downward pressures since 1973, including increasing international competition, job and wage competition from new immigrants, a sharp decline in levels of unionization and hence bargaining power, increased productivity resulting from technical innovation and automation, and the decline (in real dollar terms) of the minimum wage. Moreover, the steady decline in the number of higher-wage manufacturing jobs available during the years since 1973 remains particularly concerning. As machines have replaced workers in manufacturing and competitive global imports have entered US markets, the nation lost an average of 372,000 manufacturing jobs per year between 1985 and 2010. Taking an even longer view, the proportion of manufacturing jobs in the US economy has declined from 30 percent in 1953 to 10 percent or less currently. Union membership declined by half, from 27 percent in 1973 to 13 percent in 2013. Empirical evidence revealed that while most displaced blue-collar workers found jobs, they typically found lower-paying service economy jobs because skilled manufacturing employment grew increasingly scarce.[44]

These job losses hit high-wage blue-collar workers in stalwart industries such as automobiles and steel particularly hard. America's great industrial heartland in the upper Midwest turned into a "Rustbelt." The development of the heartland had been historically sustained by the steadily increasing productivity of workers and investments in new machinery by successful industrial firms. As the industrial heartland devolved into the Rustbelt, it hemorrhaged manufacturing jobs. In just ten years, 2000–2010, the steel-making city of Cleveland lost 17 percent of its population and auto-making Detroit a whopping 25 percent. Moreover, between 1949 and 1970 the hourly wage of the typical American worker (a forty-year-old male with a high school diploma and twenty years of experience) doubled, but since 1978 that same worker's real wage has declined by 25 percent.[45]

As experts have looked closely to find explanations for rapidly increasing inequality during periods of overall growth, geographic mobility, education, and the agglomeration economies of local areas emerged as key factors. The geographic mobility of the American workforce has long been a key to its prosperity. Prior to 1980, workers willing to move for opportunity proved more likely to experience wage increases than those who were not. Recent studies affirm what simple observation suggests: The twenty-first-century job market for professionals and other white-collar occupations is a national one while the job markets for manual and less skilled workers often remain very local. Strong ties to a home community can be a wage trap for workers because they become reluctant to move to areas where opportunities are better. Less geographic mobility also makes workers more likely to become and remain unemployed for longer periods of time.[46]

Education levels also serve as a key factor in rising inequality since well-educated individuals are generally more mobile than less educated ones. This point is buttressed by evidence showing that college graduates, the group showing the highest mobility, have the highest employment rate, while high school dropouts, the group with the lowest mobility, have the highest unemployment rates. Education facilitates mobility and both education and mobility individually promote increased earning capacity. Less educated and less mobile workers face multiple challenges for employment, much less wage growth.[47]

In his impressive book *The New Geography of Jobs*, University of California-Berkeley economist Enrico Moretti explains this new geography of inequality. He argues that the United States is now divided into three Americas: "Brain Hubs," areas which generate higher salaries for both skilled and unskilled workers; "brain drain" areas from which the brightest and most skilled have fled for the thriving "brain hubs," leaving their former locales characterized by low labor skills, low salaries, and rising unemployment; and, finally, a middle tier of areas where decisions yet unmade may determine into which of the two divergent camps they ultimately land.[48]

Moretti sees these patterns as part of the "Great Divergence" (others call it the "Great Divide"), as demographic trends push metropolitan areas and even regions nationwide toward a status as either a "brain hub" or a talent, brain, and population drain area (such as many cities in the Rustbelt and other older industrial areas). These trends have been pronounced since 1980. Well-educated people (college graduates) flock to cities already populated disproportionately by college graduates, while people with only high school degrees increasingly cluster in areas where other high school graduates are most numerous. Broadly prosperous white-collar cities and struggling blue-collar ones populate the national landscape.[49]

Abundance and the South in the Age of Inequality 105

The Great Divergence carried with it many connotations. The divergence involved not only an income divide but also an educational divide, a class divide, a complex geographic divide, racial and ethnic divides, and all manner of cultural divides. All these divides were interrelated and entangled in complex ways. Each variable in the mix was interdependent on other variables. Even complex regression models encounter difficulty sorting out causation. But after conducting such analyses and giving keen scrutiny to impressionistic evidence, Moretti concludes that technology and education loom as the key drivers of regional and local economic success in the new economy. Between 1980 and 2010, in those "brain hub" cities with a high percentage of college graduates, the incomes of those college graduates increased by over $22,000. In contrast, during the same period, the incomes of college graduates in cities with a small percentage of them grew by only $8,000. Strikingly, even service workers and high school graduates enjoyed a higher standard of living if they lived in one of the dynamic brain hubs. Moreover, these high school graduates pulled to hot economies earned sufficiently higher incomes in these booming hubs than in stagnant Rustbelt areas to more than offset the significantly higher cost of living in the brain hubs.[50]

Even more recently, the Covid pandemic which swept the nation in the Spring of 2020 encouraged smart brain hub college graduates to work from home using technology, both reducing their exposure to the Covid virus and their time for journeys to work. As a result, tech- savvy college grads began leaving the most expensive brain hubs (New York, Boston, San Francisco, and Washington, DC) for less expensive and more livable (lower housing process, less traffic congestion, and, in some cases, better weather) brain hubs, such as Austin, Dallas, Nashville, Atlanta, Tampa, Denver, and Phoenix among others.[51] The exodus of college graduates from high-cost-of-living brain hubs to lower-cost-of-living and more convenient brain hubs proved dramatic during the pandemic. Metro San Francisco lost 25,000 college graduates net in 2021, metro Washington lost nearly 20,000 net that year, and most spectacularly, metro New York lost over 100,000 college graduates net in 2021. Overall, these large and expensive metro areas lost a net of nearly 250,000 college graduates in 2021 alone. Eight of the twelve most expensive areas in the US experienced a net loss of college graduates in 2021, with New York leading the way with a net loss of over 103,000 college graduates, followed by the San Francisco–San Jose area which lost a net of over 48,000 college graduates that year, and Washington, DC which lost a net of 15,000 college graduates in 2021. But confirming Moretti's argument concerning the continuing appeal of brain hubs (just less expensive and more livable ones) to college graduates, thirty-six of the forty-two smaller-sized and less expensive metro areas showed a net gain of college graduates in 2021, with Phoenix (23,000), Austin (21,000), Houston (19,000), Denver and Tampa (each with 17,000), Nashville (16,000), and Dallas (15,000) leading the way.[52] Nonetheless, recent outmigration of college graduates from the most expensive and inconvenient brain hubs to other brain hub cities with lower costs and less inconvenience, simply illustrates the broadening appeal of brain hub cities and the advantages they offer college graduates without doing anything to uplift declining industrial blue-collar cities and rural areas.

Given the weight of the data at hand, the existence of dramatically increased inequality of opportunity seems undeniable. The Great Divergence displayed not simply a crazy quilt of local and regional differences but also a common thread of increasing inequality of both income and wealth in an era of slow economic growth. As we move well into the third decade of the twenty-first century, complaints about growing inequality within the American economic system appear credible. Inequality continues to worsen. Critics are not talking about only the bottom quarter of the population facing a wider gap between themselves and the rest of the population but the bottom 90 percent falling further and further behind the top 10 percent. Even among the top 10 percent, those most economically successful Americans, nine of ten are falling further and further behind the nation's top 1 percent. And the top one-tenth of 1 percent, today's captains of technology, finance, and entertainment, amass fortunes and earnings that might even have made the so-called "robber barons" of the Gilded Age blush.[53]

In addition to this growing economic divide, the nation is also experiencing a political divide. To be sure, it is hard to discern whether the bitterness and polarization prevalent in the nation during and shortly after the Age of Trump reflects an enduring trend or is simply the product of a series of recent events and immensely skillful political campaigns designed to polarize Americans into competing camps so party elites can gain and use power. This political and social moment might prove a brief and transient one in the nation's history. But it could also be part of an emerging trend fostered by increasing disparities of wealth and flattening levels of growth. Class, educational, racial, and gender divisions join purely geographic ones in shaping the recent political polarization. The fact that some of the forces driving increased inequality result directly from political decisions and others from growing corporate power,

Abundance and the South in the Age of Inequality   107

which has close connections to political power, suggests these changes have prompted political reactions. Perhaps what is less understandable, beyond acknowledging the growing power of large contributions in our political campaigns, is that the backlash has not been more powerful or more tightly focused.

To dramatically oversimplify the American political landscape as revealed by the 2020 election, the Blue Democrats apparently have an edge in the popular vote, having won the largest number of popular votes in seven of the last eight presidential elections. Moreover, despite high negatives among voters, Hillary Clinton received nearly four million more votes that Donald Trump in the 2016 election, and in 2020, Joe Biden garnered over seven million more votes than the incumbent Trump. But the conservative red voters have a critical strategic advantage: They typically carry more states, and thus can muster a constitutional (electoral college) majority in presidential elections without winning the popular vote. And they have, in fact, done so twice in the last twenty-five years (2000 and 2016). Moreover, Republicans still control most governorships and state legislatures and have effectively configured apportionment of those legislatures and drawn Congressional districts in a manner that makes it difficult for Democrats to increase or even maintain their Congressional representation. The sharpness of the political divide makes it hard to find shared approaches to addressing the challenges raised by slow growth and increasing economic inequality.

Solutions to the slow growth and rising inequality in the economy have, thus far, proven elusive. The patterns of growth and inequality reflect patterns of educational achievement and geographic clustering that are difficult to resolve or reverse in the short run. In the first instance, improved education for all would appear a partial but obvious remedy. But neither federal nor state governments have been willing to ramp up investment in K-12 education. The result of a challenged public school system is the flight of upper-middle-class children to private and church-supported schools, a move doubtless designed in part to give these children of comfort a better chance to remain on the favorable side of the great economic divide.

Nor have federal or state governments invested in helping children from disadvantaged backgrounds and impoverished areas achieve a better chance to get a college degree or develop valuable job skills. State funding for public universities and colleges has grown more and more stinting since the 1970s, forcing higher tuition rates as academic institutions strive to maintain academic quality. Reduced public funding also militated against expanded access for less affluent students. Apparently forgetting the importance of the GI Bill to the success of the "Greatest Generation," this disinvestment in higher education has rendered it more difficult for many to earn a college degree, a valuable credential in the competition for good jobs and higher incomes, and led too many others into accumulating a heavy debt to pay for college.

Without question, inequality in America has grown measurably worse since the 1970s, and prospects for a new convergence appear dim. For the purposes of this chapter, however, the key question remains: How does the self-image of Americans as a "people of plenty" survive, much less flourish, in the face of forty years of slow growth and deepening inequality? Can plenty serve as a unifying faith when growing inequality suggests that abundance for the few may create diminished abundance for the many? What does nearly forty years of slow economic growth and increasing inequality portend for the future?

If Potter's theory that abundance has been the dominant formative influence on the American character is correct, what will define that national character if we are no longer the people of plenty? Without that social glue of abundance, what will the nation hold together? If the nation remains in the vortex of such a sustained increase in inequality, how can abundance or plenty remain a unifying influence?

To be sure, the abundance underpinning Potter's interpretation has never been evenly shared. Much of its formative character lay in the idea that "plenty" was there for the seeking, not that it flourished among all. Yet a sustained pattern of increasing inequality through long periods of slow economic growth does raise new questions about how the mindset of American plenty can endure as patterns of inequality deepen and harden over decades. Moreover, rather than dampening or meliorating the impact of growing inequality, current political alignments tend to reinforce and even deepen the inequality divide. Pressure is rising among the disadvantaged and their advocates for more overt efforts to reverse the decades-long trend toward greater inequality, especially as it runs along racial, ethnic, and gender lines. The strength of this movement is difficult to assess given the heavily polarized political atmosphere, but intense concern about worsening inequality raises serious questions about the American perception of themselves as a people of plenty. America's Second Gilded Age, marked by the rise of great wealth and widening gaps between the top 1 percent and the rest of the nation, suggests that the very idea of plenty could ultimately become a casualty of inequality.

Abundance and the South in the Age of Inequality 109

Still, for the optimists among us, our national history suggests that the American faith in abundance can survive economic ups and downs and even sharp social divisions. The true promise of plenty lies as much in its psychological appeal to Americans as in tangible proof that it exists on the ground. Modern brain science teaches that emotions tend to override reason in human decision making.[54] The survival of plenty's appeal may depend on just that: retaining its promise to the American people in an era of economic anxiety.

Notes

1. David M. Potter, *People of Plenty: Economic Abundance and the American Character* (Chicago: University of Chicago Press, 1954).
2. Frederick Jackson Turner, "The Significance of the Frontier in American History," in *Annual Report of the American Historical Association for the Year 1893* (Washington, DC: American Historical Association, 1894), 199–227. For an overview of where Turner's interpretation stands after nearly a century of revision, see William Cronin, "Revisiting the Vanishing Frontier: The Legacy of Frederick Jackson Turner," *Western Historical Quarterly* 18, no. 2 (1987): 157–176.
3. Turner, "The Significance of the Frontier," 199–227.
4. Turner, "The Significance of the Frontier," 199–227.
5. Chilton Williamson, *American Suffrage: From Property to Democracy, 1760–1860* (Princeton: Princeton University Press, 1960); Merrill Peterson, *Democracy, Liberty, and Property: The State Constitutional Conventions of the 1820s* (Indianapolis: Bobbs-Merrill, 1966); Fletcher M. Green, *Constitutional Development in the South Atlantic States, 1776–1860: A Study in the Evolution of Democracy* (Chapel Hill: University of North Carolina Press, 1930).
6. Steven Hahn, *A Nation without Borders: The United States and Its World in an Age of Civil Wars, 1830–1910* (New York: Penguin, 2016), 79–113.
7. Colin Woodward, *American Nations: A History of the Eleven Rival Regional Cultures of North America* (New York: Penguin, 2011).
8. William W. Freehling, *Becoming Lincoln* (Charlottesville: University of Virginia Press, 2018), 14–80.
9. Turner, "The Significance of the Frontier in American History," 199–227.
10. Potter, *People of Plenty*, 142–165. Lacy K. Ford, "Frontier Democracy: The Turner Thesis Revisited," *Journal of the Early Republic* 13, no. 2 (1993): 144–163 provides a comprehensive reassessment of Turner's thesis on the one hundredth anniversary of its publication. Earlier efforts to rehabilitate Turner's interpretations include Stanley Elkins and Eric McKitrick in "A Meaning for Turner's Frontier, Part I: Democracy in the Old Northwest," *Political Science Quarterly* 69, no. 3 (1954): 321–353, and "A Meaning for Turner's Frontier, Part II: The Southwest Frontier and New England," *Political Science Quarterly* 69, no. 4 (1954): 565–602.

11. Potter, *People of Plenty*, 142–165.
12. Potter, *People of Plenty*, 91–110.
13. Potter, *People of Plenty*, 74–90.
14. Potter, *People of Plenty*, 91–110. Important early criticisms of Turner on these points emerged from Benjamin F. Wright, "Democracy and the American Frontier," *Yale Review* 20 (1930): 349–365.
15. Potter, *People of Plenty*, 111–127.
16. George Frederickson, *The Black Image in the White Mind: The Debate over Afro-American Character and Destiny, 1817–1914* (New York: Harper and Row, 1971), 43–70; George Frederickson, *White Supremacy: A Comparative Study in American and South African History* (New York: Oxford University Press, 1981), 150–162; Lacy K. Ford, "Making the 'White Man's Country' White: Race and State Constitutions in the Jacksonian South," *Journal of the Early Republic* 19, no. 4 (1999): 713–737.
17. Potter, *People of Plenty*, 128–134.
18. Potter, *People of Plenty*, 166–188.
19. Potter, *People of Plenty*, 111–127.
20. Potter, *People of Plenty*, 172–187.
21. Potter, *People of Plenty*, 164–186.
22. Potter, *People of Plenty*, 78–141.
23. Potter, *People of Plenty*, 189–208.
24. Potter, *People of Plenty*, 195–196.
25. Potter, *People of Plenty*, 195–196.
26. David M. Kennedy, *Freedom from Fear: The American People in Depression and War, 1929–1945* (New York: Oxford University Press, 1999), 10–217; William Leuchtenburg, *Franklin D. Roosevelt and the New Deal, 1932–1940* (New York: Harper's, 1963), 1–117; Robert J. Gordon, *The Rise and Fall of American Growth: The U.S. Standard of Living since the Civil War* (Princeton: Princeton University Press, 2016), 535–555.
27. Roosevelt quoted in Leuchtenburg, *Franklin D. Roosevelt and the New Deal*, 41.
28. Leuchtenburg, *Roosevelt and the New Deal*, 143–196; Zachery D. Carter, *The Price of Peace: Money, Democracy, and the Life of John Maynard Keynes* (New York: Random House, 2020), 286–307.
29. Potter, *People of Plenty*, 120–125.
30. Arthur Meyer Schlesinger, Sr., *The Rise of the City, 1878–1898* (New York: Macmillan and Co., 1933).
31. Oscar Handlin, *The Uprooted: The Epic Story of the Great Migrations which Made the American People* (Boston: Little Brown, 1951); John Higham, *Strangers in the Land: Patterns of American Nativism, 1860–1925* (New Brunswick: Rutgers University Press, 1955); C. Vann Woodward, "The Age of Reinterpretation," *American Historical Review* 66, no. 1 (1960): 1–19.
32. Louis Hartz, *The Liberal Tradition in America* (New York: Harcourt, 1955), 35–86.
33. Daniel Boorstin, *The Genius of American Politics* (Chicago: University of Chicago Press, 1953), 29–35, 163–170.

Abundance and the South in the Age of Inequality 111

34. Gordon, *The Rise and Fall of American Growth*, 329–532, 538–589.
35. Joseph E. Stiglitz, *People, Power, and Profits: Progressive Capitalism for an Age of Discontent* (New York: W. W. Norton & Company, 2019), 22–236; Gordon, *The Rise and Fall of American Growth*, 389–521, 605–642; Sean Wilentz, *The Age of Reagan: A History, 1974–2008* (New York: HarperCollins, 2008), 73–322.
36. Gordon, *The Rise and Fall of American Growth*, 652–655.
37. Enrico Moretti, *The New Geography of Jobs* (Boston: Houghton Mifflin, 2012), 73–120; Gordon, *The Rise and Fall of American Growth*, 339–592.
38. Gordon, *The Rise and Fall of American Growth*, 25–328.
39. Gordon, *The Rise and Fall of American Growth*, 331–532; Alan Brinkley, *The Publisher: Henry Luce and the American Century* (New York: A. A. Knopf, 2010).
40. Gordon, *The Rise and Fall of American Growth*, 566–639; Krugman, *Arguing with Zombies: Economics, Politics and the Fight for a Better Future* (New York: W. W. Norton & Company, 2020), 259–296; Joseph Stiglitz, *The Price of Inequality* (New York: W. W. Norton & Company, 2012), 1–34.
41. Gordon, *The Rise and Fall of American Growth*; Krugman, *Arguing with Zombies*; Stiglitz, *The Price of Inequality*.
42. Thomas Picketty and Emmanuel Saez, "Income Inequality in the United States, 1917–1998," *Quarterly Journal of Economics* 118 (2003): 1–39.
43. Gordon, *The Rise and Fall of American Growth*, 645–648.
44. Moretti, *The New Geography of Jobs*, 22–30; Gordon, *The Rise and Fall of American Growth*, 643–644. See also Enrico Moretti and Pat Kline, "People, Places and Public Policy: Some Sample Welfare Economics of Local Economic Development Programs," *Annual Review of Economics* 6 (2014): 629–662.
45. A sampling of the literature on this subject includes: Thomas J. Sugrue, *The Origins of the Urban Crisis: Race and Inequality in Postwar Detroit* (Princeton: Princeton University Press, 1996); Anne Trubek, ed., *Voices from the Rustbelt* (New York: Picador, 2018); Jonathan Metzl, *Dying of Whiteness: How the Politics of Racial Resentment Is Killing America's Heartland* (New York: Basic Books, 2019); J. D. Vance, *Hillbilly Elegy: A Memoir of a Family and Culture in Crisis* (New York: HarperCollins, 2016).
46. David Autor, David Dorn, and Gordan Hansen, "The China Shock: Learning from Labor-Market Adjustment to Large Changes in Trade," *Annual Review of Economics* 8 (2016): 205–240.
47. Moretti, *The New Geography of Jobs*, 178–214.
48. Moretti, *The New Geography of Jobs*, 73–120.
49. Moretti, *The New Geography of Jobs*, 121–242.
50. Moretti, *The New Geography of Jobs*, 226–229. But see also David Autor, David Dorn, and Gordon Hansen, "When Work Disappears: Manufacturing Decline and the Fall of Marriage Market Value of Young Men," *NBER Working Paper* 231712, 2018.

51. Emily Badger, Robert Gabeloff, and Josh Katz, "Coastal Cities Priced out Low Wage Workers, Now College Graduates Are Leaving Too," *New York Times*, May 16, 2023.
52. Badger, Gabeloff, and Katz, "Coastal Cities Priced out Low Wage Workers."
53. Moretti, *The New Geography of Jobs*, 154–177.
54. Jonathan Haidt, *The Righteous Mind: Why Good People Are Divided by Politics and Religion* (New York: Random House, 2012).

PART III

UNDERSTANDING SLAVERY, RACE, AND INEQUALITY IN THE AMERICAN SOUTH

5

The Problem of Slavery Reconsidered

The South, the Nation, and a Reflection on "The Travail of Slavery"

In the early 1960s a distinguished group of southern historians collaborated to publish a collection of essays, *The Southerner as American*, dealing broadly with the dual identity of southerners, especially white southerners, as both American and southern.[1] The growing momentum of the direct action phase of the civil rights movement, the increasing isolation of the American South as a last political redoubt of de jure white supremacy outside of Rhodesia and South Africa, and the South's status as a growing embarrassment to the United States in its Cold War competition for the hearts and minds of "colored" peoples around the world gave the volume special salience. Edited by Charles Sellers, best known at the time as the biographer of James K. Polk and a perceptive student of the Jacksonian-era American party system, also authored the contribution, "The Travail of Slavery," which proved the most enduring essay in the volume. Seller's essay struck a chord among a growing cohort of white southerners (though still hardly a majority) who felt some sense of collective guilt over the region's history of slaveholding and its continuing embrace of racial segregation. The essay also hit a nerve among recalcitrant southern whites who saw either nothing to apologize for in the region's collective behavior or felt that it had suffered enough economically to expiate any lingering guilt.[2]

For Sellers, the travail of slavery lay in the question of how southerners could be good democrats and good Christians and still defend slavery as a bedrock social and economic institution. In his essay, Sellers offered a well-grounded historical argument that the antebellum American South's commitment to defending slavery contradicted its revolutionary-era heritage of "democracy" and its early nineteenth-century embrace of

115

evangelical Christianity. Attempting to square these values – values of democracy and Christianity – with a full-throated defense of slavery created a tension, perhaps even an element of cultural dissonance, which Sellers termed the "travail of slavery." This travail, Sellers argued, created deep and suppressed guilt among white southerners.[3]

A native of North Carolina, Sellers completed his undergraduate degree at Harvard before earning his doctorate in history from the University of North Carolina, Chapel Hill. He then joined the faculty at Princeton before leaving the Ivy League for the University of California-Berkeley. Well-researched in manuscript collections, scholarly monographs, and other materials, Sellers' influential essay nonetheless took his key examples of the proslavery argument from familiar figures: John Calhoun in politics, George Fitzhugh in sociology, and James Thornwell in religion. Scholars working in the more than half century since Sellers' essay appeared have mined even more sources and found more nuance and subtlety in slaveholder statements.[4] But in fairness, Sellers' brief essay recognized that the proslavery argument was complicated and varied across space and time, and that the argument touting slavery as a positive good (rather than a necessary evil) gained significant traction chiefly after 1835, and that it faced considerable opposition from within the white South even over the last two antebellum decades.[5]

Influenced by the psychological literature of the post-World War II era, Sellers pondered the deep emotional and psychological impact of the cognitive dissonance affecting liberty-loving, freedom-proclaiming, God-fearing, and Bible-reading slaveholders, who, Sellers believed, clung to slavery even though they somehow knew or suspected that it was dead wrong. Slaveholders could, and did, find, in Sellers' view, rationales for holding slaves but none that could really convince them. Sellers argued that slaveholding was inconsistent with either Christian morality or the political freedoms proclaimed in the Declaration of Independence and protected by the United States Constitution.

For Sellers, the post-secession emancipation of slaves by self-action, war, presidential proclamation, and constitutional amendment also represented an emancipation of the white southern conscience from guilt, anxiety, and tortured allegiances – an end to the agony of arguing strained positions at odds with their American and Christian heritage. Sellers maintained that the resolution of the slavery question by force of arms lifted an ideological burden from white southerners, and perhaps even freed them from the guilt of defending a highly visible, if all too convenient, sin.[6] Sellers advanced a plausible argument, but it ignored that

The Problem of Slavery Reconsidered 117

for many slaveholders, and other white southerners, emancipation also meant the loss of slave property, the loss of their primary labor force, and the loss of racial and political control (however temporarily), and raised deeply troubling questions about how to maintain white supremacy in a society without slavery. Moreover, Sellers' interpretation downplayed the frustration and deprivation that defeat imposed on white southerners.[7]

All contributors to Sellers' volume accepted the notion that southerners were also Americans and that the dualism of being both southern and American remained a conundrum which white southerners struggled to resolve. Sellers, like many other historians of the time, worked in the long shadow cast by Harvard political scientist Louis Hartz, whose *The Liberal Tradition in America* shaped the understanding of both American history and American life during the first decade after its appearance in 1955. Part of a larger search for roots of American exceptionalism that flourished in the aftermath of World War II, Hartz's sweeping overview emphasized, at least in round terms, the strength of the liberal tradition in the United States from the time of the Declaration of Independence forward. Moreover, Hartz insisted that a broad liberal consensus dominated American political thought throughout the nation's history.[8]

But in his search for an internal foil for liberal hegemony in America, Hartz looked for a conservative tradition in a society whose distinctiveness was largely defined by slavery: the American South. Hartz believed that he had found efforts to create a "reactionary enlightenment" in the antebellum American South during the first half of the nineteenth century, as the powerful slaveholding elite, which Hartz believed controlled politics in the region (even though this elite appeared to have popular sanction for its efforts), sought ideological shelter by steering away from the nation's liberal heritage and toward more conservative doctrines. Hartz termed this effort the "great reaction," which he dated to the era of the nullification crisis fomented by South Carolina the late 1820s and early 1830s and continued down to the time of secession and Civil War.[9]

Hartz's work exerted a strong influence on Sellers' essay by positing a liberal norm that white southerners embraced even as they were increasingly challenged to offer a conservative defense of slaveholding. Hence the "travail" occasioned by the tension of maintaining a liberal tradition in a slaveholding society. In the end, Hartz concluded, even the tragically flawed slaveholding South could not and would not entirely repudiate the "liberal" values of its Revolutionary heritage. The "Reactionary Enlightenment," perhaps never much more than an idea in Hartz's fertile mind, never enjoyed a coherent identity in the prewar South. The inability

118   *Understanding the American South*

of white southerners to repudiate the principles of the Declaration lay at the heart of what Sellers described as the travail of slavery, at least in terms of political ideology.[10]

Ultimately, in the two decades after Sellers' essay and Hartz's volume appeared, an explosion of scholarship examining the ideological origins of the American Revolution and the era of the early republic concluded that "republicanism" rather than liberalism best defined the ideological origins of the American nation. Eighteenth-century Americans saw property as lying at the heart of its political system, yet they did not view property as giving men a stake in society and hence earning a right to have a say in how they were governed. Instead, property rendered its owners "independent," uniquely able to remain uncontrolled and uncorrupted by patronage and manipulation because they could provide a competence or sufficiency for themselves and their family without dependence upon patrons, estate-holders, capitalists, and speculators.[11]

The idea of a good republican society embraced by the founders carried with it social and economic dimensions as well as political values. Political corruption loomed as a grave danger to republican government when too much of the population was dependent upon others for their livelihood. Dependency produced a vulnerability to influence, manipulation, and the other temptations of corruption. Independent men – and American republicanism proved a very male-centered ideology – could remain unbought and unbossed no matter how strong the allurements power-hungry politicians used to woo them. At least according to republican theory, extreme economic and social inequalities in society were signs of aristocratic power or excessive government patronage. Yet republican ideology was not a leveling ideology. It allowed for a broad range of wealth and occupations. But it nonetheless held that societies producing extremes of wealth and poverty but lacking a broad middle-range of occupations, such as family farmers, shopkeepers, and artisans in the United States, were not likely to sustain successful experiments in republican government.[12]

This may seem a digression into the history of early American popular political thought, but it is necessary to understand how scholars' understanding of Sellers' essay evolved as the premise of Hartzian liberalism as the ideology of the American founding eroded within a decade after Sellers published "Travail." Yet even though thoughtful scholars conceded that eighteenth- and early nineteenth-century American politics hardly cherished liberalism and democracy as those concepts were commonly understood in mid-twentieth-century America, those scholars adapted Sellers'

The Problem of Slavery Reconsidered 119

arguments to suggest that the existence of slavery nonetheless created tension between those who defended slavery while also embracing the republican values that had shaped the Jeffersonian and Jacksonian political and ideological world. After all, slavery bred inequality; it fostered, as Jefferson suggested, a fondness for the power of mastery (as dangerous an expression of power as any other), and it barred a dangerously large proportion of the population from enjoying even the minimal rights of citizenship and blocked any avenue for attaining those rights that others might have.

Over time, however, some proponents, especially slaveholding proponents of republican values, grew comfortable with some degree of inequality, and increasingly southern politicians used republicanism's suspicion of dependency to render slavery a viable alternative to the dangers of a large, free, yet readily manipulated population such as the English peasantry (or later the working class). Moreover, by the Jacksonian era, American republicanism had gradually replaced property holding and militia service with "whiteness" and maleness as the appropriate measures of entitlement to suffrage and citizenship. This proved a nationwide trend, but it emerged with special vigor across most of South. As republicanism gradually embraced the idea that independence and political rights rested on "whiteness," all adult white males gained privileges regardless of economic or social status. Thus, for many white southerners of the Jacksonian era, the answer regarding how slavery could be squared with democratic values proved simple: Democracy was intended only for white men.[13]

Hence white southerners defended slavery as a system which defined truly dependent laborers out of the body politic while also letting almost all white men in. Still, within nineteenth-century southern politics, a subject Sellers knew exceedingly well, partisan differences emerged over how independence was best maintained. The Whig party, which emerged in the 1830s in opposition to President Andrew Jackson and his supporters (who shortened their party name from Democratic-Republicans to just Democrats), saw the expansion of material wealth and moral probity as the best methods of defending independence and virtue in an expanding republic. Whigs advocated the process of collective uplift, of material and moral progress, and expanding the economic and educational base of republicanism. Jacksonian Democrats, on the other hand, thought that independence was best served by using the power of government to prevent concentrations of power and wealth which might threaten individual autonomy (hence Jackson's popular "war" against the Bank of

120 *Understanding the American South*

the United States). Jackson's veto of the bank's charter threated the very financial stability of the Union, Whigs declared, but Democrats praised Old Hickory for killing a monster that threatened the autonomy of independent producers.[14]

From an ideological standpoint, slaveholders found it easy to reconcile slaveholding with republican theory even if founders such as Madison and Jefferson had emphasized inconsistencies and even incompatibilities between slaveholding and republicanism. Slavery solved the "dependency" problem inherent in republicanism for southern society by defining the dependent working class, or at least the bulk of it, out of the body politic on the bases of race and enslavement. Slavery bolstered the "independence" of masters and their households, regardless of the size of their holdings. Moreover, as manufacturing became a larger part of the northern economy, proslavery proponents expressed concern over the influence of dependent wage laborers in "free labor" society. Champions of free labor and upward mobility, such as Abraham Lincoln, who entered politics as a Whig, retorted by ridiculing the southern definitions of independence as one resting on some men taking their living "from the sweat of other men's brows" when those men had no meaningful opportunity to "rise." In Sellers' view, the contradiction between either a democratic ethos or a devotion to republican values and a commitment to slavery represented nothing less than a conscience-rending contradiction faced by many white southerners.[15]

Even more conscience-rending for white southerners, Sellers insisted, stood the stark contradiction of values presented by evangelical Christianity and slaveholding. The growing strength of evangelical Christianity in the early nineteenth-century South emerged as the second pillar of Americanism in Seller's case for a "travail of slavery." Evangelicalism promoted values decidedly different from those of republicanism, a civic ideology which carried a measure of moral content but barely touched on issues of religion or salvation. In contrast, evangelical Christianity, with its message of personal relationships with God, salvation, and eternal reward for faith, usually evidenced by good works during one's lifetime, carried a personal and emotional message on values and moral responsibility that ran even deeper than the civic code of republicanism.[16]

As the grip of evangelical Christianity, and even to a lesser degree the nonevangelical varieties of Christianity, strengthened their grip on antebellum southern society, and religious arguments defending slavery often found themselves in tension (or openly at odds) with the overtly

The Problem of Slavery Reconsidered

racist or profit-driven arguments supporting the institution. This tension, Sellers opined, "defined the Old South's central dilemma." In Sellers' view, the religious proslavery argument championed the "familial view of the peculiar institution," while the economic and racial arguments for slavery contradicted the paternalist approach on key points. Proponents of the race and profit arguments assumed that the logic of white supremacy justified their absolute power over members of an "inferior" race. But southern whites touched by the evangelical movement countered that those Christian slaveholders proved to be "good," caring stewards of their dependents. These would-be paternalists balked at the severe punishments of slaves which remained all too common, and sometimes offered stinging critiques of slaveholders' sexual behavior as mulatto children appeared on many plantations. As the antislavery critique from the North intensified, the external criticism galvanized the white South into a defensive posture, and the argument that Christian paternalism offered the best method of slave control, and perhaps the only morally defensible one, gained traction.[17]

Ironically, as evangelical religion strengthened nationwide, it pushed North and South in very different directions. In the slaveholding South, it spawned wider and wider support for the notion that a generous application of Christian "paternalism" provided the "reform" required to render slaveholding both compatible with Christian morality and defensible to the larger world. In the North, Protestant evangelical Christianity generated many reform movements (including Sabbatarianism and temperance), while also providing the critical moral foundation, and no small portion of the activists, for the abolition movement. Certainly not all northern evangelicals were abolitionists and not all abolitionists were evangelicals, but evangelicals and their values certainly lent much support and energy to growing abolition sentiment in the North.[18]

As antislavery sentiment grew in the North, paternalist ideology gained strength in the South. Yet even before abolitionist William Lloyd Garrison's "immediatism" gained a following in the North after 1833, occasional northern criticism of slavery left many white southerners stung by attacks on their morality, no matter how glancing the blows. During the Missouri debates of 1820, Georgia Senator Freeman Walker insisted that the slaveholding states "yielded to none on the practice of benevolence and humanity," and North Carolina's Nathaniel Macon defended slaveholding, noting that aging slaves in the South "are better taken care of than any poor in the world, and treated with decent respect by all their white acquaintances." South Carolina's William Smith, an

Understanding the American South

Upcountry cotton planter, went even further, shocking his Senate audience by claiming, in direct and intentional contradiction of the famous words of Thomas Jefferson, that the "the whole commerce between master and slave is patriarchical" and insisting there was often "nothing but the shadow of slavery left" among whites and enslaved Blacks who had grown up together.[19]

A decade and half later, after Garrison began publication of *The Liberator*, South Carolina's John C. Calhoun articulated the South's special sensitivity to the relentless moral critique of slaveholding emanating from the abolition petition and mail campaigns of the mid-1830s. Calhoun argued that the abolition petition and mail campaigns mounted a "war" of "a very different character" against the South. Calhoun insisted that the abolitionists had launched a "war of religious and political fanaticism ... waged not against our lives but our character. The object is to humble and debase us in our [own] estimation, and that of the world in general, to blast our reputation, while they overthrow our institutions." In such a war, Calhoun declared, "we cannot remain here in an endless struggle in defense of our character, our property, and our institutions." The slaveholding South, Calhoun insisted, "must meet the enemy at the frontier ... it is our Thermopylae." The result of the constant outpouring of abolitionist propaganda would be, Calhoun predicted, that "in the course of a few years" the next generation of northerners will "have been taught to hate the people and institutions of nearly one-half of this Union, with a hatred more deadly than one hostile nation ever entertained towards another." Calhoun thought it easy "to see the end" of such hatred: "We must become, finally, two peoples."[20]

Sellers' provocative interpretation of slaveholder attitudes suggests that white southerners grappled with a variety of concerns regarding slavery, but his essay comes up well short of proving that white southerners overwhelmingly felt guilt over holding slaves or living in a slaveholding society. Since the publication of Sellers' groundbreaking essay, two generations of historiography on slavery, slaveholders, and the Old South have added richness and complexity to our understanding of slaveholder attitudes and ideology, both complicating and ultimately weakening Sellers' case for slaveholder guilt. To be sure, some antebellum white southerners considered slavery a moral wrong. But these same white southerners often reasoned that they could not find a safe and affordable way to eliminate it. Sellers hit closer to the point when he recognized that southerners often held conflicting attitudes toward slavery. Beyond the question of the morality of slavery in the abstract, questions

The Problem of Slavery Reconsidered   123

arose about the economic vitality of slavery over the long term, over white safety in a society with a large number of enslaved Blacks, and over the moral responsibilities of masters toward their slaves in areas of daily treatment and religious instruction. Moreover, whatever reservations southern whites held about slavery, they usually proved reluctant or unwilling to give up the economic benefits slavery brought to the region or to accept the risks they associated with the presence of large, free, Black populations.[21]

Sellers, of course, was hardly the first or only student of the Americans South to talk about the guilt and anxiety generated by slavery, and that substantial body work was well surveyed by Gaines M. Foster in 1990.[22] Historian William Dodd, a committed southern progressive writing in the early twentieth century, discussed southern attitudes toward slavery in terms of ambiguous moral sentiments.[23] More famously, in 1941, as the South emerged from the Great Depression, Charlotte-based journalist W. J. Cash's classic *The Mind of the South* observed with great passion that the South had been menaced "by the specters of defeat, shame, of guilt – a society driven by the need to bolster its morale, to nerve its arm against waxing odds, to justify itself in its own eyes and the eyes of the world." In "its secret heart," Cash claimed, the South suffered from "a powerful and uneasy sense of the essential rightness of the nineteenth century's position on slavery."[24] Despite all the criticism of Cash's remarkable volume, one written with great emotional power if not scholarly precision, it likely influenced Sellers' formulation of his "travail" argument more than two decades later. Six years before Sellers' essay appeared, noted Civil War historian Bell I. Wiley judged "a sense of guilt over slavery" as one reason for the "inordinate quarrelsomeness among Confederates" during the Civil War.[25] And Foster found the idea of southern guilt a steady thread in C. Vann Woodward's well-known essay "The Search for Southern Identity." In that essay, Woodward argued the South not only failed to persuade the nation that slavery was a "positive good" but also "failed even to convince itself." Indulging momentarily in psychohistory, Woodward ventured that the white South suffered "the torments of its own conscience until it plunged into catastrophe to escape."[26] Surely, if just this once, Woodward mistook outcomes for intentions.

After the publication of Sellers' essay in 1960, historians plunged into the topic, drawing heavily on Sellers' provocative insights but using them more as matter for comment and speculation than detailed investigation. In his classic 1966 monograph on the nullification crisis in South Carolina, *Prelude to Civil War*, historian William Freehling identified

124   *Understanding the American South*

what he perceived as deep anxiety and ambivalence among slaveholders even in the heavily slave South Carolina Lowcountry. Freehling used the word guilt far more often than Sellers had, even referring at times to the "acute guilt" he believed South Carolina planters felt. And, in Freehling's view, after the failure of nullification to unify the South, white South Carolinians embraced the proslavery argument and sought to gain tighter control over their slaves. Freehling suggested that these efforts were successful enough that by 1861, they had "probably eased the guilty consciences of many slaveholders."[27]

Two years later, Freehling's mentor and distinguished historian of slavery and sectional conflict, Kenneth Stampp, attributed Confederate defeat, at least in part, to a "weakness of morale." Stampp portrayed defeat as a "reward" which offered white southerners "a way to rid themselves of the moral burden of slavery." He used the weakness of white resistance in occupied areas, the failure of guerilla movements to emerge after Appomattox, and the white population's initial acquiescence to the end of slavery as evidence that guilt had been lifted by defeat and emancipation. Yet surely the loss of over 300,000 lives, the deprivation extracted by a prolonged war, the inexorable and destructive march of Sherman's blue-clad army across much of the deep South, and the seemingly endless capacity of the Union to support the war effort may also have had much to do with the weakening of Confederate will and resistance and the acceptance of defeat and emancipation. In short, white southerners' recognition that they were soundly defeated or badly "beaten," as South Carolina journalist Ben Robertson later phrased it, may have had more to do with acceptance of the war's results than a release from guilt.[28]

Over time, Sellers' essay attracted less and less enthusiasm from the profession as historians working on a variety of different issues found far fewer reservations about slavery and a far stronger embrace of its benefits among white southerners than Sellers had acknowledged. Instead, the three decades of scholarship following Sellers generally found that southerners readily adapted their political ideology to defend slavery against external criticism. White southerners felt less guilt over slavery than concern for white safety and less ideological whiplash than a sense that the American North was advancing toward a political radicalism never entertained by the founders.

Nevertheless, the theme of "guilt over slavery" remained a steady undercurrent in the study of the pre-Civil War South. In the late 1980s, a group of southern historians contributed a volume, *Why the South Lost*

The Problem of Slavery Reconsidered

the Civil War, that again posited moral unease over slavery as a source of ambivalence toward the Confederacy itself. According to the authors, this ambivalence enhanced other divisions within the hastily formed Confederacy, and together these divisions helped doom the Confederate war effort to failure. Apparently, in the eyes of these scholars, the great irony of southern history was that slavery provided a strong justification for secession but left white southerners too ambivalent about the institution to make the sacrifices the war required.[29]

The most powerful refutation of Sellers' travail thesis emerged from the impressive scholarly corpus of Eugene Genovese and Elizabeth Fox-Genovese, who argued that by the early nineteenth century slaveholders had thoroughly repudiated their liberal, revolutionary heritage to build a conservative, hierarchical social order willing and able to defend the region's political rights and intellectual and cultural virtues. Genovese and Fox-Genovese saw white southerners as seeking a genuine embrace of a traditional social order and political conservatism, a society at odds with the rest of the United States and not bashful about defending itself (and slavery) from the mounting criticisms of the northern bourgeois world. Genovese's early work focused on the precapitalist, hierarchical nature of the antebellum southern social order and explaining how the very presence of slave labor in the society led the region toward a more nonbourgeois social order that stood outside the increasingly capitalist society of the free labor North. In Genovese's view, the precapitalist nature of the slaveholding economic order grew largely from its reliance on personal dominion (styled as paternalism) as the chief mechanism for labor control. The slaveholders' level of personal control established the Old South as a nonmarket-driven society, and hence conservative and seigneurial, resembling, though not duplicating, landed aristocracies in other parts of the world.[30]

Over time, the work of Genovese and Elizabeth Fox-Genovese evolved, focusing less on its precapitalist mode of labor control and more on the impact of slavery on the entire southern social order and on the conservative values heavily influenced by the southern version of Protestant Christianity. In the minds of Genovese and Fox-Genovese, James Thornwell replaced George Fitzhugh as the Old South's leading social thinker, and the influence of conservative religious leaders loomed as more important than that of political theorists. Still, Genovese and Fox-Genovese had little patience with Seller's guilt hypothesis, arguing that conservative religious white southerners generally embraced their role as moral stewards of their "dependents" without hesitation.[31]

Indirectly, my own *Deliver Us from Evil* (2009) offered a contribution to the "travail of slavery" debate. The book argued that there was no one southern view of slavery and that seeing the Old South as a monolith that changed little over time was wrong-headed and misleading. Instead, the so-called Old South was constantly being made, unmade, and remade by people and events while different parts of the region evolved differently. White southerners held a wide variety of different views on the moral, economic, and political propriety of slaveholding, and that those views both differed across subregions of the South and evolved significantly over time. Moreover, tensions over various issues related to slavery were very much a part of everyday life and these tensions covered a much broader set of attitudes and feelings than simply guilt, which played only a marginal role in white southerners' evaluation of slavery as an institution. The book concluded that the Old South grappled with tensions, contradictions, inconsistencies, and dilemmas regarding slavery and did so mostly with relatively little guilt but with considerable greed, fear, anxiety, arrogance, concern, uncertainty, and divided allegiances.[32]

In the upper South, the ideological tension between the republican ideals of the founding generation and the existence of slavery loomed large during the early national era and proved the source of much political debate. But the practical importance of maintaining an appropriate racial balance in the region's population arguably loomed even larger. As the continued use of slave labor appeared less critical to the economic future of the region with the comparative decline of tobacco as a cash crop, many upper South political leaders sought a demographic reconfiguration of the region. They sought such a reconfiguration through the colonization of free Blacks and some slaves combined with a vigorous diffusion of slaves across the South, a diffusion driven by the sale of enslaved people from the upper South to the booming cotton regions of the lower South. Such a demographic reconfiguration did not promise to diminish the ideological tensions between slaveholding and the founders' republican ideals nationally or even in the South, but it would enhance the safety of whites in the upper South, slow the growth of the region's free Black population, bring an infusion of capital into the region through the sale of enslaved people, and widen avenues of prosperity for free whites in region, particularly in towns, cities, and other areas not dominated by plantation agriculture. While ideological reservations about slavery persisted in the upper South to a much greater degree than in the lower South, the travail of slavery in the upper South lay in how to "whiten" the region gradually to protect and enhance white safety

The Problem of Slavery Reconsidered

and open new economic opportunity without sacrificing precious capital invested in slaves or the subregional economies of those portions of the upper South where slavery remained much more profitable than available alternatives (such as Virginia's cotton-growing Southside).[33]

In the lower South, anxiety about slavery hinged even more on concerns about white safety than on ideological or moral or economic reservations about slavery. Concern about white safety focused not only on the dangers of insurrection but also on individual acts of slave violence and other forms of slave resistance, and hence ultimately on the difficulty of managing a large and growing enslaved Black population. As periodic cotton booms recurred across the lower South, anxieties related to the growing size and proportion of the enslaved Black population in developing areas waxed and waned with the latest staple profits and most recent gossip on the local grapevine. As the cotton economy penetrated ever more subregions of the lower South, "finding the appropriate balance between economic prosperity and white safety became the chief question concerning slavery in the region." Lower South whites searched for an answer which "allowed whites to have as much of both as possible," but such an answer "remained elusive."[34]

As the antislavery attack on the South intensified after 1833, the lower South sought to resolve any lingering tensions about slavery, including the tension between profit and safety (or greed and fear), through an ideological transformation of the region based on a broad acceptance of paternalism as the ideology of slaveholding, at least as far as defending the region against criticism from the outside, if not in the actual practice of managing slaves. Armed with concepts of demographic reconfiguration (whitening through slave sales and colonization) in the upper South and the ideological reconfiguration (the broad embrace of paternalism as the ideology of slaveholding) in the lower South, the South appeared to have grappled with the problem of slavery and found mechanisms for preventing any of these problems from emerging as a debilitating travail.[35]

Across the last decade or so, a spate of recent scholarship aggressively replaced not only Genovese's portrait of the slaveholding South as a region embracing an anachronistic precapitalist social order but also asserted that the Old South stood as a leader, indeed a driving force, in the emergence of global capitalism. This new literature, now frequently referred to as the "New History of Capitalism," positioned southern slaveholders at the forefront of a world capitalist expansion. This expansion, driven by the high market value assigned certain staple commodities (especially cotton) and a hugely profitable international trade in these staples, left enslaved Black labor as a critical piece of the emerging global economy. According to Sven Beckert's Pulitzer Prize-winning *Empire of Cotton: A Global History*, the global expansion of cotton production, including the explosion of cotton production across the deep South during the first half of the nineteenth century, facilitated the growth of global capitalism even though manufacturing was concentrated in select pockets, which included the northern part of England and the American North. While this joint march of slavery and capitalism seems an improbable contradiction to both classical and Marxist economists, these new accounts highlight a key point: Slavery, both as a trade and as a labor force, proved immensely profitable. Related works by Walter Johnson, Edward Baptist, Joshua Rothman, Caitlin Rosenthal, and others insisted that the dynamics behind American capitalism lay, to a large degree, in the powerful, and often brutal, hands of slaveholders in the American South rather than in efforts of entrepreneurs and industrialists in the free labor North.[36] Ultimately, writing in the 1619 Project, sociologist Mathew Desmond labeled the emerging nineteenth-century economy as "Slavery's Capitalism."[37] Apart from the rigorous debate over whether the southern slaveholders or free labor entrepreneurs and bankers drove American capitalism in the mid-nineteenth century, southern slaveholders' relentless pursuit of wealth through expanding across more and more land, acquiring more and more slaves, expanding investment in profitable staples, and securing new markets involved the expulsion of Native Americans from traditional tribal lands, and the persistence of an active internal slave trade triggered a desire for territorial expansion richly described by Steven Hahn in *A Nation without Borders* (2016) as a contested world of nations without borders, involving nation-states in the competition for land, opportunity, and wealth during the long nineteenth century. Ironically, this process of relentless expansion eventually led to the sectionalization of the American economy and ultimately, for a brief time, a split in the American polity.[38]

Guilt over slaveholding did not loom large in these recent studies of the expansion of cotton capitalism and the role of nation-states in creating a global economy. Whatever reservations antebellum white southerners may have held about slavery – that it was not safe, that it was not morally defensible, that it corrupted white society, and that it proved difficult to defend in an increasingly free labor nation – were overwhelmed by the apparent profitability of enslaved labor and the value of enslaved Blacks as a commodity for trade. Slavery stood as the centerpiece of a

The Problem of Slavery Reconsidered 129

profitable, wealth-producing economic system that could not and would not be easily replaced. As Michael O'Brien, the esteemed intellectual historian of the Old South, concluded, the southern slaveholding elite built a vast "imperial regime" that spread from South Carolina to Texas and whose ultimate failure deserves no sympathy even if it does require understanding.[39]

The very notion of the slaveholding South as an empire is an intriguing one. Arguably O'Brien's youth in a post-World War II Great Britain that was reluctantly yielding much of its once vaunted empire gave him the opportunity to personally understand both the appeal and burdens of imperial projects, and perhaps to appreciate the near inevitability of their eventual decline and fall.[40] The intellectuals and politicians of the Old South knew the history of republics well, so they also knew the history of empires. They risked all in 1860–1861 to save all – to prolong their hegemony – and lost. They did not perceive their decision as a form of disguised suicide but as a calculated gamble for long-term triumph. They were more overconfident than guilty, more bold than timorous, and more arrogant than foolish. That the southern slaveholding regime may have survived longer by remaining inside the Union stands as a reasonable counterfactual argument, even with the free soil Republicans in power. But slaveholders and their allies were playing a long game for triumph rather than simply survival. Their gamble was wrong-headed as well as just plain wrong. But they failed more because the Union army and resistant and rebellious enslaved Blacks brought decisive force to bear against them than because they could not justify the morality of their cause to a questioning world.

In pondering the so-called travail of slavery, post-Civil War generations of white southerners displayed more resentment than guilt, more determination to defend the lost Confederate cause as honorable than to struggle with collective guilt, and more eagerness to defend segregation and maintain white supremacy than to ponder the enduring moral evils flowing from both slavery and racism. The long dominant Cult of the Lost Cause presumed and taught an honorable Old South defeated by a greedy and rapacious North sustained by raw economic and military power. The guilt-ridden South of Sellers' essay appeared occasionally in the troubled conscience of the odd southern white progressive or liberal, but it hardly defined the region's collective response to defeat and emancipation, whether in 1865 or 1877 or 1896 or 1919 or 1948 or even 1964, and perhaps even beyond.

To be sure, a measure of guilt over slavery can be found in some white southerners across many generations. Even during the antebellum era,

130 *Understanding the American South*

those who defended slavery as a necessary evil, arguably the most common view in the upper South and not uncommon in the lower, conceded a degree of moral hazard in accepting slavery as a basis for a society. Even the self-described paternalists of the late antebellum lower South sometimes grappled with the morality of slaveholding and clutched Christianity as a safeguard against moral criticism from others. Defenders of the prevailing postbellum racial caste system sometimes drew critiques from indigenous boosters who saw the rigidity of the caste system as a barrier to the full commercial success of the New South. But seldom did these doubts challenge the prevailing social order or shape debate over its future. The weight of southern guilt varied over time and place and person but rarely emerged as a controlling influence.

The true burden of southern whites across the postbellum decades was not guilt but grief. Or grief-inspired anger. White southerners grieved their defeat, their failure, and grew angry at being defeated (and even humiliated) by the power and might of the Yankees and by the sense of rightness and righteousness that the Yankees drew from their victory, their sense of being more fully American and better than their benighted southern adversaries. White southerners in turn recoiled at the northern scorn and hauteur. But all this rebellion grew not from guilt but from anger and grief, from losing rather than from moral travail. They suffered from being losers not from being sinners. Their travail was not from guilt but from defeat – abject defeat, outright surrender – not from the moral burden of having defended slavery.[41]

In accessing degrees of guilt, as in many things, Abraham Lincoln understood much that others did not. As Union victory neared, Lincoln deemed the guilt for slavery as both national and shared. In April 1864, in a letter to a Kentuckian, Lincoln declared that "[i]f God now wills the removal of a great wrong, and wills also that we of the North, as well as you of the South, shall pay fairly for our complicity in that wrong, impartial history will find therein new cause to attest and revere the justice and goodness of God." By pronouncing "American slavery" a national sin, Lincoln implied that both sides were paying for their sins with the sufferings of war.[42]

Nearly a century after Lincoln's letter, as part of the Civil War centennial observance, southern poet and novelist Robert Penn Warren crafted a perceptive extended essay on the sectionalized legacies of the Civil War, legacies still influential after a hundred years. Writing in 1961, Warren's first sentence boldly declared that "[t]he Civil War is, for the American imagination, the greatest single event of our history." As plans for the

The Problem of Slavery Reconsidered

centennial observance unfolded, Warren's declaration seemed entirely reasonable. At great human cost, the Civil War saved the Union. With more than a little national hesitation and reluctance and bitter opposition from the seceders, but with vigorous assistance from enslaved Blacks themselves, the war also abolished slavery. But, as Warren noted, "it did little or nothing to abolish racism." And it is doubtful that the war and emancipation could have done so, even if trying to abolish racism had been a war aim. Yet with slavery abolished, Warren contended, the defining sectional difference had been eliminated and "a new feeling about union was possible."[43]

But the benefit of hindsight allowed Warren to see that shared sectional guilt was hardly the legacy assumed by North or South during the first century after the war. As Warren weighed the psychological costs of war, he concluded that the war's results had indeed imposed a great psychological impact on both South and North, but that impact nudged them in very different directions. The war, according to Warren, gave the North a "treasury of virtue" and the South a "Great Alibi," neither a worthy tribute to human costs of the war but nonetheless legacies readily embraced in their respective sections.

Warren lamented that the "treasury of virtue" victory had bestowed upon the North not only gave northerners a sense of moral superiority over the wayward and benighted South but also a sense that victory, wealth, and power constituted the inevitable American destiny.[44] Through the "treasury of virtue," the North had been "redeemed." The "treasury of virtue" gave capitalism and democracy an unchecked power which they did not always use wisely, and Warren fretted that a new "treasury of virtue" resulting from victory in World War II lured northerners to embrace Henry Luce's idea of an "American Century," one in which unbridled American power and impressive American wealth stood as the envy of the world. As an American as well as a southerner, Warren regretted that the hubris of victory may have corrupted the northern winners every bit as much as slavery had corrupted and defeat traumatized the white southern losers. In the end, the greatest treasure captured by the American North with its victory was its standing as a "Galahad among nations." The resulting "marriage of victory and virtue," both Warren and the influential Protestant theologian Reinhold Niebuhr feared, lent the North and the nation an "illusion of innocence," leaving the nation struggling to fathom the inevitable "irony of history."[45]

Yet Warren's lament over the North's interpretation of its victory in the American Civil War was surpassed by his deep sorrow that defeat had given the American South "the Great Alibi," a ready-made excuse for all its woes, for its persistent racism and embrace of Jim Crow, for its lingering indifference to poverty, white as well as Black, for the slow and unshared progress of its economy, and most of all, for its resentment of all things not "southern" or "not cherished by white southerners." Or, more simply put, Warren lamented the South's resentment of defeat and all that came with it. After all, it was so un-American to lose, or at least so Americans felt in 1961.[46]

In Warren's view, the Great Alibi "explains, condones, and transmutes everything." It turned the "common lyncher" into a "defender of southern tradition" and "any rabble-rouser" into "the gallant leader of a thin gray line of heroes." It excused pellagra and hookworm, crop liens and illiteracy. It turned "blood-lust rising" from boredom and "resentful misery" into a "high sense of honor." The Great Alibi turned defeat into a fictitious victory (of sorts) and excused all manner of defects and transgressions. And the Great Alibi became the great excuse for persistent racism, segregation, and Jim Crow. The Great Alibi "rusts away" the will to face racism because all had been predetermined by history – by history and defeat.[47]

The Great Alibi explains and excuses the South's tendency to never accept responsibility for its own problems, always looking for an external scapegoat to blame for its woes. Southern politicians became especially expert at the latter, blaming "outsiders" for creating the South's problems, or compounding them, or for simply standing in the way of solutions. Moreover, the South yearned to participate more fully in the twentieth-century American dream, by which it meant economic prosperity. But worse than its alibis lay the South's inability to confront its most serious problems directly. For many years it was unable to see segregation as a problem (a fault of Warren himself in his earlier years). In that sense, racial difference and, more to the point, racism stood not as an alibi but as a denial. And a people living in denial (white southerners) are arguably worse than a people living in deception (the northerners' embrace of treasury of virtue).[48]

After three score plus years since Warren offered his centennial musings, it seems much less likely that a consensus would emerge today that the American Civil War was "the greatest single event of our history," though it would still be a contender. World War II, with its vanquishing of Nazis and Fascists, the maturing of the nation's "Greatest Generation," the building (of necessity) the most productive economy the world had ever seen, and the apparent fulfillment of Henry Luce's promised "American Century" would provide vigorous competition.

The Problem of Slavery Reconsidered

Moreover, the success of the post-World War II civil rights movement which brought democracy and full legal and political rights, at least in theory, not only to Black Americans but to all races and genders, might also be in the mix.

In 2005, the respected southern historian James Cobb tackled the question of defining the "Southern Identity" across two centuries. In part, Cobb's study revealed that at most points in the region's history, it enveloped two very different, and usually antagonistic, identities, one white and one Black. The white identity seemed romantic, defensive, wounded, and racist. It stood as an effort to justify the South's historic position in the American Union and to applaud the evolving postbellum New South as the region that increasingly embraced a tripartite identity: a romantic and vaguely chivalrous version of the Old South's "Lost Cause," an optimistic vision for the New South's gospel of prosperity (even when that prosperity was not widely shared among whites as well as Blacks), and a dominant white society insistent on establishing and maintaining white supremacy in the New South as firmly as it had been entrenched in the Old.[49]

Other scholars, speaking with entirely unsouthern accents, contributed different understandings of the South. Nearly fifty years after Robert Penn Warren's *Legacy*, Michael O'Brien, having published his two-volume magnum opus on the intellectual life of the Old South, left the field of southern history to tackle the intellectual challenges of the Adams family. But before leaving the South as a field of study, O'Brien, a native of Great Britain who spent much of his career in the American academy before returning to Cambridge University, published a collection of his short essays, conference commentaries, and book reviews in a volume aptly titled *Placing the South*. Eclectic as always, O'Brien suggested that the level of national support for white supremacy that existed between 1900 and 1960 rendered it unlikely that any road taken by white southerners in the aftermath of the Civil War could have offered a plausible alternative to the dominance of white supremacy in the American South and much of the rest of America. Arguments for viable alternative paths, O'Brien concluded, presented "hardly a plausible case at the bar of history."

Yet O'Brien offered a thoughtful new understanding of southern guilt, the very issue raised by Sellers. Growing up in postwar Britain, O'Brien saw guilt as the human condition, the burden of broken people, people decimated by war and death, the only kind of British people who had survived two world wars. In contrast, proud and achieving slaveholders from a century earlier had little or no such appetite for guilt, even after defeat and emancipation. But the context provided by O'Brien suggests

134 *Understanding the American South*

that a retrospective guilt may have crept into the minds of a new generations of defeated white southerners as war memories receded and the distance from the war lengthened in popular minds some years later, and especially among those still living in the heart of southern evangelical culture, in which admissions of guilt are commonplace, especially if followed by pleas for forgiveness. O'Brien did not argue that such guilt was pervasive in the New South but simply that it could easily be explained in the consciences of people such as Jack Cash and Lillian Smith and others who felt charged with sorting out their region's conscience.[50]

Over the course of a long career, Charles Sellers morphed from a crew-cut Associate Reformed Presbyterian growing up on a family farm near Charlotte, North Carolina and matured into a fine historian of antebellum politics and drifted further left politically, moving away from political history and growing more interested in the economic and social change that undergirded politics, ideas he presented fulsomely in his *The Market Revolution.*[51] Yet none of his fine body of work piqued national curiosity as much as the idea of a "travail of slavery." In the final analysis, however, racism sustained white supremacy long after slavery was destroyed without much travail expressed except from white supremacy's victims and scattered numbers of troubled, dissenting whites.

Unlike slavery, racism in America cannot be described as simply "was" but as a still "is."[52] There can be no disputing that racism was, but also is, a national "sin," or, for the less theologically inclined, a problem or burden or tragedy, or maybe all the aforementioned. It stands as the major stain on the greatness of the world's longest-standing democracy and, more prosaically, the America of all patriot dreams. And even the politics of the twenty-first century reflect the persistence, or even a powerful resurgence, of racism though a larger percentage of Americans than ever before now rise to combat racism. The travail of American democracy was and is racism, our persistent national sin. It remains the challenge of our past, present, and future, but, most importantly, of "now."

Notes

1. Charles G. Sellers, "The Travail of Slavery," in Charles G. Sellers, ed., *The Southerner as American* (Chapel Hill: University of North Carolina Press, 1960): 40–71.
2. Sellers, "Travail of Slavery," 40–51; Charles G. Sellers, *James K. Polk*, Vol. 1, *Jacksonian, 1793–1843* (Princeton: Princeton University Press, 1957); Charles G. Sellers, *James K. Polk*, Vol. 2, *Continentalist, 1843–1846* (Princeton: Princeton University Press, 1966).

The Problem of Slavery Reconsidered 135

3. Sellers, "The Travail of Slavery," 40–51.
4. Sellers, "The Travail of Slavery," 52–67.
5. Sellers, "The Travail of Slavery," 44–70.
6. Sellers, "The Travail of Slavery," especially 61–67; James Oakes, *The Ruling Race: A History of American Slaveholders* (New York: Knopf, 1982), 96–122.
7. Sellers, "The Travail of Slavery," 40–71.
8. Louis Hartz, *The Liberal Tradition in America* (New York: Harcourt Brace Jovanovich, 1955), 1–113.
9. Hartz, *The Liberal Tradition in America*, 145–177. In the end, this conservative rebellion was defeated by the power of the Union army, the strength and breadth of a diversified northern economy, the political skill of Abraham Lincoln, and widespread resistance from enslaved people that weakened the Confederate war effort.
10. Hartz, *The Liberal Tradition in America*, 158–200.
11. Gordon Wood, *The Creation of the American Republic, 1776–1787* (Chapel Hill: University of North Carolina Press, 1969); Robert E. Shalhope, "Toward a Republican Synthesis," *William and Mary Quarterly* 29, no. 1 (1972): 49–80; Robert E. Shalhope, "Republicanism and Early American Historiography," *William and Mary Quarterly* 39, no. 2 (1982): 334–356; Jack Rakove, *James Madison and the Creation of the American Republic* (Glenview, IL: Little Brown, 1990).
12. Drew R. McCoy, *The Elusive Republic: Political Economy in Jeffersonian America* (Chapel Hill: University of North Carolina Press, 1980), 48–75 and 136–165.
13. George M. Frederickson, *The Black Image in the White Mind: The Debate on African American Characters and Destiny* (New York: Harper Row, 1971), 43–70; Harry L. Watson, *Liberty and Power: The Politics of Jacksonian America* (New York: Farrar, Straus, and Giroux, 1990); William J. Cooper, Jr., *Liberty and Slavery: Southern Politics to 1860* (New York: McGraw Hill, 1983); Lacy K. Ford, "Making the 'White Man's Country' White: Race and State Constitutions in the Jacksonian South," *Journal of the Early Republic* 19, no. 4 (1999): 713–737; David Roediger, *Wages of Whiteness: The Making of the American Working Class* (New York: Verso, 1991).
14. Sean Wilentz, *The Rise of American Democracy: Jefferson to Lincoln* (New York: W. W. Norton & Company, 2005), 359–419; William J. Cooper, Jr., *The South and the Politics of Slavery, 1828–1856* (Baton Rouge: Louisiana State University Press, 1978), 23–224; Michael Holt, *The Rise and Fall of the American Whig Party: Jacksonian Politics and the Onset of the Civil War* (New York: Oxford University Press, 1999); Harry L. Watson, *Liberty and Power: The Politics of Jacksonian America* (New York: Hill and Wang, 1990); J. Mills Thornton, *Politics and Power in a Slave Society: Alabama, 1800–1860* (Baton Rouge: Louisiana State University, 1978).
15. Watson, *Liberty and Power*, 42–72; Cooper, *Liberty and Slavery*, 96–119; Lacy K. Ford, "The Popular Ideology of the Old South's Plain Folk: The Limits of Egalitarianism in a Slaveholding Society," in Samuel Hyde, ed.,

136   *Understanding the American South*

with an introduction by John B. Boles, *Plain Folk of the South Reconsidered* (Baton Rouge: Louisiana State University Press, 1997), 205–227.

16. Joyce E. Chaplin, "Slavery and the Principle of Humanity: A Modern Idea in the Early Lower South," *Journal of Social History* 24 (1990): 299–315; Christine Leigh Heyrman, *Southern Cross: The Beginnings of the Bible Belt* (New York: Knopf, 1998), 117–160.

17. Willie Lee Rose, "The Domestication of Domestic Slavery," in William Freehling, ed., *Slavery and Freedom* (New York: Oxford University Press, 1982), 18–36; Jeffrey Robert Young, *Domesticating Slavery: The Master Class in Georgia and South Carolina, 1679–1837* (Chapel Hill: University of North Carolina Press, 1999), 123–160; Erskine Clark, *Dwelling Place: A Plantation Epic* (New Haven: Yale University Press, 2005), especially 133–152; and Lacy K. Ford, *Deliver Us from Evil: The Slavery Question in the Old South* (New York: Oxford University Press, 2009), 141–172.

18. For an overview on northern reform, evangelicalism, and abolition, see James Brewer Stewart, *Holy Warriors: The Abolitionists and American Slavery* (New York: Hill and Wang, 1976).

19. "Speech of Freeman Walker," January 19, 1820, *Annals of Congress*, 16th Congress, 159–175; "Speech of Nathaniel Macon," January 20, 1820, *Annals of Congress*, 16th Congress, 1st Session, 219–232; "Speech of William Smith," January 26, 1820, *Annals of Congress*, 16th Congress, 2nd session, 259–275.

20. John C. Calhoun, "Remarks on Abolition Petitions," March 9, 1836, in Clyde N. Wilson, Shirley Bright Cook, and Alexander Moore, eds., *The Papers of John C. Calhoun*, Vol. 13, *1835–1837* (Columbia, SC: University of South Carolina Press, 1980), 91–110.

21. Lacy K. Ford, Jr., "Reconfiguring the Old South: 'Solving' the Problem of Slavery, 1787–1838," *Journal of American History* 95, no. 1 (2008): 95–122.

22. Gaines M. Foster, "Guilt over Slavery: A Historiographical Analysis," *Journal of Southern History* 56, no. 4 (1990): 665–694.

23. William Dodd, *The Cotton Kingdom: A Chronicle of the Old South* (New Haven: Yale University Press, 1919), 146.

24. Wilbur J. Cash, *The Mind of the South* (New York: Alfred A. Knopf, 1941), 66.

25. Bell I. Wiley, *The Road to Appomattox* (Memphis: Memphis State College Press, 1956), 102–105.

26. C. Vann Woodward, "The Search for Southern Identity, 1960," in Woodward, ed., *The Burden of Southern History* (Baton Rouge: Louisiana State University Press, 1960), 3–25.

27. William W. Freehling, *Prelude to Civil War: The Nullification Controversy in South Carolina, 1816–1836* (New York: Harper and Row, 1966), 72, 360.

28. Kenneth Stampp, "The Southern Road to Appomattox," in Kenneth Stampp, ed., *The Imperiled Union: Essays on the Background of the Civil War* (New York: Oxford University Press, 1980), 246–269; Ben Robertson, *Red Hills and Cotton: An Upcountry Memory*, with a new introduction by

The Problem of Slavery Reconsidered   137

Lacy K. Ford, Jr. (Columbia, SC: University of South Carolina Press, 1991), Southern Classics Reprint Edition, ix–xliv.

29. Richard E. Berringer, Herman Hattaway, Archer Jones, and William Still, Jr., *Why the South Lost the Civil War* (Athens, GA: University of Georgia Press, 1986).

30. The strongest expressions of these positions appeared in Eugene Genovese's *The Political Economy of Slavery: Studies in the Economy and Society of the Slave South* (New York: Pantheon Books, 1965), *The World the Slaveholders Made: Two Essays in Interpretation* (New York: Pantheon Books, 1969), and *Roll, Jordan, Roll: The World the Slaves Made* (New York: Pantheon Books, 1974), and Elizabeth Fox-Genovese and Eugene Genovese, *Fruits of Merchant Capital: Slavery and Bourgeois Property in the Rise and Expansion of Capitalism* (New York: Oxford University Press, 1983).

31. Eugene Genovese and Elizabeth Fox-Genovese, *Fatal Self-Deception: Slaveholding Paternalism in the Old South* (Cambridge: Cambridge University Press, 2011); Elizabeth Fox-Genovese and Eugene Genovese, *The Mind of the Master Class: History and Faith in the Southern Slaveholders' World View* (Cambridge: Cambridge University Press, 2005); Elizabeth Fox-Genovese and Eugene Genovese, *Slavery in White and Black: Class and Race in Southern Slaveholders' New World Order* (New York: Cambridge University Press, 2008).

32. Ford, *Deliver Us from Evil*, especially 3–18 and 505–536.

33. Ford, *Deliver Us from Evil*, 76–77, 359–389, 535–536.

34. Ford, *Deliver Us from Evil*, 200–203.

35. Ford, *Deliver Us from Evil*, 532–536.

36. See Sven Beckert and Seth Rockman, eds., *Slavery's Capitalism: A New History of American Development* (Philadelphia: University of Pennsylvania Press, 2016), 1–27.

37. Sven Beckert, *Empire of Cotton: A Global History* (New York: Alfred A. Knopf, 2014). See Mathew Desmond, "Capitalism," in Nicole Hannah-Jones, ed., *The 1619 Project: A New Origin Story* (New York: The New York Times Company, 2021), 165–185.

38. Steven Hahn, *A Nation without Borders: The United States in an Age of Civil Wars, 1830–1910* (New York: Penguin Books, 2016).

39. Michael O'Brien, *Conjectures of Order: Intellectual Life and the American South, 1810–1860*, Vol. 2 (Chapel Hill: University of North Carolina Press, 2004), 1199.

40. Michael O'Brien, *Placing the South* (Jackson: University Press of Mississippi, 2007); Lacy Ford, "Placing Michael O'Brien: A Review Essay," *The Southern Quarterly Review* 47 (2008): 121–129.

41. Michael O'Brien, *Conjectures of Order*, Vol. 2, 781–876.

42. Abraham Lincoln to A. G. Hodges, Esq., April 4, 1864, in Richard N. Current, ed., *The Political Thought of Abraham Lincoln* (Indianapolis: Bobbs-Merrill, 1967), 297–300.

43. Robert Penn Warren, *The Legacy of Civil War: A Centennial Meditation* (New York: Random House, 1961).

44. Warren, *The Legacy of Civil War*, 53–56.

45. Warren, *The Legacy of Civil War*, 59–76; Reinhold Niebuhr, *The Irony of American History* (New York: Scribner's, 1952).
46. Warren, *The Legacy of Civil War*, 53–59.
47. Warren, *The Legacy of Civil War*, 54–55.
48. Robert Penn Warren, "The Briar Patch," in Twelve Southerners, *I'll Take My Stand: The South and the Agrarian Tradition* (New York: Harper, 1930), 246–264.
49. James C. Cobb, *Away Down South: A History of Southern Identity* (New York: Oxford University Press, 2005), 130–235.
50. Michael O'Brien, *Placing the South* (Jackson: University Press of Mississippi, 2007).
51. Charles Sellers, *The Market Revolution* (New York: Oxford University Press, 1991).
52. Michael Gorra, *The Saddest Words: William Faulkner's Civil War* (New York: W. W. Norton & Company, 2020), 353–356.

6

The Legacy of W. E. B. DuBois

Slavery and Race in Southern and American History

Beyond dispute, W. E. B. Du Bois stands as one of the leading intellectuals of the twentieth century. By any estimation, he holds a place in the highest echelon of American intellectuals, in the rarified atmosphere occupied by a mere handful. Moreover, as Annette Gordon-Reed has rightly noted, Du Bois "carried himself as if he were the Negro race."[1] And he spent almost the entirety of his long and seemingly tireless life trying to help the world respect and understand that race. Du Bois is well known among students of history for his conflict with Booker T. Washington over the appropriate educational paths for Black Americans, for his role as a founder of the NAACP, for his editorship of *The Crisis*, for his dedication to socialism in several of its guises, and for his decision to live outside the United States (Ghana) near the end of his long and productive life.[2]

Prior to the appearance of his magnum opus, *Black Reconstruction in America*, in 1935, Du Bois was already widely known as the author of the lyrical epic *The Souls of Black Folk* (1903). In his opening "Forethought" written for that book, Du Bois offered a prophetic word, declaring to his readers that "the problem of the Twentieth Century is the problem of the color line." Rarely do the prophetic pronouncements of intellectuals hold up to the test of time or the shifting judgments of history as well as Du Bois' declaration. Yet Du Bois' prediction about the color line rang true for the ninety-seven remaining years of the twentieth century and continues holding its force more than two decades into the twenty-first century. *Souls of Black Folk* remains widely taught in American colleges and universities, and it stands over a century after its publication as a powerful story of the Black experience in America in the late nineteenth century, a

140   *Understanding the American South*

tale of struggle and sorrow, of achievement and setback, of triumph yet more often tragedy, and ultimately of the unmistakable "two-ness" of life for Black Americans. *Souls* is a powerful and moving prose hymn to the endurance and disappointment of Black Americans in the increasingly segregated nation and firmly segregated South which emerged after the collapse of Reconstruction. That collapse left former slaves with "nothing but freedom." Du Bois' prose evokes striving and struggle met with disappointment, sadness, tragedy, and, yes, anger.[3]

Accepted widely over time as a must read for educated citizens, *Souls of Black Folk* stands as a coming-of-age story, both for Du Bois and his race. As told by Du Bois the story rivals in richness Mark Twain's creation of a fictional "Jim," who, though already an adult, came of age along with the much younger Huck in *Huckleberry Finn*, with the critical exception that DuBois' stories were not fiction. *Souls* served as a literary anthem for a race, a people, and DuBois used it to offer readers a penetrating glimpse through what he termed "the veil." The veil, according to DuBois, separated the Black world from the white world and permitted whites to remain deliberately ignorant of the travails of life in the Black world, the life beyond the veil, and complacent about the superiority of their own lives and culture, without facing life on the other side. The veil hid and distorted reality, arguably for both whites and Blacks.[4]

Du Bois became aware of the veil, not when he journeyed into the undeniably racist South, but as a youth in his hometown of Great Barrington, Massachusetts. In *Souls*, Du Bois described the pain of his learning experience. At his school, boys and girls purchased "gorgeous visiting cards" costing ten cents a package to exchange with each other. According to Du Bois, the exchange proved "merry" until one girl, "a tall newcomer, refused my card, refused it peremptorily, without a glance." It was at that moment of rejection, Du Bois recalled, then and there "with a certain suddenness" came the recognition that "I was different from the others, ... shutout from their world by a vast veil." Du Bois went on to confess that he had "thereafter no desire to tear down that veil." Yet his confrontation with the veil made him intensely competitive (and eager to use his intellectual gifts), as he declared that "the sky was bluest when I could beat my mates at examination time, or beat them at a foot race, or even beat their stringy heads."[5]

Beyond the veil which racism and racial separation placed between Americans defined as white and Americans defined as Black emerged Du Bois' argument for the "two-ness of life for the Black American – the challenge of being both an American and a Negro." The dilemma of the

The Legacy of W. E. B. DuBois

Black race, Du Bois insisted, lay in its "double-consciousness," in being part of a people which must "ever feel its two-ness – an American, a Negro; two souls, two thoughts, two unreconciled strivings." These two "warring ideals in one dark body" survived, in Du Bois' words, only by "dogged strength." "The history of the American Negro is the history of this strife, this longing to attain self-conscious manhood, to merge his double self into a better and truer self," wrote Du Bois.[6] Du Bois' biographer, David Levering Lewis, judged the "permanent tension" between being American and being a Negro so well articulated by Du Bois as a "revolutionary conception."[7] The American Negro, Du Bois pleaded, does not want either American or Negro to triumph over the other but to "make it possible for a man to be both a Negro and an American, without being cursed and spit upon by his fellows, without having the doors of Opportunity closed roughly in his face." Posited over a century ago, the "two-ness" of Black life survives today as a racial concept that has been normalized and even understood as an interpretation of the challenge of being both Black and American.[8]

From a practical standpoint, *Souls of Black Folk* intensified the ongoing dispute between Du Bois' advocacy for equality and full opportunity (and, at this point is his career, the integration of the races) and Booker T. Washington's advocacy of a separate but someday equal approach aided by vocational education and gradual uplift through material progress. The controversy between the two had flourished for a decade, but Du Bois boldly attacked Washington in *Souls*, leaving no doubt about his feelings on the matter. Washington emerged as a Black leader, Du Bois argued, at moment when "the nation was a little ashamed of having bestowed so much sentiment on Negroes and was [now] concentrating its energy on dollars."[9] Washington's program of practical vocational education for Blacks, the conciliation of the South, and "silence" on matters of civil and political rights drew broad white support nationally. Washington's "Atlanta Compromise" speech, which declared that "in all things purely social we can be as separate as five fingers yet one as the hand in all things essential to mutual progress," sounded the notes a strong majority of white Americans wanted to hear. From Washington's standpoint at least, his strategy perhaps purchased Black Americans some breathing space and modest advancement in a broader world that was asserting white supremacy with ever greater vigor, not merely in the South but nationwide.[10]

Du Bois, however, fiercely opposed the narrowness and conservatism of Washington's agenda as did many other Black leaders of the time, not

142 *Understanding the American South*

to mention those liberal white leaders who sought full citizenship for Blacks. But no others were as consistently and forcefully outspoken on the matter as Du Bois. Among other things, Du Bois saw Washington as the voice of "triumphal commercialism" among Black leaders. Washington, Du Bois insisted, "represents in Negro thought" an "old attitude of adjustment and submission." Du Bois critiqued Washington's economic agenda as one of submission to commerce and capitalism, a "gospel of work and money." But the heart of Du Bois' fierce disagreement with Washington grew from his strenuous objection to abandoning the pursuit of three items he viewed as crucial to Black equality: political power, civil rights, and the higher education of "negro youth." In stark contrast to Washington, Du Bois countered with his own program, which included: "the right to vote," civil equality, and "the education of youth according to ability." The last of these clearly stood as the centerpiece of Du Bois' idea for cultivating the "Talented Tenth" of the nation's Black population through education of a very different sort to enable this rising Black elite to provide the leadership Blacks needed to regain and defend rights and enjoy financial success.[11]

Du Bois' argument with Washington proved ongoing and grew visceral at times. Du Bois remained an advocate of an educational strategy designed to facilitate the development of the Talented Tenth and to emphasize the need for political rights and civil equality to protect and defend whatever gains Black Americans might make economically. Du Bois traveled in broad intellectual and cultural circles and had access at times to significant funding from some of the nation's liberal philanthropists, funding which proved critical to the writing of *Black Reconstruction*. Those who followed Du Bois carefully knew about his determined advocacy for the "Talented Tenth" and that he was increasingly influenced by Marxist economic ideas. Du Bois frequently referred to both Black and white workers as "the proletariat" through his entire career, and over time, his advocacy of the Talented Tenth diminished in comparison to his championing of the proletarian cause.[12]

Less well known than *Souls of Black Folk* remains Du Bois' caustic but perceptive 1920 essay "The Souls of White Folk," intended as a brief counterpart to *Souls of Black Folk*. In this essay, Du Bois identified the concept of whiteness as not merely the tool of racism but its essence. "The discovery of personal whiteness among the world's peoples is a very modern thing," Du Bois asserted, linking it to the imperialism spreading around the globe during what Eric Hobsbawm termed "The Age of Empire" (the late nineteenth and early twentieth century). Why

The Legacy of W. E. B. DuBois

143

was whiteness so desired, Du Bois queried? Answering his own question, he observed "that whiteness is the ownership of the earth forever and ever." Domestically, whiteness was most often visualized in "the strut of the Southerner, but in the rest of the world, it came from the white Europeans as they colonized the 'colored' people of Africa and Asia." Imperialism, in Du Bois' view, appeared to be an inevitable by-product of capitalism. "The world today is trade," Du Bois insisted, and the "world has turned shopkeeper; history is economic history, living is earning a living." Du Bois devoted the bulk of the essay to how economic colonialism triggered World War I and how the horrible casualties that destabilized the world were caused by competitive imperial desires for world domination of "trade." Du Bois not only advanced his argument for the created (and falsely valued) concept of "whiteness," which he saw as closely linked to an imperialism in which the imperialists were "white," and the imperial world ruled by the privileges of whiteness. While Du Bois also offered a forceful Marxist critique of the economics of imperialism, he increasingly saw both capitalism and imperialism as a crusade for a world ruled by "whiteness," and thus by white efforts to dominate the world's "colored" peoples.[13]

Before beginning to draft *Black Reconstruction* in 1934, Du Bois left the *Crisis* and the NAACP when controversy erupted over his apparent embrace of "segregation without discrimination" as the best avenue for Black progress. The mere separation of the races did not necessarily embody inequality, Du Bois argued, it was only systematic and systemic discrimination that produced inequality. To be sure, in the American South, a region replete with discrimination, segregation produced a racial hierarchy of white over Black, but Du Bois argued that segregation with equality and without discrimination might prove a salutary means of promoting Black progress without constant hindrance from white prejudice. For the NAACP, an organization which had long championed integration and whose Board included whites and Blacks and which had long been dedicated to the principle of racial equality, Du Bois' new position sounded too much like Black separatism. This difference of opinion cost Du Bois the editorship of the *Crisis* and related tensions prompted him to resign from the NAACP.[14]

As Du Bois severed ties with the NAACP, he negotiated a two-year fellowship from the liberal Rosenwald Foundation to support his upcoming book on Reconstruction. In a decision that other scholars of his and later generations quarreled with, Du Bois decided to largely eschew archival research and rely as much as possible on published materials and

144 *Understanding the American South*

government reports. This was a decision based on time pressures from his publisher and sponsor, and the difficulty Black scholars faced when trying to access repositories, especially in the South, where the majority of archival treasures covering the period in question were housed. But while *Black Reconstruction* was not grounded in extensive archival research, its power emerged from its original and bold interpretations backed by evidence from a plethora of government documents, reports, and legislative proceedings. Du Bois was not writing a monograph but an interpretive synthesis based on extensive research.[15]

For his interpretations, Du Bois drew heavily on expanding those he first presented much earlier in his career in a paper presented at the AHA annual meeting in 1905. Du Bois' revised AHA paper was published in 1910 in the *American Historical Review* (*AHR*), the leading scholarly journal in the field. In this early essay, Du Bois argued that "negro agency" had been a key to solving the many problems the nation faced during Reconstruction.[16] In Du Bois' 1910 account, "[t]he Freedmen's Bureau, Negro schools and the Negro church" led the fight for Black progress and Black equality during Reconstruction. Of the last two sources, the Black church presented the case for Black agency most strongly even during slavery, as Black Christianity flourished under the slaveholders' watch. Slaveholders sometimes approved and sometimes failed to understand what they saw, and sometimes they sought to repress movements they saw as covert plots to undermine, escape, or overthrow slavery itself. After emancipation, Black churches emerged as centers of community organization and political activity across the South, and they remained a critical entity for Black agency through Reconstruction and beyond.[17]

In Du Bois' eyes, the Freedmen's Bureau, a federal initiative supported chiefly by national and southern Republicans, encouraged Black labor to enter fair agreements with white landlords and pressured white landowners to accept and honor such agreements, as the bureau sought to bring the southern economy back into production as quickly as possible after the war. The bureau also joined the white missionaries in launching efforts to educate the region's former enslaved Black population, which was largely, though not completely, unschooled.[18] But progressive measures for Black improvement were thwarted when whites quickly returned to power across most of the South with the blessing of President Andrew Johnson during the period of Presidential Reconstruction. Black Codes approved by southern white politicians at the state level quickly relegated the freedpeople to a condition of dependence and vulnerability. Du Bois conceded that for many reasons it was not the time to "expect

The Legacy of W. E. B. DuBois

cool thoughtful action from the white South." After all, Du Bois allowed, "their economic condition was pitiable, and the fear of negro freedom genuine," but, Du Bois insisted, "[i]t was reasonable to expect something less than repression."[19] Once Congressional Reconstruction took fully took hold in 1868, the newly formed southern Republican party, powered by Black suffrage, won control of southern states again and breathed new life into "Black" Reconstruction. Du Bois' positive reassessment of Republican Reconstruction and the tragedy of its demise in the mid-1870s dominated much of his account in *Black Reconstruction*.[20]

But while his *AHR* essay remained on the record, it met silence after publication as the so-called Dunning School, named after William Archibald Dunning, the Columbia University professor who insisted that Black rule in the South during Reconstruction stood as a lurid era of ignorance, incompetence, corruption, and venality, dominated Reconstruction historiography for decades. The Dunning School offered an interpretation suffused with racial prejudice and stood as a solid phalanx of tribute to the cultural fictions of white supremacy. The school Dunning and his protégés developed cast a long shadow over the historiography of Reconstruction for many years until directly disputed by Du Bois' work.[21]

Nearly twenty years after his *AHR* essay, as Du Bois prepared to begin his work on *Black Reconstruction*, a few works appeared that began to gradually distance their authors from the Dunning School. Altheous Taylor, a young Black professor at Fiske University, wrote two monographs, one on *Reconstruction in South Carolina* (1926) and a second on *Reconstruction in Virginia* (1928), which contradicted Dunning School assertions that Reconstruction-era Republican state governments in the South were corrupt, incompetent, and irresponsible.[22] Moreover, a general history of South Carolina during Reconstruction by two progressive white southerners, Robert H. Woody and Francis Butler Simkins, drew heavily on Taylor's work to help them produce an account of *Reconstruction in South Carolina* (1932) that was remarkably balanced for its time. Simkins and Woody emphasized that while state finances were a shambles after the recession of 1873, Black legislators were hardly responsible for the situation, and that the general record of Republican Reconstruction, hated as it was by Palmetto state whites, led to progressive changes in the education system and the structure of local government and to other democratic reforms.[23] The works of Taylor as well as Simkins and Woody spoke, to varying degrees, from the point of view of the freedpeople, and suggested the need for fair-minded treatments devoid of biting racial prejudice and just plain poorly researched history.

146   *Understanding the American South*

None these revisionist works received broad attention, but they revealed that inside the academy younger historians were beginning to break away from the Dunning orthodoxy even though the reactionary Dunning School remained dominant. Simkins and Woody at least, and most others in the profession, had not yet escaped quite far enough to embrace Du Bois' more radical conclusions, but they were beginning to challenge, however cautiously, the Dunning paradigm of Reconstruction as a "Tragic Era" marked by incompetence, corruption, and outright thievery.[24]

Du Bois' *Black Reconstruction in America, 1860–1880* appeared in 1935 as a book of a different type, yet one that was powerful and ultimately (though not immediately) remarkably influential in its own way. *Black Reconstruction* offered a bold new interpretation of the Reconstruction era, one both original and challenging in its argument. Many historians had portrayed Reconstruction as a period of Black mischief, misrule, corruption, and incompetence in the South, and continued to do so. Instead, Du Bois argued exactly the opposite. He built his book on a strategy of not only telling the story of the period from the perspective of the Black actors in the drama of the period but also by offering a broad, sweeping reinterpretation of the Reconstruction era, contradicting the exaggerations and prejudices of the Dunning School virtually every step of the way.[25]

The findings Du Bois presented in *Black Reconstruction in America* in 1935 stood as a sharp challenge to the prevailing historical interpretations and leading interpreters of Reconstruction history. Today, Du Bois' once radical interpretations have become commonplace in Reconstruction scholarship, though perhaps less commonly taught in public schools, where influence is often exercised by local politicians and state legislators who still flinch at the true story of slavery and Reconstruction. No quick summary can do justice to Du Bois' account, and certainly not to his often elegant and lyrical prose, but the main revisionist arguments offered by Du Bois reconfigured the way later generations of historians viewed not only Reconstruction but also slavery. Du Bois' story focused on what later scholars termed "Black agency," the active agency of the freedpeople, and what they did and tried to do for themselves and not simply on what was done to them, or even, on occasion, for them. It took nearly three decades for Du Bois' interpretation to fully take told, and arguably time for a new generation of scholars and a new atmosphere for champions of civil rights to emerge.[26]

Du Bois focused on several key portions of the Reconstruction process in *Black Reconstruction*, rejecting received interpretations, ones born more from turn of the twentieth-century racism than balanced assessment of evidence. For Du Bois, the leading topic of Reconstruction was always the labor question. He started the book with his account of the southern plantation economy and how the freedpeople, with support from the newly created Freedman's Bureau and other northern champions of free labor, worked to obtain a measure of autonomy and financial reward in the absence of slavery. In his assessment of slaveholders, Du Bois was frank and to the point. But rather than begin with harsh judgments, he first offered concessions to the humanity of the exploiters as well as the exploited. "The Slavery of Negroes in the South," Du Bois contended, was "not usually a deliberately cruel and oppressive system." However, he maintained that it was difficult to "conceive as quite true the idyllic picture of a patriarchal state" offered repeatedly by slaveholders and later by former slaveholders. "The victims of southern slavery," Du Bois contended, "had adequate food for their health, and shelter sufficient for a mild climate." In fact, Du Bois judged that the material condition of enslaved Blacks compared favorably with the "worst class of laborers in the slums of New York and Philadelphia and the factory towns of New England." But Du Bois argued that it was also true that "Negro slaves" found themselves in the worst position "among modern laborers" because they "represented in a very real sense the ultimate degradation of man" as "they were part of a system inconsistent with modern progress." Workers, Du Bois insisted with justified indignation, were "not real estate" and slaves were "the ultimate exploited" workers in a world filled with exploitation.[27]

Once the idea of land redistribution on a large scale was rejected by Congress, the question of how the southern proletariat, as Du Bois termed it, could exercise its long-suppressed power to create a new society loomed as critical. But poor whites, Du Bois argued, seemingly preferred "poverty to equality with the Negro" rendering a "labor movement in the South impossible." The predictable poor white reluctance to collaborate with free Blacks provided early evidence that common whites were eager to claim whatever small privileges their whiteness offered, especially in contradistinction with the choices available to Blacks.[28]

After the emancipation of the South's large supply of formerly enslaved Black labor, which included slave Black men, women, and children over the ages of ten or twelve, shrank because of family decisions about work for hire made by the freedpeople. Once emancipated, and with white ability to coerce labor reduced if not eliminated, the freedpeople valued their expanded opportunities for family life and autonomy

148 *Understanding the American South*

and reduced the labor available from women and children significantly, creating what white employers perceived as a labor shortage. Such Black agency reshaped the postbellum agricultural labor market in the South despite frequent confrontation with white landowners throughout Reconstruction and beyond.[29]

In fact, except for the brief period of Presidential Reconstruction, Black freedom and the continued need for labor gave the freedpeople a modicum of bargaining power with landowners (who had the land itself and often access to credit as leverage) in negotiations for yearly labor agreements. Absent property ownership, Black families typically preferred a working arrangement (often tenancy) that allowed the greatest autonomy other than landownership. But white landowners often sought something of a first approximation of slavery, giving the landlord as much control as possible. Negotiation produced a complex, crazy quilt result that left neither side particularly satisfied with the final arrangements. Over the course of the Reconstruction era, cotton production remained well below prewar highs, contributing to the economic malaise which settled in across the South.[30]

A second area in which Du Bois recognized the importance of Black agency involved the question of Black political participation. After gaining the franchise, Black communities organized to vote. Churches joined with Union Leagues, northern military officers, and white missionaries from the North in efforts to organize Black voters down to the precinct or ballot box level. Black voters represented at least a plurality of voters in every deep South state and a majority in South Carolina. Thus Black involvement in the Republican party played a major role, not only putting Republicans in power in southern states but also in shaping policies that improved opportunities for freedpeople and also for formerly free Blacks, who often played key roles in the postbellum Republican party in the South during Reconstruction.[31]

Du Bois offered the insight, now commonplace, emphasizing that violence and intimidation played central roles in white efforts to dampen or extinguish Black political involvement. Whether through early Ku Klux Klan efforts right after war or again in the 1870–1872 period when Klan activity rose to the level that required deployment of federal troops to suppress the white terror organization, and when local white militias, rifle clubs, Red Shirts, and a revived Klan and other murderous rogue bands used intimidation and violence to overthrow Republican Reconstruction in 1874 and 1876. For Du Bois, Black participation in politics, like the activism that flourished in the South during Reconstruction, remained an

The Legacy of W. E. B. DuBois 149

essential precondition for the true triumph of democracy, not merely in the South but in America, and to the extent that such participation was denied or diminished, the denial pushed the nation deeper into the hands of a racist capitalist oligarchy.[32]

Du Bois also offered a persuasive denial of the conservative white allegation that responsibility for the alleged financial malfeasance and corruption that occurred in the South during Reconstruction lay at the feet of a corrupt Republican party and its heavily Black constituency. Du Bois found that most of the large state debts incurred by Republican governments in the southern states resulted from bond issues to finance economic development, with a focus on railroad building (a national mania during the period). The collapse of the economy during and after the Panic of 1873 led to defaults and financial embarrassments that few observers in either party or of either race had foreseen. Both Republicans and white Democrats supported state funding for railroad development, and close analysis revealed that Black legislators were seldom in the committee positions needed to take the lead in pushing bond measures and other state fiscal assistance to improvement projects.[33]

Overall, the Black constituencies in the southern Republican party advocated a progressive economic and social agenda, including public education for all, lien laws that gave priority to the laborer, stronger structures for county (local) government, and the integration of the state militia. They also inched toward more progressive social policies. South Carolina, for example, passed its first and only law legalizing divorce during Reconstruction, and Palmetto state Conservatives soon repealed the law after Reconstruction ended and divorce remained illegal in the state until 1948.[34]

Today, all of Du Bois' points, fair compensation for labor, energetic political mobilization, support for universal public education, democratic county government, state support for transportation improvement, and a generally pro-development economic policy draw mainstream support and have become touchstones of sound government policy. Finding the tax base to support such an economic program during Reconstruction proved a challenge, however. Antebellum southern state governments had offered minimal state services, but the existing tax burden fell primarily on slaveowners through a tax on slave property and a tax on land. Once enslaved property left the tax rolls with emancipation, the tax burden fell heavily on land, arousing the ire not only of large landowners (usually men who were previously large slaveholders as well) but also on yeoman farmers and other white landowners who had shouldered only

150   *Understanding the American South*

a small portion of the antebellum tax burden. Taxpayer unions, leagues, and conventions protested the higher taxes of the Reconstruction era and readily (if wrongly) blamed Black politicians for their higher taxes, especially as the bills for railroad building and bond indebtedness came due.[35]

Ultimately, Du Bois concluded, the related problems of state debts and the floating of large bond issues to build railroads were not exclusively the result of corrupt Republican regimes. Instead, in Du Bois' view, the untimely end of Reconstruction in the South resulted from an alliance of white southerners with northern capitalists seeking to rebound from deep recession and gain access to capital. They engaged, both nationally and regionally, in a counter-revolution to restrain democracy in the interest of capital formation. The thirst for access to or control of capital was hardly confined to the South but, in fact, sparked even greater exertions across the nation to facilitate expansion and profit-seeking in the West, even at the risk of military struggle with Mexico as well as the native tribes of the western portion of the continent.[36]

In many respects, Du Bois' interpretations strike current students of history as the standard fare of modern scholarship and even good textbooks, because so much of the Reconstruction scholarship of recent decades has confirmed and deepened interpretations that made Du Bois' *Black Reconstruction in America* so bold, original, and challenging. Du Bois' radical scholarly insurgency became standard fare for the best of late twentieth century and early twenty-first century scholarship in the field.

Contrary to lingering popular perceptions, however, Du Bois' *Black Reconstruction* was not ignored when it appeared in 1935, though the popular press and larger intellectual community paid more attention to its publication than did professional historians and specialized scholarly journals. As noted by Du Bois' biographer, David Levering Lewis, only *Time* magazine among the mainstream press in the North failed to review Du Bois' book.[37] Lewis Gannett, a friend of Du Bois, wrote a highly favorable review for New York's influential *Herald-Tribune*, declaring *Black Reconstruction* one of the finest books "written in English in recent years." Gannett judged the book an "attempt to rewrite the history of the Civil War as well as Reconstruction" through an "impassioned attack upon the slave-minded historians who have blackened the story of Reconstruction, and an eloquent plea for a just recognition of the historic role of the American Negro."[38]

Yale history professor William MacDonald reviewed Du Bois in the Sunday *New York Times* and argued that Du Bois had good reason to

The Legacy of W. E. B. DuBois

offer a "a rancorous onslaught" on the existing historiography on Civil War and Reconstruction. MacDonald criticized *Black Reconstruction* as "as discursive as it is repetitious" but admitted that it was "nevertheless a remarkable book." MacDonald opined that "one puts down this extraordinary book with mixed feelings." Du Bois' work stood, in MacDonald's estimation, as "beyond question the most painstaking and thorough study ever made" of "the Negro's part in Reconstruction." Yet MacDonald insisted on offering praise with caveats. For example, there was

no need to accept the author's view about racial equality in order to recognize the imposing contribution which his work made to a critical period of American history, nor need one be a Marxist to perceive that in treating the Negro experience as a part of the American labor movement in general, he has given that movement an orientation very different from what it commonly had.

Still, MacDonald somehow interpreted Du Bois insistence that there can "be no compromise" in "the fight for absolute equality" as a warning of a coming "deadly racial struggle."[39]

Praise for *Black Reconstruction* flowed from a variety of sources other than the *Times* and *Herald-Tribune*. The New York *Daily Mirror* claimed that the book lit a "long burning torch on humanity's highroad," while the other Hearst daily in New York, the *American*, concluded that the work "should disturb complacent historians."[40] In his three-page review in the *Saturday Review of Literature*, William Garrison Villard, frequently an opponent of Du Bois in the tense infighting that marked life inside the NAACP, and the one NAACP Board member Du Bois held most responsible for his departure from that organization, nevertheless called *Black Reconstruction* a "remarkable book" and praised Du Bois for recovering an accurate portrayal of southern state legislatures during Reconstruction.[41] Moreover, the *Saturday Review* ran advertisements for Du Bois' book, calling it the "only book so far that tells of those bitterly partisan events [Reconstruction] from the point of view of the Negro," and touting the book's "combination of judgment and research,"[42] which "together make it a signal contribution to the writing of American history." Perhaps even more surprisingly, the white progressive editor of the Raleigh *News and Observer*, Jonathan Daniels, son of Josephus Daniels, Woodrow Wilson's secretary of the navy, praised Du Bois for correcting previous historical accounts of Reconstruction by developing a strong case that "the Negro played a great part" in the Reconstruction effort to set "not only Negroes but the white proletariat free."[43]

Understanding the American South

A few years after the publication of *Black Reconstruction*, Du Bois received respectful attention both from a promising young southern historian, C. Vann Woodward, and a mid-career historian, Howard Beale, who served as Woodward's advisor at the University of North Carolina, Chapel Hill. At age twenty-seven, Woodward wrote Du Bois, expressing appreciation for *Black Reconstruction* and seeking Du Bois' advice regarding revision of his doctoral thesis on Tom Watson, the Negro, and agrarian revolt in Georgia. Woodward thanked Du Bois for the incredible "insight which your admirable book" provided.[44] Five years after the book's publication, Beale commented positively on Du Bois' *Black Reconstruction* in his 1940 state of the historical literature article in the *AHR*. Beale's *AHR* article assessed the state of Reconstruction historiography and suggested new directions for study. At times critical in his assessment of Du Bois' magnum opus, Beale declared it "too wordy," and he judged it "distorted by insistence upon molding facts into a Marxian pattern." But he praised Du Bois for the "freshness" of his argument and hailed him for presenting "a mass of material formerly ignored that every future historian must reckon with." Beale noted Du Bois' use of Charles and Mary Beard's idea of the American Civil War as a Second American Revolution and thought the concept had considerable value. Beale politely chided Du Bois for his failure to recognize "the importance in Southern life of the yeoman farmer, who was neither slaveowner or poor white," and because Du Bois wrongly portrayed "the Negro and certain whites of the rural South as a typical proletariat," a portrayal which Beale argued "distorted" the reality of life during Reconstruction.[45]

Already in his mid-sixties when *Black Reconstruction* was published, Du Bois lived twenty-eight years after it appeared, and for many of those years he remained an active intellectual champion of racial equality and mounted increasingly acid critiques of capitalism and colonialism from a position clearly on the left. He remained fond of Marxist economic thought but was unafraid to criticize the efforts of communist governments when he thought them unfaithful to the ideals of democracy and racial equality. Du Bois opposed American entry into World War II. In 1950, he agreed to serve as chair of the newly formed Peace Information Center (PIC), an organization dedicated to supporting the Stockholm Peace Appeal for nuclear disarmament by the United States, a movement also supported by occasional statements from physicist Albert Einstein. The PIC quickly drew the attention of the Truman Justice Department which required Du Bois, as its chair, to register as an agent of a foreign government. Du Bois, busy with his usual schedule and objecting

The Legacy of W. E. B. DuBois

153

in principle to the requirement, never registered. In 1952, after the PIC Board voted to close the organization, the Justice Department put Du Bois on trial for failing to register. Ultimately, the presiding judge dismissed the charges against Du Bois before the case went to the jury and shortly after Albert Einstein's name had appeared on Du Bois' witness list.[46]

In 1958, Du Bois' passport, revoked eight years earlier during his PIC years, was restored when the United States Supreme Court declared, in a 5–4 decision, the denial of passports on political grounds unconstitutional. Almost immediately, Du Bois and his wife Shirley Graham Du Bois left the country for visits to the Soviet Union and China among other destinations. Du Bois met with Khrushchev and Mao and later visited Ghana. Two years before his death in 1963, Ghana offered Du Bois a chance to serve as supervising editor of a new encyclopedia of the African diaspora. Once funding was approved, Du Bois accepted and lived the final two years of his very long life in Ghana.[47]

Whatever his travel and activities, Du Bois remained curious about whether his earlier written work, especially *Souls of Black Folk* and *Black Reconstruction*, retained influence in the American academic and intellectual world. While on a speaking tour on the Pacific Coast in 1951, Du Bois was introduced to Leon Litwack, then a promising young graduate student in history at the University of California-Berkeley and later himself the author of a Pulitzer Prize-winning book on Reconstruction. When queried, Litwack informed Du Bois that his mentor, Kenneth Stampp, a young professor at Berkeley who had just published a book on the coming of the Civil War, taught Du Bois' work eagerly in his classes. Du Bois professed himself "impressed and astonished" upon hearing the news. In many respects Du Bois' encounter with a young Leon Litwack revealed what was slowly becoming a trend in slavery and Reconstruction historiography. Attention to Du Bois work led to the sincerest form of academic flattery: the advent of widespread reconsideration of and focus on the role of Black agency as crucial to understanding slavery, the Civil War, and Reconstruction.[48]

Du Bois' connection to future scholars of the Reconstruction era and the Black American experience more generally flowed most directly through his emerging friendship with John Hope Franklin, a Black historian, educated first at Fiske before taking a doctorate from Harvard in 1941. Despite facing widespread discrimination early in his career, Franklin published aggressively, with his first major work, *The Free Negro in North Carolina, 1790–1860* (still a model state-level study),

154   *Understanding the American South*

being followed up in 1947 with the first edition of *From Slavery to Freedom*, a comprehensive history of the Black experience from the colonial era to the present. Franklin first met Du Bois when the latter was passing through North Carolina on his way to Baltimore and stopped to see the president of North Carolina A&T. Franklin later spoke at both Du Bois' eightieth birthday celebration in 1948 and at his ninetieth birthday celebration, both held at the Mayflower Hotel in New York. In the early 1950s, Franklin become a public figure in his own right when he joined Thurgood Marshall's team of experts mounting evidence for school desegregation in the *Brown* v. *Board* case.[49]

Moreover, Du Bois lived to see Kenneth Stampp, the Berkeley professor he heard lauded some five years earlier, publish arguably the first revisionist account of slavery. While chiefly relying on white sources (politicians, slaveholders, and nonslaveholders), Kenneth Stampp's *The Peculiar Institution: Slavery in the Ante-Bellum South* (1956) appeared as one of the earliest works by a mainstream white scholar that paid attention to how the actions of enslaved Blacks, especially acts resisting the master's authority in large ways and small, shaped the evolution of the institution of slavery. Stampp's chapters on "A Troublesome Property" and "To Make Them Stand in Fear," chapters appearing early in the book, established a pattern of enslaved Blacks resisting white authority, and by doing so, shaping and reshaping white efforts to manage such resistance.

With the civil rights movement gaining momentum through the direct action campaign of the Southern Christian Leadership Conference and the emergence of a new generation of scholars, combined with the nation's postwar need to win favor among the "colored" people of the world in Asia, Africa, and elsewhere in its global competition with communism, white Americans outside the South began to look at both the nation's history and its current reality with less favor. With these changes lending momentum, Stampp's work quickly replaced Ulrich Bonnell Phillips' *American Negro Slavery* as the standard work on slavery in the scholarly canon.[50] A decade later, Stampp published a concise synthesis, *The Reconstruction Era* (1967), which also quickly replaced the lingering remnants of the Dunning School as the standard scholarly summary of the period, even if it did not necessarily come to dominate school textbooks. Once again, Stampp's awareness of Du Bois' contributions and their emphasis on Black agency during Reconstruction stood as a belated tribute to *Black Reconstruction*.[51]

The growing inclusion of Du Bois' insights in each new round of revision of slavery and Reconstruction history owed much, but not all, to

The Legacy of W. E. B. DuBois 155

the growing success of the postwar civil rights movement, especially the commitment to nonviolence and direct action advocated by the Reverend Martin Luther King and the Southern Christian Leadership Conference. Initially as reluctant as many Old Testament champions of justice (including Moses), King, eloquent, committed to nonviolence, and successful with the Montgomery Bus Boycott, attracted the support of white liberals outside the South and impressed even those isolated southern liberals who understood the truth of his words but were too often reluctant to face the full wrath of the South's recalcitrant white majority, a majority moved by a complicated mix of racism and self-interest.

The drama and tone of the fight for civil rights during the early 1960s was perhaps best exemplified by King's well-known "Letter from Birmingham Jail," written in March 1963 to a group of white religious leaders, Christian and Jewish, many of whom labeled themselves as racial moderates but who had criticized the Southern Christian Leadership Conference's choice to bring the direct action campaign to Birmingham, where the commissioner of public safety, Eugene "Bull" Conner, stood ready (and arguably eager) to meet direct action with confrontation. Unsurprisingly, as the leader of a movement driven at its core by Black agency, King's letter to the local white clergy explained why his movement must proceed on its own time rather than allow white leaders to set the schedule or determine the strategy required for the pursuit of racial equality.[52]

King explained to the religious leaders that their cries of "Wait!" had gone on for too long when "you are harried day and night by the fact that you are Negro, living constantly at tiptoe stance, never quite knowing what to expect next, and are plagued by inner fears and outer resentments, when you are forever fighting a sense of 'nobodiness' – then you will understand why we find it difficult to wait." The time had come, King insisted, "when the cup of endurance runs over, and men are no longer willing to be plunged into the abyss of despair." Black "impatience," King observed, resulted directly from white intransigence. Moreover, King, drawing on twentieth-century liberal Christian theologian Paul Tillich, argued that "sin is separation" and segregation is a product of man's "awful estrangement, his terrible sinfulness."

Addressing the white religious leaders' argument that the timing was not right for direct action in Birmingham, King expressed a different understanding of time:

[We] must use time creatively, in the knowledge that the time is always ripe to do right. Now is the time to make real the promise of democracy and transform our pending national elegy into a creative psalm of brotherhood. Now is the time to

156   *Understanding the American South*

lift our national policy from the quicksand of racial injustice into the solid rock of human dignity.

"I am in Birmingham," King declared, "because injustice was there. I cannot sit idly by in Atlanta and not be concerned about what happens in Birmingham. Injustice anywhere is a threat to justice everywhere."[53]

King also confessed that he had become "gravely disappointed with the white moderate." He suggested that "the Negro's greatest stumbling block in his stride toward freedom is not the White Citizens' Council or the Ku Klux Klanners, but the white moderate, who is more devoted to 'order' than to justice" and who "paternalistically believes he can set the timetable for another man's freedom." King thought that true white moderates would understand "that law and order exist for the purpose of establishing justice."[54]

King concluded, as was his bent, on notes of reconciliation, predicting that:

One day the South will know that when these disinherited children of God sat down at lunch counters, they were in reality standing up for what is best in the American dream and for the most sacred values of our ... heritage, thereby bringing our nation back to those great wells of democracy which were dug deep by the founding fathers in ... the Constitution and the Declaration of Independence.

"Let us all hope," King wrote, "that the dark clouds of racial prejudice will soon pass away and the deep fog of misunderstanding will lift from our fear drenched communities, and that at some not too distant tomorrow the radiant stars of love and brotherhood will shine over our great nation with all their scintillating beauty."[55]

The pathos, and the success, of the post-World War II civil rights movement doubtless moved many talented scholars to take up historical research related to civil rights issues in earlier periods to deepen our collective understanding as well as to clear up long-held distortions and misunderstandings. A significant proportion of these scholars decided to work in the closely related fields of slavery and Reconstruction history. With the ground already broken by the work of Stampp and earlier scholars, an outpouring of new scholarship appeared, first concentrating on the institution of slavery and then developing a sharper focus on Reconstruction.

Du Bois' theme of Black agency was picked up and vigorously advanced by a young Marxist historian, Eugene Genovese, appearing first in his book on the economics of slavery, *The Political Economy of Slavery* (1965), but much more fulsomely in his epic account of slavery

The Legacy of W. E. B. DuBois 157

in the antebellum American South, *Roll, Jordon, Roll: The World the Slaves Made* (1974). In *Roll, Jordan, Roll*, Genovese explained how slave resistance to their oppression initiated an ongoing cycle of accommodation to resistance followed by resistance to the new accommodation and the further accommodation to the latest resistance and so on. Genovese's empirical work revealed that slave resistance not only influenced production patterns on plantations and farms but also created living space for slave families and religious life and community formation that lay largely beyond the vision of slaveholders.[56]

Other scholars of slavery reported similar findings. John Blasingame wrote convincingly about the formation and influence of slave communities. Herbert Gutman published a landmark book on the slave family, refuting Department of Health, Education, and Welfare Secretary Daniel Moynihan's contention that slavery had debilitated the Black family. Albert Raboteau and others wrote eloquently about slave religion and the role that Black American Christianity played in creating and sustaining Black communities through both slavery and Jim Crow. Other works addressed the slaves' effectiveness as industrial workers in the Old South and as artisans and laborers in cities. Ira Berlin's early work extended these findings to tell the story of free Blacks in the antebellum South in his highly regarded *Slaves without Masters*.[57] Later in his career, Berlin wrote an impressively researched and largely convincing interpretation treating the evolution of slavery as a New World institution by analyzing the slave experience in the New World by generations moving from the Charter, to the Atlantic, to the Revolutionary, to the Migration, to the Freedom generations. Berlin's work told the story of slavery through generations of enslaved experiences rather than through the standard political or economic periodization that previously characterized studies of slavery.[58]

While signs of a political backlash against the civil rights movement were appearing on the horizon, within the academy penetrating revisionist works on Reconstruction proliferated, with almost all reflecting the influence of Du Bois' work some four decades earlier by affirming the importance of Black agency. Reflecting Du Bois' priorities in *Black Reconstruction*, a major focus of scholarship over the last third of the twentieth century landed on the transition from enslaved to free labor and the changing nature of labor arrangements and bargaining power for both the freedpeople and landowners. Econometric works by Gavin Wright, Roger Ransom, Richard Sutch, and others used quantitative methods to suggest qualitative frameworks concerning Black labor the

158   *Understanding the American South*

post-bellum South. Eric Foner, Barbara Fields, Pete Daniels, Joseph Reidy, Jacqueline Jones, Julie Saville, Vernon Burton, Tracey McKenzie, Tera Hunter, and many others shed much new light on the issue of labor during Reconstruction, describing the many and changing arguments and demands made by freedpeople and landowners, and, after the restoration of white Democratic rule in the South by the 1880s, on the creation of a system of tenancy, sharecropping, and day labor that was to varying degrees unsatisfactory to all.[59]

Also following a major Du Bois' theme, another flurry of scholarship highlighted the importance of Black political involvement and white determination to limit Black participation or eliminate it all together. Pioneering works by Michael Perman, Michael Les Benedict, William Gillette, Laura Edwards, and others highlighted the political volatility of Reconstruction and the surge of African American political activity that almost remade the South before the reaction took place.[60] At the state level, Joel Williamson wrote an impressive early study of South Carolina during Reconstruction covering a gamut of topics. Focusing on state-level politics, Thomas Holt's book on Black-majority South Carolina teased out important differences among Palmetto state Republicans, and even some sharp differences among African American politicians. Mulattos and people of color who had been free before the war, and perhaps even owned property, held a disproportionate number of leadership positions in the Republican-controlled legislature and often found themselves occasionally at odds with Black members who were former slaves on farms and plantations and who tended to be more focused on rural labor issues.[61] George Rable and Allen Trelease, among others, focused on the role of white violence and intimidation in the overthrow of Republican Reconstruction in the South and opening the path for white control and the creation of a "Solid South."[62]

A number of works focused on yet another Du Bois theme, the sheer drama of daily life for African Americans, especially but not only those in the South, as they lived with danger, frustration, and nervous anticipation, the emotion King described as living "constantly on tiptoe stance" throughout the Reconstruction era and beyond. Foremost among these works remains Leon Litwack's Pulitzer Prize-winning *Been in the Storm So Long*. Few books on African Americans since Du Bois' work had captured the emotional, psychological tension, the "two-ness," of African American life during the nineteenth century with such empathy and passion.[63]

In 1989, drawing on the outpouring of scholarly monographs and valuable interpretations together with significant original research, Eric Foner's

The Legacy of W. E. B. DuBois 159

award-winning *Reconstruction: America's Unfinished Revolution* (1989) emerged as the definitive account of the Reconstruction era. At the time of publication of *Reconstruction*, Foner acknowledged his great debt to Du Bois' work, which predated Foner by more than a half century and suggested similar lines of argument and a strong emphasis on Black agency as a driving force behind many of the gains Blacks made during the era. In sum, Foner offered an empirically rich account that seconded Du Bois' insistence that the tragedy of the era was not Reconstruction but its overthrow and the restoration of white supremacy in the South (with the complicity of many northerners) and the nation's acceptance of the return to white rule.[64]

By the early 2020s, several generations of professional historians have reaffirmed Foner's *Reconstruction* as the definitive work on the period while conducting new research illuminating new dimensions of the story. The world of mainstream scholarship has continued to elaborate on the broad outlines of Foner's interpretations, and indirectly on the central thrusts of Du Bois' much earlier work, fleshing out many issues with fresh insights and exploring new avenues of inquiry as well. Among historians, the question of Black agency is now taken as a given. It has enriched not only the answers given but also the questions asked in historical scholarship.

Yet the larger story of race relations since the appearance of Foner's landmark work in 1989 is bifurcated and disappointing. The ups and downs of the American economy (and there have been several since 1990) combined with the seemingly relentless increase in economic inequality, an inequality manifesting a strong racial component, increasingly haunts the American landscape. Additionally, police violence against African Americans and increasing evidence that the national system of correction and detention has and is now creating a "carceral" state, which is disproportionately Black, raises pressing questions about a growing racial divide in the nation. Incidents of white racist violence grow more common. In the author's home state there was the Charleston Massacre of 2015, when a lone white supremacist, Dylan Roof, killed nine Black people who welcomed him and engaged with him in a Bible study at Charleston's historic Mother Emanuel AME Church. Among Roof's victims was Mother Emanuel's beloved pastor, the Reverend Clementa Pinckney, who was also a state senator known in the halls of the State House for his grace and goodwill to all. Even though a strong majority of the Palmetto state's citizenry rallied and finally persuaded the state legislature to remove the Confederate battle flag from the State House grounds, such tragedies remain a persistent and disturbing problem.[65]

160   *Understanding the American South*

Many voices of protest in the twenty-first century have come from the growing African American middle class and its successful literati. In 2015, Ta-Nahisi Coates, an award-winning journalist for *The Atlantic* and author, published *Between the World and Me*, crafted as a letter to his son about his life and the lessons learned from it. The story begins with Coates' childhood in drug-ravaged Baltimore, where Coates grew up in a middle-class household. His father was a former Black Panther who became a publisher and worked as a librarian at Howard University. Coates' parents used corporal punishment to deter their son from involving himself in the temptations and violence of the world beyond home, that of the streets, whether from gangs or police. Coates writes of his childhood as largely one of physicality and fear. A different portion of the world opened to Coates when he became a student at Howard University in Washington. Coates termed "the Yard" at Howard as the "Mecca," where people of different colors (but mostly colors other than white) flourished in the privilege and freedom and presumed safety of the Yard and Howard. The glory of the Mecca, which Coates saw as a center of Black civilization worldwide, was precisely that it stretched beyond the United States into Africa and Asia. Coates fell in love with and at the "Mecca." While at Howard, Coates charted a course for his future career as a writer. He left Howard after five years without a degree but with a determination to pursue a career in journalism and writing.[66]

Coates' loving confessional and the cautioning instructions to his son that comprise *Beyond the World and Me* revealed the new race and class tensions that surfaced or resurfaced with a vengeance in the early twenty-first century. Coates' deepest source of alienation from America came from exactly the type of incident that has grown too common in twenty-first century America. Black police officers in Prince George County, Virginia, an affluent suburb of Richmond which was also one-third African American, pursued, shot, and killed Prince Jones, a Black friend of Coates from Howard and a young man of upper-middle-class status, ambition, and values, in a case of mistaken identity. Haunting fears from such tragedies, times the unthinkable becoming thinkable, came through in his letter to his son.[67]

Yet perhaps the critical advice Coates gave to his son came near the end of his letter when he reminded his son that his life, his world, his experience, no matter his achievement, would be as a Black man, but also that it would not be his father's experience. His son was not growing up on the mean streets of Baltimore during a drug epidemic. The son's father is a MacArthur Fellow and internationally known writer. Coates knew

The Legacy of W. E. B. DuBois 161

that his son's life was not lived on or near Baltimore's mean streets, and that as the son of an accomplished middle-class writer and professor, his son would face different challenges – as well as the lingering threat of becoming another Prince Jones. Coates' advice to his son was to learn from his elders' experience but also to recognize that different difficulties would lie ahead and that race and racism would still be among them. But his son's preparation could not be informed only by the past but also by the now and an anticipation of the future.[68] Our history, personal and collective, influences but does not dictate the now, nor the now the future, it simply tells us where we have been if we listen.

Following the success of her first book, *The Warmth of Other Suns*, on Black migration from the South to Chicago and other northern cities, former *New York Times* reporter and writer Isabel Wilkerson revived an older perspective on race and racism in America with her second book, *Caste: The Origins of Our Discontent*.[69] By engaging in a comparative study of a culture with an exceedingly well-defined caste system (India), and the caste system imposed in Nazi Germany, where the new caste system emerged full-blown in the 1930s, and comparing those systems to the race-based system of segregation and inequality that reemerged in the United States after the Reconstruction era ended, Wilkerson found that the United States had nurtured into being a full-blown racial caste system that proved difficult to dismantle. The chief characteristic of a caste system was its impermeability. No amount of success, education, or wealth could alter one's caste, not in India, and, Wilkerson argued, not in the United States, not even in the twentieth and twenty-first centuries.[70] With her book, Wilkerson revived an understanding of race and social hierarchy in America that had flourished among sociologists during the 1930s and 1940s but quietly fell into disuse thereafter.[71] With *Caste*, Wilkerson rediscovered an interpretive concept which explained how a rigidly defined caste system conferred a formal social status on people which one could never escape, alter, discard, or lose. You were what you were – forever and ever. In the American caste system, Blacks were designated as inferior regardless of achievement or attainment and whites were deemed superior regardless of wealth, occupation, or education. Not only did the American caste system assign Blacks to a permanent and inescapable position as an inferior class but it also conferred on whites all the privileges of "whiteness" regardless of social class or achievement or character.[72]

Wilkerson emphasized that such rigidity retained great appeal among the American white working class and rural whites because it conveyed a status above Blacks regardless of wealth, income, or occupation, a status that could neither be forfeited nor attained. It was this rigidity, or inflexibility, of caste that provided many whites the great comfort of knowing they were not society's bottom rail. Instead, they were always superior to a certain group of "others." And, as Wilkerson observed, it was often lower- or working-class whites who embraced their caste identity most fiercely and that became annoyed or angered in the extreme if Blacks or even other whites attempted to suggest otherwise.[73]

But in addition to the appeal of a racial caste system to working-class whites, Wilkerson noted, even some middle-class whites often expressed disbelief and even distress when faced with high-achieving or affluent Blacks and still tried to impose caste burdens on them or treated them as imposters or inferiors to safeguard their own privilege. In 1997, when John Hope Franklin visited Washington to accept the Medal of Freedom, the nation's highest civilian honor, from President Bill Clinton, he endured two experiences that revealed assumptions of white privilege. At a Washington club, a woman asked him to "fetch" her coat for her, having mistaken Franklin for a coat-checker, and a white man gave Franklin his car keys and asked him to retrieve his car, mistaking Medal of Freedom-winner Franklin for a parking valet.[74]

The power of whiteness as a concept has also shaped much of the best recent scholarship on the growing plight of the white working class. Jonathan Metzl, a medical doctor, attributed the ravaging of the white working class during the opioid epidemic to the cherished privileges of whiteness. In his *Dying of Whiteness*, Metzl found that many working-class whites were simply unwilling to work with Blacks and Hispanics to seek political measures addressing the loss of working-class jobs and the decline of working-class communities if it meant forming a coalition that crossed caste lines. It was an embrace of white privilege that led them into a white opioid epidemic which often led to death.[75]

As Coates suggested in his advice to his son, the challenges of the 2020s are not the problems of the 1860s and 1870s, or even of the 1950s and 1960s. Works such as those of Coates and Wilkerson bring some of the main themes of Du Bois' long and controversial life to the fore once again, revealing their persistent relevance in American life across many decades. After all, many years earlier Du Bois had used the term "whiteness" to explain the caste phenomena that Franklin described experiencing. And the concept of whiteness has now become a commonplace of recent historical scholarship.

For our purposes in the twenty-first century, what matters most about Du Bois' body of work, including *Black Reconstruction*, is not what it

The Legacy of W. E. B. DuBois 163

argued and what it did not, but the work it inspired and the continued relevance of Du Bois' central themes. In addition to his perceptive recognition of Black agency, a theme that lent originality and fresh perspectives to *Black Reconstruction*, the lingering influences of Du Bois' work also reflects the durability of *Souls of Black Folk* and other writings emphasizing the "two-ness" of the African American experience. Moreover, Du Bois was among the first historians to use the term "whiteness" to reflect a creed or an ideology, an ideology that could be expressed through a caste system. Many, though certainly not all, of the racial problems and tensions of the twenty-first century revolve around an updated version of this creed of whiteness, around the existence of "white privilege," including the right to vote, job opportunities, and fair housing, and many other "privileges," some perhaps small but looming large to those who have benefited from their persistence. The willingness of many whites to fight politically and culturally to defend the remaining vestiges of whiteness, or white privilege, contribute significantly to the political polarization and economic division challenges of our time. Somehow, more than three-quarters of a century ago, W. E. B. Du Bois understood.

Notes

1. Annette Gordon-Reed, "The Color-Line," *New York Review of Books*, August 19, 2021.
2. David Levering Lewis, *W. E. B. Du Bois: A Biography* (New York: Holt, 2009). All citations in this chapter refer to this one-volume edition.
3. W. E. Burghardt Du Bois, *The Souls of Black Folk: Sketches and Notes* (Chicago: McClurg and Co., 1903); Lewis, *W. E. B. Du Bois*, 191–204; Eric Foner, *Nothing but Freedom: Emancipation and Its Legacy* (Baton Rouge: Louisiana State University Press, 1983).
4. Du Bois, *Souls of Black Folk*, 4–22.
5. Du Bois, *Souls of Black Folk*, 4.
6. Du Bois, *Souls of Black Folk*, 5.
7. Lewis, *W. E. B. Du Bois*, 194–195.
8. Du Bois, *Souls of Black Folk*, 5.
9. Du Bois, *Souls of Black Folk*, 22–30.
10. Du Bois, *Souls of Black Folk*, 22–53. For an overview of Du Bois' sharp differences with Booker T. Washington, see Lewis, *W. E. B. Du Bois*, 152–215.
11. Du Bois, *Souls of Black Folk*, 25–29.
12. Lewis, *W. E. B. Du Bois*, 201–211.
13. Du Bois, "The Souls of White Folk," originally published in *The Independent*, August 10, 1920. The essay is reprinted in W. E. B. Du Bois, *Writings*, Library of America (New York: Penguin Books, 1987), 923–938.
14. Lewis, *W. E. B. Du Bois*, 546–545.

164 *Understanding the American South*

15. Lewis, *W. E. B. Du Bois*, 579–583.
16. W. E. Burghardt Du Bois, "Reconstruction and Its Benefits," *The American Historical Review* 15 (July 1910): 781–799; Lewis, *W. E. B. Du Bois*, 576–578.
17. Du Bois, "Reconstruction and Its Benefits," 781–782.
18. Du Bois, "Reconstruction and Its Benefits," 783–786.
19. Du Bois, "Reconstruction and Its Benefits," 784.
20. Du Bois, "Reconstruction and Its Benefits," 789–799.
21. William Archibald Dunning, *Essays on the Civil War and Reconstruction and Related Topics* (New York: The MacMillian Company, 1898). Dunning, from his perch at Columbia University, was even more influential as a mentor and advisor than as an author. Works in the so-called Dunning School include: Walter Lynwood Fleming, *Civil War and Reconstruction in Alabama* (New York: Columbia University Press, 1905) and E. Merton Coulter, *Civil War and Readjustment in Kentucky* (Chapel Hill: University of North Carolina Press, 1893). An earlier work by journalist turned historian James S. Pike, *The Prostrate State: South Carolina during Reconstruction* (New York: D. Appleton and Company, 1874), also shaped Dunning's views and those of later historians of the Dunning School.
22. Alrutheous A. Taylor, *The Negro in South Carolina during Reconstruction* (Washington, DC: The Association for the Study of Negro History and Life, 1924); Alrutheous A. Taylor, *The Negro in the Reconstruction of Virginia* (Washington, DC: The Association for the Study of Negro History and Life, 1926).
23. Francis B. Simkins and Robert H. Woody, *South Carolina during Reconstruction* (Chapel Hill: University of North Carolina Press, 1932).
24. Claude G. Bowers, *The Tragic Era: The Revolution after Lincoln* (Boston: Houghton Mifflin, 1929). Bowers had no training as a historian nor used the historical method but was successful at writing popular histories.
25. W. E. B. Du Bois, *Black Reconstruction in America, 1860–1880* (New York: Harcourt Brace, 1935). All citations in this chapter are to Du Bois, *Black Reconstruction in America, 1860–1880* (New York: The Free Press, 1992), with an introduction by David Leavering Lewis.
26. Du Bois, *Black Reconstruction*, passim.
27. Du Bois, *Black Reconstruction*, 3–83.
28. Du Bois, *Black Reconstruction*, 17–31.
29. Du Bois, *Black Reconstruction*, 84–181.
30. Du Bois, *Black Reconstruction*, 182–324. For a good overview of modern scholarship on the topic, see Gavin Wright, "The Strange Career of the New Southern Economic History," *Reviews in American History* 10, no. 4 (1982): 164–180; Gavin Wright, *Old South, New South: Revolutions in the Southern Economy since the Civil War* (New York: Basic Books, 1986); Gavin Wright, "American Agriculture and the Labor Market: What Happened to Proletarianization?" *Agricultural History* 62, no. 3 (1988): 182–209; Harold Woodman, "The Political Economy of the South: Retrospects and Prospects," *Journal of Southern History* 67, no. 4 (2001): 789–810; Roger Ransom and Richard Sutch, *One Kind of Freedom: The Economic*

The Legacy of W. E. B. DuBois

Consequences of Emancipation (Cambridge: Cambridge University Press, 1989).

31. Du Bois, *Black Reconstruction*, 325–525.
32. Du Bois, *Black Reconstruction*, 670–709.
33. Du Bois, *Black Reconstruction*, 580–636.
34. Du Bois, *Black Reconstruction*, 637–667; Janet G. Hudson, "From Constitution to Constitution: South Carolina's Unique Stance on Divorce, 1868–1895," *South Carolina Historical Magazine* 98 (January 1997): 75–96.
35. J. Mills Thornton III, "Fiscal Policy and the Failure of Radical Reconstruction in the Lower South," in J. Morgan Kousser and James M. McPherson, eds., *Region, Race, and Reconstruction: Essays in Honor of C. Vann Woodward* (New York: Oxford University Press, 1982), 349–394.
36. Du Bois, *Black Reconstruction*, 526–636; Steven Hahn, *A Nation without Borders; The United States and Its World in an Age of Civil Wars, 1830–1910* (New York: Penguin, 2016).
37. Lewis, *W. E. B. Du Bois*, 584–592.
38. Lewis Gannett, "Books and Things," *New York Herald-Tribune*, June 13, 1935.
39. William MacDonald, "The American Negro's Part in the Reconstruction Years: A Survey of the Period between 1860 and 1880 by Professor W. E. Burghardt Du Bois," *Sunday New York Times*, June 18, 1835.
40. Lewis, *W. E. B. Du Bois*, 584. *The Daily Mirror* and *The World* were both Hearst newspapers.
41. Oswald Garrison Villard, "Black Controversy," *Saturday Review of Literature*, January 18, 1936.
42. *Saturday Review of Literature*, June 19, 1935.
43. Jonathan Daniels, "Book Review of Du Bois, *Black Reconstruction*," *Book of the Month Club News* (July 1935); Charles W. Eagles, *Jonathan Daniels and the Evolution of a Southern Liberal* (Knoxville: University of Tennessee Press, 1982).
44. C. Vann Woodward to W. E. B. Du Bois, April 3, 1938, in Michael O'Brien, ed., *The Letters of C. Vann Woodward* (New Haven: Yale University Press, 2013), 60.
45. Howard K. Beale, "On Rewriting Reconstruction History," *American Historical Review* 45 (July 1940): 807–827.
46. Lewis, *W. E. B. Du Bois*, 688–695.
47. Lewis, *W. E. B. Du Bois*, 696–714, esp. 707–709.
48. Leon F. Litwack, "Trouble in Mind: The Bicentennial and the Afro-American Experience," *Journal of American History* 74 (September 1987): 315–337, especially 335–336; Lewis, *W. E. B. Du Bois*, 694.
49. John Hope Franklin, *Mirror to America: The Autobiography of John Hope Franklin* (New York: Farrar, Straus and Giroux, 2005); and Andrew Yarrow, "John Hope Franklin, Scholar of African American History, Is Dead at 94," *New York Times*, March 25, 2009.
50. Kenneth Stampp, *The Peculiar Institution: Slavery in the Ante-Bellum South* (New York: Alfred A. Knopf, 1956), especially 46–191.

166   *Understanding the American South*

51. Kenneth Stampp, *The Era of Reconstruction, 1865–1877* (New York: Alfred A. Knopf, 1965).
52. Martin Luther King, Jr., "Letter from Birmingham Jail," *Christian Century* 80 (June 12, 1963): 777–783. For background on King's life and emergence as a civil rights leader prior to Birmingham, see Taylor Branch, *Parting the Waters: America in the King Years* (New York: Simon and Schuster, 1988), see especially 673–755, and David Leavering Lewis, *King: A Biography* (Urbana: University of Illinois Press,1970). For more on the background of Birmingham, see J. Mills Thornton III, *Dividing Lines: Municipal Politics and the Struggle for Civil Rights in Montgomery, Birmingham, and Selma* (Tuscaloosa: University of Alabama Press, 2002), 141–289.
53. King, "Letter from Birmingham Jail."
54. King, "Letter from Birmingham Jail."
55. King, "Letter from Birmingham Jail."
56. These themes permeated the early work of Eugene D. Genovese, *The Political Economy of Slavery: Studies in the Economy and Society in the Slave South* (Middleton, CT: Wesleyan University Press, 1961), and especially *Roll, Jordon, Roll: The World the Slaves Made* (New York: Random House, 1974).
57. John W. Blassingame, *The Slave Community: Plantation Life in the Antebellum South* (New York: Oxford University Press, 1972); Herbert G. Gutman, *The Black Family in Slavery and Freedom, 1750–1825* (New York: Random House, 1976); Albert Raboteau, *Slave Religion: The "Invisible Institution" in the Antebellum South* (New York: Oxford University Press, 1978); Richard Wade, *Slavery in the Cities: The South, 1820–1860* (New York: Oxford University Press, 1962); Robert Starobin, *Industrial Slavery in the Old South* (New York: Oxford University Press, 1970); Ira Berlin, *Slaves without Masters: The Free Negro in the Antebellum South* (New York: Pantheon Books, 1974).
58. As Berlin's career progressed, he emerged as one of the nation's foremost historians of slavery. See Ira Berlin, *Many Thousands Gone: The First Two Centuries of Slavery in North America* (Cambridge, MA: Harvard University Press, 1998); Ira Berlin, *Generations of Captivity: A History of African American Slaves* (Cambridge, MA: Harvard University Press, 2003); Ira Berlin, *The Making of African America: The Four Great Migrations* (New York: Viking, 2010).
59. Wright, *Old South, New South*; Ransom and Sutch, *One Kind of Freedom*; Foner, *Nothing but Freedom*; Barbara J. Fields, *Slavery and Freedom on the Middle Ground: Maryland during the Nineteenth Century* (New Haven: Yale University Press, 1987); Jacqueline Jones, *Labor of Love, Labor of Sorrow: Black Women, Work, and the Family, from Slavery to the Present* (New York: Vintage Books, 1985); Pete Daniel, *The Shadow of Slavery: Peonage in the South, 1901–1969* (Urbana: University of Illinois Press, 1990); Orville Vernon Burton, *In My Father's House Are Many Mansions: Family and Community in Edgefield, South Carolina* (Chapel Hill: University of North Carolina Press, 1987); Julia Saville, *The Work of Reconstruction: From Slave to Wage Laborer in South Carolina, 1860–1870* (New York:

The Legacy of W. E. B. DuBois   167

Cambridge University Press, 1994); Tera W. Hunter, *To 'Joy My Freedom: Southern Black Women's Lives and Labors after the Civil War* (Cambridge, MA: Harvard University Press, 1998); Joseph P. Reidy, *From Slavery to Agrarian Capitalism in the Cotton Plantation South: Central Georgia, 1800–1880* (Chapel Hill: University of North Carolina Press, 1995); John C. Rodrigue, *Reconstruction in the Cane Fields: From Slavery to Free Labor in Louisiana's Sugar Parishes, 1862–1880* (Baton Rouge: Louisiana State University Press, 2001); Leslie A. Schwalm, *A Hard Fight for We: Women's Transition from Slavery to Freedom in South Carolina* (Urbana: University of Illinois Press, 1997). See also, Robert Tracy McKenzie, "Southern Labor and Reconstruction," in Lacy K. Ford, ed., *A Companion to the Civil War and Reconstruction* (Malden, MA: Blackwell, 2005), 366–385.

60. Michael Perman, *Reunion without Compromise: The South and Reconstruction, 1865–1868* (Chapel Hill: University of North Carolina Press, 1973); Michael Perman, *The Road to Redemption: Southern Politics, 1869–1879* (Chapel Hill: University of North Carolina Press, 1984); Michael Les Benedict, *A Compromise of Principle: Congressional Republicans and Reconstruction* (New York: W. W. Norton & Company,1974); William Gillette, *Retreat from Reconstruction, 1869–1879* (Baton Rouge: Louisiana State University Press, 1979); Laura Edwards, *Gendered Strife and Confusion: The Political Culture of Reconstruction* (Urbana: University of Illinois Press, 1997).

61. Joel Williamson, *After Slavery: The Negro in South Carolina during Reconstruction, 1861–1877* (Chapel Hill: University of North Carolina Press, 1965); Thomas Holt, *Black over White: Negro Political Leadership in South Carolina during Reconstruction* (Urbana: University of Illinois Press, 1977).

62. George Rable, *But There Was No Peace: The Role of Violence in the Politics of Reconstruction* (Athens: University of Georgia Press, 1984); Allen Trelease, *White Terror: The Ku Klux Klan Conspiracy and Southern Reconstruction* (New York: Harper and Row, 1971).

63. Leon F. Litwack, *Been in the Storm So Long: The Aftermath of Slavery* (New York: Knopf, 1979).

64. Eric Foner, *Reconstruction: America's Unfinished Revolution* (New York: Oxford University Press, 1988).

65. For more on the 2015 Charleston Massacre, see Jennifer Berry Hawes, *Grace Will Lead Us Home: The Charleston Church Massacre and the Hard, Inspiring Journey to Forgiveness* (New York: St. Martin's Press, 2019) and Matt Ford and Adam Chandler, "'Hate Crime': A Mass Killing at a Historic Church," *The Atlantic*, June 19, 2015.

66. Ta-Nehisi Coates, *Between the World and Me* (New York: One World, 2015), 5–71.

67. Coates, *Between the World and Me*, 75–88.

68. Coates, *Between the World and Me*, 114–132.

69. Isabel Wilkerson, *The Warmth of Other Suns: The Epic Story of America's Great Migration* (New York: Vintage, 2010); Isabel Wilkerson, *Caste: The Origins of Our Discontents* (New York: Random House, 2020).

70. Wilkerson, *Caste*, 39–98.
71. John Dollard, *Caste and Class in a Southern Town* (New Haven: Yale University Press, 1937); Hortense Powdermaker, *After Freedom: A Cultural Study in the Deep South* (New York: The Viking Press, 1939); Allison Davis, Burleigh Gardner, and Mary Gardner, *Deep South: A Social Anthropology Study of Caste and Class* (Chicago: University of Chicago Press, 1941); Gunnar Myrdal, *American Dilemma: The Negro Problem and Modern Democracy* (New York: Harper Row, 1945).
72. Wilkerson, *Caste*, 159–174, 178–189.
73. Wilkerson, *Caste*, 311–349.
74. Peter Applebaum, "John Hope Franklin, Scholar and Advocate," *New York Times*, March 28, 2009; Andrew L. Yarrow, "John Hope Franklin, Scholar of African American History, Is Dead at 94," *New York Times*, March 25, 2009. See also Franklin, *Mirror to America*.
75. Jonathan Metzl, *Dying of Whiteness: How the Politics of Racial Resentment Is Killing America's Heartland* (New York: Basic Books, 2019).

7

An American Elegy

The American South during the Ages of Capital and Inequality

In the second volume of his monumental four-volume sequence covering the history of the world since 1789, *The Age of Capital: 1848–1875*, the great British historian Eric Hobsbawm treats the American South in his chapter on "Winners" rather than in his corresponding chapter on "Losers." While Hobsbawm's choice might, at first glance, seem an obvious one to the descendants of the nearly four million enslaved Blacks who were emancipated (and the male freedmen granted suffrage by the Reconstruction-era constitutional amendments), the term hardly captured the feelings of freed people once the post-Reconstruction era produced promises betrayed, dreams deferred, and suffrage stolen. And for white southerners across two or three generations, and some recalcitrant southern whites down to this very day, and doubtless more than a few historians of the American South working from a variety of perspectives, the treatment of the South in the "Winners" chapter would have seemed, at best, savagely ironic, and at worst downright insulting.[1]

At a quick glance, however, the prevailing logic behind Hobsbawm's decision seems sound. He was writing about the United States with the Confederate rebellion quelled, the Union saved, slavery abolished, enslaved Blacks freed, democracy expanded, and the reconstructed American nation poised to transform its economic identity from that of a thriving agricultural and commercial republic to a fledgling industrial power. In view of these developments, Hobsbawm's inclusion of the American South (as well as the North) in his account of the Age of Capital's winners seems entirely logical but not without its measure of irony. The irony of the characterization invites investigation of Hobsbawm's brief

169

170 · *Understanding the American South*

but penetrating interpretation of the region's mid-nineteenth-century journey toward and away from the Civil War.

In Hobsbawm's mind, the exact nature of the conflict between the American North and American South which ultimately produced a bloody Civil War remained a critical and largely unanswered question despite a voluminous historical literature dealing with the topic. Sectional disagreements over slavery had been present since the founding of the republic and had been settled through tense negotiations and hard-earned compromises. Open warfare between the sections hardly seemed inevitable, in Hobsbawm's view, and a negotiated coexistence entirely possible, at least in theory. Instead of bloody conflict, a peaceful coexistence between an expanding capitalist free labor economy in the North and profitable slave labor agricultural one in the South might have been achieved. Even an increasingly belligerent South could have been calmed by a carefully negotiated separate peace, especially since the very isolation that drove white southerners toward disunion also awaited an independent slaveholders' republic on the world stage. Only the foolish who truly believed rather than merely proclaimed that cotton, rather than capital, was king failed to recognize the growing isolation and vulnerability of slaveholding regimes. The answer to the question of why the American Civil War erupted, Hobsbawm contended, lay in the long struggle between North and South not so much to settle their longstanding internal differences over slavery but for control of the vast American West. Or, differently put, the war resulted from a struggle for control of the continental empire looming through settlement and statehood for the western territories.[2]

For the first five decades of the nineteenth century, the South tried mightily to reorient the developing pattern of American commerce along a North–South axis, focusing on the Mississippi River as the main transportation artery with the port of New Orleans as the ultimate commercial destination. The southern effort even enjoyed a large measure of success as cotton production exploded in the fertile lower Mississippi valley and New Orleans emerged as one of the world's major ports centered on the cotton trade that drove the global economy.[3] But the southern effort to cut the North off economically from its potential hinterland in the West proved doomed with the emergence of the railroad as the nation's dominant mode of transportation in the 1840s and 1850s. Railroads depended heavily on large capital investment (which northern merchants and financiers either had or could readily access through their British and European connections). Moreover, railroads ran east–west as readily as north–south and larger demographic factors tilted trade lines toward

The South during the Ages of Capital and Inequality   171

the horizontal axis. As railroads established themselves as the dominant mode of transportation, the development of east–west railroads helped decide the economic development question decisively in favor of the North.[4]

Yet while the North had population, resources, skilled labor, and capital on its side in any economic competition with the South, the South remained a formidable political opponent. As a "virtual semi-colony" of the British, who stood as both the chief financiers and the primary customers for southern cotton, the South, with its export-oriented economy, remained an ardent supporter of free trade. On the other hand, the increasingly industrial North wanted protection for its emerging industry. Faced with an increasingly disadvantageous economic position within the Union, the South was left to fight its battles in the realm of politics.[5] Increasingly, southern politicians insisted that the right to own slaves must exist in the West even in areas where it was unlikely to thrive, not because they held out great hope that a slave-based economy could flourish there but because they needed a political guarantee for the equality of the slaveholding states within the Union.[6] Indeed, Hobsbawm argued, by the late antebellum era, the strength of the South in the Union lay in politics; the region still comprised half the states in the Union as late as 1850. Moreover, southern politicians had proven skilled in playing the game of Washington politics while also remaining successful in sustaining support for slavery among the bulk of the region's white population despite perennial concerns over white safety and scattered protests that enslaved Black labor limited white opportunity.[7]

Still, from an economic standpoint, the South presented little threat to the booming northern economy. Yet in many respects the motives behind northern ambition were framed more by ideology (albeit an ideology closely tied to economic concerns) than simple economic self-interest. Hobsbawm argued that, by the mid-nineteenth century, a "consensus" emerged among "bourgeois liberals" in the North that the institution of slavery stood in opposition to "History's march of progress," even if those liberals were mostly not in favor of immediate abolition. In the United States, bourgeois liberal values found concentrated expression during the 1850s in the political movement supporting "free soil, free labor, free men." This message, an ideology of upward mobility, became the rallying cry of the new Republican party as it was formed and grew rapidly to gain ascendency in the American North during the last antebellum decade. The free labor movement valued the right to rise and the ability of all men to benefit from the value of their labor, whether property owner or laborer. While often critics of slavery, and staunch opponents of its expansion, champions of the free labor ideology nonetheless generally opposed political and social equality for Blacks, both enslaved and free.[8]

The rapid emergence of the free labor ideology after 1854 caught Democrats off-guard and they had no political answer for it, as most northern Whigs and many northern Democrats shed their traditional party skins and flocked to the Republican banner during the late 1850s. The loss of political leverage the South needed to protect itself from northern control pushed the slaveholding South to ever more aggressive assertions of its "rights." The Old South's increasingly aggressive stance demanding equal protection for slavery in the territories strengthened the Republican cause in the North by giving credence to the growing northern suspicion that a southern "slave power conspiracy" was afoot trying to rob free white northerners of their right to avoid slave competition in the territories. Between the appeal of free labor ideology with its promise of upward social mobility and the threat of the so-called slave power conspiracy to thwart opportunity for northern whites by forcing them into competition with enslaved Blacks, northern whites rallied behind the Republican's pledge to keep slavery out of the remaining territories.[9]

The sudden and dramatic collapse of the Second American Party System in the 1850s left even crafty southern politicians at a loss. They had mastered the art of using the two-party system to protect slavery. But the formation of a largely sectional party capable of winning an electoral college majority left them without leverage – except for the radical threat of secession. In many respects, the South's cause was lost even before the Civil War began. The economic destiny of the nation had shifted from South to North. The long-time sectional balance in American politics had evaporated with the rise of the Republican party.[10]

The Civil War itself took over 700,000 lives, Union and Confederate, or about one in six men of fighting age. It advanced the cause of liberty by freeing nearly four million enslaved Blacks, though it took Union success on the battlefield, self-emancipation by enslaved Blacks and their military service, Lincoln's Emancipation Proclamation, and the Thirteenth Amendment to fully grant that freedom. The war also left later generations with legacies of bravery and heroism and devotion to the cause from soldiers, both Union and Confederate, who carried the fight. But as it was fought, the war generated anxiety, sacrifice, fear, and even hatred among both Union and Confederate populations. Actual deprivation affected more and more areas of the South as the war progressed. As

The South during the Ages of Capital and Inequality 173

the challenge of reconstructing the nation, given its much-needed "new birth of freedom" by the Union victory and emancipation, loomed, the restored republic nevertheless remained baptized in the blood of too many dead, wounded, and disabled soldiers.[11]

For formerly enslaved Blacks in the South, the Reconstruction process, and the resulting amendments promised many opportunities. It promised not only freedom but all those things that made freedom attractive: mobility, the right to marry, fundamental legal and citizenship rights including the right to vote (for males), and the right to own property. And certainly, the right most valued by the prewar Republican party: the right to enjoy the fruits of one's own labor (free labor) seemed at hand. With the passage of the Thirteenth, Fourteenth, and Fifteenth Amendments to the US Constitution and the rise of the Republican party, powered by the infusion of Black male voters into the electorate, to political control in most southern states, the Reconstruction era represented the high tide of Black influence on the southern politics. Substantial social progress was made during the 1868–1877 era, with Black male voting rights affirmed, Black candidates elected to state and local offices across the South, state spending, taxation, and debt policies altered, and broader social services and educational opportunities offered.[12]

Yet even during Reconstruction, southern white recalcitrance remained a difficult challenge to overcome. White Democrats opposed most Reconstruction-era reforms and complained about high taxes, especially on property (most of which was white owned), and whites constantly leveled charges of corruption against Republican regimes and particularly Black officeholders. White terror, whether in the form of the Ku Klux Klan, ad hoc white mobs, or other forms of extra-legal violence, also took their toll on Republican regimes, as did intimidation and outright fraud at the ballot box. Federal enforcement of Black civil and voting rights remained critical to Republican success. But when the Depression of 1873 began to divert national attention away from the problem of reconstructing the nation, federal support for southern Republicans diminished. By 1877, Republicans had withdrawn the federal support (including military support) needed to keep Republican regimes in control of southern states. White Democrats returned to power touting their terror and intimidation-driven victory as "redemption" and moving quickly to diminish Black political clout in the region.[13]

While Reconstruction lasted (until 1877), Black hopes for full equality had been realized in some instances, but after the collapse of Reconstruction hopes for equality rapidly diminished. In the post-Reconstruction South,

174   *Understanding the American South*

white-controlled governments devoted to maintaining white suprem-
acy controlled almost all the former Confederate states. The Second
Founding's early promise of full citizenship, including voting rights for
Blacks, disappeared and gradually assaults on other rights of Black cit-
izens proceeded as the Jim Crow system gradually took hold across the
South.[14]

For the American North, the Union victory in the war secured the West for
northern-style, free labor capitalism. But the combination of Confederate
defeat in 1865 and the national abandonment of Reconstruction in 1877
left the entire South not merely defeated but angry. As Hobsbawm per-
ceptively observed, the South remained "agrarian, poor, backward and
resentful; whites resenting the never-forgotten defeat and Blacks the disfranchisement and ruthless subordination imposed by whites when reconstruction ended."[15] The war and Reconstruction left Black southerners
with "nothing but freedom," not even the opportunity to vote in most
cases, much less the property on which true independence and autonomy
depended. For the white South, the defeat of the Confederacy and the
emancipation of slaves forced a radical transformation of the prevailing
system of plantation agriculture and left the entire region without the capital (the wealth formerly invested in slave property) it needed to thrive in
the international "Age of Capital."[16]

Under the circumstances, any imaginable resurrection of the old plantation system, or even large-scale commercial agriculture of any kind,
depended on organizing the region's large quantity of cheap, and mostly
Black, labor. As a result, whites thought the freedpeople too valuable as
agricultural labor to lose to the North or West, but the newly freed Black
workers remained too despised by whites, who owned almost all the land,
to acquire anything like equality or even fairly negotiated labor contracts.
Fearing competition from the large population of former slaves, potential white immigrants steered clear of the American South. After emancipation, indigenous white southern labor faced direct competition in the
workplace from recently freed slaves – the dreaded prospect that had
kept many slaveless whites loyal to slaveholding regimes before the war.
The reorganization of southern agriculture after emancipation proved a
story of experimentation with a variety of labor-intensive modes of production that succeeded in giving southerners of both races a subsistence,
but which also locked the American South into a pattern of economic
backwardness and poverty that plagued the region for decades.[17]

The early promise of Reconstruction, which included the possibility of
property redistribution in the defeated Confederacy and full bargaining

The South during the Ages of Capital and Inequality   175

rights in the tens of thousands of individual and family negotiations between Black workers and white landowners, had configured and reconfigured the southern agricultural labor system on an annual basis across the cotton South. The thousands upon thousands of individual and family labor negotiations which occurred annually remain hard to categorize because of their number and variation from locale to locale. But as economic historian Gavin Wright has argued, broad patterns became discernible. Blacks across the South clearly preferred becoming landowners, but only very limited numbers acquired property once federal land redistribution proposals failed. But failing property ownership, Black families sought a labor arrangement which gave them as much independence from daily white supervision as possible. This generally meant seeking some sort of tenancy agreement which involved paying rent to the landowner while also agreeing to provide some labor to other portions of the white-owned farm or plantation during busy seasons of the year. Blacks who successfully secured such arrangements had usually leveraged their ownership of a mule, or some tools, or the presence of working-age children as proof of reliability and creditworthiness. Black households lacking such leverage or other tangible evidence of reliability were often left to take a share of the crop as their wage or to work as day laborers. In most southern states, state laws held that sharecroppers were laborers rather than renters. Single men, especially those without visible proof of past success, usually found themselves working for wages, though single men who had succeeded in building a good work reputation in white eyes sometimes received premium wages. Over time, a patchwork quilt of labor arrangements covered the South exhibiting numerous subregional and local variations.[18]

Initially, as these new labor and credit arrangements took hold during the postbellum era, southern Blacks moved south and west toward the Black belt of the lower South and away from upland farming areas as active communication networks and larger Black populations in pre-war Black belt areas attracted Black in-migrants from other parts of the South. Yet with the advent of commercial fertilizers after the war, the locus of cotton production in the South shifted away from the southwest back to the southeast, where a large tenant and sharecropping labor force emerged that included whites as well as Blacks.[19]

Cotton production in the region increased dramatically between 1880 and 1920 despite the end of slavery. But the increased production often landed in a flooded world market in which producers from different parts of the world who had seized market share during the Civil War and

176   *Understanding the American South*

its immediate aftermath remained active competitors of southern cotton growers for decades. Still, in the cash-poor, credit-starved South, concentrating on cotton as the main cash crop made sense to lenders. But the greater commitment to cotton pulled farm acreage and farm operators of all types away from the production of foodstuffs, forcing families and individuals into a greater dependence on the market for subsistence in an era of fluctuating staple prices. In sum, the very sustenance of many cotton growers hinged on the annual ups and downs of the world cotton market.[20]

With the new lack of self-sufficiency in foodstuffs layered on a general shortage of capital in the postwar years, agricultural credit emerged as a key determinant of economic success in the South. Local merchants and cotton buyers (often the same people) generally controlled the flow of credit within the region, though even these merchants usually depended on lines of credit from northern financiers and commission houses. Particularly in the upland South, town merchants often made nice profits from trading cotton and the provision of credit to growers. These merchants soon invested in various town-building ventures, such as cotton mills, to diversify. In the Black belt, towns remained sleepy trading centers, only slightly less "rural" than the sprawling hinterlands they served, and local economic clout, such as it was, generally remained with the large landholders. Blacks seeking credit often found themselves vulnerable to unscrupulous lenders and local authorities who would not usually take their complaints seriously.[21] Urban settings across the South, where full-fledged, formal segregation took hold during the 1890s, witnessed the emergence of a small class of Black professionals and educators and ministers who often provided leadership for local Black communities. Their influence with local white leaders proved limited, but the emergence of this small Black middle class offered modest sums of capital to their communities and served as a breeding ground for future leaders and civil rights advocates.

The overall credit shortage in the region and lack of collateral that many growers (white as well as Black) brought to the transaction led to the rise of the crop-lien system in which growers mortgaged their future crop (or their share of it) to secure supplies and provisions for the year's operations. As the dean of southern historians, the late C. Vann Woodward, once observed, the crop-lien system, which advanced credit based on the future value of a crop not yet produced turned the South into a "vast pawn shop."[22] The uncertainty of the future crop's value and the power that local merchants had in the lending environment led to

The South during the Ages of Capital and Inequality   177

high interest rates being charged through the lien system. Tenants (white as well as Black) who had little or no collateral found it hard to ever get out of debt and simply eked out a living year by year with little chance for accumulation or even escape from debt.

To make matters even worse for the postwar rural South, the loss of all the capital invested in enslaved Blacks – capital which had proven relatively liquid in the prewar era when an active internal slave trade flourished in the region – and the corresponding decline in land values left the region bereft of the capital it needed to sustain thriving commercial agriculture. Simply put, even white southerners were left with a dearth of capital, the very thing they needed to participate actively in the boom of the age. As American industrialization accelerated and the British moved even deeper into the second empire, this dearth of capital at the very time capital was most valued left southerners ill-equipped to participate vigorously in the late nineteenth-century miracle of industrialization.[23]

To the extent that the South sought to industrialize, it stood very much at the mercy of northern capital and expertise. Still, portions of the South turned to industrialization for some ray of hope – and income. However warily, southern business leaders accepted dependency on northern capital that, to an extent, rendered the South a "colonial economy" of the North, an unhappy position for white southerners smarting deeply at Confederate defeat but one born of necessity.[24] To a large extent, industrialization in the American South depended on infusions of northern capital and expertise, on Yankee investors, engineers, and entrepreneurs, with the South chiefly supplying low-skilled labor, industrial sites, and much local managerial and recruiting talent. The rise of the textile industry in parts of the postbellum South stood as the prototypical example of southern industrialization: a northern industry fleeing south for lower costs, drawing significantly on northern capital and expertise, relying on a willing but low-skilled local white workforce, and supported by the organizational and managerial efforts of a cadre of local boosters and investors drawn from small-town merchants, cotton traders, bankers, and professionals of the upland South. The exercise of town-building provided customers for local merchants and helped sustain a rising middle class of managers and small-town professionals to support the enlarged local community.[25]

Beginning as early as 1880 but burgeoning between 1895 and 1920, textiles mills spread through the Piedmont of the two Carolinas and into parts or Georgia and Alabama as well, even creeping into southern Virginia. The industry provided much-needed but low-wage jobs

178 *Understanding the American South*

for white workers in white-majority sections of the South. Eventually, both indigenous and migrating textile firms, Burlington Mills, Springs Industries, and Dan River Mills and Cannon Mills as examples of the former and J. P. Stevens and Company as an example of the latter, formed a key portion if the southern business leadership. These companies ranged from firmly to fiercely anti-union and shaped short- and long-term regional attitudes toward organized labor significantly.[26]

The post-Civil War South was not a monolith, even if it seemed so at times. Pockets of industrialization driven by indigenous southern entrepreneurs also gained a foothold in the region, even as they often proved exceptions that served to highlight the rule. Southern entrepreneurs often found rapprochement with the needed northerners and partnered with them. Moreover, as manufacturing gained a modest foothold in the South, debate flourished in the region over whether Black labor was suited for factory work. In the white belt areas where the textile industry emerged, the large numbers of poor and noninheriting whites made it possible to create a heavily white factory workforce. However, in other industries, especially iron and steel, where Black labor gained a foothold prior to the Civil War, the debate carried meaning. For the most part, however, Black labor remained largely confined to agriculture and to the processing of agricultural goods and natural resources until the Great Migration of the World War I era when large numbers of southern African Americans moved North to fill factory jobs.[27]

Dependence on outside capital and expertise revealed weaknesses in the southern economic infrastructure that plagued it for at least three-quarters of a century, if not down to the present day. There were exceptions, of course, most notably the tobacco industry in the North Carolina Piedmont, where first chew and then smokes made from bright-leaf tobacco commanded a large customer base. Eventually mass-produced, machine-rolled cigarettes from the Duke family's American Tobacco Company (and others) produced some of the great Gilded Age fortunes in the South. Even after the American Tobacco trust was splintered by court decision, the region enjoyed the benefits of the successful cigarette industry. Duke family wealth built a great university of national reputation out of a small Methodist college. Duke money also built an important regional electric utility, Southern Power (later Duke Power and even more recently Duke Energy) that literally powered the industrialization of the Carolina Piedmont and remains an economic and corporate influence down to the present day. R. J. Reynolds emerged

The South during the Ages of Capital and Inequality   179

from Duke's shadow to become a leading seller of cigarettes and funded a college of his own, Wake Forest.[28]

And, of course, there was the miracle of Coca-Cola (and the Woodruff family) in Atlanta, producing, bottling, distributing, and most importantly marketing the popular soda drink across the region, nation, and ultimately the world. Ironically, like cigarettes, Coca-Cola was a consumer product, relatively simple to produce, and only somewhat difficult to distribute, whose success lay in marketing, using all the new and emerging forms of advertising. Like the Dukes in the North Carolina Piedmont, the presence of Coca-Cola money joined location to help make Atlanta the business capital of the New South. The success of both Coca-Cola and Camels depended more on marketing than on infrastructure, innovative engineering, or skilled labor.[29]

But despite such scattered success stories and the modest but significant spread effects they created, industrial development in the South lagged in comparison to that of the North. The Age of Capital left the South behind, trailing the front-runners badly. Surely the region looked, and felt, more like an economic loser than a winner. As late as 1938, with the nation locked in the throes of the Great Depression, President Franklin Roosevelt termed the South the "nation's number one economic problem."[30] Doubtless some southerners bristled at the label, but both statistics and experience confirmed its accuracy. Per capita income in southern states lagged that of the rest of the nation through the World War II era, and to an extent down to the present day. This legacy of economic backwardness, of being branded a laggard when it came to matching the vaunted American standard of living, left the postwar South suffering, both economically and psychologically. It enhanced a mindset of inferiority that fueled resentments but did little to stimulate better economic performance.

The mindset question gripped the postbellum white South for decades, if not a century. Defeat produced anger, bitterness, frustration, defiance, and a (largely denied) sense of inferiority. It generated a culture of the "Lost Cause," a culture of defeat and defiance. The Lost Cause was a broad and evolving argument that the Old South's cause had been noble, and its fight heroic, but its cause lost, not because it was wrong or immoral or defended with insufficient courage, but because the North's numbers and wealth and ultimately power prevailed. Might prevailed over right, as many white southerners saw it. Theirs was an attitude of bitter, resentful, and defiant losers. The attitude infected the culture so deeply that it became a burden in its own right – one of the many burdens of southern history, and a burden that lingers, in various forms and disguises, even today.[31]

In addition to becoming a cottage industry in the South as writers and scholars churned out Lost Cause arguments hither and yon, the apologia penetrated popular culture and politics as well. David Ward Griffith's silent movie *Birth of a Nation* convinced a willing national audience during the World War I era that the freeing of slaves unleashed a terrible scourge of ignorance and rapacity on the white South that justified even Ku Klux Klan terror against Blacks as a means of maintaining order. Such efforts ultimately facilitated a national reconciliation between North and South, but it proved a reconciliation born of and resting on the oppression of Blacks and their exclusion from the political process.[32]

In politics, successful southern politicians learned to combine resentment of Yankees with the time-tested politics of race to win elections and avoid addressing more fundamental economic and educational issues plaguing the American South. Southern politicians protested the arrogance or snobbery of "Yankees" while also convincing their constituents that maintaining white political solidarity remained essential to maintaining the racial status quo. Even when class or economic differences among whites surfaced in southern state politics, as they did from time to time, either the conservative or the populist side inevitably turned to the safe harbor of race in their efforts to staunch the opposition. An anti-Black, anti-Yankee, post-Civil War South did much to hold itself hostage to the past, both as a means of honoring it and of avoiding an honest reckoning with the present and an adequate preparation for the future.

The burden of defeat haunted the South psychologically for at least a century, if not down to the present day. The white South hid its hurt, its identity as a loser in the Old South's great gamble for independence behind a reputation for hospitality, an alleged devotion to honor, and hyper-patriotism. As C. Vann Woodward explained in the early 1950s, the South had experienced defeat, being branded a loser, and seeing the prevailing myth of American exceptionalism shattered as far as the South was concerned. For many white southerners, the idea of being "losers" rather than "winners" fastened an identity on the South that left them angry and defiant. This identity proved a heavy burden in the optimistic, can-do world of American culture, and increasingly so during the post-World War II era when talk of an American Century took center stage. White southerners were fully American, yet somehow less than, somehow the poor country cousins of the real Americans, somehow the neglected stepchildren of America. These whites did their best to make

The South during the Ages of Capital and Inequality   181

their uniqueness a virtue but it never quite worked, either for the rest of the nation or for themselves.

As Woodward pointed out in his influential essays, the South could have taught the nation many lessons: lessons about defeat, poverty, and failure (even if white southern ambitions had been imperial and racist). But white southerners often led the way in encouraging the American hubris that did not serve the nation well over the long term. The American can-do attitude morphed into a "can do no wrong" attitude that led the United States into a Cold War against communism and serious international misadventures. Southerners often tried to out-do other Americans in their patriotism and in their support for overseas adventure, especially if that adventure involved use of the nation's impressive military might – as if having their butts kicked in the mid-nineteenth century made southerners especially eager to kick butt worldwide in the mid-twentieth. It was an impulse that led men as different as Dean Rusk, William Westmoreland, and Lyndon Johnson into humbling experiences.[33]

The period Hobsbawm labeled the "Age of Capital" and its aftermath produced economic success that encouraged the United States and Great Britain, as well as other nations, into modern imperial adventures. This was a repeat performance for the British but new adventures for others, and especially so for the fiercely republican United States. Ironically, as Hobsbawm's Age of Capital roared ahead, Confederate defeat brought an abrupt end to the American South's imperial ambition, both for the western territories of the United States and other parts of the hemisphere. The end of slavery brought the end of plantation-empire ambition, southern style.[34] As a region, the South's loss of imperial ambition happened suddenly and was not voluntary, but it was complete. In 1865, a war-ravaged South was vanquished rather than victor, it needed a plan for rehabilitation and uplift. But there was no Marshall Plan forthcoming. Northern capital trickled down to its internal southern colony as prospects for profit appeared, often with high tribute charged and little done to positively reconfigure the southern social hierarchy. For southerners so inclined, the pursuit of empire turned them toward the nation's emerging world ambitions, and many southerners became apologists for the expansion of American power around the globe. The Ugly American of the mid-twentieth often spoke with a southern accent.

After three-quarters of a century of economic stagnation after Confederate defeat and the emancipation of the enslaved, being a part, even if in a trailing position, of the American economic juggernaut at long last proved advantageous for the American South. During the post-World War II economic boom, most southern states finally made significant gains on the national average in per capita income. To do so, southern states marketed themselves as low-cost, low tax, nonunion competitors for manufacturing jobs. Moreover, they aggressively sought federal investment (especially military installations) and offered substantial state-financed tax breaks and job-training programs and state-funded technical education to lure private industry southward. They courted and received international investment, particularly from Europe. These new postwar southern economic development strategies took advantage of the larger dynamism of the American economy during the postwar boom. The pro-development coalitions in the southern states were led by a progressive element (even if still strictly pro-segregation through the 1950s) in southern society and they deserved this label to an extent, since their opponents (chiefly agricultural interests and owners of existing textile mills) proved obdurate and hidebound conservatives.[35]

By the late 1960s, the success of the civil rights movement accelerated the movement of companies and jobs to the South as desegregation reduced corporate unease at investing in a region characterized by a system of American-style apartheid. As a result, the South gained significant ground on the national average in terms of per capita income and standard of living. Quality of life considerations involving weather, the advent and spread of air conditioning, improving public schools, emerging technical education, and advantageous cost-of-living differentials boosted the movement of American prosperity south. In fact, this burst of Sunbelt prosperity embraced not just the states of the former Confederacy but a larger swath of the nation that stretched from the South Atlantic coast across the nation to California, and the future finally seemed to be in the hands of those regions where the weather was warm and unions weak. But since the post-World War II boom wound down during the Oil Crisis of the mid-1970s, the South's economic performance compared to that of the nation quickly grew increasingly mixed, and the convergence of per capita income of southern states on the national average slowed dramatically and even halted in many portions of the South.[36]

During the 1980s, the Sunbelt boom both stalled and splintered, at least as far as the South was concerned. Per capita income in states from South Carolina to Louisiana, excepting Florida, generally matched the modest national average in growth but failed to converge further on that average. This stalled convergence had much to do with the emergence of low-wage international competition for manufacturing jobs as the rest of the world began to pursue international variants of the "southern

The South during the Ages of Capital and Inequality 183

strategy" for economic development. Also, the persistence of low educational and skill levels in the southern workforce, and the lack of long-term investment in the technology and human capital that sparked much economic growth in the larger American economy, contributed to the slowing and stalling of the South's convergence on the national standard of living.[37]

The splintering effect of these shifting growth and development patterns in the American South grew increasingly pronounced. Florida and Virginia seemingly escaped "the South," at least as it is defined in terms of per capita income. The flow of a highly skilled population from the nation and world into northern Virginia (NOVA) made that area (and hence the state in average) one of the higher-income regions in the United States. Florida continued to benefit from its climate, its lack of a state income tax, and its resulting appeal to affluent retirees and maintained high growth rates. To be sure, Virginia outside of the NOVA area and the northern portion of Florida remained very southern in terms of their economic indices and social climates. Texas veered off onto its own development course. Despite having wealth-producing engines (oil and gas) and innovation (technology) in Houston, Dallas, and Austin, Texas remained statistically southern in many respects, or, more precisely, the state remained suspended between states such as Virginia and Florida which have escaped the statistical profile of the core South and states such as Alabama and Mississippi which have remained well below national averages.[38]

Apart from Virginia, Florida, and to a lesser extent Texas, progress in the remaining states of the old Confederacy has been scattered and piecemeal. Cities such as Atlanta (Georgia), Nashville (Tennessee), and the Research Triangle area and Charlotte (North Carolina) have served as nodes of prosperity and wealth creation in their respective states. But even though these cities serve as nodes of prosperity, their states still profile as southern states. States of the core South, such as South Carolina, Alabama, Mississippi, Louisiana, and Arkansas, continue to struggle not only with per capita income but with other social welfare and educational measures of well-being. To a degree, these trends have made the twenty-first-century South a parallel to the rest of the nation, in which booming urban areas propelled by innovation and technology contrast with stagnant or declining small and middle-sized towns and rural areas. As the first two decades of the new century revealed, there are two Americas, but they are no longer simply North and South.

In his important work, *The New Geography of Jobs*, labor economist Enrico Moretti provided hard data that reveals, despite increasing

184 *Understanding the American South*

public rhetoric about the declining value of a college degree, that college graduates still earn far more over a lifetime than high school graduates. But Moretti's data also show that smart (college-educated) labor earns its largest premium when it clusters in areas with large numbers of other smart workers, rather than choosing areas with fewer smart workers and more workers lacking college degrees. Smart workers do best when they gravitate to areas with lots of other smart workers (smart cities). In an almost textbook example of how agglomeration economies improve individual firm performance and benefit locales where they exist, smart workers earn more in smart cities precisely because the presence of those smart workers attracts the businesses and industries that need them. Their concentration is itself an engine of growth. Hence the educational divide also becomes not only a socio-economic divide but also a geographic divide. The growing income gap between the well educated and those with less education in an increasingly knowledge-driven economy and the geographic concentration of each creates areas of "haves" and areas of "have-nots." The South has too few areas with a disproportionate number of haves and too many with a large proportion of have-nots. These geographically concentrated groups see both current reality and the future very differently, leading to a great political divide – and resulting polarization – as well as a troubling economic divide.[39]

How does this thumbnail history of economic development in the American South connect with Hobsbawm's *Age of Capital*, defined as 1848–1875? Arguably, the South's persistent challenge in economic development grows from deep roots in the southern economy during the Age of Capital. These roots grow from the low level of labor skills in the mid-nineteenth-century South, and even more directly from the region's lack of indigenous capital in the aftermath of emancipation. These factors have shaped the region's economic evolution since that time. Across several generations, southerners have learned that a lack of capital is limiting, pushing individuals, firms, and states into the beggar's line – seeking "handouts" of capital for development and having to offer very generous terms, whether in the form of low wages, or large tax breaks, or infrastructural development packages, or loose environmental and business regulations, or most often all the aforementioned. Portions of the South that were deeply embedded in the plantation staple economy of the nineteenth century have, with only a few exceptions, also found it difficult to create the human capital needed for success in post-industrial economies. Poverty, low levels of education, and limited job skills have

The South during the Ages of Capital and Inequality 185

left portions of the South trailing desperately behind the demands of the twenty-first century economy.

Yet clearly the South of the twenty-first century is hardly a uniform region. Northern Virginia, southern Florida, metropolitan Dallas, Houston, Atlanta, Nashville, Charlotte, the Research Triangle, affluent coastal areas of Florida, Georgia, and South Carolina, mountain enclaves such as Asheville and Greenville, major university towns, and state capitals do reasonably well. Western Virginia, eastern North Carolina, South Carolina's rural Lowcountry and Pee Dee region, much of southern Georgia and south Alabama, the bulk of Mississippi, much of Louisiana, including flood-battered New Orleans, and parts of Arkansas east and south of the booming northwest Arkansas region, an area whose development remains powered by Wal-Mart and Walton family investment, struggle to approach national norms in measures of income and economic well-being.[40]

Arguably no one really knows who or what holds the keys to a prosperous economic future for a region or nation. But the weight of the accumulated evidence teaches skepticism about the idea that cheap, unskilled labor can any longer drive economic success while that same evidence strongly indicates that technological innovation, high levels of entrepreneurial energy, effective communication skills, and access to investment capital are of utmost importance. Even if knowledge does not guarantee success, there is little reason to believe that the failure to invest in human capital will not be punished by the global development marketplace. In many southern states, the once effective development strategy of low, nonunion wages, low taxes, location subsidies, and favorable regulation, a strategy that moved the region toward the national average in per capita income, no longer works. Instead, policies supporting more and better education, innovation hubs, and a quality of life that appeals to smart workers and creative entrepreneurs and the experts they must recruit will be required to thrive in the twenty-first-century economy.

According to Moretti, this new divide in the United States, which he labels the "Great Divergence," is that between metropolitan areas, especially those which attract innovative and technology-savvy people, and other cities, small towns, and rural areas where plentiful, low-cost labor once fueled successful agricultural and manufacturing local economies, but which now find themselves lagging behind in the twenty-first-century knowledge and technology economy. Recent evidence has suggested that during and since the Covid pandemic, smart workers, often able to work remotely, are moving away from high-cost-of-living cites which have grown overcrowded and migrated to smaller, smart cities for convenience and enhanced purchasing power (cities such as Nashville and Charlotte), but very little evidence indicates a move toward less smart cities. Moretti argues persuasively that the economy of the late twentieth and early twenty-first century rewards "smart" workers, not cheap ones. Education raises income, but so does location in areas where high levels of education prevail. College graduates who live in locales with high percentages of other college graduates make more money than college graduates who live among mostly high school graduates. Intriguingly for policymakers, Moretti argues that there remains a middle ground in this divergence, areas that could go either way, and these are mostly cities that still must make the shift from industry to high technology and are trying, and appear to have some prospect for success, but have not yet achieved it.[41]

The overall lack of indigenous capital in the region remains a handicap – a handicap that has plagued the South since the Civil War. Current efforts to attract outside investment are arguably more effective than during earlier periods due to mature and well-articulated capital markets nationally and worldwide as well as more favorable racial, political, and business climates across the southern states. But the underdevelopment of human capital in the region, compared to other parts of the United States and some other parts of the world, remains a significant challenge that is both difficult and expensive to address.

Human capital development is a problem that too often begs for a short-term fix, such as crash job-training programs or technology "bootcamps" that serve to produce skill-proficient employees for specific jobs. Technical schools and community colleges across the South have made significant progress in these areas, both in delivering basic skill improvement and needed specialized technical skills, and, when called for, quick ramp-up job-training programs for relocating industry. But while these efforts achieve a measure of success in the short term, they only bring local human capital up to the minimum required for the current level of demand. They do not lead to the creation of a rich pool of talent needed to attract high-end investment in knowledge economies.

Why then do southern states not do more to develop indigenous human capital? The answers are complex. Improving human capital takes time. Human capital is difficult to develop because it requires improvement at all levels of the existing educational system, and southern school systems tend to rank in the bottom quartile of school systems in the United States. For the individual southern states, those systems are expensive to maintain and even more expensive to improve. Serious improvement in such

The South during the Ages of Capital and Inequality   187

educational systems requires the allocation of large amounts of public money to K-12 systems and a similar emphasis on increasing the percentage of residents with college degrees and sustaining a meaningful commitment to adequate state funding of public research universities, which, after all, provide most of the high-end talent innovative firms crave. Such funding increases, however, would require the generation of additional resources (often through taxes) or the reallocation of existing resources (cuts elsewhere to fund education). This decision is not only difficult for budgetary reasons but also for political ones. Citizens (voters) are often eager to procure human capital development for themselves or their children while broad improvement of human capital requires making a broad and significant investment for everyone. The latter is, in turn, expensive, and it often takes many years to generate visible improvement. Economic underdevelopment is not simply a capital shortage problem or even a human capital shortage problem. It is a people problem, a problem of citizens and voters and politicians. And it is also a problem of social vision.

In sum, the challenge of human capital development is a historical and political challenge with an expensive solution. In areas or regions (like much of the American South) in which large portions of the population were denied access or given only limited access to educational opportunity (often of low quality) over generations, human capital deficits remain impediments to sustained economic progress. Ambitious programs to enhance human capital often find little political support in areas which have historically underinvested in human capital because their skill deficits are large. Areas which see rich social and economic dividends from human capital in terms of productivity and innovation are willing to fund more such development, but areas in which older industrial and agricultural economies operated effectively for many years without high levels of human capital often do not see the value of such investment. To them, their journey looks longer and even more expensive.

Over forty years ago, economic sociologist Immanuel Wallerstein aptly described this pattern as the development of underdevelopment, a condition in which regions that find themselves underdeveloped often embrace habits and practices and even strategies that make it even more difficult to escape underdevelopment. They often find themselves in an underdevelopment trap in which a lack of capital and the impact of low incomes restrict the society's ability to invest in human capital, whether education or job skills, leaving the region with little to market to outside investors except low wage rates and loose regulation, inviting still another generation of underdevelopment and even exploitation.[42] Portions of the

188   *Understanding the American South*

American South have a long legacy of the development of underdevelopment to overcome, an enduring legacy of the misguided actions and reactions dating to the Age of Capital and its enduring aftermath. This legacy lingers as a darker side of the cataclysm that saved the Union and ended slavery but did not sustain a meaningful "reconstruction."

Notes

1. Eric Hobsbawm, *The Age of Capital: 1845–1875* (New York: Random House, 1975), 135–154.
2. Hobsbawm, *Age of Capital*, 136–143.
3. Adam Rothman, *Slave Country: American Expansion and the Origins of the Deep South* (Cambridge, MA: Harvard University Press, 2005); Walter Johnson, *River of Dark Dreams: Slavery and Empire in the Cotton Kingdom* (Cambridge, MA: Harvard University Press, 2013).
4. John Lauritz Larson, *Internal Improvements: National Public Works and the Promise of Popular Government in the Early United States* (Chapel Hill: University of North Carolina Press, 2001); John Lauritz Larson, *Bonds of Enterprise: John Murray Forbes and Western Development in America's Railway Age* (Iowa City: University of Iowa Press, 1984). See also George Rogers Taylor, *The Transportation Revolution, 1815–1860* (New York: Rinehart, 1951).
5. Hobsbawm, *Age of Capital*, 141–143.
6. Steven Hahn, *A Nation without Borders: The United States in an Age of Civil Wars, 1830–1910* (New York: Penguin Books, 2016); Matthew Karp, *This Vast Southern Empire: Slaveholders at the Helm of American Foreign Policy* (Cambridge, MA: Harvard University Press, 2016); Rothman, *Slave Country*; James David Miller, *South by Southwest: Planter Emigration and Identity in the Slave South* (Charlottesville: University of Virginia Press, 2002); Daniel Dupre, *Transforming the Cotton Frontier: Madison County, Alabama, 1800–1840* (Baton Rouge: Louisiana State University Press, 1997); and Christopher Morris, *Becoming Southern: The Evolution of a Way of Life: Warren County and Vicksburg, Mississippi, 1770–1860* (New York: Oxford University Press, 1995).
7. Hobsbawm, *Age of Capital*, 141–142.
8. Hobsbawm, *Age of Capital*, 140–143.
9. Eric Foner, *Free Soil, Free Labor, and Free Men: The Ideology of the Republican Party before the Civil War* (New York: Oxford University Press, 1970); Sean Wilentz, *The Rise of American Democracy: From Jefferson to Lincoln* (New York: W. W. Norton & Company, 2006); Michael Holt, *The Rise and Fall of the American Whig Party: Jacksonian Politics and the Onset of the Civil War* (New York: Oxford University Press, 1999); Harry L. Watson, *Liberty and Power: The Politics of Jacksonian America* (New York: Hill and Wang, 1990); William Freehling, *The Road to Disunion: Secessionists Triumphant 1854–1861*, Vol. 2 (New York: Oxford University Press, 2007); William E. Gienapp, *The Origins of the Republican Party, 1852–1856* (New York: Oxford University Press, 1987).

The South during the Ages of Capital and Inequality   189

10. David Potter, *The Impending Crisis: America before the Civil War, 1848–1861*, completed and edited by Donald E. Fehrenbacher (New York: HarperCollins, 1976); James McPherson, *Battle Cry of Freedom: The Civil War Era* (New York: Oxford University Press, 1988); Michael Holt, *The Political Crisis of the 1850s* (New York: Wiley, 1978); William Gienapp, *The Origins of the Republican Party, 1852–1856* (New York: Oxford University Press, 1987).

11. Drew Gilpin Faust, *The Republic of Suffering: Death and the American Civil War* (New York: Random House, 2008); Eric Foner, *The Fiery Trial: Abraham Lincoln and American Slavery* (New York: W. W. Norton & Company, 2010); Elizabeth Varon, *Disunion! The Coming of the American Civil War, 1789–1859* (Chapel Hill: University of North Carolina Press, 2008); Reid Mitchell, *Civil War Soldiers* (New York: Penguin, 1988); Reid Mitchell, *The Vacant Chair: The Northern Soldier Leaves Home* (New York: Oxford University Press, 1993).

12. Eric Foner, *The Second Founding: How Civil War and Reconstruction Remade the Constitution* (New York: W. W. Norton & Company, 2019), 21–123; Leon F. Litwack, *Been in the Storm So Long: The Aftermath of Slavery* (New York: Knopf, 1979).

13. Eric Foner, *Reconstruction: America's Unfinished Revolution* (New York: Oxford University Press, 1988); George Rable, *But There Was No Peace: The Role of Violence in the Politics of Reconstruction* (Athens, GA: University of Georgia Press, 1984); Allen Trelease, *White Terror: The Ku Klux Klan Conspiracy and Southern Reconstruction* (New York: Harper and Row, 1971).

14. Foner, *Second Founding*, 125–168.

15. Hobsbawm, *Age of Capital*, 156.

16. Hahn, *A Nation without Borders*, 44–77; Sven Beckert, *Empire of Cotton: A Global History* (New York: Alfred A Knopf, 2014); and Hobsbawm, *Age of Capital*, 186–192.

17. Gavin Wright, *Old South, New South: Revolutions in the Southern Economy since the Civil War* (New York: Basic Books, 1986); Gavin Wright, "American Agriculture and the Labor Market: What Happened to Proletarianization?" *Agricultural History* 62, no. 3 (1988): 182–209; Harold Woodman, "The Political Economy of the South: Retrospects and Prospects," *Journal of Southern History* 67, no. 4 (2001): 789–810; Roger Ransom and Richard Sutch, *One Kind of Freedom: The Economic Consequences of Emancipation* (Cambridge: Cambridge University Press, 1989).

18. Wright, *Old South, New South*; Wright, "American Agriculture and the Labor Market"; Woodman, "The Political Economy of the South"; Ransom and Sutch, *One Kind of Freedom*.

19. Harold D. Woodman, *New South-New Law: The Legal Foundations of Credit and Labor Relations in the Postbellum Agricultural South* (Baton Rouge: Louisiana State University Press, 1995); Harold D. Woodman, "One Kind of Freedom after Twenty Years," *Explorations in Economic History* 38, no. 1 (2001): 48–57.

20. Wright, *Old South, New South*, 17–80; Edward L. Ayers, *The Promise of the New South: Life after Reconstruction* (New York: Oxford University Press, 1992), 104–213.

190   *Understanding the American South*

21. David L. Carlton, "The Revolution from Above: The National Market and the Beginnings of Industrialization in North Carolina," *Journal of American History* 77 (1990): 445–475.
22. C. Vann Woodward, *Tom Watson; Agrarian Rebel* (New York: Macmillan, 1938), 110.
23. Ralph V. Anderson and Robert E. Gallman, "Slaves as Fixed Capital: Slave Labor and Southern Economic Development," *Journal of American History* 64 (June 1978): 47–66.
24. Woodward, *Origins of a New South*, 291–320.
25. David L. Carlton, *Mill and Town in South Carolina, 1880–1920* (Baton Rouge: Louisiana State University Press, 1982).
26. Peter J. Wood, *Southern Capitalism: The Political Economy of North Carolina, 1880–1980* (Durham, NC: Duke University Press, 1986), especially 22–93; Burke Davis, *War Bird: The Life and Times of Elliott White Spring* (Chapel Hill: University of North Carolina Press, 1987); Louise Pettus, *The Springs Story, Our First Hundred Years* (Fort Mill, SC: Springs Industries, 1987); Walter Y. Elisha, *Standing on the Shoulders of Visionaries: The Story of Springs Industries, Inc.* (Princeton: Princeton University Press, 1993); Timothy W. Vanderburg, *Cannon Mills and Kannapolis: Persistent Paternalism in a Textile Town* (Knoxville: University of Tennessee Press, 2013); Robert S. Smith, "Mill on the Dan: The Riverside Cotton Mill, 1882–1901," *Journal of Southern History* 21 (February 1955): 38–66.
27. Wright, *Old South, New South*, 156–197.
28. Robert F. Durden, *The Dukes of Durham, 1865–1929* (Durham, NC: Duke University Press, 1975); Nannie M. Tilley, *The R. J. Reynolds Tobacco Company* (Chapel Hill: University of North Carolina Press, 1985); Allan Brandt, *The Cigarette Century: The Rise and Fall and Deadly Persistence of the Product That Defined America* (New York: Basic Books, 2007).
29. Mark Pendergast, *For God, Country and Coca-Cola: The Definitive History of the Great American Soft Drink and the Company That Makes It* (New York: Basic Books, 2013); H. W. Brands, *Masters of Enterprise: Giants of American Business from John Jacob Astor and J. P. Morgan to Bill Gates and Oprah Winfrey* (New York: The Free Press, 1999), 195–210.
30. David L. Carlton and Peter A. Coclanis, *Confronting Southern Poverty in the Great Depression: The Report on Economic Conditions of the South with Related Documents* (Boston: Bedford Books, 1996), especially 1–37.
31. Gaines M. Foster, *Ghosts of the Confederacy: Defeat, the Lost Cause, and the Emergence of the New South* (New York: Oxford University Press, 1985); Charles R. Wilson, *Baptized in Blood: The Religion of the Lost Cause, 1865–1920* (Athens, GA: University of Georgia Press, 1980); Thomas L. Connelly and Barbara L. Bellows, *God and General Longstreet: The Lost Cause and the Southern Mind* (Baton Rouge: Louisiana State University Press, 1982).
32. Melvyn Stokes, *D. W. Griffith's The Birth of the Nation: A History of the "Most Controversial Motion Picture of All Time"* (New York: Oxford University Press, 2007); Jack Temple Kirby, *Media-Made Dixie: The South in the American Imagination* (Baton Rouge: Louisiana State University

The South during the Ages of Capital and Inequality 191

Press, 1978); Edward D. C. Campbell, Jr., *The Celluloid South: Hollywood and the Southern Myth* (Knoxville: University of Tennessee Press, 1981).

33. C. Vann Woodward, *American Counterpoint: Slavery and Racism in the North-South Dialogue* (New York: Little, Brown, 1971).

34. Michael O'Brien, *Conjectures of Order: Intellectual Life and the American South, 1810–1860*, 2 vols. (Chapel Hill and London: University of North Carolina Press, 2004); Michael O'Brien, *Placing the South* (Jackson: University Press of Mississippi, 2007), 3–40, 48–52; Lacy Ford, "Placing Michael O'Brien: A Review Essay," *The Southern Quarterly Review* 47 (Fall 2008): 121–129.

35. Bruce Schulman, *From Cotton Belt to Sunbelt: Federal Policy, Economic Development, and the Transformation of the South, 1938–1980* (New York: Oxford University Press, 1991); James C. Cobb, *The Selling of the South: The Crusade for Industrial Economic Development, 1936–1980* (Baton Rouge: Louisiana State University Press, 1984).

36. Schulman, *From Cotton Belt to Sunbelt*; Cobb, *The Selling of the South.*

37. Edward Glaeser and Kristina Tobio, "The Rise of the Sunbelt," *Taubman Center Policy Briefs*, Harvard University (May 2007), 106; David Goldfield, "Writing the Sunbelt," *Organization of American Historians' Magazine of History* 18 (October 2003): 5–10; Richard Florida, "The State Story: Growth without Growth," *The Atlantic*, April 4, 2011.

38. "Personal Income by State," Bureau of Economic Analysis, US Department of Commerce, www.bea.gov/data/income-saving/personal-income-by-state; "Per Capita Income by State," Infoplease, www.infoplease.com/business/poverty-income/capita-personal-income-state.

39. Enrico Moretti, *The New Geography of Jobs* (Boston: Houghton Mifflin, 2013), 154–177.

40. "Personal Income by State," Bureau of Economic Analysis, US Department of Commerce; "Per Capita Income by State," Infoplease.

41. Moretti, *The New Geography of Jobs*, 178–214.

42. Immanuel Wallerstein, "The Rise and Future Demise of the World Capitalist System: Concepts for Comparative Analysis," *Comparative Studies in Society & History*, 16 (September 1974): 387–415; Immanuel Wallerstein, *The Modern World System IV: Centralist Liberalism Triumphant, 1789–1914* (Berkeley: University of California Press, 2011).

8

Transforming Southern History

The Role of Women Historians

At a time when the exceptional scholarly and administrative career of Drew Gilpin Faust, who held prominent interpretive positions in southern and American history while entering an administrative career that brought her to a successful eleven-year presidency at Harvard University, gains public attention for her coming-of-age memoir, *Necessary Trouble: Coming of Age at Midcentury*, which reached the bookstores and, more importantly, Amazon in 2023. The memoir describes young Drew Gilpin's rebellion against her conservative background and that of her region, as she boldly aligned with pro-civil rights and antiwar activists. Quite possibly, Faust's memoir explains the importance of women historians in the same manner of William Faulkner "telling" about the South in the novel *Absalom, Absalom*. But Faust also left us a career of magnificent scholarship which surely might explain much about southern and women's history if it was all we had at hand for the task. But many women historians, Black and white, have also helped us understand what stories we need to "tell" about women, Black and white, and their relationship to the American South. And today's scholars of the American South are accepting the challenge of undertaking the work that remains at hand.[1]

The question of how and when women historians transformed the field of southern history, and I would argue transformed it toward richness and inclusivity, must begin by explaining how, why, and when women historians worked their way onto the playing field of history and historiography. The World War II labor shortage prompted the popular "Rosie the Riveter" advertising campaign, which made its mark on the blue-collar world with appeals for women to enter the wartime labor force while able-bodied men were away in the theaters of war. Then,

The Role of Women Historians

early in the 1950s, men were back in the labor pool in large numbers, and the postwar baby boom kept many women of child-bearing age out of the workforce for a time. A fictional depiction of the postwar household emerged from network television's 1950s saga *The Honeymooners.* The popular show featured Ralph Kramden, a New York City bus driver (played by Jackie Gleason), and neighboring city sanitation worker Ed Norton (Art Carney), who earned blue-collar wages while their wives Alice (played by Sheila McCrae) and Trixie (Jane Kean) assumed the full responsibilities of being "homemakers," as the term entered American popular culture, while also rescuing Ralph and Ed from their weekly foolishness.[2]

After a brief period of adjustment, the postwar boom led to income growth and high levels of employment while also luring more and more Americans, including more women, into the peacetime labor force. Economists have labeled the post-World War II years (1948–1973) as the "Great Boom" or the "Great Expansion," but by whatever name, it triggered one of the longest and strongest periods of economic growth (and rising incomes) in American history. By the late 1960s, more women pushed into the nonhousehold workforce and into sales, pink-collar, and secretarial jobs, but also more and more women made impressive forays into middle-class and professional jobs, jobs often requiring college degrees, most often serving the public education system and the helping professions. Still, the role of women in the academy, and especially departments of history, remained marginal compared to that men (and mostly white men) through the decade.[3]

But Nobel Prize-winning economist Claudia Goldin, who has successfully addressed questions of labor economics with frequency and success, has labeled the emergence of more highly educated women in the workforce in larger numbers, beginning as early as the late 1960s, as a harbinger of a "Quiet Revolution" of women in the workforce during the late 1970s. According to Goldin, three evolutionary periods preceded the advent of the "Quiet Revolution." The first evolutionary phase extended from the late nineteenth century until 1930 and focused on women chiefly as piece goods workers in manufacturing enterprises. Usually unmarried, these women workers gained only small benefit from any human capital they acquired, and they often left the labor force upon marriage. During Goldin's second phase, which ran from the 1930s to 1959, the labor force participation rate for married women over age thirty-five increased significantly and the proportion of women employed rose dramatically from 26 percent in 1930 to 47 percent by 1950. Additionally, rates

194   *Understanding the American South*

of high school graduation increased by 1950 as did the availability of
labor-saving home appliances which enabled women to spend less time
on household chores and more time to enter the workforce. In phase
three, 1950–1970, labeled by Goldin as the "roots of revolution," more
married women worked but were often still primarily earners of second
incomes in the late 1960s.[4]

Beginning in the latter half of the 1970s, however, Goldin's "Quiet
Revolution" emerged, and it persisted, with varying levels of strength,
well into the twenty-first century. Marriage age, college graduation,
and professional school enrollment passed turning points in the early
1970s, and expectations concerning future work and life satisfaction
increased. Levels of college graduation for women soared during the
1960s as women began to marry later in life. The quiet revolution of
middle-class women in the workforce proceeded vigorously during the
1970s and 1980s. By the 1990s, rather than simply jobs, most women
sought employment as part of a long-term career that would bring a
"fundamental aspect of their satisfaction in life" and locate "their place
of work as an integral part of their social world." The availability of
oral contraceptives further allowed women more choice about when to
enter and exit and reenter the labor force. Moreover, the quiet revolution
flourished as female participation in the labor force and opportunities
to gain entry to high-earning occupations continued to grow. Taking a
longer view, the "quiet revolution" was set in motion by generations
born in the late 1940s (baby boomers), and it still yielded an ongoing
transformation of the workforce over at least a generation.[5]

By the 1960s, the broad postwar prosperity of the boom years encouraged more women to enter the professions, including the history profession at the college and university level, doubtless in part motivated
by the growing success of both the women's movement and the civil
rights movement, each of which gave women encouragement to challenge the status quo. Still, during the 1950s and 1960s, men, and overwhelmingly white men, dominated the field of American history at the
university level. Even as more women entered the history profession and
engaged in active scholarship, it took a decade or longer for change to
gain momentum. Yet as the first generation of women historians began to
make their mark, the second generation became more and more involved
in a broad wave of scholarship as well as increased interest in departmen-
tal and administrative issues. Women "pioneered" topics such as gender
and women's history and the history of sexuality. These "topics broadened over time to include new methodological frameworks which were

The Role of Women Historians 195

soon broadly embraced." Over time, even male historians changed their approach to addressing many topics.[6]

According to empirical data, the breaking down of gender barriers proceeded slowly. But findings of a longitudinal study completed in the twenty-first century indicated that "the growth in women historians" coincided with "the broadening of research agendas and an increased sensitivity to new topics and methodologies in the field." Moreover, the study's analysis of recent history dissertations identified strong "correlations between advisor/advisee gender pairings and choice of dissertation topic." The data for the final third of the twentieth century revealed the anticipated results. The share of women earning doctoral degrees rose steadily from only 12 percent in 1966 to 32 percent by 1980, to a high of 45.3 percent in 2010, before sliding downward modestly in 2014 to 42.9 percent. Also, the trajectory of women's degrees and publications improved steadily. By 2010, women completed 46 percent of all dissertations and published 37 percent of all published journal articles. Moreover, in the twenty-first century, while male historians still focused on topics related to political and intellectual history, military history, and so-called Big History (i.e., the study of history on a large scale), women historians researched and wrote about a greater diversity of topics related to gender, patterns of consumption, family and households, sexuality, the US civil rights movement, and the "cultural turn." Moreover, women historians led decisively in the arena for pathbreaking work in women's and gender history. Among the 100 articles identified as well-respected in the field of women and gender history, only seventeen articles were written by men, and five of those were co-authored with women. The remaining eighty-three articles were written by women. Additionally, women's and gender history attracted the largest increase in the share of subject area specialists between 1975 and 2015.[7]

The rise of women historians to leadership positions in professional historical organizations, however, came slowly. Not until 1987 did the first woman president of the AHA of the second half of the twentieth century emerge when Natalie Zemon Davis was elected president. During the 1990s, three women, Caroline Walker Bynum, Nannie Louis Tilley, and Joyce Appleby, were elected AHA president. Five women were elected to the AHA presidency in the first decade of the twenty-first century. Then, between 2010 and 2021, six of the next twelve AHA presidents elected were women, seemingly achieving a final measure of equity and balance for women in the nation's leading historical organization. In the Organization of American Historians (OAH), only five women were

196 *Understanding the American South*

elected as president during the 1960s and 1970s. However, during the 1980s, two highly regarded women, Gerda Lerner and Anne Firor Scott, were both elected president of the OAH, and during the 1990s three women, Mary Frances Berry, Joyce Appleby, and Linda Kerber, served the OAH as president. In the first decade of the twenty-first century, the OAH elected five women (Darlene Clark Hine, Jacquelyn Hall, Vicki Ruiz, Nell Irvin Painter, and Elaine Tyler May) to serve as president, and in the second decade of the new century four women (Alice Kessler Harris, Patricia Limerick, Nancy Cott, and Joanne Meyerowitz) served as president of the OAH.[8]

When viewed in more subjective terms, however, the emergence of women historians as leaders in the profession (and to approximate parity in numbers of men in the profession) has been a long, slow, obstacle-filled climb to influence in the profession. And it has not been a purely numbers game but rather the unfolding of fresh, and often penetrating, questions being posed by women historians exploring topics of inquiry where male historians have seldom ventured. The climb to influence involved a first wave of women historians who relied on their determination and drive to become pioneers in the field even if they could only gain a foothold in the larger profession as long as male administrators and senior faculty either did not or would not see the need for change. But, over time, the talent and dedication of female historians' research and teaching, as well as growing political pressure for equal rights, helped open doors for women in the academy. Their climb was hard and slow. By the 1980s, however, women had gained a firm foothold in the profession. By the 1990s, their footholds were secure, and they pushed for greater opportunity and recognition. And by the early 2000s, the percentage of women faculty, the prominence of their research and publication records, and their leadership positions on professional associations revealed a long journey of ascent that, perhaps above all else, brought a needed diversity and balance not only to the history profession but to university life.

In my area of study, the history of the nineteenth-century American South, a combination of frustration and initiative stirred to generate progress for women historians, white and Black. Talented and accomplished women historians pried their way into a male-dominated field, opening new research horizons of race, gender, class, and identity into the study and writing of southern history, and opening doors to a scholarly profession that previously had been almost completely a white male domain. Still, for several decades the history profession remained a realm dominated by male historians. Openness and gender balance, or a ratio

The Role of Women Historians 197

approaching it, took decades to achieve, but both Black and white women historians broadened and enriched the perspectives of long-studied questions of southern history while also opening many compelling new issues for study.

This chapter focuses not so much on the power of numbers as on the increasing potency of the compelling historical research and analysis that captured the profession's attention and insured women historians' place at the table for future scholarship. While it is not possible to allocate attention in these pages to all women historians, Black or white, who contributed to the literature, as a historian of the nineteenth-century American South, I attempt to highlight the opportunities and insights which insightful women historians have brought to key portions of the historiography of the nineteenth-century American South, especially during the decades of the 1970s through the 1990s, and set the stage for an even more fulsome cacophony of women's voices in the literature and the profession in the twenty-first century.

During the early stages of seeking careers in history, women did pathbreaking work on the history of the American South long before the post-World War II decades, and these women encountered high hurdles to achieve even modest recognition. Yet they also worked to open doors for women scholars who followed by engaging critical topics in southern history. For the purposes or this chapter, three women scholars, all members of the pioneering generation, Marjorie Mendenhall, Julia Cherry Spruill, and Guion Griffis Johnson, stood among those women studied in Anne Firor Scott's *Unheard Voices: The First Historians of Southern Women* (1993). These "First Historians" held prominence because they broke, or began to break, barriers that slowed or stymied the progress of women historians in the field of southern history. These first female southern historians faced many obstacles, and perhaps the most difficult to overcome remained the reluctance of almost entirely male college faculties to accept women historians as tenure-track faculty. A brief study of three of these talented women, and the barriers they overcame, the sacrifices they made, and the results they achieved opened new insights into the challenges the first southern women historians faced. Focusing on the efforts of three women of the "pioneering" generation, this chapter first explores these three examples of women historians who only belatedly gained recognition for the value of their work.[9]

Born in 1900 in Randleman, North Carolina, Marjorie Mendenhall grew up in nearby Greensboro and attended the North Carolina College for Women (located in Greensboro). Mendenhall was voted "brainiest" among eighty female graduates of the college, and at age twenty, she quickly accepted a job teaching high school in Roanoke Rapids, NC. While there, Mendenhall spent one of several summer terms studying at Harvard. She soon moved back to Greensboro to teach at the North Carolina College of Women while continuing to work summers at Harvard before spending cuts at Greensboro prompted Mendenhall to teach for a year at Winthrop College in South Carolina. A year later, Mendenhall received funding from the Social Science Research Council which led to her acceptance into the PhD program in history at the University of North Carolina, Chapel Hill.[10]

While researching her dissertation, Mendenhall published several refereed essays. "The Southern Women of a Lost Generation" in the *South Atlantic Quarterly* (1934) lured Mendenhall to argue that postbellum southern women of the "plain people" worked to lead the postwar South away from drudgery and to meaningful work, especially those efforts which improved education in the region.[11] In 1937, Mendenhall published a second essay, on "The Rise of Southern Tenancy," in the *Yale Review*. The article maintained that tenant farming existed in the South before the Civil War as well as after, and thus had long been a part of the hard lives of many rural southerners, including women as well as men. In 1939, Mendenhall completed her impressive dissertation, "The History of South Carolina Agriculture, 1790–1860." After being passed over for positions elsewhere, Mendenhall accepted a teaching position at the Bradbury school in Massachusetts. But in 1942, Mendenhall married widower Blake Applewaite, a merchant in Wilmington, NC, who brought a measure of economic stability to Mendenhall's life and household, which included her oft-complaining mother. With World War II mobilization gaining momentum, the new Mrs. Applewaite took a leading role on the home front, working with the Red Cross, and remaining active, as she long had, in the Presbyterian church. But Blake Applewaite died suddenly in 1945, and even though Marjorie tried to keep his business afloat for over two years, she was forced to close shop in 1947. She sold the business and moved, with her sometimes disagreeable mother, back to Greensboro, where she accepted a teaching position at Guilford College.[12]

In 1949, Marjorie Mendenhall Applewaite accepted a teaching position in sociology at Florida State University, but she soon returned to North Carolina, where she purchased an old house in Chapel Hill. She turned her purchase into a boarding house for college students as well as a residence for her aging mother and herself. The University of North

The Role of Women Historians

Carolina hired Applewaite to teach a few freshman classes and she participated in the university's extension program. But Marjorie quickly realized that the University of North Carolina's leadership (overwhelming male) had little interest in hiring women. In 1960, after a trip to Germany to teach for the University of Maryland's extension program, she returned to Chapel Hill prematurely, reportedly suffering from depression. The medication she took damaged her immune system and in 1961, Marjorie Mendenhall Applewaite died from a minor infection in her sixty-first year. Family members remembered Marjorie as a woman who did not flatter or manipulate. Her stepdaughter asserted frankly that Marjorie's "honesty may have been off putting to many other colleagues."[13]

Julia Cherry was born in Rocky Mount, North Carolina, in 1899, where her father served as the local postmaster and her mother worked as a teacher in the public schools and remained a devoted Christian Scientist. Active in service to the community, Julia's mother supported both women's suffrage and birth control, causes outside the norm in Rocky Mount, making Mrs. Cherry a community activist by Tar Heel state standards. Following her mother's path, Julia was a suffragist in high school, and upon graduation at age sixteen, she enrolled in the North Carolina College for Women. The 1920 college yearbook reveals both Julia Cherry and Marjorie Mendenhall as leaders in the literary society, the chorus, and the women's basketball team. The 1920 yearbook also revealed a developing relationship between Cherry and Corydon Spruill, a male student at Chapel Hill who won a Rhodes Scholarship. Upon graduation, Spruill soon left for Oxford, and Julia quickly accepted a teaching position at Rocky Mount High.[14]

After Cherry completed two years of teaching and Spruill finished his academic work at Oxford, he returned to Chapel Hill and married Cherry. Corydon Spruill soon accepted a faculty position at the University of North Carolina, beginning a career of favor and progress at Chapel Hill. Julia Cherry Spruill soon met members of the University of North Carolina's talented history faculty, arguably the most respected faculty of its discipline in the South, and she entered the masters' program in history there. She soon joined Howard Odum's team of sociological investigators while also beginning her own major research project studying southern women of the colonial period. She quickly landed two research grants which enabled her to undertake research at Harvard's Widener Library, and she eventually published five articles and her completed monograph appeared in book form as *Women's Life and Work in the Southern Colonies*. She produced a carefully researched volume that

200   *Understanding the American South*

remained the best work done on southern women of the colonial era for at least two decades if not longer.[15]

Cherry Spruill had concluded that "only a limited amount of research had been attempted in the whole field of the social history of the South," and those like herself who wanted to venture into social history had to do the hard spade work largely by themselves. And she did. When her book appeared, Howard Mumford Jones of Harvard, writing in the *Boston Evening Transcript*, argued that her book worked to "illuminate a history" because the reader has the confidence that the author had gone so far in ascertaining what the facts are in human terms, rather than because the author told her audience what she wanted them to hear. Harvard's Arthur Schlesinger Sr. called Cherry Spruill's book a "model of research and exposition" and "an important contribution to American social history." The reviewer for the *William and Mary Quarterly* judged the book one "[w]hich feminists have been waiting for" since men had too often "expunged women's work from the record." Despite the book's early and fulsome praise, however, Cherry Spruill's book received less attention once research focused on political and ideological forays into origins of the American Revolution nudged scholarship on women of the colonial and Revolutionary eras into the background. However, in 1972, Norton publishing brought out a new paperback version of Cherry Spruill's book on southern women of the colonial period usable for classroom audiences and it sparked new interest in her pathbreaking work.[16]

As the years passed, Cherry Spruill increasingly assumed a heavy domestic load as her husband's university administrative responsibilities increased. She played an active role in campus life, serving as president of the University Women's Club and the local chapter of the American Association of University Women. After a long career as a devoted spouse and a respected, if not always active historian, Julia Cherry Spruill died in 1986, two years before her husband. Upon his wife Julia's death, Corydon Spruill donated funds to endow the Julia Cherry Spruill Chair in women's history for the History department at the University of North Carolina, Chapel Hill, and in 1984, the Southern Association of Women Historians established a book prize named in Cherry Spruill's honor.[17]

Raised in Greenville, Texas, where her mother was the only woman in town with a college degree, Guion Griffis and her sisters all attended the Baylor College for Women, and Guion graduated at age twenty. The Baylor College of Women immediately named Guion a faculty member in its school of journalism. Guion actively pursued a journalism degree from the well-respected school of journalism at the University of Missouri

The Role of Women Historians

and quickly returned to the College of Women. After Guion returned to her native state, she quickly organized the Texas High School Press Association, and in 1923 she married Guy Benton Johnson, a Baylor journalist who had reported on the activities of the Ku Klux Klan in Texas.[18]

North Carolina sociologist Howard Odom offered Guy Johnson a fellowship at Chapel Hill, and Guion quickly demanded employment from Odom for herself, and he obliged. Almost immediately both Guion and Guy enrolled in the PhD program in sociology at Chapel Hill, though Guion eventually moved to the history department to develop her passion for documentary research. Her work eventually led to a dissertation on the economic life of antebellum North Carolina that prompted Odom to assign Guion Johnson to work on the Sea Islands of South Carolina, which she published in 1930 as *The Social History of the Sea Islands with Special Reference to Saint Helena's Island, South Carolina*. Soon after completing her Saint Helena's Island book, Guion returned to work on her primary research project, a book that became *The Social History of Antebellum North Carolina* (1937). Guion's work moved beyond traditional political categories to examine religion, education, the social life of enslaved Blacks, the court system, the press, the life of free Blacks, and much else. For example, Johnson dealt directly with the fact that the third most common justification for divorce petitions in early North Carolina was "cohabitation with a negro."[19]

Both Johnsons were recruited by Swedish sociologist Gunnar Myrdal to study caste relations in the American South as part of his larger project on *The American Dilemma* and its laser focus on race. Guion Johnson was assigned to draft a section on the development of racial ideologies. After their work with Myrdal ended, the Johnsons returned to North Carolina. But unwilling to accept the university's low-ball salary offers, Guion Johnson accepted a teaching position at the American History and Naval Strategy program. In 1944, Guy Johnson moved to Atlanta to lead the Southern Regional Council's efforts and Guion accepted a position there with the Georgia Council of Social Welfare.[20]

After moving back to Chapel Hill at the end of Guy's post at the Southern Regional Council, his open liberalism on race seemed to bother a disagreeable faction on the University of North Carolina Board of Trustees. But Guion organized a counter-move to join as many women's organizations as she could. Joining the American Association of University Women, the Young Women's Christian Association, and several benevolent outreaches of the Methodist church, she also created a

202   *Understanding the American South*

North Carolina Council of Women's organization, which made its presence felt at the state legislature. Yet Guion Johnson never abandoned her scholarship. In 1957, she published "The Ideology of White Supremacy, 1876–1910" in the *Journal of Southern History*, and the next year published "The Changing Status of the Negro" in the *Journal of the American Association of University Women*. By the early 1960s, Guion Johnson's committee work and organizational talent lead her to chair a committee on voluntary associations for North Carolina's Governor Commission on the Status of Women, and in 1967 she published a study of volunteers called *Volunteers in Community Service*.[21] The stories of Mendenhall, Cherry Spruill, and Johnson, as delineated by Anne Firor Scott, did much to keep the early contributors front and center in the minds of those scholars who have worked in the field of southern history, and certainly revealed that Scott had a keen sense of the achievements of her predecessors.[22]

From a personal standpoint, as a young doctoral student at the University of South Carolina beginning his research on an antebellum South Carolina topic in the late 1970s, I encountered Marjorie Mendenhall's excellent University of North Carolina dissertation on the "The South Carolina Economy from 1830–1890." There was still a dearth of South Carolina-specific work on agriculture, but Mendenhall's dissertation revealed careful analysis, rigorous data collection, thorough research, and keen insights on the economic and social aspects of rural South Carolina before the American Civil War. I recognized immediately that it was an immensely valuable piece of work. And I wondered, at least at the time, why Mendenhall's work had not garnered more attention, even belated attention, than it had. Moreover, just a few years earlier, as a first-year graduate student, a graduate seminar on the colonial period introduced me to Cherry Spruill's book on southern women during colonial period (and republished by Norton in 1972).

At least in the field of southern women's history, it was the early work of Anne Firor which established her as the leading expert of an emerging field and a recognized figure and leader for women in the profession. First, she emerged as one of the first women historians to established herself as a leading authority in the field of southern history. After she graduated from the University of Georgia at age nineteen, she then earned her masters' degree from Northwestern. She soon moved to Washington, DC to take a job with the National League of Women Voters. She later revealed that when employed at the National League of Women Voters during World War II, she worked with "still-powerful, aging suffragists,"

The Role of Women Historians

but also with contemporary women, born in the 1920s, who were determined to make a difference with their lives. "People see what they are prepared to see," Firor later observed, and "these women were teaching me to see things that other historians had overlooked."[23]

After World War II ended, Anne Firor married Andrew Scott, a former naval pilot, and Anne joined Andrew as he headed off to Harvard (to study political science) and she headed to Radcliffe to study history. Over the next decade Anne bore three children and followed her husband's career. With her doctorate in hand and their three children arriving, the family followed her husband's career from one campus to the next. Firor Scott taught at Haverford College and then in a part-time position at the University of North Carolina at Chapel Hill. In 1960–1961, Anne agreed to fill in at Duke University, and she eventually joined the full-time faculty at Duke, making her the first woman ever to join Duke's history department.[24]

In 1970, Anne Firor Scott published *The Southern Lady: From Pedestal to Politics, 1830–1930*. The book's title and its century-long scope carried a powerful message, and its subtitle's journey of women in the America South from the so-called pedestal, a revered place of favor, through a struggle to obtain a place at the ballot box and the negotiating table, provided women with a hard-earned place at the bar of electoral politics. Firor Scott's account of the "Southern Lady's" journey from pedestal to politics told a compelling story of how more affluent women had long created (and had created for them by male counterparts) the image of southern white women as standing on a pedestal, holding an elevated and uniquely feminine position in the southern social pecking order. Yet by the early twentieth century, a pedestal no longer seemed an appropriate place to stand while other white southern women led a progressive campaign championing the causes of better education, better sanitation, political reform, and seeking the right for women to vote. And in the American South, it was primarily middle-class women who led the drive for the right to vote and who voted disproportionately when it became possible for them to do so.[25]

Anne Firor Scott portrayed upper- and middle-class women who stood on the pedestal as accepting the declared ideal, though arguably not the reality, presented to the white women who represented the planter and business elite. Those women on the pedestal may not have fully understood or admitted the problems many other southern women faced. The interactions of these elite women with enslaved Black women and lower-class white women left those women on the pedestal with awareness and often even sympathy with women who faced harsh circumstances. Still, Firor Scott perceived that many antebellum southern white women found slavery an "evil." She, while focusing on upper-class women, also explored enslaved and free Black women and white women of hardscrabble backgrounds. Overall, however, Firor Scott concluded that southern women of the antebellum era accepted white male fealty to the image of protecting women. But white male protection gave its benefits, such as they were, chiefly to upper- and middle-class white women and largely to the white men who made the decisions. Despite the comforts these antebellum white women sometimes enjoyed, southern women often experienced, as Mary Chestnut's diary revealed, that the protection offered by southern white men remained cold comfort.[26]

Firor Scott understood the image of southern white men as depicted by Union soldier J. W. DeForest during his postwar assignment in the South Carolina Upcountry. DeForest identified the "central trait" of a white male southerner as that of being a "devil of a fellow." In fact, DeForest held that being a "chivalrous Southern" required an intense respect for "virility." A white southerner, DeForest contended, "will forgive any vice of any man who is manly," while southern whites also admired "vices" that he termed "exaggerations of the masculine." A reputation for "vigorous manly attributes," DeForest claimed, will bring a white man respect among his peers. Given these facts, DeForest concluded puckishly, it "will be a very long time before they will establish female suffrage" in the South.[27]

As portrayed by Firor Scott, the coming of the Civil War, and the war itself, accelerated the process of change throughout the South. As the pressure of war pressed hard on Confederate women, calls for white women to nurse injured soldiers or to scrap out hard meals for subsistence multiplied. Moreover, Union forces led by General William Sherman destroyed Confederate supply lines as he marched through the lower South winning victory after victory and forcing Confederates on to defend ever narrower pieces of ground. But the southern Civil War patriarchy died hard. Even after surrender, at a Charleston Board of Trade meeting in 1867, as Firor Scott discovered, the meeting held that "it was the woman's mission to make the home happy, to keep burning the lamp of religion," and to "teach men virtue." Yet the Board insisted that women's nature should "never be lowered to the arena of politics and party strife." And if DeForest's characterization held any truth, teaching southern white men virtue proved a tall order.[28]

The Role of Women Historians   205

Firor Scott's work revealed that after the Civil War middle class women faced a variety of challenges. Some women went to work, others joined voluntary associations or engaged in social uplift activities. Other women dedicated themselves to church work and still others to literary societies and temperance movements. Perhaps the most common activity, as the wartime years receded, centered on the growth of middle-class women membership in Women's Clubs and support for education.[29]

By the early twentieth century, the cohort of middle-class women who supported the women's suffrage movement faced considerable opposition within the white community. White males held that politics was a "man's endeavor," partly owing to a concern that Black voters, whether male or female, must be kept away from the ballot box. For Firor Scott, the woman's right to vote was a pivotal crusade. The right to vote emerged just as some women tried to break out of their narrow sphere, even when it appeared a pedestal, and asserted the right to vote. Even after the Nineteenth Amendment passed Congress and was returned to the states, only four southern states ratified it (Texas, Arkansas, Tennessee, and Kentucky). Once the ratified amendment granted women the right to vote, some southern women moved quickly to take advantage of it.[30]

Some twenty years after the publication of *The Southern Lady*, Firor Scott produced *Natural Allies: Women's Associations in American History* in 1991, exploring the multitude of women's associations and their influence on American history. She noted that her research led her to more and more encounters with women's groups that had played important social roles. Soon, Firor Scott realized that many such organizations had long promoted the causes of orphans, school lunches, and improved sanitation, among many other progressive measures. "It soon became clear that women's associations were literally everywhere," she wrote, "known or unknown, famous or obscure; young or ancient; auxiliary or freestanding; reactionary, conservative, liberal, radical, or a mix of all four; old women, young women, Black women, white women, women from every ethnic group, every religious group had their societies." Before long, "as the scope, magnitude, and diversity of this phenomenon came into view, I realized that it lay at the very heart of American social and political development."[31]

Elizabeth Anne Payne, historian at the University of Mississippi, later maintained that Anne Firor Scott "was the mother" of "looking at women in a different way, not in relation to their fathers, husbands, and children, but in the community." In Firor Scott's work, Payne

206 *Understanding the American South*

emphasized, "women's friendships" revealed "their roles in church and in reform circles." Firor Scott recognized the value of conveying "the everyday experiences of women ... [that] gave meaning and texture to their lives."[32] In 2013, President Barack Obama awarded Anne Firor Scott a National Humanities Medal. The award praised her "groundbreaking research spanning ideology, race and class" and noted that she had "helped open the floodgates both for women historians and women's history."[33]

Anne Firor Scott lived some ninety-seven years before her death in 2019. Commenting on the growing numbers of women historians, she noted that in 1958 three women historians could fit in one hotel room, but within twenty years over 2,000 women would attend their national women's meetings. Firor Scott's daughter, Rebecca Scott, a highly regarded historian of Latin America at the University of Michigan, spoke of her mother's "love of manuscripts" which "drew her to the voluminous collections of family papers of planters, politicians, and Confederate soldiers," archived by admiring descendants. In the archives, Rebecca Scott recalled, her mother found "the overlooked letters and diaries of wives and daughters. In her hands, these brought to light a very different and far less demure 'southern lady,' one who had played a vital role in economic, political, and social life."[34]

Within Anne Firor Scott's lifetime, women historians writing southern history engaged a rich variety of topics that were hardly demure and not limited to women. By the late and 1970s and 1980s in particular, a new group of leading women scholars addressed gender issues but they also addressed many topics that went well beyond gender.[35] Just as women's history expanded the hard-won territory established by Firor Scott and others, the civil rights movement's success appeared in both the academy and across the nation. Darlene Clark Hine emerged as one of the first Black women historians who focused on the American South. After earning her degree at Kent State in 1970, Hine took a position at South Carolina State University in Orangeburg, SC. Hine then worked from 1974 to 1979 as an assistant professor and an associate professor from 1979 to 1985 at Purdue University. From 1985 to 2004, Hine served as the John A. Hannah Professor of History at Michigan State University at East Lansing, and from 2004 to 2017, Hine held a Board of Trustees Professorship at Northwestern University. Much of Hine's success emerged from her work establishing and building programs. She established one of the first doctoral programs in comparative Black history at Michigan State and she helped edit an important series on African

The Role of Women Historians   207

American history in the United States, "Milestones in African American History."[36]

But in addition to all Hine's institution building, she emerged as a scholar advancing important arguments. For example, in her 1989 article, "Rape and the Inner Lives of Black Women in the Middle West: Preliminary Thoughts on the Culture of Dissemblance," Hine argued that a "culture of dissemblance," which she defined as the "the behavior and attitudes of Black women that created the appearance of openness and disclosure but actually shielded the truth of their inner lives and selves from their oppressors," explained why "African American women developed a code of silence around intimate matters as a response to discursive and literal attacks on black sexuality." Hine presented a diversified list of "reasons Black women might have migrated North," but she concluded that "sexual violence and abuse" stood as the principal trigger for migration. Hine's work built an early but strong foundation for the study of Black history, especially Black women's history, and made her a leading contributor to its emergence as an academic discipline. Later, Hine served as president of the OAH in 2001–2002, and in 2013 President Barack Obama awarded Hine with a National Humanities Medal.[37]

By the 1980s, and occasionally even earlier, women historians studying the American South pushed their way into the forefront of major issues in the field, but especially on issues of slavery, race, and women (Black and white). Catherine Clinton's sprightly written *The Plantation Mistress: Woman's World in the Old South* appeared in 1982. Coming from a trade press, Clinton's book reached an eager readers' market. Appropriately, Clinton's introduction paid homage to Julia Cherry Spruill and Anne Firor Scott as pioneering women scholars, positioning Clinton to establish a new interpretive role with her study of plantations mistresses. In her fast-paced volume, Clinton's research efforts focused on examining "the personal records of planter families" which yielded "rich and abundant source materials" and explained the key roles played by "plantation women in this critical period of southern history." Clinton's *The Plantation Mistress* certainly laid the groundwork for further, more extensive inquiries, but she boldly sketched the broad outlines of the subject. Her conclusion was that plantation mistresses lived in a trap of controlling enslaved Black labor, especially labor required in or near the Big House, and leaving white women on the plantation feeling like the "slave of slaves."[38]

As presented by Clinton, the position of the plantation mistress required the support of an authoritative male spouse. Preferable male

208   *Understanding the American South*

spousal candidates required high moral character and good financial prospects, but all too often those very standards disqualified, or threatened to disqualify, many white male candidates. Philandering with enslaved women, Clinton contended, proved a common practice among white male plantation owners and heirs, and in some cases, the white male household heads would not relinquish a Black concubine, whether a coerced sexual partner or an acquiescent one. Several of Clinton's chapters focused on sexual relations between white men and both white and Black women, who too often found themselves forced to comply with white male preferences and passions.[39]

Moreover, Clinton rightly concluded that the challenges facing white women were "in no way comparable to the sexual exploitation Black women" faced from white men. Enslaved Black females found themselves manipulated by owners and "forced into unwanted liaisons" which illustrated "one aspect of the master's power over his slaves." Clinton's assertions seemed both plausible and deeply troubling. The reach of white supremacy had snared poet and writer William Gilmore Simms, who suggested that "the practice" of interracial sex safeguarded "white women." But Clinton countered in her chapter on "The Sexual Dynamics of Slavery," with an exposition from Mary Boykin Chesnut of Camden. "God forgive us," Mary Chesnut lamented, "[b]ut ours is a monstrous system, a wrong and iniquity. Like the patriarchs of old, our men live all in one house with the wives and their concubines; and the mulattos one sees in every family partly resemble the white children. Any lady is ready to tell all the fathers of the mulatto children in everybody's household but their own." A slaveholder, in Mary Chesnut's words, ran "a hideous harem under his own roof with his lovely white wife, and his beautiful and accomplished daughter." Writing late in the antebellum era, Chesnut mused, "You see Mrs. Stowe did not hit the sorest spot. She makes Legree a bachelor."[40]

Jane Turner Censer captured attention in the field when she published "'Smiling Through Her Tears': Ante-Bellum Southern Women and Divorce" in the *American Journal of Legal History*. Censer's pathbreaking article highlighted the difficulty even privileged white women faced when seeking to obtain a divorce in the antebellum American South. A few years later, Censer published *North Carolina Planters and their Children* (1984). Using a close study of more than 100 North Carolina families, Censer's study revealed North Carolina women to have been doting parents who emphasized to their children the importance of education and achievement and the wise use of time and money. Moreover,

Censer's evidence revealed that southern planters, at least in their relations with their children, were caring, affectionate, and familial in tone. Yet Censer found that planters rarely cultivated empathetic relationships with their slaves. North Carolina planters also encouraged their children to cultivate autonomy and independent decision making, and most children of the North Carolina planter elite married within their class. Censer won a National Humanities Center Fellowship in 1983–1984, and after a long and successful career in southern history, Censer was elected president of the Southern Historical Association in 2017.[41]

In 1982, Barbara Fields' pathbreaking essay in *Race, Region, and Reconstruction: Essays in Honor of C. Vann Woodward*, advanced as a foundational premise that race was an artificial intellectual construct, while class, the social and political material circumstances of people belonging to a specific social group, was social and economic reality. Fields' provocative presentation stirred much discussion, but more than that, it identified race, class, and gender as defining themes of study that took hold for many years and is still influential. For Fields, class proved defining. It proved hard for southern historians, for whom race had been a dominant issue for many years, to accept race as something more invented than real, while class, as defined by Marxist intellectuals, stood as undeniably real. Some scholars compromised. They accepted class as real but nevertheless still accepted race as "real" as well. Over time, however, southern intellectual historian Michael O'Brien convinced many scholars (including this author) that the argument between race and class was itself a part of a larger set of social and economic and political constructs, and that neither race nor class was real, but rather both are ideological constructs. Fields continued her influence on the field with her 1985 monograph *Slavery and Freedom on the Middle Ground: Maryland during the Nineteenth Century*, which explored the experience of slavery and emancipation in a border state that remained in the Union but which contained no small number of proslavery southern whites.[42]

Other women historians also gained traction with books about enslaved Black women and free Black women, arguing that gender made an important difference in their historical experience, including the conclusion that enslaved Black women often became victims of sexual violence. For example, Debra Gray White's *Aren't I A Women* brought attention to enslaved Black women throughout the nineteenth century. In White's account, published in 1985, the impact of the expansion of slavery throughout the lower South had a devastating impact on enslaved Black families. According to White, southern Black women sorted mental

210 *Understanding the American South*

or psychological images of other Black women as Jezebels, taking an aggressive stance to do all they could to defy slaveholder orders and desires, contrasted with images of the superficially complaint "Mammys" who placated slaveowners and found ways of accommodating masters and their families. Enslaved Black women as Jezebels exhibited a defiant spirit, a sharp tongue, and an angry streak, while the agreeable Mammy was talkative and light-hearted perhaps but cagey, while carefully avoided defying or even evading white authority.[43]

Similarly, Suzanne Lebsock won recognition, and the Bancroft Prize, for *The Free Women of Petersburg* (1984), her book on the lives of free whites and free Blacks of this Virginia city. As Lebsock wove together the experiences of individual women of both races, she revealed how both groups of women helped drive significant changes in the antebellum Petersburg economy. Change came in part because of the growing presence of the institution of slavery and property ownership. Lebsock discovered that women sought economic security as well as the comfort of religious faith while they took care to protect the interests of other women. Accepting of male dominance and materialism, women in Petersburg nonetheless opened spaces where they could exert a subversive influence with enslaved Black labor and arguably even create an insurgent female culture. Duke University's Anne Firor Scott praised Lebsock for exploring how the lives of free Black women differed from those of white women and how Lebsock found ways to explore lives "in illuminating detail."[44]

While Jacqueline Jones' first book, *Soldiers of Light and Love: Northern Missionaries and Georgia Blacks, 1865–1873* (1980), focused on northern white missionaries trying to educate free Blacks in Georgia during eight years of Reconstruction, her second book, *Labor of Love, Labor of Sorrow: Black Women, Work, and the Family from Slavery to the Present*, published in 1986, garnered much attention for addressing issues of race, gender, and labor, and won Jones the Bancroft Prize that year. Jones examined enslaved and free Blacks facing hardships in the nineteenth-century America South. Anticipating themes that emerged over later portions of her career, Jones moved beyond race to explore the impact of class and gender on women in the American South. Highlighting the experiences of the majority of nineteenth-century Black women, Jones' comprehensive account of the lives of toil told the story of women and work in the nineteenth century. As Jones focused on the Black family in the nineteenth century, the *New York Times Book Review*'s assessment of her work stood as a tribute to the importance and quality of her scholarship. In her review, Toni Morrison, acclaimed novelist and later Nobel Prize winner for literature, applauded Jones for delivering a "perceptive, well-written," myth-shattering book, pointing out that "[r]ather than simply looking at data, Miss Jones sees them."[45]

Born in 1948, Jacqueline Jones grew up in Christiana, Delaware, a small town about twelve miles from Wilmington, even though residents spoke with unmistakable southern accents. Her parents were comfortably middle class. Delaware still followed the familiar southern social patterns, so Jones attended segregated schools. Black students in Christiana attended a small, segregated school. Jones' family held values different from most Christiana residents but did little to disrupt the status quo. For instance, Christiana's local Presbyterian church, which the Jones attended for years, heard the local pastor denounce "civil-rights activists, welfare mothers, and antiwar protesters." After graduating from high school, Jones left the religious and social faiths she had been taught as a youth and worked relentlessly to find her own voice of conscience.[46]

Jones' mature scholarship expressed an "existential urgency – whether on race, gender, poverty, inequality, or injustice – that society has failed to adequately address." Jones always sought accountability and regularly challenged the country to discover its best self. In 1992, Jones broadly focused work on *The Dispossessed: America's Underclasses from the Civil War to the Present*, published by Basic Books, won the Bancroft Prize in history and was a finalist for the Pulitzer Prize. One reviewer of *The Dispossessed* insisted that Jones' "central objective" was to "dismantle the myth of the culture of poverty" by writing with "moral fire." Jones retired in 2021, the author of nine books, as she prepared to assume the presidency of the AHA that year.[47]

Among the first southern women historians of her generation to gain prominence among her peers stood Carol K. Bleser. Bleser was a native of New York who went South to attend Converse College, a women's college located in Spartanburg, South Carolina. She married Edward Blesser, a particle physicist who worked at the Brookhaven National Laboratory in Suffolk County, New York. After obtaining her doctorate in history at Columbia University, Bleser accepted a faculty position at Colgate University in central New York for fifteen years (1970–1985), and then she accepted an endowed chair at Clemson University in upstate South Carolina and closer to the sources of southern history.[48] While Bleser's scholarship on southern history initially focused on the South Carolina Land Commission and its work redistributing land in rural areas of the Palmetto state during Reconstruction, her interest in the role

212 *Understanding the American South*

of women in southern history occupied her for the rest of her career. Bleser's much anticipated 1982 book, *The Hammond's of Redcliffe*, examined the Redcliffe plantation through the generations from James Henry Hammond down through the family to *Time* editor John Shaw Billings in the twentieth century.[49]

But the bulk of Bleser's scholarly work focused on social history questions dealing with the nineteenth-century American South, and in particular exploring the thoughts and actions of James Henry Hammond, a leading slaveholding radical and advocate of secession. In 1988, Bleser published an edited version of Hammond's diaries, *Secret and Sacred: The Diaries of James Henry Hammond, a Southern Slaveholder*. The diaries revealed much about Hammond's political thoughts and ambitions, but his diary also revealed his scandalous personal life. Hammond's private life, openly revealed by Bleser, included Hammond's notorious sexual assault on an enslaved Black woman by whom Hammond fathered a female child. Later, Hammond followed this assault with forced sexual intercourse with the twelve- year-old daughter of his earlier victim. Moreover, Hammond's political troubles emerged from his sexual intimacies with Wade Hampton II's four daughters, who were all teenagers (ages 12–19) when Hammond's dalliances with them began. Hammond excused his behavior by claiming that Hampton's four daughters all engaged in voluntary, intimate physical activity with Hammond, which he revealed in his "secret and sacred" diary. These actions "extended to everything short of direct sexual intercourse" and were carried on for two years with "great regularity," Hammond insisted. He admitted "permitting my hands to stray unchecked into the most secret and sacred regions" and included "every intimacy but the ultimate" without complaint from the four Hampton daughters. Ultimately, Hampton's daughters revealed their violation by Hammond to their father, Wade Hampton II, who did his best to keep Hammond's conduct out of the public eye, perhaps to protect his daughters' reputations. Hammond seemed initially to prefer a direct confrontation with Hampton, but the latter, one of the richest and most respected South Carolinians, may have chosen to protect his own reputation as a father rather than confront Hammond. None of Hampton's four daughters ever married. And after some fifteen years passed with Wade Hampton II's death in 1857, Hammond returned to public life, where he delivered his much-quoted "Cotton is King Speech" in the US Senate.[50]

In 2001, Carol Bleser, a more than thirty-year veteran of service to the field of southern women's history, a field she did much to define, boldly observed at a conference on southern women's history at her undergraduate institution, Converse College in (Spartanburg, South Carolina), that "by 2050, there will not be a separate southern women's culture; there will be only an American culture with no significant differences for women, north or south." One reviewer revealed a strong reluctance to concur with Bleser's assertion, suggesting that "the work of historians, however, is not to predict the future as much as to interpret the past." Other historians of the twenty-first century might go even further and argue that it is essential that a separate women's culture must flourish in the South, whether to sustain the field of women's history or simply the cause of women's rights. But Bleser had a legitimate question about the region sustaining a single, separate southern women's culture, as opposed to multiple and competing women's cultures.[51]

In 1988, Elizabeth Fox-Genovese generated one of the most compelling works of scholarship to appear in the late 1980s, *Within the Plantation Household: Black and White Women of the Old South*. Still near the very beginning of the path, also taken by her husband Eugene Genovese, away from Marxism and toward conservatism, Fox-Genovese studied the lives of Black and white women on southern plantations that included suggestive portraits of plantation life as a key to understanding a world of white freedom and Black slavery. Like Eugene Genovese's understanding of the enslaved Black experience in the plantation world, Fox-Genovese saw the plantation as an integrated work of enslaved Blacks and privileged whites, but one in which whites held almost all the power and enslaved Black men as well as Black women could negotiate only around the edges for maneuvering room or breathing space, or take bold actions, such as running away or resisting violently against great odds. And even within the plantation household, white women were expected to subordinate their opinions, and even their grievances, rather than contradict prevailing white male authority. The plantation household created a moving, complicated combination of strong forces and weak forces that might puzzle even modern physicists.[52]

Fox-Genovese's book on the plantation household both broadened and deepened Catherine Clinton's earlier portrayal of plantation mistresses. Fox-Genovese studied both white women and Black women, moving beyond the focus of plantation mistresses, and included in her narratives not on only both races but also interaction with both genders. Enslaved Black women, Fox-Genovese insisted, shaped the plantation household partially in their own images, sometimes receiving punishment for resisting the white household's wishes in return. At other times, enslaved Black women resisted bondage, and regularly looked for ways to either escape or find more tolerable means of resisting from within it. White women, despite all their limitations and their reliance on enslaved Black women, often considered themselves, as Fox-Genovese reported, as the "Slave of slaves" because of their dependence on the work performed by enslaved Black women.[53]

Within the Plantation Household revealed both Fox-Genovese's remarkable combination of gifted storytelling and the exercise of her rigorous analytical powers. One such insight that Fox-Genovese shared revealed the process by which the enslaved endured slavery. Enslaved Blacks pushed against boundaries yet submitted at times to the harsh or even cruel discipline imposed by slaveholders and their hired overseers in the interest of survival. Numerous accounts, including those of Fox-Genovese and Genovese, told horrid tales of the brutal violence and harsh oppression, and of hard-working, unappreciated Black women bearing physical or psychological marks of frequent physical and psychological punishments. Enduring the powerlessness and horror enslaved Blacks experienced from dislocation and separation of families led to more than occasional efforts of enslaved Blacks to escape to freedom, sometimes for only a short while, to escape the hardships of plantation life, and sometimes to risk a clean break from slavery forever.[54]

Fox-Genovese's work, again partially like Genovese's *Roll, Jordan, Roll*, connected Christianity to enslaved Black life in the Old South. With most Protestant denominations willing to support evangelical efforts to enslaved Blacks, Black Christians used the church for their own purposes, while also recognizing that white tolerance, however guarded, of Black Christians often allowed them to work for their own purposes. Arguably the historian's story tells much about white women and enslaved Black women and men. Yet Fox-Genovese wrote her history, at least most of the time, as the omnipotent storyteller.[55]

Over time, Elizabeth Fox-Genovese's impressive scholarship and personal political leanings moved away from the Marxism of her early career and moved toward social and political conservatism. Fox-Genovese's rejection of mainstream feminist beliefs coincided with her conversion to Roman Catholicism in 1995. She explained her acceptance of the Catholic Church not as a sharp break with the past but as a gradual move. Fox-Genovese's political realignment triggered sharp criticism from the left and even some centrist analysts. In *Feminism without Illusion* (1991), Fox-Genovese argued that feminism combined with the nation's confidence in individualism yielded "at best a mixed blessing for women who, freed from community domination, faced society with inadequate protection." By 1996, following the publication of Fox-Genovese's *Feminism Is Not the Story of My Life*, other writers treated Fox-Genovese harshly in the public press. The left-liberal *Nation* magazine blamed Fox-Genovese for "pursuing public policies that serve only upper-class women" while ignoring evidence that "feminists have fought desperately and exhaustively for paid leave and comprehensive [insurance] coverage." Both conservative and business lobbies as well as those who championed "family values," the *Nation* writer argued, "have cheated working mothers of decent maternity leaves and benefits." Fox-Genovese's public scholarship, and her identity with the Roman Catholic Church, along with her eventual political alignment with Republicans Dick and Lynne Cheney as conservative intellectuals, identified a full turn from academic Marxism to cultural conservativism. In 2003, President George W. Bush bestowed Fox-Genovese with the National Humanities Medal. Elizabeth Fox-Genovese died in 2007 at age sixty-five after battling multiple sclerosis for several years. Prominent Black historian Nell Painter observed that Fox-Genovese's work elevated "America's women's history to a new level of investigation."[56]

Perhaps no woman historian of the American South has enjoyed as much impact on the historical profession or the larger academic world as Drew Gilpin Faust. As president of Harvard from 2007 to 2018, Faust expanded financial aid and sought to enhance access to Harvard College for students of all economic backgrounds. She proved a strong advocate for increased federal funding for scientific research, and she enhanced Harvard's international reach. Additionally, Faust led a successful capital campaign, restructured university governance, raised the profile of diversity and inclusion at Harvard, and led the university through a period of significant financial challenges. Since 2018, Faust served as Arthur Kingsley Porter University Professor, still teaching courses and writing until her retirement in May 2023. Previously, Faust had served as founding dean of the Radcliffe Institute for Advanced Study (2001–2007). Earlier in her career Faust was Annenberg Professor of History at the University of Pennsylvania.[57]

As a historian, Faust authored six books, and arguably the most influential of her work remains *This Republic of Suffering: Death and the American Civil War* (2008), which, among much else, presented readers with the enormous death tolls of the American Civil War. For this work, Faust won the 2009 Bancroft Prize, and *This Republic of Suffering* served as the basis of a 2012 Emmy-nominated episode of the PBS's American

216   *Understanding the American South*

Experience documentaries titled *Death and the Civil War*, directed by prominent filmmaker Ric Burns.[58]

Early in her career Faust established herself as a scholar who immersed herself in archival sources and raised important new questions concerning her research findings. Her work produced fresh insights and Faust expressed her findings in clear and evocative prose. Over the course of her productive and distinguished career, Drew Faust emerged as a pioneer in at least four distinct subfields of nineteenth-century American and southern history: First, the intellectual history of the Old South, especially proslavery ideology; second, the almost Faulknerian concept of "mastery" and "design" sought by southern planters for their plantation worlds, personified in the life of James Henry Hammond; third, the history of women and gender in the American South; and fourth, the social and cultural history of the Civil War, particularly that conflict's overwhelming scale of suffering and death. Faust has not merely contributed to historical knowledge or merely told old stories extremely well but she has also changed questions and moved narratives in new directions.

Highlighting the Old South's preoccupation with proslavery ideology, early in her career Faust revealed how the region's antebellum intellectuals mounted a vigorous campaign to rationalize the proslavery argument. In her first book, *A Sacred Circle: The Dilemma of the Intellectual in the Old South*, Faust worked against the then prevailing assumption that the slaveholding elite of the Old South produced no "intellectual history." While the "mind of the South" had been a twentieth-century preoccupation of many writers and scholars, few scholars had probed the disturbing and, to modern sensibilities, retrograde proslavery mind. But in the five white southerners that Faust studied, and who fashioned themselves a "sacred circle" of proslavery intellectuals, the politician Hammond, the novelist William Gilmore Simms, the agricultural reformer Edmund Ruffin, and the college professors Nathaniel Beverly Tucker and George Frederick Holmes, Faust uncovered and humanized a cadre of intellectual critics of the society they were in the process of building and questioning as they built. Their failed struggle to manage any permanent "institutionalization of intellect" arguably turns out little different than pursuing the life of the mind in many other eras. Even more lasting, Faust helped forge a new interpretation of proslavery ideology. Rather than ungraspable "odd" defenders of the twin evils of slavery and white supremacy, the myriad writers who fashioned an elaborate justification of slavery in the antebellum era were, on the whole, believers in an organically conservative, hierarchical worldview, not only manipulating the Bible but also offering a theory of history and human nature to defend racial slavery as a vision of social order. Their views were rendered no less racist or abhorrent, but, in Faust's handling, their defense of such a system of exploitation became comprehensible as rational thought.[59]

In her biography of James Henry Hammond, Faust found a figure through which all the contradictions of the Old South flowed; he was a brilliant and handsome sexual predator who abused his slave women at the same time as arguing for a blending of modernization and tradition in a society heading, if not plunging, toward destruction. Faust focused on the talents, aspirations, and persistent moral obtuseness of Hammond, whose relentless ambition, unbridled selfishness, and wanton moral turpitude ran throughout his career. In many respects, Faust's Hammond and his "design for mastery" echoed in real life antebellum South Carolina the later fiction of William Faulkner's *Absolom, Absolom*. Faulkner's character, Thomas Sutpen, whose arrival in fictitious Yoknapatawpha with an unrevealed background but whose propitious marriage and relentless energy, created for the fictitious "Sutpen's Hundred" a design for mastery, albeit one arguably even coarser than Hammond's reality.[60]

By the 1990s, Faust turned the social history of the Old South into her third book, *Mothers of Invention: Women of the Slaveholding South in the American Civil War*. Faust's research revealed how white women experienced the suffering and brutality of war and defeat and concluded that white southern women, who wrote hundreds to thousands of letters to men at the front, and who also feared losing all that they had, may have weakened the Confederate cause by revealing how life at back home was falling apart. While Faust's bold interpretation contradicted the prevailing Lost Cause apologias focusing on female devotion to the Confederacy, it also suggested why Confederate morale faltered so badly as the war's prospects deteriorated, and why it was not hard to understand why the Confederate cause collapsed so miserably.[61]

Faust's *Mothers of Invention* suggested her next topic: *This Republic of Suffering: Death and the American Civil War*. Experts now estimate the war's death count at nearly 750,000 for both Union and Confederate soldiers and sailors as well as still uncounted numbers of enslaved Black and civilian casualties. Faust's pathbreaking new study wiped away nostalgia and sentimentality. The American Civil War was itself brutal, savage, and deadly on both the Union and Confederate sides. Faust's book, published in 2008, wrote of the withering sacrifice of over 600,000 soldiers and uncounted thousands of civilians and enslaved Blacks in 1861–1865. And we now know, through expert demography and record

218 *Understanding the American South*

analysis, that the death toll more closely approximated 750,000. In a mode both analytical and elegiac, Faust removed the veil from a subject that has never fit into the sentimentalized Civil War demanded by many enthusiasts. Americans, North and South, Black and white, Faust demonstrated, could not achieve the "good death" of their fallen loved ones, since huge numbers of slain soldiers were never identified by name or even the location of their graves. Above all, with this book, Faust achieved a rare kind of historical writing: unforgettable descriptions of what we have not wanted to see, intertwined with a presentation of death on an almost incomprehensible scale.[62]

Shortly following the acclaim for Faust's *This Republic of Suffering*, Black historian Nell Irvin Painter, who has written about many broad cultural and political topics that revealed her remarkable talent for cultivating diversity, published *The History of White People* in 2010. With Painter's emphasis on "white people" as an invented category, she frequently accepted an invitation to lump certain nonwhites into the category of "whiteness," while defining Black Americans and Hispanic Americans conspicuously outside, chiefly on the basis of race. The category "White People," Painter argues, embraces just enough people as "white" to portray a majority of Americans as successful, bright, imaginative, hard-working, patriotic, and, perhaps most importantly, a group which resides well outside the "welfare state." Those in the whiteness "category" do not need political or economic assistance from that welfare state. In sum, as Painter maintains, the idea of "White People" is simply to align a healthy majority on one side while ignoring the vast number of ethnic and racial minorities on another. As Painter points out, no matter how well grounded or how flawed, the device of "White People" has political appeal.[63]

Most recently, a cohort of women journalists and women scholars, as well as an equally robust cohort of male scholars and journalists, assumed a leadership role in arguing for a dramatic reinterpretation of slavery, secession, Civil War, and Reconstruction, ending, most importantly, with a new interpretation of capitalism and its controversial place in American historiography. Beginning in 2019, this dramatic shift in the focus on capitalism emerged from the *New York Times*' Nicole Hannah-Jones' 1619 Project, and ultimately, in 2021, Hannah-Jones' book *The 1619 Project: A New Origins Story*, which emphasized the arrival of the first Blacks in 1619 who eventually became enslaved after first arriving in Virginia. Over time, the presence of Black labor sparked white designs of enslaved Blacks working in the tobacco fields in seventeenth-century

The Role of Women Historians

Virginia and Maryland. By the 1720s, enslaved Black laborers worked in the rice fields of Lowcountry South Carolina.[64]

According to champions of *The 1619 Project*, enslaved Black labor eventually emerged as critical to the rebellion of the thirteen American colonies against British rule and challenged the validity of Thomas Jefferson's plea for independence based on "life, liberty, and pursuit of happiness" rather than a nation based on enslaved Black labor and white supremacy ideology. Moreover, *The 1619 Project* argued that enslaved Blacks produced the bulk of the cotton that drove the nineteenth century's world economy and provided the capital needed to finance capitalism's expansion. *The 1619 Project* mounted an aggressive argument that enslaved Black labor became so central to world capitalism that it should be appropriately termed "Slavery's Capitalism." Thus "Slavery's Capitalism" established the rise of modern capitalism along a path different from that articulated by even British Marxist historian Eric Hobsbawm some fifty years earlier. Moreover, the concept of "Slavery's Capitalism" evoked vigorous objections from economists, economic historians, and historians who have offered impressive evidence and well-articulated arguments that raise serious doubts about the concept of "Slavery's Capitalism."[65]

Leading American historians, including Gordon Wood, James McPherson, Sean Wilentz, and Victoria Bynum took issue with the 1619 interpretation and made the argument that the 1619 Project authors had replaced historical accuracy with ideology.[66] Victoria Bynum blasted *The 1619 Project* from the left. Speaking from an avowedly socialist perspective, Bynum argued that by the nineteenth century, "racist dogma was deeply entrenched and practiced with special urgency among elite Southerners whose wealth and leisure depended on slavery." But, Bynum contends, white confidence in white racial superiority resonated as well among non-slaveholding whites who defined their freedom from chattel slavery on racial grounds as part of belonging to the "superior" race. No matter "how successful slaveholders were in inculcating the common people with racism," Bynum contends, the notion that all whites "that harbored racial prejudice was a priori historically responsible for slavery" remains little more than a "rhetorical device" designed to render "racism timeless and immutable" as presented by the 1619 Project. Bynum's dissent from the thrust of the 1619 Project reminds us that the work of women historians often reveals dissent among scholars of the same gender and race. And wherever a scholar stands on any particular issue, healthy debate survives.[67]

220   *Understanding the American South*

As controversial scholarship, such as the work emerging from the *1619 Project* for example, moves more deeply into the third decade of the twenty-first century, women historians enter a broad range of scholarly debates and speak with expertise on a broad range of historical issues. They sometimes disagree with each other just as male historians do. At this point, however, few historians would hazard to guess concerning what new issues will emerge, who will be on what side of an issue, and that increasingly, differences of opinion are not as likely as previously to fall along strictly gender lines. Moreover, as women historians as well as women in other disciplines increasingly enter senior academic leadership positions, they face making critical leadership decisions regularly. With tensions evident and confrontation looming within larger society as well as the academy, its leaders must listen to all its members and make their choices carefully and wisely.

Notes

1. Drew Gilpin Faust, *Necessary Trouble: Growing Up at Midcentury* (New York, 2023).
2. "Rosie the Riveter," April 23, 2010, *HistoryCom Editors*; "The Honeymooners," *Wikipedia*.
3. Robert J. Gordon, *The Rise and Fall of American Growth: The U.S. Standard of Living since the Civil War* (Princeton: Princeton University Press, 2016), 605–639; Joseph E. Stiglitz, *People, Power, and Profits: Progressive Capitalism for an Age of Discontent* (New York: W. W. Norton & Company, 2019), 32–46.
4. Claudia Goldin, "The Quiet Revolution That Transformed Women's Employment, Education, and Family," *American Economic Association Papers and Proceedings* (May 2006): 1–21.
5. Goldin, "The Quiet Revolution."
6. Goldin, "The Quiet Revolution."
7. Stephan Risi et al., "Diversifying History: A Large-Scale Analysis of Changes in Researcher Demographics and Scholarly Agendas," *PLOS One* (2022), https://doi.org/10.1371/journal.pone.0262027; Robert B. Townsend, "What the Data Reveals about Women Historians," *Perspectives on History*, May 10, 2010; Patricia Albjerg Graham, "Women Historians in Academia: The 1970 Rose Report," *Perspectives on History*, May 20, 2020.
8. AHA, "Presidential Addresses," www.historians.org/about-aha-and-member ship/aha-history-and-archives/presidential-addresses/by-year; www.oah.org/about/governance/oah-executive-board/pastpresidents.
9. Anne Firor Scott, ed., *Unheard Voices: The First Historians of Southern Women* (Charlottesville and London: University of Virginia Press, 1993), 16–46, 54–57.
10. Firor Scott, *Unheard Voices*, 16–18.

The Role of Women Historians   223

52. Elizabeth Fox-Genovese, *Within the Plantation Household: Black and White Women of the Old South* (Chapel Hill: University of North Carlina Press, 1988).

53. Fox-Genovese, *Within the Plantation Household*, 1–191.

54. Fox-Genovese, *Within the Plantation Household*.

55. Fox-Genovese, *Within the Plantation Household*, esp. 232–234, 327–328.

56. Elizabeth Fox-Genovese, *Feminism without Illusions: A Critique of Individualism* (Chapel Hill: University of North Carolina Press, 1992); Elizabeth Fox-Genovese, *Feminism Is Not the Story of My Life* (New York: Knopf Doubleday, 1996); Elaine Woo, "Elizabeth Fox-Genovese, Feminist Turned Conservation, 65," *Los Angeles Times*, January 24, 2007. Susan Faludi's comments in the *Nation* quoted therein.

57. "After Nearly 50 Years in Academia, Former University President Drew Faust Retires From Teaching," *The Crimson*, July 28, 2023, www .thecrimson.com/article/2023/7/28/drew-faust-harvard-retires.

58. Drew Faust, *This Republic of Suffering: Death and the American Civil War* (New York: Knopf, 2009).

59. Drew Faust, *A Sacred Circle: The Dilemma of the Intellectual in the Old South* (Baltimore: The Johns Hopkins University Press, 1977).

60. Drew Faust, *A Design for Mastery: James Henry Hammond and the Old South* (Baton Rouge: Louisiana State University Press 1982).

61. Drew Faust, *Mothers of Invention: Women of the Slaveholding South in the American Civil War* (Chapel Hill: University of North Carolina Press, 1996).

62. Faust, *This Republic of Suffering*, esp. 32–101.

63. Nell Irvin Painter, *The History of White People* (New York: W. W. Norton & Company, 2010).

64. The 1619 Project, *New York Times Magazine*, www.nytimes.com/ interactive/2019/08/14/magazine/1619-america-slavery.html; Nicole Hannah-Jones, ed., *The 1619 Project: A New Origins Story* (New York: The New York Times Company, 2021); Desmond, "Capitalism," in Hannah-Jones, ed., *The 1619 Project*, 165–185.

65. The best one-volume summation of the "New History of Capitalism" arguments is found in Sven Beckert and Seth Rockman, eds., *Slavery's Capitalism: A New History of American Development* (Philadelphia: University of Pennsylvania Press, 2016), especially 1–27; Edward Baptist, "Toward a Political Economy of Slave Labor: Hands, Whipping Machines, and Modern Power," in Beckert and Rockman, eds., *Slavery's Capitalism*, 31–61; Caitlin Rosenthal, "Slavery's Scientific Management: Masters and Managers," in Beckert and Rockman, eds., *Slavery's Capitalism*, 62–86. See also Rosenthal's, *Accounting for Slavery: Masters and Management* (Cambridge, MA: Harvard University Press, 2019) and Joshua D. Rothman, "Contours of Capitalism: Speculation, Slavery and the Economic Panic in Mississippi, 1831–1841," in Beckert and Rothman, eds., in *Slavery's Capitalism*, 122–145. See also Rothman's book, *Flush Times and Fever Dreams: A Story of Capitalism and Slavery in the Age of Jackson* (Athens, GA: University of Georgia Press, 2012), 157–208. On criticism from economic historians, see Alan L. Olmstead and Paul W. Rhode, "Cotton,

224 *Understanding the American South*

Slavery, and the New History of Capitalism," *Explorations in Economic History* 67 (2018): 1–17; Peter A. Coclanis, "Slavery, Capitalism, and the Problem of Misprision," *Journal of American Studies* 52 (2018): 484–511; Eric Hilt, "Economic History, Historical Analysis, and the 'New History of Capitalism'," *Journal of Economic History* 77 (2017): 511–536; and Gavin Wright, "Slavery and Anglo-American Capitalism Revisited," *Economic History Review* 73 (2020): 353–383. See also James L. Huston, "Slavery, Capitalism, and the Interpretations of the Antebellum United States: The Problem of Definition," *Civil War History* 63 (June 2019): 119–156. For an overview, see Lacy Ford, "A New Historiography for the Old South? Slavery and Capitalism, White Elites and Enslaved Blacks," *Reviews in American History* 50 (December 2022): 442–467.

66. Kattie Mettler, "Five Historians Say the 1619 Project Should Be Amended. 'We Disagree' says the New York Times," *Washington Post*, December 22, 2019. The five historians who wrote asking for amendment were Gordon Wood, James Oakes, Sean Wilentz, James McPherson, and Victoria Bynum.

67. Eric London, "Historian Victoria Bynum on the Inaccuracies of the New York Times' 1619 Project," *World Socialist Website*, October 30, 2019, www.wsws.org/en/articles/2019/10/30/bynu-o30.html.

9

The Fraying Fabric of Community

The Unraveling of Southern White Working-Class Culture

In 2016, the appearance of J. D. Vance's *Hillbilly Elegy* created a literary and political stir with its highly personalized account of how distinct regional cultures, in his case southern Appalachian culture, contributed to the rise of dysfunctional behavior in working-class communities not only in the American South but in its diaspora. *Hillbilly Elegy*, a compelling tale of Vance's journey from his Appalachian coal-mining family and his steel-town Ohio upbringing to the United States Army, the Ivy League, and his West Coast career with a leading investment firm, became a *New York Times* bestseller and made Vance a minor national celebrity on the lecture and talk show circuits, and now, after a successful candidacy in 2022, an incumbent Republican United States senator from Ohio. The book itself offered a native son's caring but often savagely critical exposé of "hillbilly" culture, the dysfunction that Appalachian culture helped breed even when relocated to an Ohio industrial town. In *Hillbilly Elegy*, Vance also presented his view that the government programs designed to help the less fortunate cope with their problems created instead a culture of pervasive "cynicism" that disincentivized work and education in traditional working-class communities.[1]

Many other analyses, both scholarly and otherwise, have identified the weakening or even the disintegration of white working-class culture in the American South and sought to identify the underlying reasons. While a few analyses share Vance's emphasis on the pernicious effects of government intervention, more studies point to material concerns and diminishing psychological support from the culture itself. Regardless of how readers evaluate Vance's conclusions, many white southerners of my baby boom generation must admit being at least mildly surprised at

226 *Understanding the American South*

the suddenness with which the culture of working-class white southerners came apart during the half century after the civil rights movement ended apartheid in the American South. In addition to desegregation, multitudes of low-wage manufacturing jobs across several of the region's dominant industries disappeared in the face of improving technology and global wage competition. While not the only factors at work disrupting southern white working-class communities, these two developments contributed much to reshaping the lives and culture of many white working-class southerners.[2]

But before going forward with the analysis, two important caveats must be entered. First, the white southern working class had already experienced significant changes during the first two postwar decades, well before desegregation occurred, global competition reached its zenith, and a computer-led technology revolution further mechanized production. The national postwar economic boom, aided by aggressive new state-level economic development strategies, led to a significant diversification of industry and the creation of better-paying manufacturing jobs in the American South. Moreover, improved technology and the full integration of the South into the national market drove agricultural employment to decline to less than 20 percent of its prewar levels, freeing up farmers and farm workers to move into manufacturing and service jobs. Across the South, per capita income not only increased substantially but the regional average took major strides toward closing the large and longstanding gap between the South and the rest of the nation. On balance, the quarter century-long postwar boom brought improved standards of living and broadened horizons for white southern workers.[3] Also, as automobile ownership grew more widespread in the region, southern white workers gradually grew less tied to specific working-class communities and commuted to work in factories at some distance from their residences. In the textile regions of the Carolinas in particular, many mills gradually sold off their village housing after the Fair Labor Standards Act of 1938 precluded counting housing expenses as part of worker wages. The mill housing was often sold to older, often retired, members of the mill's working community, and the mills hired workers who commuted to the plant by car. The rise of the automobile and commuting certainly diminished any community's ability to exercise influence on workers except through related experiences in church, school, or recreational activities, or through family ties.[4]

Second, the southern white working class as a social group admittedly defies easy definition. In fact, upon first review, the southern white

The Unraveling of Southern White Working-Class Culture 227

working class might be more readily defined by what they were not. They were not white collar, nor salaried, nor college graduates. Yet many categories of white "worker" required more fulsome description. The diversity of blue-collar jobs held by white southern workers, their different and evolving residential patterns, the different levels of pay and types of working conditions they experienced, their widely dispersed geographic locations across the region, and their lack of a unified or coherent voice speaking publicly on their behalf (a role labor unions played in other parts of the country) renders generalizations about white southern workers difficult. The term southern white working class envelops textile workers once housed in mill villages across the Piedmont, including the Carolinas, Georgia, Alabama. and southern Virginia, steel workers in Birmingham and its surrounding environs, coal miners living in hills and hollows near the mines in eastern Kentucky and West Virginia, workers in cigarette-manufacturing plants in North Carolina and Virginia, and furniture makers in North Carolina, Virginia, and Tennessee, not to mention the multitude of skilled blue-collar tradesmen who worked as carpenters, stone masons, machinists, mechanics, construction workers, heating and air-conditioning workers, plumbers, and so on all across the region. All could be properly characterized as working-class people or blue-collar workers. Yet their circumstances were different in many ways, from wages to control of the workplace. Occupation, rather than income, arguably provides a better guide to a worker's actual position within the larger society, but for the purposes of this chapter the term white southern working class is used to envelop all the groups mentioned here and more. While their individual experiences differed widely, together they formed the white southern working class. Nonetheless, it is important to caution that the term "working class" is a broad rubric and that not all groups within it share anything close to similar experiences.

The culture of the southern white working class, like all cultures, always had its serious flaws (its deep racism foremost among them), but it also possessed many strengths that helped sustain workers through both normal and difficult times. The culture valued hard work and thrift, and usually displayed a deep willingness to share – at least with other members of its own race and class and occasionally beyond. The culture valued family, usually extended as well as nuclear. It generally had strong ties to Protestant Christian churches, especially evangelical and Pentecostal churches. Religion often held great emotional power in white southern working-class culture. Working-class communities projected a strong sense of right and wrong even if the lives led by inhabitants

228 *Understanding the American South*

waivered to considerable degrees in faithfulness to their culture's professed values. As is the case with most communities, its saints and sinners were the same people.

Yet despite its seemingly strong and deep roots, roots much heralded in its songs and stories, this culture proved quite fragile in the face of modernity's full-out assault – whether in the form of popular culture, changing sexual mores, or, more recently, the temptation of drugs such as crystal meth and opioids. Nor did the culture shed much of its historic racism and xenophobia while acquiring new vices. A caricature that contains too many grains of truth holds that the battered remnants of the southern working-class cling to buying lottery tickets for hope, viewing YouTube videos for entertainment, and swallowing Percocet for comfort. Hard work and education get less attention. Like all negative stereotypes, this characterization reveals the culture's characteristic abuses rather than its dominant characteristics, but it does evoke concern over the erosion the culture's core values.

These trends and other related developments have both produced and revealed a high level of dysfunction across vast swaths of southern white working-class culture and in its diaspora. Why did the culture prove so fragile, so vulnerable? Why did its strengths yield so rapidly? Why did the institutions and traditions that gave the culture ballast fail so thoroughly and so quickly? These questions deserve answers or at least attempts at understanding even if the judgments rendered seem harsh and unflinching.

To start with the obvious comparison, in other parts of the nation labor unions served as community entities that provided some ballast, an organized presence in and voice for working-class communities. Outside the South, union halls often served as community centers and the unions themselves stood as promoters and guardians of worker interests. But the labor movement had always been comparatively unsuccessful in the American South, especially among white workers; so much so, in fact, that white southerners' reluctance to unionize became an integral part of the region's development strategy, evidenced by the almost universal passage of "right-to-work" laws by southern states during the 1950s and state development leaders continually touting abundant "nonunion" labor as one of the region's development assets. As a result, unions were notably lacking in the region at a time when they might have provided something of a stabilizing social influence and a buffer (albeit a weakening one) against increasing economic inequality.[5]

Working-class churches supplied spiritual guidance but also served as hubs of community fellowship and support. But, while Black churches

The Unraveling of Southern White Working-Class Culture   229

which have largely remained anchors of community, southern white working-class churches have proven less effective at sustaining their communities. The diminishing role of the church in white southern working-class communities constitutes a complicated story. Some evangelical churches sought to rise with the upwardly mobile portion of working-class whites who moved, whether up within, or out of, the working class and left small towns and the countryside for newish suburbs and exurbs in large numbers. Church coffers proved easier to fill at megachurches in the suburbs, where leadership often fell to the personality-centered pulpits of the evangelical denominations. The comforts of city life had an appeal and more money supported broader church ministries. In short, much of the church went for market share and celebrity. Restoration of community feeling and service to its needy took a back seat.[6]

Churches that stayed behind in traditional working-class areas faced different challenges. The coded gospel of success that pervaded the suburban megachurches often fell on barren ground in struggling working-class communities in which wages were stagnant or declining and jobs disappearing. In the cultural realm, hard-bitten proclamations of "thou shalt not" flowing from many pulpits proved poor antidotes to the new cultural temptations offered through television, music, and movies. The economic struggles of white working-class communities made it difficult for local churches to generate budgets sufficient to both assist the community needy and provide an inviting worship experience. In an age of increased religious showmanship and television ministers reaching working-class households daily with pleas for giving, modest community churches with modest resources often experienced a decline in membership and giving, and ultimately in influence.

Moreover, and perhaps more critically, the local public schools, once strong sources of community identity and support, no longer exercised the trusted and steadying presence they had previously. The explanation for this declining influence lies in a complex and troubling story related to the white reaction to the long-overdue desegregation of the public schools in the American South. Many white southerners of all socioeconomic classes lost faith in public schools the moment they were desegregated. Perhaps more accurately, they lost much of their identity with these integrated public schools as "their" schools because sharing an identity with Black southerners was anathema to many southern whites, regardless of class. But these prevailing sentiments proved especially strong among the white working class, who had fewer resources to devote to finding alternative educational solutions.

Middle-class whites had more resources and hence more options to weigh as schools integrated than did white working-class parents. Private schools (often expensive) provided one option for higher-income whites and the portion of white students going to private schools increased significantly. Other middle-class households still preferred public schools due to the high cost of private education. For these middle-class whites, white flight to heavily white-majority suburbs surged. The clustering of middle-class white households in suburban neighborhoods created healthy property tax bases in suburban school districts. Soon, southern school districts with large white majorities and healthy tax bases became labeled as "good schools," attracting even more education-minded parents who could afford to settle in such districts.

This flight to "good schools," a term that became virtually synonymous with "white-majority schools," proved more difficult for most working-class whites to achieve. Most of these well-funded, white-majority schools emerged in suburbs, areas in which housing prices often limited working-class access. Per student funding (and hence teacher pay) in rural and heavily urban districts grew increasingly less competitive, and soon less affluent districts faced challenges in retaining and recruiting effective teachers. Moreover, the continuing racism of many whites made any integrated social activities sponsored by local schools – activities common and valued before desegregation – suddenly less desirable, especially among white working-class parents.

Moreover, whites lost confidence quickly in Black-majority public schools, and white flight from these schools popularized the concept of a "tipping point," the notion that when Black enrollment hit a certain percentage (and certainly when it became a majority), white enrollment would plummet sharply as white students fled to private and fledging church-supported schools. As schools became less tied to community identity than before, they could do little to cultivate community identity and values. The strong sense of community emanating from public schools and shaping white working-class pride diminished greatly, even if, in scattered towns, local pride and Friday night football defied the trend to some extent.

Finally, any honest probing of the vulnerabilities of southern white working-class communities must also take account of the racism that has pervaded those communities, both historically and in recent years. White working-class racism may have diminished since the demise of de jure segregation, but it has still flourished, even if dampened by pressures from the larger society, individual changes of heart, and degrees of generational change. At this point, it remains difficult to tell whether sharing employment, schools, and public spaces has diminished racism among southern white workers or simply pushed it beneath the surface, where it simmers and then boils over at key moments.

Undoubtedly, racial issues played a very large role in the evolving politics of the white southern working class. Politics often serves as a source of empowerment for struggling communities even if remedies to existing problems seldom emerge from the political process. The political decisions of the white southern working class have been much bruited for decades by historians and political scientists. Some scholars have suggested that white workers were long victims of elite manipulation and piecemeal disfranchisement. Other scholars have countered that in the political arena working-class whites in the South were largely in control of their own choices and they rather emphatically chose the benefits and privileges of "whiteness," even as their voting numbers grew fewer in number and their impact fainter, over class-based coalitions with Blacks.[7]

In sum, the traditional moorings of southern white working-class culture – church, school, and politics – shifted dramatically. Churches headed for the suburbs to chase the new money. Public schools evolved to include so much of the public that they ceased to be a source of white working-class identity. Racial resentments remained a hindrance to fuller inclusion in the larger American society and shaped political preferences. Politics retained a strong measure of identity for working-class whites in the South as party allegiances shifted from Democrat to Republican, largely due to the affinity of southern white workers for the cultural and identity politics increasingly emphasized by Republicans. Yet while the southern white working class found the cultural positions of the GOP appealing, Republicans offered little in the way of ideas, apart from opposition to immigration, to improve the declining economic position of the white working class in the South.[8]

Many southern working-class whites did not respond to highly competitive labor markets like immigrants carrying an exceptional first-generation drive to work exceedingly hard or second-generation ambition to seek education to achieve upward social mobility. Instead, they responded as disgruntled natives trying to reclaim a race-based privilege the society (or at least the government) no longer allowed. With the decline of traditional low-wage industries in the South, white working-class communities in the region experienced an accumulation of societal maladies. The new, better-paying jobs in the South, often created by outside investment (including direct international investment), low taxes, a favorable

232 *Understanding the American South*

regulatory climate, and affordable nonunion labor, grew fewer in number, required more skill, and were not reserved for whites only. These crises ran beyond unemployment and the lack of job opportunities and reached into areas of social dysfunction. It proved easy for outside observers to take a bipolar approach to these problems, either by blaming the entire social dysfunction problem on economic change or going to the other extreme to see social dysfunction as a product of engrained cultural values which enhanced if they did not create the fundamental economic challenges facing these white working-class communities.[9]

Solutions proved elusive. The economy, the government, and the public schools all seemed arrayed against the interests, values, or preferences of working-class southern whites. The politicians who catered to the class focused on expressing its resentments, but they did little to reverse the declining fortunes of people previously sustained by the benefits of whiteness. The seams of white southern working-class culture frayed rapidly. Divorce rates increased, single-parent households proliferated, teenage pregnancies rose, and ultimately the opioid epidemic – a predominately white drug culture – took its terrible toll.[10] The culture might have appeared strong enough to sustain the community through at least a couple of waves of economic shock and job losses, but it does not appear to have done so. As such, scholars might ask, what happened?

The rise of modern consumerism and popular culture through various forms of mass and social media certainly looms as one major influence. Consumerism and popular culture penetrated working-class communities, reshaping their value systems and leaving them more vulnerable to economic stress. The emergent popular culture entered the community with a vengeance, first by radio, then television, records, CDs, movies, and music videos, and then cell phones, smartphones, and more. Self-gratification, hedonism, momentary fame, and virtual communities pulled working-class teens (who later became adults) into a world whose temptations their culture hardly prepared them to resist – or even assess fairly.

Consumerism and popular culture's emphasis on immediate satisfaction, personal gratification, craving for celebrity (however fleeting), and a broader consumption orientation gradually eroded the prevailing values and work ethic of working-class communities. Regardless of whether those communities were centered on a religious faith, as many were, they almost all held the value of community. People supported others in the community and shared a belief that the work done by people in the community had inherent value and that value served as the foundation of

The Unraveling of Southern White Working-Class Culture 233

personal and community identity and dignity. Steelworkers were proud of their skill, as were printers in printing and finishing textile plants, as were the carpenters and masons and electricians who worked in the construction trades, as were operatives in textile mills. Workers took pride in the products they and their communities produced.

The intrusive message of consumerism suggested that personal identity also came from what you could buy or own or simply enjoy. This message of consumption did not triumph overnight. The initial working-class recipients of the messages veered hardly at all from their belief that their identity lay chiefly in what they did and what they produced. But over time, the next-generation workers increasingly decided to define themselves by the purchase of consumer goods and the way they spent their entertainment or amusement dollars. On its surface, this shift seemed innocent enough. For one thing, it mirrored the behavior of the larger middle class, suggesting that as living standards improved, as they did during the postwar boom, workers were acquiring middle-class values.

This seeming white working-class aspiration for middle-class lifestyles and values proved both seductive and toxic. It lured working-class whites into thinking consumption and material goods could bring them middle-class security and acceptance, and it convinced the middle class that working-class whites held the same aspirations and security enjoyed by the middle class. Lost in the years of prosperity lingered the broad recognition that education, social and business connections, and adaptability remained largely middle-class possessions. Yet over time, among the white working class, thrift yielded to extravagance, saving to spending, the long-term calculation to the rash purchase even as wage increases stalled or diminished. As fun and enjoyment grew accessible to youth so too did drugs and related temptations. All while the economic basis needed to sustain the consumption ethic eroded, leaving workers and their communities with eyes and appetites for more and wallets and purses only able to afford less.

Of course, the lack of economic and occupational opportunity itself exerted a powerful influence. Skills and adaptability became as important as work ethic even for blue-collar jobs. Deepening involvement in the global economy brought new opportunity and new industrial jobs to parts of the South but the number of lower-skill factory jobs nonetheless shrank at an alarming rate. Displaced workers often found new jobs, but they often found them in lower-paying service occupations. The average annual income for workers nationally actually fell between 1970 and 2015, creating frustration that workers were losing touch with the American dream of

234   *Understanding the American South*

prosperity and plenty. This stagnation of worker income hit the American South especially hard since incomes were already low across much of the South compared to the national average.[11] Also, finding new jobs, even those in the service industry, often required relocation, leaving small towns and rural communities and moving to larger cities, and sometimes moving out of the South altogether (as Vance's family did).[12]

For years, fellow southern historian and friend David Carlton quietly advanced a hypothesis, based on his years of study of the southern white working class and sound sociological theory, that white southern working people found it much more difficult to break the bonds of extended family and community to seek economic opportunity elsewhere than the better-educated, geographically mobile middle-class families. The logical corollary to Carlton's proposition is that once these community bonds were broken, whether among those who leave or among those left behind, the moorings of the broken community's values were severed. Given what we know about the deep community bonds and networks developed in working-class communities, Carlton's interpretation made sense, and especially so in the southern textile mill villages that Carlton studied.[13]

To be sure, the actual historical grip of "home" on common whites in the American South sometimes seemed more nostalgic than real, more a part of community lore than fact. The allures of home tugged at the heartstrings of out-migrants, but those allures often failed to either hold working-class whites at home or draw them back once they left. When viewing the movement of the southern white population on a broad chronological scope, it appears that the region's white working people have often been quite mobile. In the nineteenth century, white yeoman farmers and tenants in the southeastern states moved west to fresh cotton land in Alabama, Mississippi, Louisiana, and east Texas in droves, especially during the pre-Civil War era.[14] In fact, over half of all whites born in South Carolina between 1800 and 1850 had left the state by 1860, chiefly in search of more productive cotton land further to the southwest.[15] Then there was the massive twentieth-century Appalachian migration to the steel mills and auto-plants of the industrializing Midwest, stories highlighted by Vance's *Hillbilly Elegy*, and over a half century earlier in the popular country song "Detroit City," co-written by Mel Tillis and released in 1963 by Bobby Bare. This country hit, written from the perspective of an autoworker who moved north from Appalachia, included the lyrics: "Went to bed last night in Detroit city, and dreamed about those cotton fields and home," and "by day I make the cars and by night I make the bars ... , Lord, how I wanna go home."[16]

The Unraveling of Southern White Working-Class Culture   235

But most auto and steel workers never went home, never left the urban Midwest. Instead, they did what immigrants often do: They remade portions of the nation's industrial heartland in the cultural image of home. Even the internal movement of southern textile workers from one mill community to another raised questions about the strong local and community ties theory. Of course, in almost every case mentioned here, migrants made vigorous and partially successful efforts to reestablish their old community culture and values in a new place, forming their own communities, their own churches, and more. At the same time, Vance's personal saga of leaving the coal region of Kentucky for the steel mills and auto-plants of Ohio raises questions about whether the problems that emerged in the new communities grew out of the failure of these community replication projects – or from their success.[17]

Work by the social psychologist Jonathan Haidt has popularized a theory about cultures that supports Carlton's hypothesis and goes a long way toward explaining the "adaptability" gap between the middle and working classes in a manner that has direct application to the issues of the white southern working class. His argument is that humans are driven first and foremost by emotions. Our brains then work to develop rationales that fit best with our emotional preference while dismissing rationales that do not fit comfortably with our emotional leanings. In the process of sorting, humans usually embrace rationales that sit comfortably with their original emotional response.[18]

But if emotion is more powerful than reason, at least most of the time, or sets the foundation from which what we term "reason" later emerges, then what determines emotion? New studies in social psychology suggest that emotions flow involuntarily from our values. In Haidt's model, there are three primary sets of values, or what he terms "natural ethics": the ethic of the individual, the ethic of the community, and the ethic of the divine. College graduates readily adopt or embrace the ethic of the individual and are comfortable operating anywhere within the large sphere (generally in the United States and western Europe) where the ethic of the individual prevails. As a result, college-educated, middle-class whites move easily in search of opportunity. In contrast, the ethic of community tends to envelop the working class, those without college degrees, and those whose values come more from locale or community or extended family than education. Their emotional response to perceived threats to the values of their community often proves visceral and defensive. For those deeply enveloped in the ethic of community, moving beyond community boundaries is not only difficult but frightening. Even when economic circumstances compel geographic mobility, those who leave familiar communities are often discomfited by their unfamiliarity with the values and habits of their new location or situation.[19]

In the case of the southern white working class, Haidt's theory seems to apply. Recent economic studies show that, at least from a financial standpoint, blue-collar whites who leave their communities improve their economic position by moving to cites where wages are higher and demand for workers stronger. The appeal of higher wages may be offset to an extent by higher costs of living, but, on balance, workers are still better off financially in prosperous cities than elsewhere.[20] As a result, working-class whites find themselves choosing between maintaining community and seeking economic opportunity. Middle-class Americans remain confident they can recreate community wherever they land. But working-class Americans, and perhaps especially working-class white southerners, question or even doubt their ability to recreate their lives and networks in a new place.

Southern white working-class cultures were profoundly local, community cultures. Their values were tied to community, with relatives and friends crossing generations (in many cases dating back decades to old farming communities) with reasonably clear geographic boundaries. Yet success and even survival in the new economy often required geographic mobility. As the bold take the chance and leave, the remaining workers grow more despondent and perhaps dysfunctional. Yet even if the bold find decent jobs elsewhere, they often lose their cultural moorings and slip to dysfunctional lifestyles beyond the workplace. Outward mobility tore hard at the fabric of localist culture, pulling away not only the upwardly mobile progeny of the southern white working class but also the desperate and the adventurous. People moved to keep or seek jobs. As Carlton hypothesized, given what we know about the deep community bonds and networks developed in working-class communities, working-class whites found it much more difficult to break the bonds of extended family and community to seek economic opportunity elsewhere than did the ever-geographically mobile middle-class families. They also proved less able to successful recreate a culture in which they were comfortable after they moved.[21]

Doubtless globalization and technological advances in the larger society played a significant role in accelerating and worsening the social decline of these rural and blue-collar communities, and political decisions at the state and national level about both economic and social policy had much to do with the failure to ameliorate these problems in a timely

The Unraveling of Southern White Working-Class Culture   237

manner. But, in fact, southern white workers have consistently encouraged their political system to find the solution to their economic problems through the punishment of others, blaming their plight first on federal legislation which allowed Black workers to compete for what previously been "whites only" jobs in the segregated South and more recently blaming globalization and the arrival of hard-working immigrants for the loss of jobs. They have been quick to rally behind politicians who play to their traditional cultural identity as southern whites, with all the symbols, slogans, and trappings of that identity, but working-class southern whites have only rarely given palpable support to measures, such as affordable health care, raising minimum wages, tighter regulation of the financial sector, and reasonable policies regarding pensions and benefits, that aligned with their economic self-interests.[22]

Two decades into the twenty-first century, the white southern working class, like much of the rest of the American working class (white and Black), is struggling with both growing economic inequality and social dislocation. Over the past quarter century, such struggles among southern white workers have not been measurably different from those of workers in major industries in the older northern industrial states such as Pennsylvania, Ohio, Michigan, and Wisconsin where job loss and community disruption has been common. The problem of social decay in these communities, even if the causes range well beyond economic distress, has put the culture of such communities under the magnifying glass.[23]

The incomes of the American working class have been essentially stagnant since 1970 with little immediate prospect for reversing the trend over the long term. Global competition has certainly played a role in the stagnation of worker incomes, but that role has been much more modest than the political rhetoric would indicate. To be sure, encouraged by political rhetoric and drawing on its long-nurtured sentiments of nativism and xenophobia, southern white workers have blamed more of the decline of southern industry on globalization and immigration than is justified by hard economic analysis. Global trade and the entry of immigrants into the American workforce certainly accounted for some job losses, but research suggests that only a small portion (certainly no more than 15 percent) of the loss of manufacturing jobs in the United States can be attributed to these factors. Instead, technological innovation and the resulting decline in the proportion of manufacturing jobs required by the overall economy took its toll on American working-class prosperity. The proportion of manufacturing jobs in the American economy has cratered,

238 *Understanding the American South*

falling from 20 percent in 1980 to 10 percent of all employment by 2000. Strong empirical evidence points to improved technology and gains in the efficiency of production (which allowed American industry to produce more and more output with fewer and fewer workers) as the primary drivers of this job loss. By the second decade of the twenty-first century, only 16 percent of noncollege graduates in the American workforce were employed in manufacturing. By any careful reckoning, globalization has accounted for a much smaller share of manufacturing job losses than enhanced technology and greater production efficiency. But for workers, lost jobs are lost jobs. Even if the misattribution of the reason for such job losses clouds the path to solutions, the distress and dislocation of workers is no less real.[24]

Both classical and neoliberal economic theory suggest that the productive efficiencies led to overall economic growth and thus produced new opportunities. According to the dominant theories, over time and possibly in different places, new opportunities for displaced workers appeared in the growing economy. As matters of pure economic logic the prevailing theories are hard to dispute, but, on the ground, displaced workers faced difficult obstacles in the search for new opportunities. Their skill sets, particularly if they were long-term workers in a specific industry such as textiles or automobile assembly, were often not readily transferrable to other industries. Retraining opportunities proved hard to find, difficult to complete, and led, if anywhere, to new jobs that required moving away from long-settled communities.

In fact, recent econometric studies suggest that both classical and neoliberal theory fail to adequately account for the challenges presented by location concentration. For example, if industries were highly concentrated in specific areas, as many southern industries, such as textiles and furniture, were, the impact of employment loss proved highly concentrated, and thus proved a strong drag on the overall economy of large areas. This left displaced workers with few if any opportunities to recoup job losses without both leaving their home area and acquiring an entirely new skill set. Since industrial locations had always been concentrated to capture the benefits of external economies and economies of agglomeration, industry-specific economic damage was quite often highly concentrated in specific locales and thus difficult to distribute throughout the larger economy.[25]

Moreover, to complicate matters further, current scholarship indicates that the transaction costs of leaving communities (and even regions) while also acquiring new job skills are sufficiently high to prevent market

The Unraveling of Southern White Working-Class Culture   239

incentives from insuring that international trade does, in fact, benefit all in the long run. For working-class families, as Haidt's theory suggests, both the economic and psychological costs of moving often prove daunting. Contrary to their image as footloose and adventurous, Americans, and especially working-class Americans, tend to stay closer to home over the course of a lifetime than we might think. Over 70 percent of Americans live "in or near" the city where they grew up, and, as recently as 2015, the "typical adult" in the United States lived within eighteen miles of her or his mother.[26] Moreover, recent econometric work suggests that if the losses of employment are concentrated in a few specific industries, and if the affected industries are concentrated geographically, then the tightly focused impact of these job losses makes recovery for the locale much more difficult, and much less probable, than if the job loss is widely distributed geographically.

Without question, the long-term stagnation and decline in wages presented the southern (and American) working class with challenges that run deeper than the immediate shortage of job prospects. Recent scholarship indicates that a long-term diminution of economic prospects for a better life, or even simply the extension of the existing quality of life, takes an increasingly heavy toll on working-class communities in terms of physical and mental health. Pessimism and worry slouch into despair and desperation and the resulting depression leads to life choices that decrease life expectancy significantly. Gripping recent work from Princeton economists Anne Case and Angus Deaton suggests that long-term economic stagnation can lead to depression and despair. Depression and despair then lead to increased levels of suicide, alcohol abuse, and other drug addictions, all of which ultimately increase death rates among the effected population. These health consequences, and even death rates, are not immediately sensitive to short-term economic ups and downs, but in the longer term the absence of upward mobility, or even just a reasonable hope for it, creates serious mental and physical health problems that can produce rising death rates.[27]

These rising death rates, reversing decades of increased life expectancy, stand as a uniquely American phenomenon, one centered in heavily white working-class areas of the southern and western states. This is a trend completely without parallel in other wealthy or advanced countries. It appears that the emergence of long-term economic stagnation and decline and the resulting collapse of community constitute the requisite criteria that pushed these white workers toward escape and addiction. To date, the shortening of life expectancy has been largely confined

240   *Understanding the American South*

to America's white working class, and especially those in the South and mountain West.[28]

The resentments of southern working class, which blamed immigration and cheap global competition for diminishing opportunity, may have been misplaced, but such resentments seem understandable in view of economic changes that devalued their job skills and disrupted their home communities while offering no alternative except moving and acquiring new skill sets. As workers struggled, the nation's economic bounty flowed disproportionately to the richest one-tenth of 1 percent of Americans, who control nearly 12 percent of the nation's wealth, and in decidedly lesser amounts to the well-educated and geographically mobile middle-class. As manufacturing jobs have grown harder to find, and wages stagnated, social dysfunction among the white working class has grown – and rapidly. Even the entire geography of jobs in the US has shifted, lessening the need for working-class communities, towns, and cities on the American economic landscape. Moreover, strong econometric data suggest that the anger and frustration of the white working class is justifiable even if the white workers' diagnosis of the problems are off the mark. The evidence that wages and earnings for men without a four-year college degree has declined is overwhelming. Between 1980 and 2000 the premium for having a college degree (as opposed to simply a high school diploma) rose from 40 percent to 80 percent. Moreover, the widening gap between the earnings of high school graduates as opposed to college graduates grew from 7 percent at age twenty-two to 77 percent at age fifty-four. Aging is not kind to less educated workers.[29]

A strong case can be made that the weakening of southern white working class communities emerged directly from its long-term economic decline, a decline that provided fertile ground for the worst fruits of frustration and even desperation to grow. Without question, the long-term stagnation and decline in wages presented the southern, and indeed the entire American, working class with challenges that run deeper than the immediate shortage or attractiveness of job prospects.

Overall, the American working class and the American middle class faced fundamentally different challenges and opportunities when confronted with periods of rapid economic change. The better-educated middle class seems more nimble – better able to move and adjust. Education and the resulting broad knowledge and soft skills, as well as technological expertise and creativity, that education provides or nurtures – reflected in the career-earning disparity between Americans with a college degree and those high school diplomas (much less without high school diplomas) – helps ease

The Unraveling of Southern White Working-Class Culture 241

the strain of geographic transition. To be sure, there are a worrisome number of young college graduates working as baristas these days, but many are doing so as periods of self-discovery rather than for reasons of genuine economic hardship. For many of these middle-class twenty-somethings, the security of the family safety net looms large. The white working class finds it difficult to take their community culture with them when they move, making working-class whites more reluctant to move and more likely to embrace destructive patterns of behavior regardless of whether they stay or leave. Increasingly, the education gap, defined as those who have a college diploma and those with only a high school degree, has become a yawning chasm in terms of both earnings and health. As recently as 2017, with overall unemployment low (3.6 percent), only 64 percent of those with only a high school diploma were employed compared to 84 percent of college graduates.[30]

The broader trends of twenty-first-century culture – such as increasing numbers and proportions of digital natives, high levels of absorption in personalized technology, the expansion of the gig economy, a broadening, if still not a fully inclusive, tolerance of differences, the emergence and centrality of virtual communities, a fondness for urban living, and so forth – run counter to the traditional patterns of white working-class culture. There is certainly still a need for skilled production workers but not for as many such workers overall as in previous decades. The highly portable personal and "soft" skills of the middle class still often elude members of the working class.

Still, we must be careful not to overstate the frailty of southern white working-class culture. Many of the embattled culture's core values – neighborliness, a concern for and a desire to help others – remain visible throughout the rural and small-town South and wherever working-class communities exist. These communities often still come to life during both crises and celebrations. Some working-class communities still rally around their local public schools for athletics. For example, Friday night high school football is still a popular ritual in many communities across the South. In my native South Carolina, it is no accident that the working-class textile town of Gaffney still holds the state record for number of football state championship titles won and is still adding to the number in the post-textile era. Churches still perform their outreach and serving work, stocking food pantries, donating clothes to closets for the needy, serving the less fortunate, caring for the elderly, and attending to many of the communities' needs despite meager resources. Almost every holiday or tragedy in working-class communities yields an outpouring of generosity toward some group of people in need, from veterans suffering from post-traumatic stress disorder to cancer-stricken children. Yet, despite the signs of health and good intentions, the fraying at the seams, if not the rending, of the fabric of working-class culture remains all too visible. The seeming solidarity of the South's white working class's political support for the identity politics of Donald Trump in 2016 and again with added gusto in 2020 revealed more about the culture's challenges than its resilience.

Yet as we go round and round with analysis of the southern white working class, we often find ourselves revisiting race and racism. As much as the problems of the southern white working class have grown increasingly similar to those of the larger American working class, race still looms as the central theme of southern working-class history across generations. To understand the way in which racism and the concept of whiteness or white privilege shaped the attitudes and behavior of the southern white working class, the term "caste," an older term formerly used by scholars to label the system of de jure and de facto segregation that flourished in the American South from the 1890s into the 1960s, offers valuable insight. Decades ago, starting in the 1930s, leading sociologists, after doing substantial fieldwork in the South, described the apartheid of southern society as a "caste" system. The caste system placed whites of all socioeconomic classes in a privileged position and allowed them to enjoy privileges denied to Blacks of all socioeconomic classes. Under a caste system, escape from your born or inherited caste remained impossible no matter your personal level of success or accomplishment. In 1937, social scientist John Dollard published *Caste and Class in a Southern Town*, establishing the concept of caste as a common mode of understanding the prevailing southern racial hierarchy.[31] Decades later, as the civil rights movement in the 1950s and 1960s dismantled key portions of the caste system, both popular and academic references to caste grew less common.

In recent years, however, the term caste has enjoyed a revival due to the rediscovery of its descriptive power. The revival gained momentum through geographer Colin Woodward's use of the term to describe the "Deep South nation" in his widely read *American Nations*.[32] The resurrected term then gained widespread circulation and influence through Isabel Wilkerson's blockbuster, *Caste: The Origins of Our Discontent*, published in 2020 and heralded as a must read by Oprah Winfrey's Book Club. Wilkerson's work revived discussion of the concept of caste as we enter the third decade of the twenty-first century and thus opened new

The Unraveling of Southern White Working-Class Culture   243

understandings of the intricacies of social and racial hierarchy in the United States.[33] A caste system, Wilkerson explained, involved a dominant group "keeping the hierarchy as it is in order to maintain your own ranking, advantage, privilege or to elevate yourself above others or keep others beneath you."[34] In the American context of caste, Wilkerson detailed the essence of white privilege or the advantages of "whiteness." Race served as the basis for the American bipartite caste system. The post-slavery, segregated South, like South African apartheid and the Indian system of social stratification, operated more as a caste system than as a class hierarchy.

Wilkerson's application of the term to the modern American South hinged on the system's absolute prohibition against moving from caste to caste. Caste lines were impenetrable. Whites were a privileged caste and Blacks were an inferior one. Within both white and Black communities class divisions existed. But no American Blacks, regardless of class or education or achievement, could enjoy the same status and privilege as a white person. Local variations (and even exceptions) in the operations of the caste system emerged across the South (with New Orleans perhaps the leading example), but throughout the region the caste system insured that even poorer whites enjoyed rights and privileges denied to all Blacks. The pivotal point in a caste system was that to remain dominant all members of the group exercising power must be considered as superior to any member of the subordinate group. The caste hierarchy held no matter how bright or talented or successful the subordinate caste member may be or how lacking in talent and virtue the member of the dominant group, a member of the dominant caste must always be recognized as such, and members of the subordinate caste must always accept their defined status.[35] Wilkerson's book often made its points about the enduring caste mentality by highlighting the all too frequent instances in which whites react with disbelief or skepticism or even scorn when encountering successful and well-educated Blacks. These poignant moments served as ready reminders of the caste system's pernicious legacy. Yet the most powerful of her points lies in explaining the unrelenting anger and bitterness of the southern white working class over the desegregation of the South, the dismantling of the caste system, and the loss of white privilege.

Indigenous observers of the southern caste system recognized that nothing stood as more central to the caste system than the fact that all members of the dominant caste should enjoy privileges denied to all members of the subordinate caste. In the early 1940s, Charlotte-based journalist and writer W. J. Cash explained the power of whiteness in

244 *Understanding the American South*

the South by claiming that slavery had for many decades conferred the "dear treasure of his superiority as a white man" on white plain folk and poor whites as well as the planter and mercantile elite.[36] White southern author Lillian Smith, whose *Killers of the Dream* (1949) presented a frank indictment of lynching, claimed that the caste system in the South told working-class whites that "[n]obody can take away from you this whiteness that has made you superior ... they cannot strip your white skin off you." According to Smith, their white skin "became the poor whites most special possession."[37] Swedish economist and social scientist Gunnar Myrdal, author of the pathbreaking *An American Dilemma: The Negro Problem and Modern Democracy* (1944), observed that working-class whites "need more demarcations of caste than more upper-class whites" to secure their status as members of the dominant and privileged caste. "They are the people," Myrdal reported, "likely to stress aggressively that no Negro can ever attain the status of even the lowest white."[38]

Individual white opinions may have distanced themselves from the caste norm, but at least formally, the caste system defined all Blacks, no matter their level of education, financial well-being, or social respectability within their own community, as unfit for membership in the privileged caste. The prevailing caste system gave whites across class lines both a real and a psychological sense of power and control. It was that very status and privilege that working-class whites fought fiercely to maintain and so much resented losing.

The partial dismantling of the caste system by legislation and court decisions during the 1950s, 1960s, and beyond may have been resented by the white southern middle class, and clearly was, in fact, resented by a portion of it. But the white middle class had a variety of coping strategies at its disposal. Many middle-class whites simply took advantage of one or more of those options. Middle-class whites could segregate themselves privately. They could live in neighborhoods segregated by price, seek segregated education for their children through attendance at private schools, and segregate socially at country clubs through private invitation and selection processes. Middle-class whites also could (and did), of course, accept middle-class Blacks on grounds of their achievements. Over time, much of the middle class moved beyond exclusion to accepting Blacks on a class basis. Middle-class Blacks were welcome almost everywhere; separation by income replaced separation by race. For middle- and upper-class whites, class replaced caste in the search for social ranking.

The Unraveling of Southern White Working-Class Culture   245

But the southern white working class had fewer options. For the most part, they clung to the remnants of the fading caste system for protection and privilege and grew increasingly angry and resentful as the old caste barriers weakened or disintegrated all together. To be sure, in many ways, Blacks of all socioeconomic classes in the United States still experience many of the insults and limitations and barriers imposed by a race-based caste system, but the sweeping privilege caste used to provide for working-class whites has gradually diminished.

No candid commentator can deny that persistent racism (and white working-class frustration) plays an important role in the political alignment of southern white workers with the Republican party. The famous Lee Atwater memo, written after the 1968 presidential election, suggested that Republicans pursue a "southern strategy" by appealing, albeit in cleverly coded language, to the George Wallace voters of 1968 and other die-hard segregationists to join financially conservative white middle-class voters from the suburbs and silk-stocking districts, igniting the growth of a new Republican majority in many southern states. It took a few elections before the new strategy worked fully, but the southern white working class abandoned the Democratic party more quickly and more thoroughly than its counterparts in other areas of the country- –a major reason so few southern states have been even remotely competitive in presidential elections since Ronald Reagan's election in 1980.[39]

In fact, the political shift was so dramatic in the deep South that leading political scientists labeled it the "Great White Switch." Southern white working-class voters in the deep South abandoned their historic home in the Democratic party in droves for the Republican party of Ronald Reagan, eventually including down-ticket offices in which local Democrats had traditionally been safe, throughout the 1980s. Aided by the rise of an organized and well-funded religious right, which played to conservative cultural values rather than populist economic interests, the white working-class reaction to desegregation nonetheless triggered a tidal shift into the Republican party in the deep South. No Democratic presidential candidate except Arkansas native Bill Clinton had carried a deep South state since 1980 until Joe Biden squeaked out a narrow (10,000 vote) victory in Georgia in 2020 (due chiefly to large margins in metropolitan Atlanta). The Republican party continued to win white working-class support with defiant stances in favor of the region's traditional culture even as the GOP did little to address the economic challenges faced by hard-pressed southern working-class whites.[40]

246 *Understanding the American South*

A second phase of the "Great White Switch" of white working-class voters occurred nearly two decades later in the upper South states of Tennessee, North Carolina, and Virginia. The so-called China Trade Shock (which displaced large numbers of manufacturing employees in the South), the overall damage inflicted on the manufacturing sector by the Great Recession, and the election of the nation's first Black president in 2008, prompted rural and small-town working-class whites, residents of areas largely hollowed out by deindustrialization, to become loyal Republican voters up and down the ticket. They were drawn to Republican appeals on cultural issues including limiting gun control, defending school prayer, and supporting pro-life positions on abortion rights. In the political arena, they found themselves pitted against the increasingly prosperous residents of urban brain hubs, who trended Democratic. In Virginia, the dynamic brain hub of northern Virginia (Fairfax County) prevailed over Republican-leaning areas in the southern and western portions of the state and Virginia became a strong Democratic lean in presidential elections. In Tennessee, the growing Nashville area with its generally flourishing economy leans strongly Democratic but routinely loses to Republican majorities in the rest of the state. Similarly, in North Carolina, brain hubs such as Charlotte and the Research Triangle area lean Democratic and make the Tar Heel state competitive, but in the presidential elections of 2012, 2016, and 2020 red voters from the rest of the state have prevailed comfortably. Kentucky and West Virginia had already swung sharply Republican in the late 1990s as the Clinton administration policies toward fossil fuels drove coal industry states (including Ohio) into waiting GOP arms.[41]

Overall, the southern strategy of identity politics has continued to work well within the South, as the states of the lower South remain almost unshakably Republican. At the national level, however, the appeal of conservative identity politics has proven more limited. Nationwide, Democratic majorities have frequently emerged. In seven of the eight presidential elections since 1990, the Democratic candidate has won the popular vote. But the Republicans won two of those seven presidential elections in which Democrats won the popular vote by winning enough states to prevail in the electoral college. Moreover, the southern strategy continues to pay dividends at the state level and in nonpresidential years (due to lower Democratic turnout), in which Republicans often gain seats in Congress and retain control of governorships and state legislatures. Still, on occasion, the deep red southern states seem isolated as part of the last redoubt of conservatism in a nation moving in a different direction.

The Unraveling of Southern White Working-Class Culture   247

On balance, Democrats hold a clear if modest advantage in the national popular vote. In the South, however, Republicans have played the politics of cultural and racial identity fiercely and effectively over the past four decades, even before Fox News emerged to provide the daily dose. The power of identity politics triumphed easily over common class and economic interests that white workers shared with Black workers. The low-skilled, low-wage work that constituted too much of the manufacturing employment in the South gradually disappeared across borders and overseas or simply gave way to more high-tech, less labor-intensive methods of production. The rising presence of a new and robust Black middle class that defied southern white working-class visions of the proper social order only made matters worse. The politics of resentment took center stage with a vengeance as the treasured historical privileges of whiteness dwindled in number and quality. The bulk of this resentment turned against Blacks (as well as a rapidly growing Hispanic population) but no small amount of hostility targeted liberal or progressive politicians who supported civil rights and equal opportunity. Such southern white working-class resentment was hardly new. It had flourished for generations unto centuries. What was new was a social and political economy that did not reward whiteness as readily as it once had. As the economic foundations of white privilege weakened, white working-class frustration increased. Vanderbilt University psychiatrist and sociologist Jonathan Metzl has gone so far as to assert that working-class whites are "dying of whiteness," because of their refusal to abandon the politics of racial resentment and seek political options that might improve both working-class health and the overall fairness of the economy.[42]

The strange coalition of the southern working class with the region's business leadership to create a dominant Republican party across most of the South produced a party which has catered to the cultural values of the working class and the economic program preferred by the business community. The GOP's economic strategies have often worked against working-class economic interests, whether in the form of touting nonunion (low) wages to entice development prospects, insisting on rigorous right-to-work laws, and lowering state taxes on corporations and the affluent at the expense of public education, health care, job safety, and retirement benefits for the working class. The southern white working class has consistently shunned the obvious alternative of seeking a political coalition along economic lines to push for more government investment in working-class needs: schools, healthcare, job training, and job safety.

248 *Understanding the American South*

Deeply wounded (think personally offended) by the shrinking of white privilege in the public sphere since the 1960s, the southern white working class has essentially shied away from the notion of seeking economic remedies, except for efforts to limit the further erosion of white privilege though immigration restriction (largely aimed at Hispanics), in return for Republican protection of conservative cultural values (gun rights, the right to life, resistance to gay marriage, and even the bizarre Fox News creation, rolled out annually, the "War on Christmas"). In a very tangible way, the southern white working-class retreat from seeking coalitions capable of addressing working-class economic challenges (and there are many) has led them to an aggressive, if nonetheless fearful, assertion of identity politics. The assertive cultural conservatism of working-class southern whites, in turn, has proven effective at rallying voters to the polls but has won few allies beyond the working class. Defending the remnants of caste privilege appears to meet the psychological needs of the white working class but has left the economic cupboard increasingly bare.

So, in the final analysis, the crumbling of white southern working-class culture came partly from circumstances beyond local control – the decline in the number and percentage of manufacturing jobs needed to produce the required output – as well as from the culture's inherent weaknesses. Endemic racism stood foremost among those weaknesses, followed closely by the culture's reluctance to embrace education as a vehicle of upward mobility. Without oversimplification, the sheer advantages of being white in the long-segregated American South lent rewards, even among working-class whites, and a sense of status based on race that southern white workers prized and proved reluctant to yield. The loss of that intangible sense of belonging to the preferred race, that distinct white privilege that desegregation forced them to yield, generated resentments that fueled futility to the point of self-destruction. Finally, as a culture born to cope with scarcity and adversity, southern white working-class culture proved less prepared to manage either the temptations of consumerism or the frustrations of vanishing racial advantage. That this culture could not hold its coherence given the forces arrayed against it should not surprise us; that it gave way so quickly still does.

Notes

1. J. D. Vance, *Hillbilly Elegy: A Memoir of a Family and Culture in Crisis* (New York: HarperCollins, 2016).
2. Anne Case and Angus Deaton, *Deaths of Despair and the Future of Capitalism* (Princeton: Princeton University Press, 2020). For a conservative's view on

The Unraveling of Southern White Working-Class Culture   249

the hardening of class lines in the United States, see Charles Murray, *Coming Apart: The State of White America, 1960–2010* (New York: Random House, 2012).

3. For a multi-sided response to Vance, see Anthony Harkins and Meredith McCarroll, *Appalachian Reckoning: A Region Responds to Hillbilly Elegy* (Morgantown: West Virginia University Press, 2019). For a larger perspective, see Bruce Schulman, *From Cotton Belt to Sunbelt: Federal Policy, Economic Development, and the Transformation of the South, 1938–1980* (Durham, NC: Duke University Press, 1994); James C. Cobb, *The South and America since World War II* (New York: Oxford University Press, 2010), 52–74, 202–222.

4. David L. Carlton, "Textile Town Settles in, 1950–1974," in Betsey Wakefield Teter, ed., *Textile Town* (Spartanburg, SC: Hub City Writers Project, 2002), 209–231. See also Carlton, "The American South and the American Manufacturing Belt," in David L. Carlton and Peter A. Coclanis, eds., *The South, the Nation, and the World: Perspectives on Southern Economic Development* (Charlottesville: University of Virginia Press, 2003), 163–178.

5. James C. Cobb, *The Selling of the South: The Southern Crusade for Industrial Development, 1936–1980* (Baton Rouge: Louisiana State University Press, 1982), 5–24; Schulman, *From Cotton Belt to Sunbelt*, 63–111. For an introduction to the strength of anti-union sentiment in the post-World War II South, see Leon Fink, "Union Power, Soul Power: The Story of 1199B and Labor's Search for a Southern Strategy," *Southern Changes* 5 (March–April 1983): 9–20.

6. Paul Harvey, *Christianity and Race in the American South: A History* (Chicago: University of Chicago Press, 2016), 118–208; Mark A. Shibley, "The Southernization of American Religion: Testing A Hypothesis," *Sociological Analysis* 52 (Summer 1991): 159–174.

7. J. Morgan Kousser, *The Shaping of Southern Politics: Suffrage Restriction and the Establishment of the One-Party South, 1880–1910* (New Haven: Yale University Press, 1974); David L. Carlton, *Mill and Town in South Carolina, 1880–1920* (Baton Rouge: Louisiana State University Press, 1982); Bryant Simon, *A Fabric of Defeat: The Politics of South Carolina Millhands, 1910–1948* (Chapel Hill: University of North Carolina Press, 1998); J. Mills Thornton III, *Politics and Power in a Slave Society: Alabama, 1800–1860* (Baton Rouge: Louisiana State University Press, 1978); Lacy K. Ford, Jr., *Origins of Southern Radicalism: The South Carolina Upcountry, 1800–1860* (New York: Oxford University Press, 1988); Harry L. Watson, *Jacksonian Politics and Community Conflict: The Emergence of the Second American Party System in Cumberland County, North Carolina* (Baton Rouge: Louisiana State University Press, 1981). The foundational treatment is V. O. Key, *Southern Politics in State and Nation* (New York: Alfred A. Knopf, 1949).

8. Earl Black and Merle Black, *Politics and Society in the South* (Cambridge, MA: Harvard University Press, 1987).

9. On social dysfunction, see Sam Quinones, *Dreamland: The True Tale of the Opiate Epidemic* (New York: Bloomsbury Press, 2015).

10. See Case and Deaton, *Deaths of Despair and the Future of Capitalism*.

11. Richard A. Easterlin, "Interregional Differences in per Capita Income, Population, and Total Income, 1840–1950," in *Trends in the American Economy in the Nineteenth Century: A Report of the National Bureau of Economic Research, New York*, Studies in Income and Wealth, Vol. 24, the Conference on Research in Income and Wealth (Princeton: Princeton University Press, 1960), 73–140; Kris James Mitchener and Ian W. McLean, "U.S. Regional Growth and Convergence, 1880–1980," *Journal of Economic History* 59, no. 4 (1999): 1016–1042.

12. Joseph E. Stiglitz, *People, Power, and Profits: Progressive Capitalism for an Age of Discontent* (New York: W. W. Norton & Company, 2019), 32–46; Enrico Moretti, *The New Geography of Jobs* (Boston: Mariner Books, 2013), 178–214; Robert J. Gordon, *The Rise and Fall of American Growth: The U.S. Standard of Living since the Civil War* (Princeton: Princeton University Press, 2016), 605–639.

13. See Carlton, *Mill and Town in South Carolina, 1880–1920*, especially 82–214.

14. Adam Rothman, *Slave Country: American Expansion and the Origins of the Deep South* (Cambridge, MA: Harvard University Press, 2005), 165–216; Walter Johnson, *River of Dark Dreams: Slavery and Empire in the Cotton Kingdom* (Cambridge, MA: Harvard University Press, 2013); Edward E. Baptist, *The Half Has Never Been Told: Slavery and the Making of American Capitalism* (New York: Basic Books, 2014); James David Miller, *South by Southwest: Planter Emigration and Identity in the Slave South* (Charlottesville: University of Virginia Press, 2002); Daniel S. Dupre, *Transforming the Cotton Frontier: Madison County, Alabama, 1800–1840* (Baton Rouge: Louisiana State University Press, 1997).

15. Tommy W. Rogers, "The Great Population Exodus from South Carolina, 1850–1860," *South Carolina Historical Magazine* 68 (January 1967): 14–22.

16. Bill Malone, *Classic Country Music: A Smithsonian Collection* (Washington, DC: The Smithsonian Institution, 1990). Malone's booklet was included with *Classic Country Music: A Smithsonian Collection*, a four-disc set; Jack Temple Kirby, "The Great Southern Exodus, 1910–1960: A Primer for Historians," *Journal of Southern History* 49 (November 1983): 585–600.

17. James N. Gregory, *The Southern Diaspora: How the Great Migrations of Black and White Southerners Changed America* (Chapel Hill: University of North Carolina Press, 2005); William J. Collins and Marianne Wannamaker, "The Great Migration in Black and White: New Evidence on the Selection and Sorting of Southern Migrants," *Journal of Economic History* 75 (December 2015): 947–992; Chad Berry, *Southern Migrants, Northern Exiles* (Urbana-Champaign: University of Illinois Press, 2000).

18. Jonathan Haidt, *The Righteous Mind: Why Good People Are Divided by Politics and Religion* (New York: Vintage Books, 2012), 118–126.

19. Haidt, *The Righteous Mind*, 25–25, 121–125, 338–339. See also R. A. Shweder and Jonathan Haidt, "The Future of Moral Psychology: Truth, Intuition and the Pluralist Way," *Psychological Studies* 4 (1993): 360–365.

The Unraveling of Southern White Working-Class Culture   251

20. Moretti, *The New Geography of Jobs*, 154–177.
21. Jack Temple Kirby, *Rural Worlds Lost: The American South, 1920–1960* (Baton Rouge: Louisiana State University Press, 1986); Abigail Wozniak, "Are College Graduates More Responsive to Distant Labor Market Opportunities?" *Journal of Human Resources* 45 (4: 2010): 944–970.
22. Dan T. Carter, *The Politics of Rage: George Wallace, The Origins of the New Conservatism, and the Transformation of American Politics* (Baton Rouge: Louisiana State University Press, 1995), 294–323.
23. Case and Deaton, *Deaths of Despair*, 49–61; Moretti, *The New Geography of Jobs*, 178–214.
24. Adam Posen, "The Price of Nostalgia: America's Self-defeating Economic Retreat," *Foreign Affairs* (May–June 2021): 1–24.
25. David Autor, David Dorn, and Gordan Hansen, "The China Syndrome: Local Labor Market Effects of Import Competition in the United States," *American Economic Review* 103 (2013): 212–268; David Autor, David Dorn, and Gordan Hansen, "The China Shock: Learning from Labor-Market Adjustment to Large Changes in Trade," *Annual Review of Economics* 8 (2016): 205–240.
26. Daniel W. Drezner, "Free Trade with Benefits," *Washington Post*, April 26, 2021.
27. Case and Deaton, *Deaths of Despair*, especially 71–130.
28. Case and Deaton, *Deaths of Despair*, 33–36.
29. Case and Deaton, *Deaths of Despair*, 152–156, 257–258.
30. Case and Deaton, *Deaths of Despair*, 50–55; Thomas Picketty and Emmanuel Saez, "Income Inequality in the United States, 1917–1998," *Quarterly Journal of Economics* 118 (2003): 1–39.
31. John Dollard, *Caste and Class in a Southern Town* (New Haven: Yale University Press, 1937).
32. Colin Woodard, *American Nations: A History of the Eleven Rival Regional Cultures of North America* (New York: Penguin Books, 2011).
33. Isabel Wilkerson, *Caste: The Origins of Our Discontent* (New York: Random House, 2020). Wilkerson's account of how even the scholarly study of caste in the Natchez area during the late 1930s proved constrained by restrictions the caste system placed on African American researchers and the roles they were compelled to play to conform the system's expectations. See 245–256.
34. Wilkerson, *Caste*, 70.
35. Wilkerson, *Caste*, 224–237.
36. W. J. Cash, *The Mind of the South* (New York: Knopf, 1941), 66.
37. Lillian Smith, *Killers of the Dream* (New York: W. W. Norton & Company, 1949), 171.
38. Gunnar Myrdal, *An American Dilemma: The Negro Problem and Modern Democracy*, Vol. 2 (New York: Harper and Row, 1944), 597.
39. Black and Black, *Politics and Society in the South*, 232–275; Mathew D. Lassiter, *The Silent Majority: Suburban Politics in the Sunbelt South* (Princeton: Princeton University Press, 2006), 119–275.
40. Earl Black and Merle Black, *The Rise of Southern Republicans* (Cambridge, MA: Harvard University Press, 2002).

41. Angie Mitchell and Todd Shields, *The Long Southern Strategy: How Chasing White Voters in the South Transformed American Politics* (New York: Oxford University Press, 2019).

42. Jonathan Metzl, *Dying of Whiteness: How the Politics of Racial Resentment Is Killing America's Heartland* (New York: Basic Books, 2019).

PART IV

UNDERSTANDING HISTORY AND IRONY

10

The Irony of Southern History and the Problem of Innocence in American Life

Americans stand in a very peculiar relationship to their history. We are fond of evoking it with pride – as the inspiring story of the "City on the Hill" or the "last best hope for democracy," and as the "leader of the free world," and so on. We Americans are also readily inspired by our liberty-avowing rhetoric and documents: Jefferson's Declaration of Independence, Lincoln's Gettysburg Address, Franklin Roosevelt's assertion of the Four Freedoms, Martin Luther King, Jr.'s "I Have a Dream" speech. But we Americans are rather selective in our historical memory. Many Americans still blanch at public discussion of the less laudable aspects of our history: Indian removal, slavery and segregation, the long disfranchisement of women, the half-legal thievery of the Gilded Age, the internment of Japanese-Americans during World War II, the censorious scourge of McCarthyism and the Red Scare, the ugly backlash against the civil rights movement, the dark underside of arms-for-hostages deals, and the myriad actions of amorality and dubious legality that produced the early twenty-first-century banking bubble, just as examples.

Indeed, many Asians and Europeans believe that Americans have a poor understanding of their history. Even our own self-image tends to rank our historical consciousness as low. Americans tout themselves as pragmatic, innovative, enterprising, self-reliant, freedom-loving, and patriotic. But no popular stereotype that I know of characterizes Americans as a historically minded people. To be sure, the modern information revolution, part blessing, part curse though it is, has democratized the pursuit of family history through the availability of resources on popular websites such as GenealogyBank.com and Ancestry.com, and as a result, we no longer see family history as the exclusive provenance of elites living in scattered pockets of genealogical infatuation, such as Boston's Back Bay or the South of Broad section of Charleston. Americans, at least as far as revenues from tourism are a measure, seem intrigued by the nation's multitude of history museums and historic sites, and we have as a nation wisely invested in developing and maintaining such sites. Younger generations seemed drawn to our historic national parks for hiking and climbing. Such sites certainly constitute a major part of both our educational and recreational experience in my home state of South Carolina. But still, almost no one at home or abroad instinctively thinks of Americans as a people endowed with a deep understanding of their history. Almost none of the nation's history teachers, from middle school through college, think that Americans have nearly the knowledge of or interest in American history that they need.

Like most historians of my generation, I imbibed heavily from the elixir that the past is all we have. The future has not arrived yet, and the present is a false moment between past and future, a moment so transient and elusive that it cannot be grasped. But perhaps America's comparatively poor understanding of its past is not as much of a liability as historians think. By the first decade of twenty-first century, a large body of thought, emanating both from brain scientists and leading spiritual thinkers, cautions us that true freedom can only be found by living in the "now."[1] Our past, our memories, are just that: stories we have created for ourselves to make sense of our experiences. The marriage of modern psychology with neuroscience explains that for individuals, memories rush quickly to mind when triggered by reminders signaling to us from different parts of our brain and the immediate influence of our surroundings. This new line of reasoning holds that all we have is the present, the "now." All else is merely a construction of memories generated by our "rational" (so-called) mind to fit our emotional needs or those of our willful imagination. Differently put, the past is simply a reflection of our emotional reaction to events, a self-constructed reflection no more real than our imagination. As a result, the past is simply a false reflection generated from our minds and not a reliable guide to our future.[2]

Thus individuals, when trying to understand their own past, naturally find memories and feelings rushing in to fill the void. These memories are shaped by emotions, intervening experiences, and a variety of other factors. They are powerful, and they ring true emotionally. Most of us would admit that our personal memories are not actual "fact," much less revealed truth. But is the scholarly history provided by professional historians any better? Despite having spent the better part of a lifetime

The Irony of Southern History and Problem of Innocence 257

studying history, I readily acknowledge that the past, whether understood as a personal, familial, societal, or global story, is just that: a story constructed from available sources. Historians, the scholars in charge of piecing together evidence-based societal, national, and international stories together, work from the best available surviving documentation and present their ideas and interpretations to other experts in our fields for test and challenge. Yet even with the safeguards of archival research, vast learning, disciplinary rigor, peer review, and collaborative endeavor behind the writing of scholarly history, most historians would concede that their accounts and interpretations uncover and present valuable insights into the past rather than proclaim revealed truths.

Where the lessons of history, and a historical way of thinking, can converge with what the influential spiritual thinker Eckhart Tolle terms the "Power of Now," the virtue of being present in the moment and in touch with the larger world of being is that they can guide us in that moment if we can learn to stand apart from our experiences and observe them holistically, knowing that we can only grasp imperfectly the truths revealed.[3] After all, Tolle's sentiments do not divert far from the thoughts of Reinhold Niebuhr, arguably the leading Protestant theologian of the twentieth century, when he advised: "Living one day at a time; Enjoying one moment at a time; Accepting hardships as the pathway to peace."[4]

So, let us just assume for the moment that our critics are right, that Americans, for whatever reason, have a poor or underdeveloped or simply unsophisticated sense of their history. Does it really matter? What good is history anyway? Why should it be important to us? After all, aren't we smart, capable, reasonable people, with lots of resources and technology at our disposal? Our ability to make things anew in the twenty-fist century is considerable. Why do we really need to understand the past anyway? Can't we count on reason, logic, ingenuity, resources, and, yes, even, spoken *sotto voce*, our "power" to show us the way? Why must we listen to history's tiresome, complicated, and demanding lessons?

For much of my career, it has been my job, as well as my passion, and possibly even my calling, as a professor of history, to convince people that they should. And, as is often the case, I found it easier to begin at the personal level. During my twenty-plus years in the classroom, I regularly asked my large survey classes, with 350 people amassed in the University of South Carolina's largest auditorium classroom (at the time), the following question: "How many of you would volunteer for a case of amnesia? How many of you would be willing to suddenly forget everything you have experienced in life up until this moment, and start over with your mind a blank slate?" I usually found out quickly that virtually no one in the audience really wanted to live without any knowledge of their personal history. Even by the time we're eighteen, nineteen, or twenty years old, much less by the time we reach riper ages, most of us have learned something about ourselves that we value. We've developed some likes and dislikes and come to have some modicum of understanding about ourselves and our abilities. Most of us learn fairly early on that we aren't likely to quarterback a Super Bowl team, like Joe Montana, Peyton Manning, Tom Brady, or Patrick Mahomes, or, yet again, Tom Brady, or become the next Julia Roberts or Tom Hanks, or gain even the splendid epochs of celebrity like that of Madonna or Lady Gaga or Justin Bieber or Beyonce or Kanye West or most recently Taylor Swift; we learn that neither neurosurgery nor classical piano are likely our best career choices, though society is thankful that some few people learn that they might have the gift to do such demanding yet wonderful things. Of course, most of us learn painful lessons as well, about the loss of loved ones, about tragic accidents that snuff out lives at too early an age, about friends who are fickle and unfaithful, about abuse within families, about mental health miseries, about the whims of the job market, about the hypocrisy of societies, all societies, which profess values they don't really practice. In sum, few people would welcome amnesia at any age. We do not want to sacrifice the knowledge of our personal history; it's too important, too much a part of who we are, too much a guide for our future aspirations, too much of our self-understanding. No one wants to learn all the hard lessons all over again.

But if our personal history is important to us as individuals, so, too, is our larger history important to us as a society, a state, and a nation. We should fear collective amnesia every bit as much as personal memory loss. And ignorance of our history is exactly that: a case of collective amnesia. History is, or least should be, our collective memory. We must try to understand history if we are to make informed choices about our society's future. The great southern writer William Faulkner famously expressed this same sentiment when, in *Requiem for a Nun*, a novel about the struggle to overcome racial distrust, his character Gavin Stevens declared: "The past isn't dead, it's not even past. Yesterday isn't over until tomorrow and tomorrow began ten thousand years ago."[5] As popular as slogans such as "go for the gusto" and "have it your way" have been, and as present-centered and even "in the moment" as we often are, we lead existential lives at our own peril – and so do societies and nation-states. We are but a part of history, living links between past

The Irony of Southern History and Problem of Innocence   259

and future, and our responsibilities are huge. The hand of the past isn't dead; the past lives in us today. But, yes, the hand of the past can be a heavy hand, influencing what we can do, shaping, defining, and, yes, even limiting our choices. History is not a fascination with how things used to be but a way of understanding how things are now, and even a way of gaining insight about what things might one day become.

Moreover, I suggest in this chapter that history, when viewed with an ironic sensibility, is a way of understanding that reinforces our need for a sense of public responsibility, civility, and humility that are too often lacking in our public and political culture today. Within history as an academic discipline there are a variety of different philosophical approaches to its study. But in this chapter, I make a strong case in favor of the ironic approach to history and sketch briefly why I see an ironic understanding of history as so valuable to Americans as a people.

I start with an unidentified quotation: "Everybody understands the obvious meaning of the world struggle in which we are now engaged. We are defending freedom ... and trying to preserve justice against a system which has demonically distilled injustice and cruelty out of its original promise of a higher justice."[6] These words might resonate with any generation as it surveys the world it inhabits. Fitting as these words seem as a summation of our nation's stand against Nazis and Fascists in World War II or as a position against international terrorism in the wake of the unthinkable tragedies of September 11, 2001; they could apply in a variety of circumstances. In fact, they were written by Reinhold Niebuhr in the early 1950s as part of his reflections on the emerging Cold War. Few books have influenced historians and public intellectuals generally through the second half of the twentieth century as much as Niebuhr's classic *The Irony of American History*, published in 1950 with the hope of influencing America's conduct during the Cold War. Niebuhr supported the vigorous defense of freedom and democracy, including the use of military might if necessary, but he knew the Cold War would be a dangerous game, so he also wanted to warn the nation that it should not assume too much about the inherent goodness of its own cause. Put more directly, Niebuhr sought to curb the swaggering national pride unleashed when *Time, Inc.* publisher Henry Luce proclaimed in 1941 that the world was entering an "American Century" that would surpass in glory and grandeur of the Pax Britannica of the nineteenth century.[7]

Niebuhr's *Irony of American History* pleaded a cautionary case from the perspective of both history and Reformed theology. While he very much expected the United States to engage in the world's struggles, just

260   *Understanding the American South*

as Reformed theology expects Christians to engage the world and all its imperfections, Niebuhr cautioned against a continued American preoccupation with its national myths of virtue and innocence. He believed that Americans embraced a false or mythical history sustained by a logic in which our material prosperity stood as witness to our virtue and our unparalleled military success buttressed a belief in American innocence. In popular national myth, Niebuhr lamented, Americans believed that their nation somehow led a charmed life, free from guilt and failure. Our virtue was known by our good works which in turn testified to our virtue.[8] In later years, the well-known Catholic intellectual Garry Wills called this instinctive American faith in our own virtue and innocence nothing less than a national doctrine of "original sinlessness," an American counter-myth to the Genesis account of the Fall.[9]

Niebuhr insisted that these assumptions of national virtue and innocence, and any self-congratulatory history which sustained them, required rebuttal from an ironic view of history grounded in Augustinian or Reformed assumptions about good and evil. Ironic history, in Niebuhr's view, emphasized that human actions always produced unintended, unpredicted, and unexpected consequences. Undeniably, the roots of Niebuhr's contention were deeply grounded in the Reformed theology he professed. Saint Augustine argued for the absolute "discontinuity" between our perfect knowledge of God's will that our souls should receive grace on the one hand and "any knowledge of his purpose in the vicissitudes of life" on the other. Indeed, Augustine insisted that "all attempts to know God's purpose ... [apart from saving souls] is presumptuous."[10] Like Augustine, Niebuhr held that evil had no independent existence in God's creation; it flourished only as a corruption of the good. Humans, having all sinned and fallen short of God's glory, can do only limited, imperfect, incomplete, and corrupted good, and in that good there is inevitably evil. That's why humans need God's ongoing forgiveness. Thus, according to Augustine, and to Niebuhr, humans ended up "doing evil" not simply when they knowingly violated God's law but also through their best, most well-intentioned, and even selfless actions. As the twenty-first-century Reformed theologian Douglas Ottati puts it, sin is radical and universal in God's creation. Or to paraphrase the comic strip wisdom of Pogo: "We have met evil, and it is us."[11] It was in this theological belief – that no human endeavor was, or ever could be, completely "good" or utterly bereft of "evil" – that Niebuhr based his case for a history that emphasized an ironic understanding of the American experience.

The Irony of Southern History and Problem of Innocence   261

If the ironic approach to interpreting history is deeply rooted in the assumptions of Reformed theology, and the foremost practitioner of the ironic brand of history that Niebuhr recommended proved to be a skeptic with little time for theology: C. Vann Woodward, the late Yale professor widely regarded as the greatest southern historian of his generation. Immediately influenced by Niebuhr's work in the early 1950s, Woodward worked out an ironic interpretation of American history that carried special meaning for the history of his primary scholarly subject and native region: the American South.

Beginning with a landmark essay, "The Irony of Southern History," in 1952, Woodward argued that the southern experience, long perceived as more embarrassment than instruction to the nation, might teach Americans something they very much needed to learn. The wave of Cold War nationalism that swept all before it in 1952, Woodward agreed with Niebuhr, grew in part out of the "American legend of success, a legend that is not shared by any other people in the civilized world." America's long track record of success had left a "deep imprint" on the nation and went a long way toward explaining "the national faith in unlimited progress, in the efficacy of material means, ... and the belief in the invincibility of American arms." Abundant resources, a measure of geographic isolation, economic prosperity, and military victories, Woodward concluded, left Americans convinced of their own innocence and virtue.[12]

Against these myths of national innocence and virtue, in contrast to this legend of unsullied success and prosperity, Woodward argued, the historical experience of the American South offered a valuable or even vital counterpoint. Remember that when Woodward wrote in 1952, the South was still segregated and still stuck with a per capita income less than 60 percent of the national average. For all its poverty and nostalgic clinging to the ideology of the "Lost Cause," the white South, Woodward suggested to readers, offered America an example of a region whose people knew defeat and disappointment, sacrifice and poverty, a region whose experience stood in stark contrast to the American national faith in its innocence, virtue, power, and prosperity. Southerners were the poor country cousins of the American People of Plenty. The white South alone had known military defeat, humiliation, and enemy occupation. White southerners were Americans to be sure, but the post-secession southern experience had been, through its experience with failure and humiliation, decidedly un-American.[13]

Ironically, Woodward noted, if the southern experience was rather un-American, however, it was very worldly, very European. From the

262 *Understanding the American South*

international perspective, the southern experience was hardly provincial; instead, it was cosmopolitan. Perhaps then, Woodward argued, the South could teach the rest of the nation something about humility, about the limits of power, about the pain of poverty, about the maddening frustration that builds when a people find a social stigma fastened upon them or hear themselves branded as "losers." Woodward believed that Americans could see the southern experience as a cautionary tale, one warning them against the temptation to arrogance, to abuse of its great power, to excessive confidence in its good intentions, and to excessive faith in its military and economic power.[14]

Well, Woodward lived another forty-eight years, and through his long life he saw many of his fondest hopes that the United States might learn crucial lessons from the counterpoint of southern history blasted. Indeed, he found southerners aiding and abetting, and at times even leading, in the national refusal to learn. During the 1960s, he saw the tragedy of Vietnam unfold with a southerner as president, a Davidson graduate as secretary of state, and a South Carolinian as ranking general. Woodward soon realized that other southerners had learned different, and he believed less salutary, lessons from the region's history. They had learned that power rules, that you can't back down or out of a fight, much less admit that you're wrong, without losing face. They had learned, Woodward mused, all the wrong things. "Irony," Woodward later confessed, "had caught up with the ironist."[15]

South Carolina's own Ben Robertson, the noted New Deal-era and World War II journalist who became Edward R. Murrow's best friend, had anticipated that the white South's passive-aggressive defensiveness might produce such a refusal to learn from its history. Best known as the author of the well-received *Red Hills and Cotton*, a precocious memory of his childhood near Clemson, Robertson once explained the strong grip of tradition on the white southern mind with an apocryphal anecdote. A stranger walked down an old Charleston street and passed a "proud and beautiful" woman, sitting on the front porch of a dilapidated house, weeping. "What's the matter?" the stranger asked. "Uncle Joe is dead," the woman replied. The stranger offered his sympathy and inquired if Uncle Joe had lived in the house where the woman was sitting. "Oh no," the grieving woman replied, "he didn't live here, but my mother told me about him." Well, the stranger observed, "He must have been very close to your mother." No, the lady politely explained to the stranger, "My mother didn't know him personally – it was her mother who knew him. Her mother knew him when she was a little girl." Bewildered, the

The Irony of Southern History and Problem of Innocence 263

stranger demanded to know exactly *when* Uncle Joe had passed on. "He died at Gettysburg," replied the lady, now crying profusely, "He died at the Peach Orchard on the third day and it was all General Longstreet's fault."[16]

Ben Robertson lamented the tendency of white southerners, like the fictitious Charleston lady, to "grieve over the Gettysburg peach orchard" more than "over the poverty" of the southern people. In a speech during the summer of 1939, Robertson implored his tradition-bound Charleston audience to choose progress over tradition. "Let's try to develop a Southern passion for social justice, let's open our eyes to human suffering," he urged, "And the next time anybody mentions Gettysburg, let's get up and go plant a pine tree or pile rocks in a gully. It won't change the South, but it will change us."[17]

Woodward had not been wrong about the lessons southern history could teach; he had simply misjudged southerners' (and Americans') willingness to learn. Instead, when finally given the opportunity to share fully in the national's prosperity, southerners threw themselves headlong into its pursuit. Moreover, southerners, having experienced bitter military defeat, hardly emerged as voices of restraint in national counsels. Instead, through the Cold War, Vietnam, and beyond, southern voices have more often been those of spread-eagled patriotism. As Woodward found to his chagrin, southerners seemed to learn from their defeat that they never wanted to be caught on the poor, weak, or losing side again. Rather than being chastened by their historical experience, many late twentieth-century and early twenty-first-century southerners seemed more willing to embrace the myths of American innocence and virtue than many of their countrymen. Rather than a counterpoint to the myths of national innocence and virtue, the South had become a driving force in their reassertion.

All teachers, at any level, learn the same exasperating lesson that Woodward learned: that the lessons teachers teach are not always the lessons students learn. But that hard-recognized fact notwithstanding, I want to turn once again to history for instruction. The United States has elected five generals to the presidency, but our greatest warrior president was a civilian, a lawyer who sometimes defended railroad companies, yet a man who possessed a sophisticated understanding of war's (and life's) moral ambiguities. No American president has been more resolute or more successful in pursuit of war aims than Abraham Lincoln. Surely no president has ever had more reason to be confident of the ultimate rightness of his causes: saving the Union, freeing the enslaved. But while

264   *Understanding the American South*

resolute in his leadership, Lincoln remained cautious and wary of rash judgments concerning good and evil, even when there seemed little reason for such caution.[18]

Often Lincoln deflected the temptation of easy moralizing with humor. Early in the war, a delegation of New England ministers met with Lincoln to express their support. As they left, the pastors collectively assured the president that because his cause was just, God was surely on his side. "I would be most pleased to have God on my side," Lincoln reportedly told the departing clergy, "but I must have Kentucky."[19]

On other occasions Lincoln grappled with moral ambiguity and historical contingency more directly. In his second inaugural address, that greatest of American political speeches, Lincoln weighed the ironic dimensions, both practical and spiritual, of the crisis briefly but carefully:

Neither party expected for the war the magnitude and duration which it has already attained. Neither anticipated that the cause of the conflict might cease with or even before the conflict itself would cease. Each looked for an easier triumph ... Both read the same Bible and pray to the same God, and each evokes His aid against the other.

Now at this point, Lincoln momentarily dropped his ironic posture, doubtless overcome by his swelling scorn for the moral claims of his opponents. "It may seem strange," Lincoln injected, "that any men should dare to ask a just God's assistance in wringing their bread from the sweat of other men's faces." But even on this point Lincoln quickly shrank away from self-confident moral rebuke and sought once again refuge in irony and scripture, adding, "but let us judge not that we are not judged." "The prayers of both [sides] could not be answered," Lincoln continued. "That of neither has been answered fully. The Almighty has his own purposes."[20]

When Lincoln gave this address in March of 1865, he was only a few weeks away from finally bringing the American Civil War to a successful conclusion (Lee would surrender in early April), and he knew it. As he prepared his inaugural remarks, President Lincoln stood with unprecedented political capital and military power at his disposal. He stood before his audience in the mud and muck of Washington on that late winter day as Savior of the Union, Emancipator of nearly four million slaves, and commander-in-chief of the most powerful land army the world had ever seen. But at that moment of destiny, he chose to neither bask in the glow of his accomplishments nor look for new uses for his unrivaled military and political power. Instead, he thought of the 700,000 Americans

The Irony of Southern History and Problem of Innocence 265

who had died, nearly 400,000 on his side, nearly 300,000 on the other – all Americans in Lincoln's eyes – and chose another course.[21] Focus for a moment on words I am sure you have heard or read before but perhaps never considered in the context I am suggesting – the concluding paragraph of Lincoln's second inaugural address:

> With malice toward none and charity for all, with firmness in the right as God gives us to see the right, let us strive on to finish the work we are in, to bind up the nation's wounds, to care for him who shall have borne the battle and for his widow and his orphan, to do all which may achieve and cherish a just and lasting peace among ourselves and with all nations.[22]

Lincoln's choice of words and subject matter reflected the decision of a man humbled rather than emboldened, chastened rather than tempted, by his presence and "power" at American history's most pivotal moment. Rather than look up to find ever more evil to combat, Lincoln leaned over to find people to serve. His audience heard no rhetoric about "trampling out the vineyards where the grapes of wrath are stored" but rather about "binding up the nation's wounds," about caring for widows and orphans, about those people marginalized by the exercise of the unrivaled power Lincoln so skillfully brought to bear against his foe.[23] At this critical moment, he spoke not of power but of justice and mercy, and he spoke not with boasting confidence but with humility, offering a great national commission for harmony and concern for society's least, last, and lost.

So back for a moment to our time and place, in twenty-first century America, what does all this tell us about the lessons of irony and the value of history as a way of understanding? My undoubtedly flawed answer, but one with which I am prepared to rest my case, is that it tells those southerners eager to build a better South and a greater America that they must still humbly teach those hard lessons of southern history all over again, again, and again, knowing full well that the lessons taught will not always be the lessons learned, but teaching them anyway because we still have rocks to move and gullies to fill. Put another way, we must try, discerning as best we can the Almighty's purpose, to bend that long arc of history toward justice.

Notes

1. Eckhart Tolle, *The Power of Now: A Guide to Spiritual Enlightenment* (Vancouver: Nemaste Publishing, 1997).
2. Daniel Kahneman, *Thinking, Fast and Slow* (New York: Farrar, Strauss, and Giroux, 2011); Jonathan Haidt, *The Righteous Mind: Why Good People Are Divided by Politics and Religion* (New York: Random House, 2012).

266 *Understanding the American South*

3. Tolle, *The Power of Now*, 33–70.
4. This sentiment is at the heart of the serenity prayer, which is most often attributed to Niebuhr, who believed that he wrote it over time, doubtless including many sentiments he had heard articulated over the years. See Elisabeth Sifton, *The Serenity Prayer: Faith and Politics in Times of Peace and War* (New York: W. W. Norton & Company, 2003); see also Laurie Goodstein, "Serenity Prayer Stirs Up Doubt: Who Wrote It," *New York Times*, July 11, 2008.
5. William Faulkner, *Requiem for a Nun* (New York: Random House, 1951); Michael Gorra, *The Saddest Words: William Faulkner's Civil War* (New York: W. W. Norton & Company, 2020), 20.
6. Reinhold Niebuhr, *The Irony of American History* (Chicago: University of Chicago Press, 1952), 1.
7. Henry Luce, "The American Century," *Life*, February 17, 1941; Alan Brinkley, *The Publisher: Henry Luce and His American Century* (New York: Knopf, 2010), 260–272.
8. Niebuhr, *The Irony of American History*, 1–16, 151–174.
9. Garry Wills, *Reagan's America: Innocents at Home* (Garden City, NY: Doubleday, 1987), 278–288.
10. Garry Wills, *Confessions of a Conservative* (New York: Doubleday, 1979), 187–199, especially 190–191, and Garry Wills, *Saint Augustine: A Life* (New York: Penguin Group, 1999); Saint Augustine of Hippo, *The City of God*, trans. Marcus Dods (Peabody, MA: Hendrickson Publishers, 2009).
11. Douglas F. Ottati, *Reforming Protestantism: Christian Commitment in Today's World* (Louisville: Westminster John Knox Press, 1995); Douglas F. Ottati, *Theology for Liberal Presbyterians and Other Endangered Species* (Louisville: Geneva Press, 2006); Walt Kelly, *Pogo: We Have Met the Enemy and He Is Us* (New York: Touchstone Press, 1972).
12. C. Vann Woodward, "The Irony of Southern History," in C. Vann Woodward, ed., *The Burden of South History* (Baton Rouge: Louisiana State University Press, 1960), 187–211.
13. Woodward, "The Irony of Southern History," 140, 195–196; David M. Potter, *People of Plenty: Economic Abundance and the American Character* (Chicago: University of Chicago Press, 1954), 11–141.
14. Woodward, "The Irony of Southern History," 187–211.
15. Woodward, "A Second Look at the Theme of Irony," in C. Vann Woodward, ed., *Burden of Southern History*, 2nd edition (Baton Rouge: Louisiana State University, 1968).
16. Ben Robertson, "Forget Gettysburg," *Charleston News and Courier*, July 1, 1939, 12; Lacy K. Ford, "The Personable Journalist as Social Critic: Ben Robertson and the Early Twentieth Century South," *Southern Cultures* 4 (Winter 1996): 353–373.
17. Robertson, "Forget Gettysburg"; Ford, "The Personable Journalist as Social Critic."
18. Eric Foner, *The Fiery Trial: Abraham Lincoln and American Slavery* (New York: W. W. Norton & Company, 2010); James Oakes, *The Crooked Path to Abolition: Abraham Lincoln and the Antislavery Constitution* (New

The Irony of Southern History and Problem of Innocence   267

York: W. W. Norton & Company, 2021); William W. Freehling, *Becoming Lincoln* (Charlottesville: University of Virginia Press, 2018).

19. William E. Gienapp, "Abraham Lincoln and the Border States," *Journal of the Abraham Lincoln Association* 13 (1992): 13–46; John David Smith, "'Gentlemen, I, Too, Am a Kentuckian': Abraham Lincoln, the Lincoln Bicentennial, and Lincoln's Kentucky in Recent Scholarship," *Register of The Kentucky Historical Society* 106 (Summer–Autumn 2008): 433–470. Lincoln's reported remark is on p. 439. See also Nancy Disher Baird, ed., *Josie Underwood's Civil War Diary* (Lexington: University Press of Kentucky, 2009).

20. Abraham Lincoln, "Second Inaugural Address, March 4, 1865," in Richard N. Current, ed., *The Political Thought of Abraham Lincoln* (Indianapolis: Bobbs-Merrill, 1967), 314–316.

21. Drew Gilpin Faust. *This Republic of Suffering: Death and the American Civil War* (New York: Random House, 2008).

22. Lincoln, "Second Inaugural Address," in Current, *Political Thought of Abraham Lincoln*, 314–316.

23. Lincoln, "Second Inaugural Address," in Current, *Political Thought of Abraham Lincoln*, 316; Julia Ward Howe, "The Battle Hymn of the Republic," *Atlantic Monthly* (February 1862), 10. See also Dominic Tierney, "'The Battle Hymn of the Republic': America's Song of Itself," *Atlantic Monthly*, November 4, 2010.

Bibliography

BOOKS

Ambrose, Stephen. *Eisenhower: Soldier and President* (New York: Simon and Schuster, 1990).

Bailyn, Bernard. *Ideological Origins of the American Revolution* (Cambridge, MA: Harvard University Press, 1967).

Banerjee, Abhijit V. and Esthere Duflo. *Good Economics for Hard Times* (New York: Public Affairs, 2019).

Baptist, Edward E. *The Half Has Never Been Told: Slavery and the Making of American Capitalism* (New York: Basic Books, 2014).

Baum, Nancy. *Personal Connections in the Digital Age* (Cambridge, MA: Polity Press, 2015).

Beard, Charles and Mary Beard. *The Rise of American Civilization*, 2 vols. (New York: MacMillan, 1927).

Beckert, Sven. *Empire of Cotton: A Global History* (New York: Penguin, 2014).

Benedict, Michael Les. *A Compromise of Principle: Congressional Republicans and Reconstruction* (New York: W. W. Norton & Company, 1974).

Berlin, Ira. *Slaves without Masters: The Free Negro in the Antebellum South* (New York: Pantheon Books, 1974).

Berringer, Richard E., Herman Hattaway, Archer Jones, and William Still, Jr. *Why the South Lost the Civil War* (Athens: University of Georgia Press, 1986).

Berry, Chad. *Southern Migrants, Northern Exiles* (Urbana-Champaign: University of Illinois Press, 2000).

Black, Earl and Merle Black. *Politics and Society in the South* (Cambridge, MA: Harvard University Press, 1987).

Black, Earl and Merle Black. *The Rise of Southern Republicanism* (Cambridge, MA: Harvard University Press, 2002).

Blassingame, John W. *The Slave Community: Plantation Life in the Antebellum South* (New York: Oxford University Press, 1972).

Bleser, Carol K. *The Hammonds of Redcliffe* (Columbia: University of South Carolina Press, 1997).

Bibliography

Bleser, Carol K. *Secret and Sacred: The Diaries of James Henry Hammond* (Columbia: University of South Carolina Press, 1997).

Boorstin, Daniel. *The Americans: The Democratic Experience* (New York: Random House, 1973).

Boorstin, Daniel. *The Genius of American Politics* (Chicago: University of Chicago Press, 1953).

Boorstin, Daniel. *The Image: A Guide to Pseudo-Events in America* (New York: Vintage, 1962).

Bowers, Claude G. *The Tragic Era: The Revolution after Lincoln* (Boston: Houghton Mifflin, 1929).

Branch, Taylor. *At Canaan's Edge: America in the King Years, 1965–1968* (New York: Simon and Schuster, 2007).

Brands, H. W. *Masters of Enterprise: Giants of American Business from John Jacob Astor and J. P. Morgan to Bill Gates and Oprah Winfrey* (New York: The Free Press, 1999).

Brandt, Allan. *The Cigarette Century: The Rise and Fall and Deadly Persistence of the Product That Defined America* (New York: Basic Books, 2007).

Brinkley, Alan. *The Publisher: Henry Luce and His American Century* (New York: Alfred A. Knopf, 2010).

Brinkley, Douglas. *Cronkite* (New York: HarperCollins, 2012).

Burton, Orville Vernon. *In My Father's House Are Many Mansions: Family and Community in Edgefield, South Carolina* (Chapel Hill: University of North Carolina Press, 1987).

Butler, Jon. *Awash in a Sea of Faith: Christianizing the American People* (Cambridge, MA: Harvard University Press, 1990).

Campbell, Edward D. C., Jr. *The Celluloid South: Hollywood and the Southern Myth* (Knoxville: University of Tennessee Press, 1981).

Carlton, David L. *Mill and Town in South Carolina, 1880–1920* (Baton Rouge: Louisiana State University Press, 1982).

Carlton, David L. and Peter A. Coclanis. *Confronting Southern Poverty in the Great Depression: The Report on Economic Conditions of the South with Related Documents* (Boston: Bedford Books, 1996).

Carter, Dan T. *The Politics of Rage: George Wallace, the Origins of the New Conservatism, and the Transformation of American Politics* (Baton Rouge: Louisiana State University Press, 1995).

Carter, Zachary D. *The Price of Peace: Money, Democracy, and the Life of John Maynard Keynes* (New York: Random House, 2020).

Case, Anne and Angus Deaton. *Deaths of Despair and the Future of Capitalism* (Princeton: Princeton University Press, 2020).

Cash, Wilbur J. *The Mind of the South* (New York: Alfred A. Knopf, 1941).

Censer, Jane Turner. *North Carolina Planters and Their Children* (Chapel Hill: University of North Carolian Press, 1984).

Clark, Erskine. *Dwelling Place: A Plantation Epic* (New Haven: Yale University Press, 2005).

Clinton, Catherine. *The Plantation Mistress: Woman's World in the Old South* (New York: Pantheon Books, 1982).

Coates, Ta-Nehisi. *Between the World and Me* (New York: One World, 2015).

Bibliography

Cobb, James C. *The Selling of the South: The Crusade for Industrial Economic Development, 1936–1980* (Baton Rouge: Louisiana State University Press, 1984).

Conklin, Paul K. *The New Deal*, 3rd ed. (New York: Wiley-Blackwell, 1991).

Connelly, Thomas L. and Barbara L. Bellows. *God and General Longstreet: The Lost Cause and the Southern Mind* (Baton Rouge: Louisiana State University Press, 1982).

Cooper, William J. *Liberty and Slavery: Southern Politics to 1860* (New York: McGraw Hill, 1983).

Cooper, William J., Jr. *The South and the Politics of Slavery, 1828–1856* (Baton Rouge: Louisiana State University Press, 1978).

Croly, Herbert. *The Promise of American Life* (New York: MacMillan, 1909).

Daniel, Pete. *The Shadow of Slavery Peonage in the South, 1901–1969* (Urbana: University of Illinois Press, 1990).

Davis, Allison, Burleigh Gardner, and Mary Gardner. *Deep South: A Social Anthropology Study of Caste and Class* (Chicago: University of Chicago Press, 1941).

Davis, Burke. *War Bird: The Life and Times of Elliott White Spring* (Chapel Hill: University of North Carolina Press, 1987).

Deaton, Angus. *The Great Escape: Health, Wealth, and the Origins of Inequality* (Princeton: Princeton University Press, 2013).

Dew, Charles B. *Apostles of Disunion: Southern Peace Commissioners and the Coming of Civil War* (Charlottesville: University of Virginia Press, 2001).

Dodd, William. *The Cotton Kingdom: A Chronicle of the Old South* (New Haven: Yale University Press, 1919).

Dollard, John. *Caste and Class in a Southern Town* (New Haven: Yale University Press, 1937).

Du Bois, W. E. Burghardt. *Black Reconstruction in America, 1860–1880* (New York: Harcourt Brace, 1935).

Du Bois, W. E. Burghardt. *The Souls of Black Folk: Sketches and Notes* (Chicago: McClurg and Co., 1903).

Dunning, William Archibald. *Essays on the Civil War and Reconstruction and Related Topics* (New York: The MacMillan Company, 1898).

Dupre, Daniel. *Transforming the Cotton Frontier: Madison County, Alabama, 1800–1840* (Baton Rouge: Louisiana State University Press, 1997).

Durden, Robert F. *The Dukes of Durham, 1865–1929* (Durham: Duke University Press, 1975).

Eagles, Charles W. *Jonathan Daniels and the Evolution of a Southern Liberal* (Knoxville: University of Tennessee Press, 1982).

Edwards, Laura. *Gendered Strife and Confusion: The Political Culture of Reconstruction* (Urbana: University of Illinois Press, 1997).

Elisha, Walter Y. *Standing on the Shoulders of Visionaries: The Story of Springs Industries, Inc.* (Princeton: Princeton University Press, 1993).

Faulkner, William. *Requiem for a Nun* (New York: Random House, 1951).

Faust, Drew Gilpin. *A Design for Mastery: James Henry Hammond and the Old South* (Baton Rouge: Louisiana State University Press, 1982).

Faust, Drew Gilpin. *Mothers of Invention: Women of the Slaveholding South in the American South* (Chapel Hill: University of North Carolina Press, 1996).

Bibliography

Faust, Drew Gilpin. *Necessary Trouble: Growing Up at Midcentury* (New York: Farrar, Straus and Giroux, 2023).

Faust, Drew Gilpin. *The Republic of Suffering: Death and the American Civil War* (New York: Random House, 2008).

Faust, Drew Gilpin. *A Sacred Circle: The Dilemma of the Intellectual in the Old South* (Philadelphia: University of Pennsylvania Press, 1986).

Fields, Barbara J. *Slavery and Freedom on the Middle Ground Maryland during the Nineteenth Century* (New Haven: Yale University Press, 1987).

Foner, Eric. *The Fiery Trial: Abraham Lincoln and American Slavery* (New York: W. W. Norton & Company, 2010).

Foner, Eric. *Free Soil, Free Labor, and Free Men: The Ideology of the Republican Party before the Civil War* (New York: Oxford University Press, 1970).

Foner, Eric. *Nothing but Freedom: Emancipation and Its Legacy.* (Baton Rouge: Louisiana State University Press, 2007).

Foner, Eric. *Reconstruction: America's Unfinished Revolution, 1863–1877*, updated edition (New York: Harper Perennial Modern Classics, 2014).

Foner, Eric. *The Second Founding: How the Civil War and Reconstruction Remade the Constitution* (New York: W. W. Norton & Company, 2019).

Forcey, Charles. *The Crossroads of Liberalism: Croly, Weyl, Lippman and the Progressive Era, 1900–1925* (New York: Oxford University Press, 1961).

Ford, Lacy K. *Deliver Us from Evil: The Slavery Question in the Old South* (New York: Oxford University Press, 2009).

Ford, Lacy K. *Origins of Southern Radicalism: The South Carolina Upcountry, 1800–1860* (New York: Oxford University Press, 1988).

Foster, Gaines. *Ghosts of the Confederacy: Defeat, the Lost Cause, and the Emergence of the New South* (New York: Oxford University Press, 1985).

Fox-Genovese, Elizabeth. *Feminism Is Not the Story of My Life* (New York: Anchor, 1996).

Fox-Genovese, Elizabeth. *Within the Plantation Household: Black and White Women of the Old South* (Chapel Hill: University of North Carolina Press, 1988).

Fox-Genovese, Elizabeth and Eugene Genovese. *Fruits of Merchant Capital: Slavery and Bourgeois Property in the Rise and Expansion of Capitalism* (New York: Oxford University Press, 1983).

Fox-Genovese, Elizabeth and Eugene Genovese. *The Mind of the Master Class: History and Faith in the Southern Slaveholders' Worldview* (New York: Cambridge University Press, 2005).

Fox-Genovese, Elizabeth and Eugene Genovese. *Slavery in White and Black: Class and Race in the Southern Slaveholders' New World Order* (New York: Cambridge University Press, 2008).

Franklin, John Hope. *Mirror to America: The Autobiography of John Hope Franklin* (New York: Farrar, Straus and Giroux, 2005).

Frederickson, George. *The Black Image in the White Mind: The Debate over Afro-American Character and Destiny, 1817–1914* (New York: Harper and Row, 1971).

Frederickson, George. *White Supremacy: A Comparative Study in American and South African History* (New York: Oxford University Press, 1981).

Bibliography

Freehling, William. *Becoming Lincoln* (Charlottesville: University of Virginia Press, 2018).

Freehling, William. *Prelude to Civil War: The Nullification Controversy in South Carolina, 1816–1836* (New York: Harper and Row, 1966).

Freehling, William. *The Road to Disunion: Secessionists at Bay*, Volume 1 (New York: Oxford University Press, 1990).

Fukuyama, Francis. *The End of History and the Last Man* (New York: The Free Press, 1992).

Gaddis, John Lewis. *The United States and The End of the Cold War: Implications, Reconsiderations, and Provocations* (New York: Oxford University Press, 1992).

Genovese, Eugene. *The Political Economy of Slavery: Studies in the Economy and Society of the Slave South* (New York: Pantheon Books, 1965).

Genovese, Eugene. *Roll, Jordan, Roll: The World the Slaves Made* (New York: Pantheon Books, 1974).

Genovese, Eugene. *The Slaveholders' Dilemma: Freedom and Progress in Southern Conservative Thought, 1820–1860* (Columbia, SC: University of South Carolina Press, 1992).

Genovese, Eugene. *The World the Slaveholders Made: Two Essays in Interpretation* (New York: Pantheon, 1969).

Genovese, Eugene and Elizabeth Fox-Genovese. *Fatal Self-Deception: Slaveholding Paternalism in the Old South* (Cambridge: Cambridge University Press, 2011).

Gienapp, William E. *The Origins of the Republican Party, 1852–1856* (New York: Oxford University Press, 1987).

Gillette, William. *Retreat from Reconstruction, 1869–1879* (Baton Rouge: Louisiana State University Press, 1979).

Glickman, Lawrence B. *Free Enterprise: An American History* (New Haven: Yale University Press, 2019).

Goodrich, Carter. *Government Promotion of American Canals and Railroads, 1800–1890* (New York: Columbia University Press, 1965).

Gordon, Robert J. *The Rise and Fall of American Growth: The U.S. Standard of Living since the Civil War* (Princeton: Princeton University Press, 2016).

Gorra, Michael. *The Saddest Words: William Faulkner's Civil War* (New York: W. W. Norton & Company, 2020).

Grantham, Dewey W. *Southern Progressivism: The Reconciliation of Progress and Tradition* (Knoxville: University of Tennessee Press, 1983).

Green, Fletcher M. *Constitutional Development in the South Atlantic States, 1776–1860: A Study in the Evolution of Democracy* (Chapel Hill: University of North Carolina Press, 1930).

Gregory, James N. *The Southern Diaspora: How the Great Migrations of Black and White Southerners Changed America* (Chapel Hill: University of North Carolina Press, 2005).

Gutman, Herbert G. *The Black Family in Slavery and Freedom, 1750–1825* (New York: Random House, 1976).

Hahn, Steven. *A Nation without Borders: The United States and Its World in the Age of Civil Wars, 1830–1910* (New York: Penguin Books, 2016).

274   Bibliography

Haidt, Jonathan. *The Righteous Mind: Why Good People Are Divided by Politics and Religion* (New York: Random House, 2012).

Handlin, Oscar. *The Uprooted: The Epic Story of the Great Migrations Which Made the American People* (Boston: Little, Brown and Company, 1951).

Hartz, Louis. *The Liberal Tradition in America* (New York: Harcourt, 1955).

Heyrman, Christine Leigh. *Southern Cross: The Beginnings of the Bible Belt* (New York: Alfred A. Knopf, 1998).

Higham, John. *Strangers in the Land: Patterns of American Nativism, 1860–1925* (New Brunswick: Rutgers University Press, 1955).

Hobsbawm, Eric. *The Age of Capital, 1848–1875* (London: Widenfield and Nicolson, 1975).

Holt, Michael. *The Political Crisis of the 1850s* (New York: Wiley, 1978).

Holt, Michael. *The Rise and Fall of the American Whig Party: Jacksonian Politics and the Onset of the Civil War* (New York: Oxford University Press, 1999).

Holt, Thomas. *Black over White: Negro Political Leadership in South Carolina during Reconstruction* (Urbana: University of Illinois Press, 1977).

Howe, Daniel Walker. *What God Hath Wrought: The Transformation of America, 1815–1848* (New York: Oxford University Press, 2007).

Hunter, Tera W. *To 'Joy My Freedom: Southern Black Women's Lives and Labors after the Civil War* (Cambridge, MA: Harvard University Press, 1998).

John, Richard. *Spreading the News: The U.S. Postal Service from Franklin to Morse* (Cambridge, MA: Harvard University Press, 1995).

Johnson, Guion G. *The Social History of the Sea Islands with Special Reference to Saint Helena's Island, South Carolina* (Chapel Hill: University of North Carolina Press, 2018).

Johnson, Walter. *River of Dark Dreams: Slavery and Empire in the Cotton Kingdom* (Cambridge, MA: Harvard University Press, 2013).

Jones, Jacqueline. *Labor of Love, Labor of Sorrow: Black Women, Work, and the Family, from Slavery to the Present* (New York: Vintage Books, 1985).

Jones, Jacqueline. *Soldiers of Light and Love: Northern Teachers and Georgia Blacks, 1865–1873* (Athens: University of Georgia Press, 2004).

Kahneman, Daneil. *Thinking, Fast and Slow* (New York: Farrar, Strauss, and Giroux, 2011).

Karp, Matthew. *This Vast Southern Empire: Slaveholders at the Helm of American Foreign Policy* (Cambridge, MA: Harvard University Press, 2016).

Kelly, Walt. *Pogo: We Have Met the Enemy and He is Us* (New York: Touchstone Press, 1972).

Kennedy, David M. *Freedom from Fear: The American People in Depression and War, 1929–1945* (New York: Oxford University Press, 1999).

Kennedy, David M. *Over Here: The First World War and American Society* (New York: Oxford University Press, 1980).

Kirby, Jack Temple. *Media-Made Dixie: The South in the American Imagination* (Baton Rouge: Louisiana State University Press, 1978).

Kirby, Jack Temple. *Rural Worlds Lost: The American South, 1920–1960* (Baton Rouge: Louisiana State University Press, 1986).

Kousser, J. Morgan. *The Shaping of Southern Politics: Suffrage Restriction and the Establishment of the One-Party South, 1880–1910* (New Haven: Yale University Press, 1974).

Bibliography

Krugman, Paul. *Arguing with Zombies: Economics, Politics and the Fight for a Better Future* (New York: W. W. Norton & Company, 2020).

Larson, John Lauritz. *Bonds of Enterprise: John Murray Forbes and Western Development in America's Railway Age* (Iowa City: University of Iowa Press, 1984).

Larson, John Lauritz. *Internal Improvements: National Public Works and the Promise of Popular Government in the Early United States* (Chapel Hill: University of North Carolina Press, 2001).

Larson, John Lauritz. *National Public Works and the Promise of Popular Government in the United States* (Chapel Hill: University of North Carolina Press, 2001).

Lassiter, Mathew D. *The Silent Majority: Suburban Politics in the Sunbelt South* (Princeton: Princeton University Press, 2006).

Lebsock, Suzanne. *The Free Women of Petersburg: Status and Culture in a Southern Town, 1784–1860* (New York: W. W. Norton & Company, 1984).

Leuchtenberg, William E. *Franklin D. Roosevelt and the New Deal, 1932–1940* (New York: Harper and Row, 1963).

Lewis, David Levering. *W. E. B. Du Bois: A Biography* (New York: Holt, 2009).

Link, William A. *The Paradox of Southern Progressivism, 1880–1930* (Chapel Hill: University of North Carolina Press, 1992).

Litwak, Leon F. *Been in the Storm So Long: The Aftermath of Slavery* (New York: Alfred A. Knopf, 1979).

Logevall, Fredrik. *Embers of War: The Fall of an Empire and the Making of America's Vietnam* (New York: Random House, 2012).

McCoy, Drew R. *The Elusive Republic: Political Economy in Jeffersonian America* (Chapel Hill: University of North Carolina Press, 1980).

McCoy, Drew R. *The Last of the Fathers: James Madison and the Republican Legacy* (New York and Cambridge: Cambridge University Press, 1989).

McGraw, Thomas K. *Prophet of Innovation: Joseph Schumpeter and Creative Destruction* (Cambridge, MA: Harvard University Press, 2007).

McPherson, James. A. *Battle Cry of Freedom: The Civil War Era* (New York: Oxford University Press, 1988).

Metzl, Jonathan. *Dying of Whiteness: How the Politics of Racial Resentment is Killing America's Heartland* (New York: Basic Books, 2019).

Miller, James David. *South by Southwest: Planter Emigration and Identity in the Slave South* (Charlottesville: University of Virginia Press, 2002).

Mitchell, Angie and Todd Shields. *The Long Southern Strategy: How Chasing White Voters in the South Transformed American Politics* (New York: Oxford University Press, 2019).

Mitchell, Reid. *Civil War Soldiers* (New York: Penguin, 1988).

Mitchell, Reid. *The Vacant Chair: The Northern Soldier Leaves Home* (New York: Oxford University Press, 1993).

Moretti, Enrico. *The New Geography of Jobs* (Boston: Houghton Mifflin, 2012).

Morris, Christopher. *Becoming Southern: The Evolution of a Way of Life: Warren Country and Vicksburg, Mississippi, 1770–1860* (New York: Oxford University Press, 1995).

Myrdal, Gunnar. *American Dilemma: The Negro Problem and Modern Democracy* (New York: Harper and Row, 1945).

Bibliography

Niebuhr, Reinhold. *The Irony of American History* (New York: Scribner's, 1952).

Noble, David. *The Paradox of Progressive Thought* (Minneapolis: University of Minnesota Press, 1958).

Oakes, James. *The Crooked Path to Abolition: Abraham Lincoln and the Antislavery Constitution* (New York: W. W. Norton & Company, 2021).

Oakes, James. *The Ruling Race: A History of American Slaveholders* (New York: Alfred A. Knopf, 1982).

O'Brien, Michael. *Conjectures of Order: Intellectual Life and the American South, 1810–1860,* vol 2. (Chapel Hill: University of North Carolina Press, 2004).

O'Brien, Michael. *Placing the South* (Jackson: University Press of Mississippi, 2007).

O'Neill, William. *Coming Apart: An Informal History of the 1960s* (Chicago: Quadrangle Books, 1971).

Oshinsky, David. *A Conspiracy So Immense: The World of Joe McCarthy* (New York: The Free Press, 1983).

Ottati, Douglas F. *Reforming Protestantism: Christian Commitment in Today's World* (Louisville: Westminster John Knox Press, 1995).

Ottati, Douglas F. *Theology for Liberal Presbyterians and Other Endangered Species* (Louisville: Geneva Press, 2006).

Painter, Nell Irvin. *The History of White People* (New York: W. W. Norton & Company, 2010).

Paskoff, Paul F. *Troubled Waters: Steamboats, Disasters, River Improvements, and American Public Policy, 1821–1860* (Baton Rouge: Louisiana State University Press, 2007).

Paterson, James T. *Grand Expectations: The United States, 1945–1974* (New York: Oxford University Press, 1996).

Payne, Elizabeth Anne. *Writing Women's History: A Tribute to Anne Firor Scott* (Jackson: University Press of Mississippi, 2011).

Pendergast, Mark. *For God, Country and Coca-Cola: The Definitive History of the Great American Soft Drink and the Company That Makes It* (New York: Basic Books, 2013).

Perman, Michael. *Reunion without Compromise: The South and Reconstruction, 1865–1868* (Chapel Hill: University of North Carolina Press, 1973).

Peterson, Merrill. *Democracy, Liberty, and Property: The State Constitutional Conventions of the 1820s* (Indianapolis: Bobbs-Merrill, 1966).

Pettus, Louise. *The Springs Story, Our First Hundred Years* (Fort Mill, S.C: Springs Industries, 1987).

Piketty, Thomas. *Capital in the Twenty-First Century* (Cambridge, MA: Harvard University Press, 2014).

Potter, David. *The Impending Crisis: America before the Civil War, 1848–1861,* completed and edited by Donald E. Fehrenbacher (New York: HarperCollins, 1976).

Potter, David. *People of Plenty: Economic Abundance and the American Character* (Chicago: University of Chicago Press, 1954).

Powdermaker, Hortense. *After Freedom: A Cultural Study in the Deep South* (New York: The Viking Press, 1939).

Bibliography

Pressley, Thomas J. *Americans Interpret Their Civil War* (Princeton: Princeton University Press, 1954).

Rable, George. *But There Was No Peace: The Role of Violence in the Politics of Reconstruction* (Athens: University of Georgia Press, 1984).

Raboteau, Albert. *Slave Religion: The "Invisible Institution" in the Antebellum South* (New York: Oxford University Press, 1978).

Rakove, Jack. *James Madison and the Creation of the American Republic* (New York, HarperCollins, 1990).

Rakove, Jack. *Original Meanings: Politics and Ideas in the Making of the Constitution* (New York, Random House, 1996).

Ransom, Roger and Richard Sutch. *One Kind of Freedom: The Economic Consequences of Emancipation* (Cambridge: Cambridge University Press, 1989).

Reidy, Joseph P. *From Slavery to Agrarian Capitalism in the Cotton Plantation South: Central Georgia, 1800–1880* (Chapel Hill: University of North Carolina Press, 1995).

Reisman, David, with Nathan Glazer and Reuel Denny. *The Lonely Crowd: A Study of the Changing American Character* (New Haven: Yale University Press, 1963).

Rodrigue, John C. *Reconstruction in the Cane Fields: From Slavery to Free Labor in Louisiana's Sugar Parishes, 1862–1880* (Baton Rouge: Louisiana State University Press, 2001).

Roediger, David. *Wages of Whiteness: The Making of the American Working Class* (New York: Verso, 1991).

Ross, Jack. *The Socialist Party of America: A Complete History* (Lincoln: University of Nebraska Press, 2015).

Rothman, Adam. *Slave Country: American Expansion and the Origins of the Deep South* (Cambridge, MA: Harvard University Press, 2005).

Saville, Julia. *The Work of Reconstruction: From Slave to Wage Laborer in South Carolina, 1860–1870* (New York: Cambridge University Press, 1994).

Schlesinger, Arthur M., Jr. *The Vital Center: Our Purpose and Perils on the Tightrope of American Liberalism* (Boston: Houghton Mifflin, 1949).

Schlesinger, Arthur M., Sr. *The Rise of the City, 1878–1898* (New York: MacMillan and Co., 1933).

Schulman, Bruce. *From Cotton Belt to Sunbelt: Federal Policy, Economic Development, and the Transformation of the South, 1938–1980* (New York: Oxford University Press, 1991).

Schumpeter, Joseph. *Capitalism, Socialism and Democracy* (New York: Harper and Brothers, 1942).

Schwalm, Leslie A. *A Hard Fight for We: Women's Transition from Slavery to Freedom in South Carolina* (Urbana: University of Illinois Press, 1997).

Scott, Anne Firor. *Natural Allies: Women's Associations in American History* (Urbana: University of Illinois Press, 1992).

Scott, Anne Firor. *The Southern Lady: From Pedestal to Politics, 1830–1930* (Chicago: University of Chicago Press, 1970).

Scott, Anne Firor, ed. *Unheard Voices: The First Historians of Southern Women* (Charlottesville and London: University of Virginia, 1993).

278 *Bibliography*

Scott, Holly V. *Younger Than That Now: The Politics of Age in the 1960s* (Amherst: University of Massachusetts Press, 2016).

Sellers, Charles G. *James K. Polk, Volume I: Jacksonian, 1793–1843* (Princeton: Princeton University Press, 1957).

Sellers, Charles G. *James K. Polk, Volume II: Continentalist, 1843–1846* (Princeton: Princeton University Press, 1966).

Sellers, Charles G. *The Market Revolution: Jacksonian America, 1815–1846* (New York: Oxford University Press, 1992).

Simkins, Francis B. and Robert H. Woody. *South Carolina during Reconstruction* (Chapel Hill: University of North Carolina Press, 1932).

Simon, Bryant. *A Fabric of Defeat: The Politics of South Carolina Millhands, 1910–1948* (Chapel Hill: University of North Carolina Press, 1998).

Smith, Lillian. *Killers of the Dream* (New York: W. W. Norton & Company, 1949).

Sperber, A. M. *Murrow: His Life and Times* (New York: Fordham University Press, 1999).

Spruill, Julia Cherry. *Women's Life and Work in the Southern Colonies* (Chapel Hill, 1938).

Stampp, Kenneth. *The Era of Reconstruction, 1865–1877* (New York: Alfred A. Knopf, 1965).

Stampp, Kenneth. *The Peculiar Institution: Slavery in the Ante-Bellum South* (New York: Alfred A. Knopf, 1956).

Starobin, Robert. *Industrial Slavery in the Old South* (New York: Oxford University Press, 1970).

Stewart, James Brewer. *Holy Warriors: Abolitionists and American Slavery* (New York: Hill and Wang, 1976).

Stiglitz, Joseph. *People, Power, and Profits: Progressive Capitalism for an Age of Discontent* (New York: W. W. Norton & Company, 2019).

Stiglitz, Joseph. *The Price of Inequality* (New York: W.W. Norton & Company, 2012).

Stokes, Melvyn. *D. W. Griffith's The Birth of the Nation: A History of the "Most Controversial Motion Picture of All Time"* (New York: Oxford University Press, 2007).

Sujon, Zoetanya. *The Social Media Age* (Los Angeles: SAGE Publications, 2021).

Taylor, Alrutheous. *The Negro in South Carolina during Reconstruction* (Washington, DC: The Association for the Study of Negro History and Life, 1924).

Taylor, Alrutheous. *The Negro in the Reconstruction of Virginia* (Washington, DC: The Association for the Study of Negro History and Life, 1926).

Taylor, George Rogers. *The Transportation Revolution, 1815–1860* (New York: Rinehart, 1951).

Thornton, J. Mills. *Politics and Power in a Slave Society: Alabama, 1800–1860* (Baton Rouge: Louisiana State University, 1978).

Tilley, Nannie M. *The R. J. Reynolds Tobacco Company* (Chapel Hill: University of North Carolina Press, 1985).

Tolle, Eckhart. *The Power of Now: A Guide to Spiritual Enlightenment* (Vancouver: Nemaste Publishing, 1997).

Bibliography

Trelease, Allen. *White Terror: The Ku Klux Klan Conspiracy and Southern Reconstruction* (New York: Harper and Row, 1971).

Tye, Larry. *Demagogue: The Life and Long Shadow of Joe McCarthy* (Boston: Houghton Mifflin, 2020).

Vance, J. D. *Hillbilly Elegy: A Memoir of a Family and Culture in Crisis* (New York: HarperCollins, 2016).

Vanderburg, Timothy W. *Cannon Mills and Kannapolis: Persistent Paternalism in a Textile Town* (Knoxville: University of Tennessee Press, 2013).

Varon, Elizabeth. *Disunion! The Coming of the American Civil War, 1789–1859* (Chapel Hill: University of North Carolina Press, 2008).

Wade, Richard. *Slavery in the Cities: The South, 1820–1860* (New York: Oxford University Press, 1962).

Wallerstein, Immanuel. *The Modern World System IV: Centralist Liberalism Triumphant, 1789–1914* (Berkeley: University of California Press, 2011).

Warren, Robert Penn. *The Legacy of Civil War: A Centennial Meditation* (New York: Random House, 1961).

Watson, Harry L. *Jacksonian Politics and Community Conflict: The Emergence of the Second American Party System in Cumberland County, North Carolina* (Baton Rouge: Louisiana State University Press, 1981).

Watson, Harry L. *Liberty and Power: The Politics of Jacksonian America* (New York: Hill and Wang, 1990).

Westad, Odd Arne. *The Cold War: A World History* (New York: Basic Books, 2017).

White, Debra Gray. *Aren't I A Women? Female Slaves in the Plantation South* (New York: W. W. Norton & Company, 1985).

Wiebe, Robert. *Wiebe, The Search for Order, 1877–1920* (New York: Hill and Wang, 1966).

Wilentz, Sean. *The Age of Reagan: A History, 1974–2008* (New York: HarperCollins, 2008).

Wilentz, Sean. *The Rise of American Democracy: From Jefferson to Lincoln* (New York: W. W. Norton & Company, 2006).

Wiley, Bell I. *The Road to Appomattox* (Memphis: Memphis State College Press, 1956).

Wilkerson, Isabel. *Caste: The Origins of Our Discontents* (New York: Random House, 2020).

Wilkerson, Isabel. *The Warmth of Other Suns: The Epic Story of America's Great Migration* (New York: Vintage, 2010).

Williamson, Chilton. *American Suffrage: From Property to Democracy, 1760–1860* (Princeton: Princeton University Press, 1960).

Williamson, Joel. *After Slavery: The Negro in South Carolina during Reconstruction, 1861–1877* (Chapel Hill: University of North Carolina Press, 1965).

Wills, Garry. *Confessions of a Conservative* (New York: Doubleday, 1979).

Wills, Garry. *Lincoln at Gettysburg: The Words That Remade America* (New York: Simon and Schuster, 1992).

Wills, Garry. *Reagan's America: Innocents at Home* (Garden City, NY: Doubleday, 1987).

280

Bibliography

Wills, Garry. *Saint Augustine: A Life* (New York: Penguin Group, 1999).

Wilson, Charles R. *Baptized in Blood: The Religion of the Lost Cause, 1865–1920* (Athens: University of Georgia Press, 1980).

Wood, Gordon S. *The Creation of the American Republic, 1776–1787* (Chapel Hill: University of North Carolina Press, 1969).

Wood, Gordon S. *Empire for Liberty: A History of the Early Republic* (New York: Oxford University Press, 2009).

Wood, Peter J. *Southern Capitalism: The Political Economy of North Carolina, 1880–1980* (Durham: Duke University Press, 1986).

Woodard, Colin. *American Nations: A History of the Eleven Rival Regional Cultures of North America* (New York: Penguin, 2011).

Woodman, Harold. *New South-New Law: The Legal Foundations of Credit and Labor Relations in the Postbellum Agricultural South* (Baton Rouge: Louisiana State University Press, 1995).

Woodward, C. Vann. *The Burden of Southern History* (Baton Rouge: Louisiana University Press, 1960).

Woodward, C. Vann. *Origins of the New South 1877–1913* (Baton Rouge: Louisiana State University Press, 1951).

Woodward, C. Vann. *American Counterpoint: Slavery and Racism in the North-South Dialogue* (New Yok: Little, Brown and Company, 1971).

Woodward, C. Vann. *Tom Watson: Agrarian Rebel* (New York: Macmillan, 1938).

Woodard, Colin. *American Nations: A History of the Eleven Rival Regional Cultures of North America* (New York: Penguin, 2011).

Wright, Gavin. *Old South, New South: Revolutions in the Southern Economy since the Civil War.* (Baton Rouge: Louisiana State University Press, 1997).

Young, Jeffrey Robert. *Domesticating Slavery: The Master Class in Georgia and South Carolina, 1679–1837* (Chapel Hill: University of North Carolina Press, 1999).

ARTICLES & BOOK CHAPTERS

Anderson, Ralph V. and Robert E. Gallman. "Slaves as Fixed Capital: Slave Labor and Southern Economic Development," *Journal of American History* 64 (June 1978): 47–66.

Applebaum, Peter. "John Hope Franklin, Scholar and Advocate," *New York Times*, March 28, 2009.

Autor, David, David Dorn, and Gordon Hansen. "The China Shock: Learning from Labor-Market Adjustment to Large Changes in Trade," *Annual Review of Economics* 8 (2016): 205–240.

Badger, Emily, Robert Gabeloff, and Josh Katz. "Coastal Cities Priced Out Low Wage Workers, Now College Graduates Are Leaving Too," *New York Times*, May 16, 2023.

Beale, Howard K. "On Rewriting Reconstruction History," *American Historical Review* 45 (July 1940): 807–827.

Bellah, Robert W. "Civil Religion in America," *Daedalus* 96 (Winter 1967): 1–21.

Bibliography

Calhoun, John C. "Remarks on Abolition Petitions," March 9, 1836, in Clyde N. Wilson, Shirley Bright Cook, and Alexander Moore, eds., *The Papers of John C. Calhoun, Volume XIII: 1835–1837* (Columbia: University of South Carolina Press, 1980), 91–110.

Carlton, David L. "The Revolution from Above: The National Market and the Beginnings of Industrialization in North Carolina," *Journal of American History* 77 (1990): 445–475.

Censer, Jane Turner. "'Smiling Through Her Tears': Ante–Bellum Southern Women and Divorce," *American Journal of Legal History* 25 (January 1981): 24–47.

Chaplin, Joyce. "Slavery and the Principle of Humanity: A Modern Idea in the Early Lower South," *Journal of Social History* 24 (1990): 299–315.

Collins, William J. and Marianne Wannamaker. "The Great Migration in Black and White: New Evidence on the Selection and Sorting of Southern Migrants," *Journal of Economic History* 75 (December 2015): 947–992.

Daniels, Jonathan. "Book Review of Du Bois, *Black Reconstruction*," *Book of the Month Club News* (July 1935).

Drezner, Daniel W. "Free Trade with Benefits," *The Washington Post*, April 26, 2021.

Du Bois, W. E. Burghardt. "Reconstruction and Its Benefits," *The American Historical Review* 15 (July 1910): 781–799.

Du Bois, W. E. Burghardt. "*Souls of White Folk*," originally published in *The Independent*, August 10, 1920. The essay is reprinted in W. E. B. Du Bois, *Writings*, Library of America (New York: Penguin Books, 1987), 923–938.

Easterlin, Richard A. "Interregional Differences in Per Capita Income, Population, and Total Income, 1840–1950," in *Trends in the American Economy in the Nineteenth Century: A Report of the National Bureau of Economic Research, New York* [Studies in Income and Wealth, Volume XXIV, by the Conference on Research in Income and Wealth] (Princeton: Princeton University Press, 1960), 73–140.

Fields, Barbara J. "Ideology and Race in American History," in J. Morgan Kousser and James M. McPherson, eds., *Race, Region, and Reconstruction: Essays in Honor of C. Vann Woodward* (New York: Oxford University Press, 1982), 143–177.

Florida, Richard. "The State Story: Growth without Growth," *The Atlantic*, April 4, 2011.

Foner, Eric. "The Causes of the American Civil War: Recent Interpretations and New Directions," *Civil War History* 20 (September 1974): 197–214.

Ford, Lacy K. "Frontier Democracy: The Turner Thesis Revisited," *Journal of the Early Republic* 13, no. 2 (1993): 144–163.

Ford, Lacy K. "Inventing the Concurrent Majority: Madison, Calhoun and the Problem of Majoritarianism in American Political Thought," *Journal of Southern History* 60 (1994): 19–58.

Ford, Lacy K. "Making the 'White Man's Country' White: Race and State Constitutions in the Jacksonian South," *Journal of the Early Republic* 19, no. 4 (1999): 713–737.

Ford, Lacy K. "The Personable Journalist as Social Critic: Ben Robertson and the Early Twentieth Century South," *Southern Cultures* 4 (Winter 1996): 353–373.

Bibliography

Ford, Lacy K. "Placing Michael O'Brien: A Review Essay," *The Southern Quarterly Review* 47 (2008): 121–129.

Ford, Lacy K. "The Popular Ideology of the Old South's Plain Folk: The Limits of Egalitarianism in a Slaveholding Society," in Samuel Hyde, ed., with an introduction by John B. Boles, *Plain Folk of the South Reconsidered* (Baton Rouge: Louisiana State University Press, 1997), 205–227.

Ford, Lacy K. "Prophet with Posthumous Honor: John C. Calhoun and the Southern Political Tradition," in Charles Eagles, ed., *Is There a Southern Political Tradition?* (Jackson: University Press of Mississippi, 1996), 3–25 and 207–211.

Ford, Lacy K. "Reconfiguring the Old South: 'Solving' the Problem of Slavery, 1787–1838," *Journal of American History* 95 (2008): 95–122.

Foster, Gaines. "Guilt over Slavery: A Historiographical Analysis," *Journal of Southern History* 56, no. 4 (1990): 665–694.

Fukuyama, Francis. "The End of History," *The Public Interest* 16 (Summer 1989): 1–5.

Gannett, Lewis. "Books and Things," *New York Herald-Tribune*, June 13, 1935.

Gienapp, William E. "Abraham Lincoln and the Border States," *Journal of the Abraham Lincoln Association* 13 (1992): 13–46.

Glaeser, Edward and Kristina Tobio. "The Rise of the Sunbelt," *Taubman Center Policy Briefs, Harvard University* (May 2007): 106.

Goldfield, David. "Writing the Sunbelt," *Organization of American Historians' Magazine of History* 18 (October 2003): 5–10.

Goldin, Claudia. "The Quiet Revolution That Transformed Women's Employment, Education, and Family," *American Economic Association Papers and Proceedings* (May 2006): 1–21.

Gordon-Reed, Annette. "The Color-Line," *The New York Review of Books*, August 19, 2021.

Hine, Darlene Clark. "Rape and the Inner Lives of Black Women in the Middle West: Preliminary Thoughts on the Culture of Dissemblance," *Signs: Journal of Women in Culture and Society* 14 (Summer 1989).

Hudson, Janet G. "From Constitution to Constitution: South Carolina's Unique Stance on Divorce, 1868–1895," *South Carolina Historical Magazine* 98 (January 1997): 75–96.

Huntington, Samuel. "Clash of Civilizations," *Foreign Affairs* 72 (Summer 1993): 22–49.

Johnson, Guion G. "The Changing Status of the Negro," *Journal of the American Association of University Women* (1958).

Johnson, Guion G. "The Ideology of White Supremacy, 1876–1910," *Journal of Southern History* 31 (November 1957): 483–509.

King, Martin Luther, Jr. "Letter from Birmingham Jail," *Christian Century* 80 (June 12, 1963): 777–783.

Kirby, Jack Temple. "The Great Southern Exodus, 1910–1960: A Primer for Historians," *Journal of Southern History* 49 (November 1983): 585–600.

Lincoln, Abraham, to A. G. Hodges, Esq. April 4, 1864, in Richard N. Current, ed., *The Political Thought of Abraham Lincoln* (Indianapolis: Bobbs-Merrill, 1967), 297–300.

Bibliography

Lincoln, Abraham. "Second Inaugural Address, March 4, 1865," in Richard N. Current, ed., *The Political Thought of Abraham Lincoln* (Indianapolis: Bobbs-Merrill, 1967), 314–316.

Lincoln, Abraham. "Speech on Kansas-Nebraska Act, 1854, at the Wisconsin State Fair," in Richard N. Current, ed., *The Political Thought of Abraham Lincoln* (Indianapolis: Bobbs-Merrill, 1967), 72–76.

Litwak, Leon F. "Trouble in Mind: The Bicentennial and the Afro-American Experience," *Journal of American History* 74 (September 1987): 315–337.

London, Eric. "Historian Victoria Bynum on the Inaccuracies of the New York Times; 1619 Project," *World Socialist Website*, October 30, 2019. See www.wsws.org/en/articles/2019/10/30/bynu-o30.html.

MacDonald, William. "The American Negro's Part in the Reconstruction Years: A Survey of the Period between 1860 and 1880 by Professor W. E. Burghardt Du Bois," in Sunday *New York Times*, June 18, 1835.

Macon, Nathaniel. "Speech of Nathaniel Macon," January 20, 1820, *Annals of Congress*, 16th Congress, 1st Session, 219–232.

Malone, Bill. *Classic Country Music: A Smithsonian Collection*, Booklet (Washington, DC: The Smithsonian Institution, 1990).

Mendenhall, Marjorie. "Southern Women of a Lost Generation," *South Atlantic Quarterly* 33 (1934): 334–353.

Mettler, Kattie. "Five Historians Say the 1619 Project Should Be Amended. 'We Disagree' Says the New York Times," *The Washington Post*, December 22, 2019.

Phipps, Sheila R. "Southern Women at the Millennium: A Historical Perspective," *American Historical Review*, 109 (2004): 1596–1597.

Piketty, Thomas and Emmanuel Saez. "Income Inequality in the United States, 1917–1998," *Quarterly Journal of Economics* 118 (2003): 1–39.

Posen, Adam. "The Price of Nostalgia: America's Self-Defeating Economic Retreat," *Foreign Affairs* (May/June 2021): 1–24.

Potter, David. "Civil War," in C. Vann Woodward, ed., *The Comparative Approach to American History* (New York: Basic Books, 1968), 135–145.

Rakove, Jack. "From James Madison to Thomas Jefferson, 6 September 1787," in Robert A. Rutland, Charles F. Hobson, William M. E. Rachal, and Frederika J. Teute, eds., *The Papers of James Madison*, Vol. 10, May 27, 1787–March 3, 1788 (Chicago: University of Chicago Press, 1977), 163–165.

Roberts, Ben. "Forget Gettysburg," *Charleston News and Courier*, July 1, 1939, 12.

Robertson, Ben. *Red Hills and Cotton: An Upcountry Memory*, with a new introduction by Lacy K. Ford, Jr. (Columbia, SC: University of South Carolina Press, 1991), Southern Classics Reprint Edition, ix–xliv.

Robertson, Tommy W. "The Great Population Exodus from South Carolina, 1850–1860," *South Carolina Historical Magazine* 68 (January 1967): 14–22.

Rose, Willie Lee. "The Domestication of Domestic Slavery," in William Freehling, ed., *Slavery and Freedom* (New York: Oxford University Press, 1982).

Scott, Anne Firor. "Writing Women's History: A Response," in Elizabeth Anne Payne, ed., *Writing Women's History: A Tribute to Ann Firor Scott* (Jackson: University Press of Mississippi, 2012), 203–210.

Sellers, Charles G. "The Travail of Slavery," in Charles G. Sellers, ed., *The Southerner as American* (Chapel Hill: University of North Carolina Press, 1960), 40–71.

Shalhope, Robert E. "Republicanism and Early American Historiography," *William and Mary Quarterly* 39, no. 2 (1982): 334–356.

Shalhope, Robert E. "Toward a Republican Synthesis," *William and Mary Quarterly* 29, no. 1 (1972): 49–80.

Smith, John David. "'Gentlemen, I, Too, Am a Kentuckian': Abraham Lincoln, The Lincoln Bicentennial, and Lincoln's Kentucky in Recent Scholarship," *Register of The Kentucky Historical Society* 106 (Summer/Autumn 2008): 433–470.

Smith, Robert S. "Mill on the Dan: The Riverside Cotton Mill, 1882–1901," *Journal of Southern History* 21 (February 1955): 38–66.

Smith, William. "Speech of William Smith," *Annals of Congress*, 16th Congress, 2nd session (January 26, 1820): 259–275.

Stampp, Kenneth. "The Southern Road to Appomattox," in *The Imperiled Union: Essays on the Background of the Civil War* (New York: Oxford University Press, 1980), 246–269.

Thornton, J. Mills, III. "Fiscal Policy and the Failure of Radical Reconstruction in the Lower South," in J. Morgan Kousser and James M. McPherson, eds., *Region, Race, and Reconstruction: Essays in Honor of C. Vann Woodward* (New York: Oxford University Press, 1982), 349–394.

Turner, Frederick Jackson. "The Significance of the Frontier in American History," in *Annual Report of the American Historical Association for the Year 1893* (Washington, DC: 1894).

Villard, Oswald Garrison. "Black Controversy," *Saturday Review of Literature*, January 18, 1936.

Walker, Freeman. "Speech of Freeman Walker," January 19, 1820, *Annals of Congress*, 16th Congress, 159–175.

Wallerstein, Immanuel. "The Rise and Future Demise of the World Capitalist System: Concepts for Comparative Analysis," *Comparative Studies in Society & History*, 16 (September 1974): 387–415.

Warren, Robert Penn. "The Briar Patch," in Twelve Southerners, *I'll Take My Stand: The South and the Agrarian Tradition* (New York: Harper and Row, 1930), 246–264.

Weir, Robert M. "'The Harmony We Were Famous For': An Interpretation of Pre-Revolutionary South Carolina," *William and Mary Quarterly* 36 (1969): 473–501.

Woodman, Harold. "One Kind of Freedom after Twenty Years," *Explorations in Economic History* 38, no. 1 (2001): 48–57.

Woodman, Harold. "The Political Economy of the South: Retrospects and Prospects," *Journal of Southern History* 67, no. 4 (2001): 789–810.

Woodward. C. Vann. "The Age of Reinterpretation," *American Historical Review* 66, no. 1 (1960): 1–19.

Woodward, C. Vann. C. Vann Woodward to W. E. B. Du Bois, April 3, 1938, in Michael O'Brien, ed., *The Letters of C. Vann Woodward* (New Haven: Yale University Press, 2013), 60.

Bibliography

Woodward, C. Vann. "The Search for Southern Identity, 1960," in Woodward, ed., *The Burden of Southern History* (Baton Rouge: Louisiana State University Press, 1960), 3–25.

Wozniak, Abigail. "Are College Graduates More Responsive to Distant Labor Market Opportunities?" *Journal of Human Resources* 45, no. 4 (2010): 944–970.

Wright, Gavin. "American Agriculture and the Labor Market: What Happened to Proletarianization?" *Agricultural History* 62, no. 3 (1988): 182–209.

Yarrow, Andrew. "John Hope Franklin, Scholar of African American History, is Dead at 94," *New York Times*, March 25, 2009.

Index

1619 Project, 128, 218–220
9/11 attacks, 22, 33, 259

abolitionism, 69, 75–76, 121–122, 171
adventurism, 19, 21
advertising, 25, 94–96, 101, 179, 192
African Americans
  agency, 6, 144, 146, 148, 153–159, 163
  churches, 144, 157, 214, 228
  citizenship, 5, 7, 22, 32, 73, 76, 119,
    142, 173–174
  and civil rights, 142
  economic inequality, 97, 102
  economic opportunity, 148, 163
  educational opportunity, 139, 142, 144
  family life, 147–148, 157
  and housing, 163
  labor, 144, 147–148, 157, 174,
    178, 218
  political power, 6, 141–142, 145–146,
    148–150, 158, 173
  professional classes, 176
  violence against, 148, 159–160
  voting rights, 20, 47, 51, 142, 145,
    148–149, 163, 169, 173–174,
    205, 231
  women, 203, 207–208, 210, 213–214
Age of Capital, 7, 169, 174, 179, 181,
  184, 188
Agricultural Adjustment Act, 54
American caste system, 130, 245, 251
American Century, 3–4, 39, 66, 101,
  131–132, 180, 259

American Civil War, 3, 34, 57, 70,
  72–73, 78, 117, 130, 151, 170, 172,
  216–218, 264
  capitalism, 17, 80, 175
  ideological nature, 4–5, 16, 47–48, 56,
    73, 76, 78
  importance, 3, 13–15, 71, 78, 132, 152
  slavery, 73, 79, 123–124, 129, 150, 153
American dream, 132, 233
American exceptionalism, 3, 5, 7, 22, 40,
  79, 117, 180
American Federation of Labor. See labor
  unions
American Historical Association (AHA),
  89, 91, 144, 195
American liberal tradition, 56, 60
American Revolution, 42, 67, 69, 72, 118,
  152, 200
American South
  agrarianism, 7, 72–73, 152, 174
  agricultural labor force, 7
  capital shortages, 7, 187
  defeat of, 3, 6–7, 9, 18, 27, 46, 71, 75,
    117, 123–124, 130–134, 174, 177,
    180–182, 217, 261–263
  impact on the nation, 2, 4
American Tobacco Company, 178
American universalism, 22
anti-communism, 18–19
anti-unionism, 178, 182, 185, 228, 232, 247
antiwar protest movement, 20–21
Appalachian culture, 225
Apple, 23–24, 31

Index

Appleby, Joyce, 195–196
Articles of Confederation, 44
artisans, 75, 101, 118, 157
Asian Americans, 33
atavism, 29
Atlanta Compromise speech
(Washington), 141
atomic weapons, 40, 55
Atwater, Lee, 245
authoritarianism, 22
automobile industry, 101, 103, 234, 238
automobile ownership, 226

baby boomers, 19
Bailyn, Bernard, 42
Bank of the United States, 120
Baptist, Edward, 128
Beale, Howard, 152
Beard, Charles, 72, 152
Beard, Mary, 72, 152
Beckert, Sven, 128
Benedict, Michael Les, 158
Berlin Wall, 22
Berlin, Ira, 21–22, 157
Berry, Mary Frances, 196
Biden, Joe, 107, 245
Big Entertainment, 30
Big Media, 30
Big Money (political), 25
Black belt, 175–176
Black Codes, 144
Black scholars/scholarship, 144
Black separatism, 143
Black women historians, 206
Blackberry, 24
Black majorities, 158
Blasingame, John, 157
Bleser, Carol K., 211–212
blue-collar workers, 25, 28, 103–104, 106,
192–193, 227, 233, 236
Boorstin, Daniel, 4, 40, 56, 69–72, 76, 78,
80–83
American Civil War, 4–5, 13, 48, 68–74,
78–79
American politics, 4–5, 39, 66–67, 69,
78–83, 85, 99
bourgeois liberals, 171
brain hubs, 8, 104, 105–106, 246
Brown v. Board decision, 154
Burlington Mills, 178
Burton, Vernon, 158

Bush, George H. W., 60
Bush, George W., 27–28, 60, 215
Bynum, Caroline Walker, 195
Bynum, Victoria, 219

Calhoun, John C., 49, 61, 71, 116, 122
Cannon Mills, 178
capitalism, 16, 22, 41, 73, 83, 128
boosterism, 9, 177
expansion of, 19, 127–128
ills of, 4, 19, 25, 41, 49, 52, 80–81,
143, 152
Carlton, David, 234–236
Carter, Jimmy, 99
Case, Anne, 239
Cash, W. J., 123, 134, 243
cell phones, 3, 24, 31, 232
Censer, Jane Turner, 208
Charleston Massacre (2015), 159
chauvinism, 29
Chesnut, Mary Boykin, 204, 208
China, 18, 84, 153, 246
Christianity, 29, 116, 125, 154–155, 159,
199, 211, 227–228, 231
evangelical Protestantism, 6, 116,
120–121, 134, 214, 227, 229
and slavery, 115–116, 120–121, 130
civil rights, 83
Civil Rights Act of 1964, 20
civil rights movement, 6, 13, 20–21, 30,
57, 115, 133, 146, 154–157, 176, 182,
194–195, 206, 255
Civil War, 124
class anger, 5
class divides, 25, 93, 204
industrialization, 52
progressivism, 52–53
race, 160–161, 176, 206, 209–210, 230
Clinton, Bill, 27, 84, 162, 245
Clinton, Catherine, 207, 213
Clinton, Hillary, 28, 107
Coates, Ta-Nahisi, 160–162
Cobb, James, 133
Coca Cola, 179
Cold War, 18–23, 25, 30, 32, 56, 84, 115,
181, 259, 261, 263
college graduates, 104–105, 184, 186,
240–241
colonialism, 143, 152
communism, 18–19, 22, 26, 39, 55–56, 66,
82, 84, 152, 154, 181

Index

community/technical colleges, 18
computer industry, 23–24, 30, 226
Confederate battle flag, 159
Conner, Eugene "Bull", 155
conservatism, 4, 18, 26, 28, 41, 48, 56,
    59–60, 71, 79–80, 107, 117, 180, 248
  in America, 39, 41, 49, 56, 59, 79–82,
    99, 125, 213–214, 246, 248
  versus liberalism, 58
  in the South, 49, 57, 59, 71, 117,
    125, 216
conservative populism, 27
Constitutional Convention of 1787, 16, 60
consumerism, 101, 232–233, 248
corporate oligopolies, 23
Cott, Nancy, 196
cotton, 212
  global markets, 97, 128, 170–171
  growing, 91, 128, 148, 175, 234
  slavery, 126–128, 170, 219
  world markets, 79, 176–177
COVID pandemic, 1, 185
credit arrangements, 175–176
credit shortages, 176
Croly, Herbert, 32, 34
Cronkite, Walter, 30
crop-lien system, 176
Cult of the Lost Cause, 129, 133, 179–180,
    217, 261

Dan River Mills, 178
Daniels, Jonathan, 151
Daniels, Pete, 158
Davis, Natalie Zemon, 195
day labor, 158
Deaton, Angus, 239
Declaration of Independence, 66, 78,
    116–118, 156, 255
deficit spending, 98–99
DeForest, J. W., 204
Dell Computers, 23
democracy, 93, 115, 133–134, 149, 259
  American success of, 82, 93, 255
  economic prosperity, 93–94, 96
  expansion of, 17–18, 21–22, 41–42,
    47–48, 50, 55–56, 84, 131
  free labor, 80
  nationalism, 90
  racial equality, 152, 155–156, 169
  slavery, 94, 116, 119
  threats to, 83, 150

Democratic Party, 52, 58, 74, 90, 119, 149,
    246–247
  centrism, 27, 107
  liberalism, 27
  redistricting, 26, 107
  slavery, 76
  in the South, 59, 158, 173
  versus Whigs, 48, 57, 74–75, 120, 172
  working-class whites, 245
desegregation, 154, 182, 226, 229–230,
    243, 245, 248
Desmond, Mathew, 128
divided sovereignty, 16
Dodd, William, 123
Dollard, John, 242
Dred Scott decision, 75
Du Bois, Shirley Graham., 153
Du Bois, W. E. B., 6–7, 143, 145–146,
    148–149, 153, 156, 162
  Black Reconstruction, 6, 139, 144–146,
    150–153, 157, 163
  and Booker T. Washington, 141
  double-consciousness, 140–141
  influence of, 6, 139, 150, 153–154,
    157–159, 162
  National Association for the
    Advancement of Colored People
    (NAACP), 6, 143, 151
  Souls of Black Folk, 6, 140–142
  Talented Tenth idea, 142
  two-ness, 6, 140
Dukakis, Michael, 27
Duke Energy, 178
Dunning, William Archibald, 145, 164
Dunning School, 145–146, 154

economic inequality, 1, 5, 23–25, 51–52,
    100, 102, 106–108, 159, 240
economic prosperity, 22, 32, 74, 91–92,
    96, 104, 132, 183, 234, 237,
    260–261, 263
  agriculture, 91
  American South, 133, 182, 261
  Black Americans, 126, 133
  capitalism, 84
  manufacturing, 25
  post-World War II, 19, 59, 99–100,
    182, 194
economic slowdowns, 8, 100, 103, 106, 108
Education Act of 1958, 19
education levels, 104–105

290 *Index*

educational divide, 184
Edwards, Laura, 158
Eisenhower, Dwight, 18, 60
electricity, 100
emancipation, 3, 13, 70, 129, 172, 209
    effects of, 5, 7, 57, 79, 97, 116, 124,
        147, 174
    ideas of freedom, 16, 78, 169
    and racism, 131, 133
Emancipation Proclamation, 172
empire building, 20, 83–85, 129, 170,
        177, 181
entrepreneurism, 31, 40, 74, 128,
        177–178, 185
environmental movement, 18

Facebook, 31
Fair Labor Standards Act (1938), 226
family farms, 68
farmers/farming, 89–90, 92, 101, 118,
        149, 177
    credit systems, 176
    economic importance, 51, 73, 91–92, 97,
        169, 182, 187
    labor, 58, 70, 75, 96, 148, 170, 174–175,
        178, 226
    progressivism, 52, 58
    regulation of, 54, 59
Farmers' Alliance, 51
Fascism, 17–18, 22, 54–56, 66, 78, 83,
        98, 259
Faulkner, William, 2, 192, 217, 258
Faust, Drew Gilpin, 72, 192, 215–218
federalism, 68–69
Federalist Papers, The, 47, 67
feminism/feminists, 200, 215
Fields, Barbara, 158, 209
Fifteenth Amendment, 173
financiers, 74, 170–171
Fitzhugh, George, 49, 116, 125
Foner, Eric, 34, 158–159
Ford, Lacy K., 126
Foster, Gaines M., 123
Fourteenth Amendment, 173
Fox-Genovese, Elizabeth, 125
Franklin, John Hope, 13, 17, 153–154, 162
free labor, 49–52, 57, 68, 70, 72–73,
        75–76, 80, 84, 120, 125, 128, 147,
        157, 170–174
free market economy, 16
Freedmen's Bureau, 144, 147

freedom of religion, 54
freedom of speech, 54
freedpeople, 51, 57, 123, 126, 144–148,
        157, 169, 174, 201, 210
Freehling, William, 123
free trade, 171
French revolution, 14
Fukuyama, Francis, 22
furniture industry, 227, 238

Garrison, William Lloyd, 121–122,
        151
Genovese, Eugene, 125, 127, 156–157,
        213–215
George I, 42
George III, 41, 43
Gettysburg address, 255. *See also* Lincoln,
        Abraham
GI Bill, 18, 108
Gilded Age, 50–52, 58, 83, 106, 108,
        178, 255
Gillette, William, 158
global warming, 1
globalization, 25, 33, 59, 236–238
Goldin, Claudia, 8, 193–194
Goldwater, Barry, 27
Gorbachev, Mikhail, 21
Gordon, Robert, 102
Gordon-Reed, Annette, 139
Gore, Al, 28
government shut downs, 28
Grange, the, 51
Great Alibi, 131–132
Great Boom, 193
Great Britain, 101
    aristocracy, 24, 41, 43, 99
    Church of England, 41
    class divides, 41, 44
    government, 43
    royalty, 41, 43, 45, 99
Great Depression, 53–54, 58, 66, 78, 96,
        98, 100, 123, 173, 179
Great Divergence, 104–106, 185
Great Migration, 178
Great White Switch, 246
Greatest Generation, 108, 132
Griffith, David Ward, 180
Gutman, Herbert, 157

Habsburg empire, 15
Hahn, Steven, 128

Index

Haidt, Jonathan, 235–236, 239
Hall, Jacquelyn, 196
Hamilton, Alexander, 33, 73
Hammond, James Henry, 212, 216–217
Handlin, Oscar, 98
Hannah-Jones, Nicole, 218
Harrison, Alice Kessler, 196
Hartz, Louis, 4, 39–42, 44, 47–49, 51–53,
    55–56, 59–60, 99, 117–118
Higham, John, 98
higher education, 18–19, 25, 107–108,
    149, 186
hillbilly culture, 225
Hine, Darlene Clark, 196, 206
Hispanics, 26, 32–33, 162, 218, 247–248
    income inequality, 102
history profession, 194, 196
Hobsbawm, Eric, 7, 142, 169–171, 174,
    181, 184, 219
Hofstadter, Richard, 13
Hohenzollern empire, 15
Holt, Thomas, 158
Homes, George Frederick, 216
Hoover, Herbert, 58
human capital deficits, 187
Hunter, Tera, 158
Huntington, Samuel, 22
Hussein, Saddam, 22

identity politics, 231, 242, 246–248
immigration, 98, 231, 237, 240, 248
imperialism, 15, 20–22, 82, 84, 94, 129,
    142–143, 181
income growth, 100–102, 193
income inequality, 84, 102–103, 105
individualism, 90, 214
industrialization, 18, 28, 51–52, 58, 60,
    72–73, 80, 97, 100, 103–104, 106,
    157, 169, 171, 177–179, 184, 187,
    225, 233, 235, 237–238
inflation, 24, 99
information revolution, 255
infrastructure, 17, 57, 73–74, 90–91, 150,
    170–171
intellectual history, 195, 216
International Business Machine (IBM), 23
International Workers of the World.
    See labor unions
internationalism, 58
Islam, 22
isolationism, 58

Jackson, Andrew, 33, 47, 51, 60, 73–75,
    115, 119
Japan, 102
Jefferson, Thomas, 33, 73, 92, 96,
    119–120, 122, 219, 255
Jim Crow, 7, 20, 53, 132, 157, 174
job losses, 25, 237
John Birch Society, 60
Johnson, Andrew, 144
Johnson, Guion Griffis, 197, 200–201
Johnson, Lyndon, 21, 83, 181
Johnson, Walter, 128
Jones, Howard Mumford, 200
Jones, Jacqueline, 158, 210–211
Jones, Prince, 160–161

Kaiser Wilhelm, 17
Kansas-Nebraska debates, 76
Kerber, Linda, 196
Keynes, John Maynard, 54, 98
Khrushchev, Nikita, 26, 153
King, Martin Luther, Jr., 21, 155–156,
    158, 255
Knights of Labor. See labor unions
Krugman, Paul, 102
Ku Klux Klan, 148, 156, 173, 180, 201

labor contracts, 174
labor shortages, 148, 192
labor unions, 52–54, 58, 101, 182,
    227–228
Lebsock, Suzanne, 210
Lecompton Constitution, 75
Lerner, Gerda, 196
Lewis, David Leavering, 141, 150
LGBTQ community, 33, 248
liberalism, 4
    and economy, 16
    and politics, 16
    in United States, 13, 16–17, 19,
        23, 40–42, 47–49, 53–56, 59–60,
        82, 201
liberalism/nationalism, marriage of, 3,
    13–14, 17–19, 23, 25, 29, 131, 193,
    217, 248, 256
Limerick, Patricia, 196
Lincoln, Abraham, 9, 16, 33, 50–52,
    76–78, 82–83, 91, 120, 130, 135, 172,
    255, 263–265
Litwack, Leon, 153, 158
localism, 15, 22, 29

Index

Locke, John, 16, 41–42, 44, 47, 60
lower class, 53
lower South, 80, 97, 126–127, 130, 175, 204, 209, 246
Luce, Henry, 3–4, 39, 66, 101, 131–132, 259
lynching, 244

MacDonald, William, 150
Macon, Nathaniel, 121
Madison, James, 16, 44–47, 60–61, 120
majority minority districts, 26
manhood, 73, 141
Marshall, Thurgood, 154
Marxism, 80, 128, 142–143, 151–152, 156, 209, 213–214, 219
materialism, 39
May, Elaine Tyler, 196
McCarthy, Joseph, 30
McCarthyism, 20, 255
McKenzie, Tracey, 158
McPherson, James, 219
Mendenhall, Marjorie, 197–199, 202
merchants, 43, 170, 176–177
Metzl, Jonathan, 162, 247
Mexicans, 84
Meyerowitz, Joanne, 196
Microsoft, 23
middle class, 20, 230, 234–236, 240–241, 244
    Black Americans, 160, 176
    expansion of, 19, 177
    nuclear family, 97
    progressivism, 53
    reformism, 52
    women, 193–194, 205
military-industrial complex, 18
mill culture, 226–227, 234
miscegenation, 121, 208
Missouri Compromise, 75
Mondale, Walter, 27
Montgomery Bus Boycott, 155
morality, 85, 131
    and religion, 95, 116, 120–121
    and slavery, 69, 76, 120–122, 124–125, 127, 129–130
    in the South, 125, 181, 264
    U. S. myths of virtue, 13, 18, 48, 56, 260, 261, 263
Moretti, Enrico, 104–105, 183–186
Morrison, Toni, 211

movie industry, 30
Moynihan, Daniel, 157
Murrow, Edward R., 30, 262
Muslims, 33
Myrdal, Gunnar, 201, 244

Napoleon, Louis I, 14
National Aeronautics & Space Administration (NASA), 19
National Association for the Advancement of Colored People (NAACP), 139, 143, 151
national bank, 74
National Institutes of Health (NIH), 19
National Labor Relations Act of 1935, 54
National Recovery Act, 54
National Science Foundation (NSF), 19
nationalism
    in America, 13–18, 23, 29–30, 90, 261
    in China, 18
    in Europe, 15, 17
    obstacles to, 15–16
    in Russia, 18
nationalism/liberalism, marriage of, 17–18, 21–23, 32
Native Americans, 40, 84, 90, 128, 150, 255
Nazism, 17–18, 39, 55, 78, 98, 132, 161, 259
neoconservativism, 22
New Deal, 17, 39, 53–55, 58–59, 98, 262
Niebuhr, Reinhold, 9, 29, 131, 257, 259–261, 266
Nineteenth Amendment, 205
nonviolence philosophy, 155
North Atlantic Treaty Organization (NATO), 18
nullification crisis, 70, 117, 123–124

Obama, Barack, 27–28, 60, 206–207
O'Brien, Michael, 129, 133, 209
Odom, Howard, 201
Oil Crisis (1970s), 59, 99
opioid epidemic, 162, 228, 232
Organization of American Historians (OAH), 195–196, 207
Ottati, Douglas, 260
Ottoman empire, 15

Painter, Nell Irvin, 196, 215, 218
Palm, 24
Pandora, 31

Index

Panic of 1873, 149
paternalism, 50, 52, 121, 125, 127, 130, 156
patriarchy, 147, 210
patriotism, 32, 180–181, 263
Payne, Elizabeth Anne, 205
Pearl Harbor, 40, 54
Penn Warren, Robert, 133
per capita income, 97–98, 179, 182–183, 185, 226, 261
Perman, Michael, 158
Perot, Ross, 27
Phillips, Ulrich Bonnell, 154
Picketty, Thomas, 25
Pinckney, Clementa, 159
pink-collar workers, 193
plantation mistresses, 207, 213
plantations, 15, 126, 147, 174–175, 181, 184, 207–208, 212–214, 216
planter elites, 209
political corruption, 118
Polk, James K., 115
popular culture, 30, 81, 83, 180, 193, 228, 232
populism, 51–52, 58
Populist Party, 51
postal system, 73
Potter, David, 3, 13, 95, 97
  American abundance, 5, 89, 93–94, 96–99, 101, 108
  liberalism/nationalism marriage, 14, 18, 25, 29
  materialism, 39
  nationalism/liberalism marriage, 21
  U. S. national character, 4, 5, 40, 56, 92, 97
poverty, 7, 9, 27, 93, 118, 211, 229
  and capitalism, 81, 178
  and communism, 56
  and racism, 147, 244
  in the South, 5, 121, 132, 152, 174, 176, 180–181, 244, 261, 263
pragmatism, 53–55
progressivism, 17, 52–53, 58
property rights, 16, 41–42, 44, 46, 49, 56–57, 118
provincialism, 15–16, 262
public education, 1, 17, 95, 103, 105, 145–146, 187, 193, 225, 228, 230, 233, 240, 247
  attainment levels, 25, 52, 184, 186, 231, 235

K12 schools, 18, 103, 107, 149, 182, 185, 187, 198–199, 229, 232, 241
progressivism, 58
and race, 141–142, 161, 201, 230, 243–244, 248
and women, 203, 205, 208

Quiet Revolution, 193–194

Rable, George, 158
racial equality, 13, 76–77, 143, 151–152, 155
racial prejudice, 145, 156, 219
racial segregation, 115
racism, 134, 149, 161, 228, 248
  and Civil War, 131, 132
  and government, 94
  and slavery, 121, 129
  in the South, 140, 142, 147, 155, 181, 217, 219, 227, 229–230, 245
  and violence, 33, 159
Rakove, Jack, 44
Ransom, Roger, 157
Reagan, Ronald, 21–22, 27, 55, 59, 99, 245
recessions, 150
Reconstruction, 34, 146, 151, 153–154, 158, 161, 174, 210–211, 218
  African American political gains, 6–7, 51, 144–145, 148, 169, 173
  criticism of, 146, 149, 173
  failure of, 13, 22, 79, 140
Reidy, Joseph, 158
representative government, 16, 41
Republican Party, 26–27, 51, 57, 60, 71, 76, 119, 145, 149, 171–172, 246
  conservatism, 27–29, 53, 231, 245–248
  corruption, 150, 173
  free labor, 50–51, 57, 75–76, 144, 171, 173
  pro-business wing, 27, 52, 58
  redistricting, 27
  slavery stance, 75, 80, 129, 172
  state-level politics, 28, 107, 145, 148, 158, 173, 225, 246
  working class whites, 231, 245, 247
republicanism, 43, 48, 51, 57, 118–119, 120, 126
research universities, 187
Reynolds, R. J., 178
Robertson, Ben, 124, 262–263
Roman Catholic Church, 15–16, 214

Romney, Mitt, 27
Roof, Dylan, 159
Roosevelt, Franklin, 5, 17, 53–55, 58–59,
83, 98, 179, 255
Roosevelt, Teddy, 83
Rosenthal, Caitlin, 128
Rothman, Joshua, 128
Ruiz, Vicki, 196
rule of law, 41–42, 56, 61
Rusk, Dean, 181

Sabbatarianism, 74, 121
sanitation, 17, 193, 203, 205
Saville, Julie, 158
Schlesinger, Arthur, Jr., 39, 66, 98, 200
Scott, Anne Firor, 196–197, 202–203,
205–207, 210
Scott, Rebecca, 206
secession, 49, 69, 71, 76–77, 79–80,
116–117, 125, 172, 212, 218, 261
Second American Party System, 48,
73–75, 172
Second Party System, 83
sectionalism, 48, 68–71, 73, 76, 81, 84,
124, 128, 130–131, 170, 172
secularism, 22
segregation, 129, 132, 140, 143, 155, 161,
176, 182, 230, 242, 255
Sellers, Charles, 5–6, 115–125, 129,
133–134
Seven Years (or French and Indian) War, 43
sexism, 118
sharecropping, 158, 175
shopkeepers, 93, 118
Simkins, Francis Butler, 145–146
Simms, William Gilmore, 208, 216
Singapore, 102
sit-ins, 156
skilled labor, 7, 171, 177, 179
slave labor, 70, 72, 75, 80, 125–126, 128,
147, 171, 207, 210, 219
slave power conspiracy, 73, 75, 80, 172
slaveholder elites, 4
slaveholding elites, 117, 129, 216
slavery, 3, 68, 119, 121
assault on enslaved women, 208, 217
brutality to slaves, 16, 18, 22, 128,
214, 217
defense of, 15, 68, 75, 115–116,
119–120, 172, 209, 216
domestic slave trade, 17, 46, 127–128

enslaved women, 209–210, 213–214
expansion of, 57, 68–70, 72, 74–76, 80,
91, 129, 171–172, 209
and morality, 129–130
opposition to, 69, 76
slave resistance, 127, 157
and white safety, 123–124,
126–127, 171
smartphones, 24, 30, 232
Smith, Adam, 16
Smith, Lillian, 134, 244
Smith, William, 121
social justice, 20
social media, 1, 3, 30–31, 33, 83, 232
social mobility, 40, 50, 91–92, 98, 104,
120, 171, 239, 248
social safety net, 18, 39, 53–55, 83, 98
socialism, 21–22, 49, 54–56, 60, 139
South Korea, 102
Southern Association of Women
Historians, 200
Southern Christian Leadership Conference,
154–155
southern strategy, 183, 245–246
Soviet Union, 18–19, 21, 25–26, 39–40,
55, 82, 84, 153
Spotify, 31
Springs Industries, 178
Spruill, Julia Cherry, 197, 199, 200,
202, 207
stagflation, 99
Stalin, Joseph, 18
Stampp, Kenneth, 13, 124, 153–154, 156
states' rights, 15, 57, 70, 76
steel industry, 101, 103, 178, 225, 227,
234–235
Stephens, Alexander, 71
Stock Market Crash of 1929, 58
Sutch, Richard, 157

tariffs, 51, 57, 74
taxation, 48, 149–150, 173, 185, 187,
230–231, 247
Taylor, Altheous, 145
technology
advances, 226, 236–238
Cold War, 19, 23
decentralizing influence of, 3, 23–25
personalization of, 23–24, 30–31, 241
television industry, 23, 30
cable TV, 23, 31

Index

temperance movement, 74, 121, 205
tenant farming, 148, 158, 175, 198, 234
terrorism, 84, 259
textile industry, 177–178, 182, 226–227,
 233–235, 238, 241
Third World, 19
Thirteenth Amendment, 172
Thornwell, James, 116, 125
Tilley, Nannie Louis, 195
Tillich, Paul, 155
tobacco, 79, 95, 126, 178, 218
Tolle, Eckhart, 257
Trelease, Allen, 158
Truman, Harry S., 152
Trump, Donald, 28–29, 60, 107, 242
Tucker, Nathaniel Beverly, 216
Turner, Frederick Jackson, 89–93, 97, 109
Twitter, 31

U. S. Bureau of the Census, 91
U. S. Constitution, 16, 28, 34, 46, 48–49,
 54, 57, 61, 72, 78, 116, 156, 173
U. S. Justice Department, 152–153
U. S. Supreme Court, 25, 75, 153
unemployment, 54, 98–99, 104, 232, 241
unions, 103
United States
 big business, 58, 84
 checks and balances of power, 16, 32,
  44–47
 commercialization of, 85
 consumer culture, 17, 95–96, 101
 decentralizing currents, 15, 23–26,
  29–30, 32
 economic prosperity, 98–99, 182
 federal/state power balance, 69–70
 frontier of, 89–93, 97
 household incomes, 97, 100
 ideological issues, 68, 72, 78, 84
 and infrastructure, 149–150
 liberalism, 117–118
 national character, 40, 55–56, 66, 90, 92,
  94, 96–97, 99, 108
 and political corruption, 42–44, 118,
  145–146, 149, 173, 260
 political polarization, 1, 85, 106, 108,
  163, 184
 politics, 41, 53, 56–57, 59–61, 66,
  72–73, 83, 106, 118, 172
 public sector, 29, 52–53, 83
 republicanism, 47–48

territorial expansion, 40, 72, 74–75, 80,
 84, 99, 128
two-party system, 52, 172
vital center, 18, 21, 26–27, 39, 66
unskilled labor, 185
upper class, 52–53
upper South, 87, 91, 126–127, 130, 246
upward mobility, 25, 77, 92–93,
 172, 231

Vance, J. D., 8, 225, 234–235
Vietnam War, 20–22, 30, 262–263
virtue, in the South, 263
vocational education, 141, 182, 184
voting rights. *See* African Americans,
 voting rights; women, voting rights
Voting Rights Act of 1965, 20

Walker, Freeman, 121
Wallace, George, 245
Wallerstein, Immanuel, 187
Wal-Mart, 185
Walpole, Robert, 42–44
Warren, Robert Penn, 130–132
Washington, Booker T., 139, 141–142
Watergate, 22
Watson, Tom, 152
wealth, 57, 119, 131, 161, 179, 183
 capitalism, 41, 51, 178, 183
 concentratedness of, 24, 100, 102, 106
 and income inequality, 25, 106,
  108, 240
 privilege, 25
 from slavery, 49, 68, 97, 128–129,
  174, 219
Westmoreland, William, 181
Whig Party, 48, 51–52, 57, 74–75, 90–91,
 119–120, 172
White Citizens' Councils, 156
white elites, 15, 93, 117, 142, 203, 219,
 231, 244
white flight, 230
white moderates, 156
white privilege, 6, 9, 162–163, 243, 248
white southerners
 and identity, 115, 133
 and property ownership, 144,
  148–149, 175
 slavery guilt, 115–116, 122–126,
  128–130, 133
 and southern defeat, 130

Index

white supremacy, 115, 121, 133–134,
  145, 219
  entrenchment of, 6, 133, 141, 208
  protection of, 52, 117, 129, 174, 216
  Reconstruction, 6–7, 79, 159
white women, 197, 205, 208, 210,
  213–214, 217
white working class, 93, 119, 226,
  234–235, 237, 239, 242
  culture, 227, 229, 231–234, 236, 241, 248
  disaffection of, 8, 228–229, 232, 240
  labor dynamics, 80, 120, 225, 227, 231,
    236–237, 240–241
  progressivism, 52–53
  racism, 161–162, 229–231, 242–245,
    247–248
White, Debra Gray, 209
white-collar workers, 97, 104
whiteness, 119, 142–143, 147, 162–163,
  218, 232, 244, 247
Wiebe, Robert, 53
Wilentz, Sean, 219
Wiley, Bell I., 123
Wilkerson, Isabel, 161–162, 242–243
Williamson, Joel, 158
Wills, Garry, 9, 260
Wilson, Woodrow, 58, 83, 151

women
  and higher education, 193–195
  voting rights, 47, 199, 203–205, 255
  in workforce, 97, 194
women historians, 7, 192, 197, 202, 207,
    209, 211, 219–221
women's history, 192, 194, 200, 202, 207,
    212, 215
Wood, Gordon, 42, 219
Woodward, C. Vann, 9, 13, 123, 152, 176,
    261–263
  Age of Free Security, 40, 98
  southern defeat, 180–181, 261–263
Woodward, Colin, 242
Woody, Robert H., 145–146
workers' wages, 226
  low rates, 239–240
  unionism, 247
working-class, culture, 226
World War II, 3, 5, 55, 99
Wright, Gavin, 157, 175

Yeltsin, Boris, 21
yeoman farmers, 152, 234

Zedong, Mao, 18, 153
Zuckerberg, Mark, 31

Printed in the United States
by Baker & Taylor Publisher Services